COMPUTER NUMERICAL CONTROL

Macmillan/McGraw–Hill

Lake Forest, Illinois   Columbus, Ohio   Mission Hills, California   Peoria, Illinois

621.9023
KIE

Library of Congress Cataloging-in-Publication Data

Kief, Hans B.

   [NC/CNC Handbuch. English]

   Computer numerical control / Hans B. Kief, T. Frederick Waters.

     p. cm.

   Translation of: NC/CNC Handbuch.

   Also published in Great Britain with title: Flexible automation.

   Includes index.

   ISBN 0-02-676411-3

   1. Machine-tools—Numerical control.   2. Computer integrated manufacturing
systems. I. Title

TJ1189.K4513   1992

621.9' 023—dc20   92-3920
                                            CIP

Computer Numerical Control

Send all inquiries to:
GLENCOE DIVISION
Macmillan/McGraw-Hill
936 Eastwind Drive
Westerville, OH 43081

ISBN 0-02-676411-3

Printed in the United States of America.

1 2 3 4 5 6 7 8 9 0   RRD-C 99 98 97 96 95 94 93 92

19/7/93

PREFACE

••

The introduction of the computer, and its subsequent application to almost every sphere of modern life, has resulted in a second industrial revolution, with manufacturing at the forefront of these fundamental technological changes.

One effect of introducing computers into production engineering is reducing the "artisan skill" content traditionally required in manufacturing processes and replacing it with high-precision, computer-controlled machinery. While this reduces human error and variability in output, it does not reduce the production engineering knowledge required of either the professional engineering or shop floor worker. In fact, the reverse is true. Engineers and workers still need to understand the practical fundamentals as much as they ever did, but they also need to acquire additional skills if they are to meet the maximum level of productivity and consistent quality that can be obtained with careful application of the latest computer-assisted manufacturing techniques and hardware.

The best way to learn new skills is to start from areas of relevant knowledge that are well understood and then to logically build on these into the areas of new learning. With this in mind the authors of COMPUTER NUMERICAL CONTROL have worked together, each drawing on many years of industrial experience as well as extensive experience in teaching modern manufacturing to both technicians and undergraduate engineering students. This book, while assuming a basic understanding of conventional non-NC equipment, has been carefully structured so that a student of any age needs no prior knowledge of how computer control is applied to modern machinery.

Because the CNC subject area is so broad, most texts in this field provide either an in-depth treatment of certain specialist areas, or else give such a broad overview that they are too superficial to be of much practical use "on the job." This book is unique in that it attempts to strike a balance between these two extremes, making it both an ideal learning text and a reference work for industry. For example, after a brief overview of NC/CNC development over the past forty years, the reader is introduced to the idea of NC and the fundamentals involved in its application to manufacturing hardware. This is followed by a number of chapters which explain, in clear and well-illustrated detail, how these NC principles are applied in practice. This logical approach is then extended to the study of CNC, flexible manufacturing cells, islands and systems (FMSs), and finally through to how CNC is seen as the basic module in computer-integrated manufacturing (CIM).

Additional stand-alone chapters are included to cover such matters as preventive maintenance and personnel & training requirements, as these topics are vital to industry if they are to get the best out of their high capital investment in CNC plant. However they may be conveniently omitted when using this book as the text for basic CNC courses. This is equally true of the chapter which gives a simple practical example of computer-assisted programming. It is only intended to illustrate a practical application of the APT principle of programming, and courses specifically designed to teach machine tool programming are better served using texts specially written for this purpose. Unfortunately, many of these topic-specific books rarely consider the pros and cons of associated matters, such as whether programming is best carried out at the machine (MDI) or away from the shop floor in a production planning office. Such vital considerations are examined in detail in Chapter 8, and are typical of the uniquely practical approach to real problems adopted throughout this book.

Chapter 12 is extremely valuable to both college student and industrial technician, and should be studied in detail. It not only extensively illustrates the very wide range of modern CNC equipment used in industry today, but also explains the logic of how internationally agreed machine axis standards are established. This chapter concludes with a description of how touch probing is used for component checking on coordinate measuring machines. Many instructors may feel that, after dealing with the fundamentals of NC/CNC, they would then like to introduce the topic of "Group Technology," as this is a fundamental approach in assessing where best to target the introduction of flexible manufacturing cells and systems. This may also be an appropriate point to introduce the concept of CAD/CAM and the benefits and limitations of linking CAD with CAM systems. Chapters dealing with each of these two areas are included, and are designed to provide a clear understanding of the fundamentals involved.

Hans Kief has worked mainly in the field of CNC with the firm of Robert Bosch GmbH in Germany. He was the founder of the Germany NC Society, a visiting Professor at the University of Mannheim, and is acknowledged as one of the world's leading experts in the field of CNC manufacturing. After spending twenty years working with both British and American engineering companies Fred Waters has been engaged for a similar period in consulting, technical journalism, and in teaching advanced manufacturing at one of the largest and most prestigious academic institutions in Great Britain. He has also been a visiting professor in manufacturing at FHS, Hamburg, Germany.

Both authors travel widely in their professional capacities, and have extensive experience of current industrial practice worldwide. The authors are therefore well aware, not only of the needs of young people currently receiving training for working in the twenty-first century, but equally important, the requirements of manufacturing workers who find it necessary to be retrained in the fields of computer numerical control and flexible automation.

While the content of this book has been produced in Europe, thanks to close collaboration between the American publisher, Glencoe, the authors, and specialist equipment producers worldwide, it is a truly international text. It should therefore rapidly establish itself as the standard CNC reference work not only in colleges, universities and technical institutes, but also throughout the manufacturing industry.

Hans B. Kief, Germany
T. Frederick Waters, Great Britain

CONTENTS

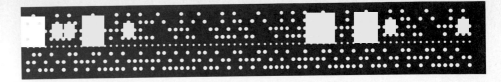

CHAPTER 1

THE EVOLUTION OF COMPUTERIZED CONTROL IN MANUFACTURING

The principle of controlling a mechanical device by sequencing information, as in today's numerically controlled (NC) machine tools, dates back to the fourteenth century when pegged cylinders were used to control the movement of ornamental figures on church clocks. Much of today's economic prosperity is founded on computerized control in manufacturing that employs this same fundamental principle.

In 1808 Joseph M. Jacquard used punched holes in sheet-metal cards, arranging them on his weaving machines in various ways, to automatically control complex weaving patterns. The presence or absence of a hole determined whether or not a needle would be activated. This method was the forerunner of the portable data carrier. Almost 55 years later M. Fourneaux patented the automatic piano player under the world-renowned name of Pianola. Using the principle of air passing through a perforated roll of paper, he was able to control and activate the keyboard mechanism. This method was further developed to control sound intensity, roll speed, and tonal characteristics.

As early as 1642 Pascal built the first mechanical calculator using gears. In 1834, Babbage completed a "difference engine," as well as a mechanical calculator capable of calculating to accuracies of six decimal places. Babbage experimented with various designs in order to realize his ideas of expanding the size and complexity of his machine. At that time he designed a machine that could not only perform arithmetic calculations, but could also perform many of the functions that modern calculators can do today, such as the storage, processing, memorizing, inputting, and outputting of data.

Over a hundred years passed before, in 1940, Aiken in the United States and Zuse in Germany used relays to develop the first electronic computing machine. Three years later, in 1943, Mauchly and Eckert built the first electronic computer, called ENIAC (Electronic Numerical Integrator and Computer). It contained 18,000 electron tubes and approximately 500,000 hand-soldered connections, weighed 30 tons, required floor space of 1613 ft^2, and had an electrical connect load of 174 kW. Programming was very difficult, and took place via 6000 switches and a prepatched board, plus a few hundred additional connections.

It was so complex that it took only a few minutes of operation for malfunctions to appear. Replacing all tubes prior to start-up would take about a week!

Only with the introduction of the transistor, developed in 1948 and put into industrial operation around 1960, could reprogrammable computers be commercially manufactured.

The transistor had the following decisive advantages over the electron tube:

- Small size
- Durability (shockproof, wearproof)
- Dependability
- Low cost
- Low energy requirements
- Low heat loss

Since that time, developments in electronics—integrated circuits (ICs) in 1959, large-scale integrated circuits (LSIs) in 1965, microprocessors in 1974, program-control data, storage techniques, and so forth—have all played an important role in the massive growth of computer development and application.

Numerical control of machine tools began with research aimed at achieving greater accuracy in the complex machining of aircraft components. The simpler, more basic developments that today constitute the bulk of numerical-control applications came later. By 1949 the concept of numerical control had been developing gradually for over 500 years, and it was at this time that John C. Parsons and the Massachusetts Institute of Technology (MIT) won a study contract from the U.S. Air Force. By then the aircraft industry had become aware that high-precision machined structural parts would be essential in order to meet the greatest possible strength-to-weight ratio for future supersonic aircraft. Manual and tracer-controlled machine tools could not meet the accuracy requirements demanded, nor could existing techniques readily accommodate the many and frequent engineering design changes inherent in advanced aircraft development. Therefore this initial study contract concerned the development of a system for machine tools that could control the position of their leadscrews directly from the output of a computer. This output would then serve to automatically operate the machine tool without manual intervention. Parsons and his associates proposed three essential steps to realize this objective:

- The use of a computer to calculate the path of the cutting tool, and storage of the computed cutter-path data on punched cards
- The use of a reading device at the machine tool to automatically read the punch cards

- The use of a control system that would continuously output the appropriate data to servomotors which were attached to the machine tool's lead screws

In 1952 the first numerically controlled machine tool, a Cincinnati Hydrotel vertical-spindle milling machine, was successfully demonstrated at MIT. The machine-control unit was built with electron tubes, controlled three axes, and received its data via binary-coded punch tapes. Because highly complex shapes were required, very precise mathematical description and voluminous mathematical computations were necessary, which, if executed manually, would have taken years to complete. Therefore the utilization of a computer was absolutely essential for the generation of accurate and rapid cutter-path data. These data were then transmitted as coded instructions onto punch tape.

Indeed, it may be claimed that using a computer to free human effort from tedious computations, and coupling it with manufacturing hardware, has virtually initiated a second industrial revolution.

Since 1952 the development of computer-utilization techniques has been continuous. By 1954 the development of a symbolic language called automatically programmed tool (APT) had begun. This was a specially devised symbolic language capable of transmitting to the control computer an accurate description of the shape of a required piecepart, together with the machining instructions necessary to make it.

In the same year the Bendix Company bought the patent rights from Parsons and built the first industrially produced NC machine tool, using electron tubes. In 1957 the Air Material Command of the U.S. Air Force began using numerically controlled machine tools, leading to the establishment of a cooperative project between the Aerospace Industries Association (AIA) and MIT. Since that time MIT and others, notably Illinois Institute of Technology Research Institute (IITRI), have worked on this APT symbolic language, resulting in more advanced versions of the basic language being introduced that are capable of coping with defining and machining more complex surface profiles. The prime objectives of IITRI's APT long-range development program were the extension of the APT system capability and the development of new applications for the APT language. This work continued until 1971.

By this time general industry had begun to recognize the potential advantages of numerical control, and this forced them to look more closely at their own manufacturing problems and how this new technology might help improve their existing production methods. It was quickly realized that the vast majority of metal-removal problems, such as hole drilling, turning, and straight-line milling, did not require such sophisticated computational facilities, controllers, or NC machine tools. However, the application of even the most basic form of APT to simple component geometries proved to be both cumbersome and costly.

Therefore many simpler, special purpose languages were developed, most of them, however, still derivatives of APT.

The NC machine tool is now nearly 40 years old and has been successfully used for simple manufacturing applications, such as point-to-point drilling and two-axis contouring, as in turning, as well as for highly complex·multiaxis duties. Indeed, NC machines are also now in use for inspection, wire harness making, electronic component insertion, electrodischarge machining, flame cutting, coil winding, glass and textile material cutting, and many other diverse areas of application.

As in most areas of life, the computer has influenced and, in part, fundamentally changed the original technology to which it has been applied. This is especially true in the case of the microprocessor since it was first applied to computer numerical controllers (CNCs) in 1976. CNC has taken giant leaps forward in line with progressive microprocessor developments. Together with the electronic modules for data storage and impulse generation, the microprocessor forms the switching and computational center of all modern CNC controls. The high switching speed of these elements is sufficient to carry out several different functions and computational tasks without interfering with the work tempo of the connected machine tool, but if one microprocessor should prove inadequate to perform all functions required within the maximum allotted time cycle, then a second or even a third unit may be added, either in tandem or alternatively dedicated to specific tasks.

Modern computing technology has made a major impact on engineering design and manufacture and has assisted in significantly reducing design and production costs, inventory levels, and lead times, as well as increasing productivity, quality, capital equipment utilization levels, and so on. Based upon this technology a vast array of equipment has been developed by various industries and research institutes in order to support specific design and manufacturing needs. These computer-based developments are now being integrated into industry by the introduction in 1982 of Flexible Manufacturing Systems (FMSs), for example, and subsequently the more comprehensive concept of computer-aided engineering (CAE).

Although computer technology—computer-aided design (CAD) and computer-aided manufacture (CAM)—has demonstrated significant potential for improving the productivity of both design and manufacture, there has been a gap between the available technologies and the general understanding of how to use them most effectively. The bulk of the above developments are not well coordinated and contain a great deal of overlap in terms of their intended functions. For example, CAD/CAM systems have their strength in the ability to digitize geometric definition. Nevertheless the CAM part is mostly limited to NC/CNC programming and cutter center-line data generation, whereas other related elements of CAM, such as process planning, group technology, materials-resource planning, and production control are usually not included. This may, in part, be due to these various technology elements being products of many different specialist software package suppliers and developers.

Unfortunately, software technology also reflects differing viewpoints in terms of the perception of its different functions in a manufacturing enterprise. The interrelationships and linking of these various software packages therefore becomes extremely difficult. It has thus been a major development objective since 1986 to link as many of these various elements together as possible to support the operation of a completely integrated design and manufacturing plant of the type implied by the often misunderstood term computer-integrated manufacturing (CIM).

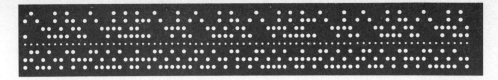

CHAPTER 2
WHAT IS NC?

After studying this chapter you should understand:

1. What is meant by NC and how it differs from CNC.
2. The types of electronic modules used in modern controllers.
3. The various control modes used by NC machines.
4. How NC programs are structured.
5. How the various data-input devices used with NC equipment work.

Numerical control (NC) is a specialized form of automation. Specifically, automatic machine tools are programmed to perform an ordered sequence of events at a predetermined rate to produce a piecepart with entirely predictable results and physical parameters.

2.1 THE DEVELOPMENT OF NC

The operation of most mechanical devices requires some form of control, whether manual, automatic, through a computer program, or by remote control. Manufacturing machines need control systems that primarily repeat well-defined movements with high precision and in a minimum of time, permitting the mass production of products of uniform quality with a minimum of human intervention.

For mass production such automated machinery is frequently arranged sequentially so that, at each stage, an additional operation or operations may be carried out. This type of manufacture is the most efficient yet devised and has been the norm in the automobile industry, where production volume justifies the huge capital investment involved. It is usually termed a **transfer line**.

The basic types of control used in both mass production and NC machine tools are listed in Table 2–1.

A control system which has been designed according to traditional principles is referred to as a mechanical, electrical, pneumatic, or hydraulic control, depending on the classification of its main components. These controls, despite having stood the test of time, do have a major disadvantage in that their sequence of operations is fixed. Alterations to operational sequence due to product changes cause considerable downtime while the electrical circuitry and mechanical elements of the control are being changed to achieve the new control characteristics required. A major portion of setup time is needed to effect adjustment of control devices to suit the geometry of the new job. Adjustable cam disks and cam rails, combined with microswitches to keep movement within defined limits, are common for this purpose, and although such adjustable mechanical elements are versatile, their adjustment procedure can be very time-consuming. For this reason it is also common practice to exchange the complete cam rail and cam disks in order

TABLE 2–1   Basic types of machine tool control.

| CONTROL TYPE | TASK | STORAGE FOR | | PROGRAM |
		GEOMETRICAL INFO.	MISC. FUNCTIONS	GENERATION
Mechanical C	Positioning, continuous path	Cam disk	Cam disk	Design office (Tool design)
Cam C	Positioning	Cam rail	Control	Design office (Tool design)
Plugboard C	Positioning	Cam rail	Plugboard	Workshop/machine shop
Tracer C	Linear or continuous path	Template or model	Template or model (Tool design)	Production planning and design office
Line Tracer C	Continuous path	Drawing	Drawing	Product design
Playback C	Continuous path	Magnetic tape	Magnetic tape	Original path recording Workshop/machine shop
NC	High precision positioning and continuous path C.	Punched tape, magnetic tape	Decade switch, punched tape, magnetic tape	Production planning
CNC	Like NC but more complex for FMS control.	Punched or Magnetic tape or floppy disk. Internal memory (RAM, bubble)	Punched or mag tape Internal RAM or bubble	Production planning or machine shop

to minimize setting time. Setup time also includes the time required for manually changing cutting tools and machine-operating parameters, such as spindle speeds and feed rate, as well as setting up piecepart clamping fixtures.

For these economic reasons, machines with traditional controls do not therefore lend themselves to flexible manufacturing. Not surprisingly, a new control concept has been developed, which meets the following criteria:

■ No manual intervention necessary during the machining process
■ Storage of part programs that are quickly retrievable
■ No cam disk/limit switch devices
■ Precisely defined and simultaneous movements of as many machine axes as possible
■ Quickchange tooling and autochange feed and spindle speed facilities

This new controller concept demands programmable machines that offer rapid and error-free response to changing manufacturing demands and which are "controlled by numbers," as all information is supplied in a digital format.

All NC machine tools need numerical data for controlling the relative motion between cutting tool and piecepart, the component dimensions normally emanating directly from engineering drawings—the geometric data. Other digitized numerical data define feed rates, spindle speeds, tool identification numbers, and miscellaneous functions to perform such operations as tool or work changing, or coolant control—the technological data.

The combination of all this numerical information in a sequence understood by the machine tool's controller is called a **part program**, and the process of creating data in a correctly structured format is called **programming** *(Fig. 2–1, p. 8).*

Numerical controls use standard microelectronic modules which have been developed for computer hardware. Except for special modules needed in servocontrol circuits, no individual modules are necessary, in contrast to traditional controls, which employ only components tailored to suit one specific control function. In modern NC controllers extensive control and calculation tasks are performed by one or more integral microprocessors. These are termed computer numerical controllers (CNCs).

CNCs have expandable memories that can store large numbers of programs, plus subroutine and correction data. Sophisticated graphic displays and dynamic simulation have also now become available as a result of the extensive memory capacity being built into current CNCs.

Within only a few years, the capability and efficiency of machine controllers has increased to such an extent that the name "numerical control" is no longer appropriate; "computer numerical control" is more accurately descriptive.

The fundamental differences between NC and CNC are more fully discussed in Chapter 7.

FIGURE 2–1   The principle of Manual NC Programming. Geometrical and technological data are combined step-by-step on a program sheet and then fed directly into the machine's controller or data carrier.

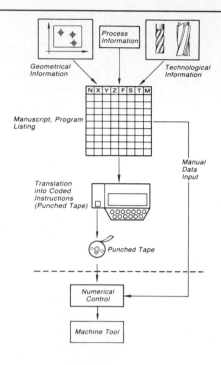

2.2 NC AXES

Machine tools have a combination of both linear and rotary axes. To control these axes digitally each NC axis needs:

- An electronic path-measuring system
- A numerically controllable drive system

Both must be directly linked to the machine's numerical control.

An NC continuously compares target positional values with actual values (measured by the machine's path-measuring systems), and then sends signals to the appropriate axis drive to eliminate any discrepancies between the two values. This is called "closed loop" control *(Fig. 2–2)*.

2.3 HARDWARE

The hardware comprising a CNC is made up of microprocessors (16-bit and 32–bit technology) and integrated circuits (ICs). Some controls incorporate special custom-designed very large scale integrated circuits (VLSIs) developed to meet the customer's specific needs, and provided they are required in sufficiently large quantities. They offer increased compactness, reliability, and ease of maintenance. In addition to a CNC's microprocessor(s), its electronic memory modules are also of major importance.

FIGURE 2–2   Geometrical data processing via closed-loop control.

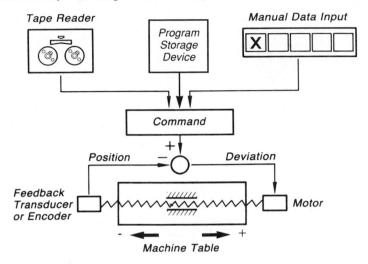

Several types of memory modules are employed *(Fig. 2–3, p. 10):*

- ROMs and EPROMs are used to store unalterable sections of the CNC operating system, as well as "canned cycles" and fixed routines.
- EEPROMs store data that is generated at the time of installation of the CNC operating system, such as specific machine parameters, special cycles, and subroutines. Although EEPROM contents are protected, later modification is possible.
- RAM modules are used in every CNC to store programs and correction data. They have extendable storage capacities ranging from 16 to more than 500 Kbytes.

The individual functions within a controller usually have their own card(s) that are installed in a card rack and interconnected by internal buslinks *(Fig. 2–4, p. 11).*

Electrical interference can cause an NC to malfunction; it is therefore advisable to keep all electronic equipment in a housing offering electromagnetic and electrostatic protection. The housing should also be dust and grease proof, as deposits of even the smallest particle on the circuit boards can endanger the integrity of the whole controller. For this reason air cooling of the electronic racks is not permitted, even if the air is filtered, because if the filters should become blocked, cooling would cease.

FIGURE 2–3   Electronic modules used in today's NCs.

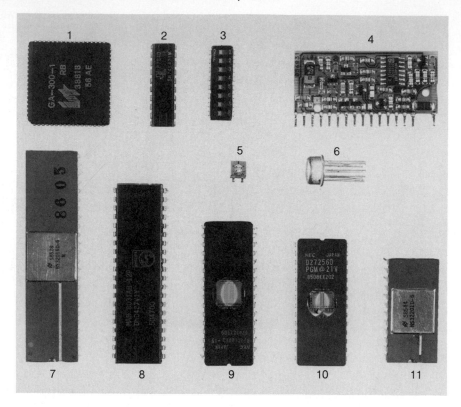

1=Custom-Designed Module (ASIC)
2=TTL Module (e.g. RAM, ROM)
3=DIP Switch
4=SMD Module
5=Potentiometer
6=D/A Converter

7=Microprocessor, 32/16 Bit
8=CMOS Module (electronic clock)
9=EPROM, 1 MBit
10=EPROM, 256 KBit
11=Periphery Module (FPU)

2.4 SOFTWARE

Modern NC controllers may be considered as special-purpose computers for the control of machine tools or robots. Like any other computer, the NC needs an operating system, sometimes referred to as the system software. It must be specifically designed for the type of machine that it is destined to control, because the kinematics and general operating characteristics of every machine type are unique. The software controls all functions of the machine and its efficiency of operation and manages all local programming at the machine tool and graphic simulation of the cutting process if available. Special test and self-diagnostic software and software to achieve interfacing to mainframe computers can all be bought as commercial software packages.

FIGURE 2–4   Multilayered plug-in card incorporating many electronic module devices.

An important aspect of any NC software should be its versatility, that is, its ability to cope with machine-specific variations within a given machine type. Typical variants are the number of NC axes to be controlled, the operational characteristics of the tool magazine and changer mechanisms, and the possible existence of a tool-monitoring system.

Modern controllers also offer integrated programming languages similar to BASIC and PASCAL, thus allowing machine tool manufacturers to readily incorporate their own know-how into the control of their machines. The machine-tool builder can even influence the form of the graphics that are displayed on the controller VDU screen, and can therefore create appropriate graphics to depict special customer's tooling.

2.5 CONTROL MODES

There are four specific control modes on NC machines, and their differences should be clearly understood *(Fig. 2–5, p. 12)*.

2.5.1 POINT-TO-POINT CONTROL

To reach a desired position, all axes independently rapid-traverse until each axis has reached its programmed target value. Clearly, no cutting

---

FIGURE 2–5   The four types of control mode.

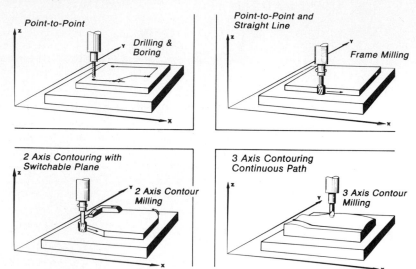

can occur during traverse and it commences only when the target position has been reached.

This control mode which is both simple and low cost is typical of that used on drilling and punching machines.

2.5.2 STRAIGHT-LINE CONTROL

In the straight-line control mode each axis may be programmed individually to any desired feed rate. However this mode is of limited interest because its application is restricted and its price unattractive.

Its area of operation tends to be restricted to component handling and to use as an automation aid in the form of an NC module for controls with a programmable memory.

2.5.3 TWO-AXIS CONTOURING CONTROL

This is a simplified, two-dimensional version of the full three-axis control mode dealt with in Section 2.5.4.

2.5.4 THREE-AXIS CONTOURING WITH CONTINUOUS PATH CONTROL

Continuous path control, or contouring systems as they are often called, provide accurate spindle positioning at any point in space because all NC axes are precisely controlled at all times, both individually and in exact relation to each other.

A software package called an "interpolator" coordinates the movement of each axis by calculating target points along the intended path and then controlling the relative motion of the axes to ensure that the target point for each axis is reached simultaneously—see Section 2.6 for a more detailed study of interpolation.

Depending on the number of simultaneously controlled axes, there are 2, 3, or multipath controllers.

Successive 2-D interpolation in each of the three principal planes (XY, XZ, and YZ) is called 2½-D path control, and simultaneous interpolation of these axes is termed 3-D path control.

The various types of continuous path systems are used to control such machine tools as turning and machining centers, or any other NC machine used to remove material continuously over the surface of a component, as in the milling of a cam, for example. Contouring may also be applied to flame cutting, sawing in a continuous path, welding, spark erosion machines, and other processes such as the application of adhesives.

2.6 TYPES OF INTERPOLATION

During positioning, all programmed axes move simultaneously at the specified feed rates until each axis has reached its destination. All drives start together, but without an interpolator individual destinations are reached successively according to the path traveled.

However, an interpolator coordinates these axis motions in such a way that the programmed path is constantly maintained from the beginning to the end of the movement. Interpolation may be achieved in several ways.

2.6.1   LINEAR INTERPOLATION

With linear interpolation the spindle axis is moved rectilinearly from profile start to finish *(Fig. 2–6)*. In effect the desired profile is broken up into a large number of straight lines, and the larger the number of lines the closer becomes the path of the spindle to the specified profile *(Fig. 2–7, p. 14)*. Theoretically, linear interpolation can be achieved for any number of simultaneously moving axes. On machine tools it is possible to interpolate up to five axes (X, Y, and Z to determine a spatial point, and two rotational movements, such as A and B, relating to the rotational control of the tool spindle). By control of these five axes, any profile or solid curve can be generated.

FIGURE 2–6   Linear interpolation.

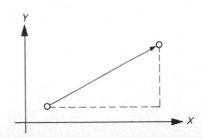

FIGURE 2–7   Continuous path approximation.

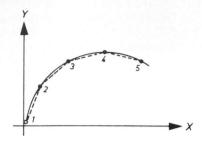

When very close approximation to a given profile is required, the resulting large number of necessary intermediate points results in a greatly increased volume of data processing, and when it extends to three or more axes the number of necessary calculations becomes prodigious. Theoretically, all path-control problems can be solved by continuous path approximation via linear interpolation, but circular, parabolic, and spline interpolation result in a major reduction in the volume of data to be processed, and simpler programming is thereby facilitated.

2.6.2   CIRCULAR INTERPOLATION

This type of interpolation is limited to the plane of the principal machine surface. Inclusion of rotary axes in circular interpolation is not feasible. For spatial interpolation, that is simultaneous movement of three or more axes, circular interpolation is not used.

If a profile in the XY, XZ, YZ plane is composed of circular arcs, only the end points and the arc center need be programmed. All required intermediate points are calculated by the interpolator via circular interpolation *(Fig. 2–8)*.

2.6.3   PARABOLIC INTERPOLATION

A spatial parabola is made up of three points *(Fig. 2–9)*. Point P2 is the midpoint between P4 and P5, and P5 is the midpoint between P1 and

FIGURE 2–8   Circular interpolation.

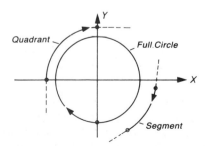

FIGURE 2–9   Parabolic interpolation.

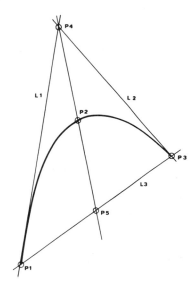

P3. P1 is known from the preceding block of data; P2 and P3 are entered together in two successive data blocks. The transition between two successive parabolas blends well if their tangents at P3 are identical.

Basically parabolic interpolation is useful only with four or five axes machining, since the data required for simultaneous multiaxis movements are only reduced significantly compared to linear interpolation, when profiles are highly complex.

2.6.4   SPLINE INTERPOLATION

The blending of mathematically definable curves is called spline fitting, the transition between the curves being formed tangentially. With this type of interpolation complex geometries can be programmed using far fewer program-data blocks than would be the case with linear interpolation, but the precise procedure can be mathematically complex and is beyond the scope of this book.

2.7   WORKING WITH NC MACHINE CONTROLLERS

The commercial success of NC machines depends, in part, on the user-friendliness of their controllers. "Help" menus and input dialogues build operator confidence, assist in the prevention of operator errors, enhance safe machine operation, and minimize machine downtime.

Modern NC controllers are generally highly user-friendly as the machine-tool builder can use a familiar integrated programming language to program user aids and tailor them to each machine type, as well as have access to the system graphics to provide easily comprehensible comments. After the user has become familiar with the new control, any software package which contains user learning aids may be deleted, thus freeing additional memory space for program storage.

The great complexity of current NC controllers should not be evident to the user, and only a minimum of commands, in a logical order, should be necessary to operate the machine correctly.

The dialogue mode of modern controls makes data input both fast and reliable. It should be recognized that even highly automated machines will from time to time still require a degree of manual intervention. For example, modifications of feed rates, spindle speeds, and miscellaneous functions are sometimes necessary because it is often possible to optimize these parameters only by machining a test-piece, and noting vibration, chip formation, surface finish, and so on. Furthermore, when a tool breaks or wears unacceptably the operator may be required to intervene quickly, change the tool manually, input new tooling data, and finally make the new tool recommence the interrupted cut.

2.8 THE PART PROGRAM

The control of an NC machine is performed by a part program. This program contains, among other things, details of the individual machining steps, in the order needed to produce the required part. (The storage medium is a data carrier such as a punched or magnetic tape). The NC controller works through the data by processing each program block of information sequentially and it receives the information either directly from the data carrier or from the controller's internal memory if the program has been preloaded at an earlier time.

An important prerequisite for the rapid introduction of NC machines was the adoption of a standardized program format, and at a relatively early stage agreement was reached on the use of an internationally standardized code based on International Standards Organization (ISO) recommendations. In the United States programming predominantly follows either the Electronics Industries Association (EIA) RS 244 standard or the RS 358, ISO compatible standard.

2.8.1 PROGRAM FORMAT

Data are entered by program blocks normally consisting of several words each—see Chapter 9. Block and word length may vary from block to block, only the programming of new data being necessary, as all existing commands are obeyed until countermanded. Each block starts with a designatory address letter N plus a sequential number. As an introduction to "word address" program format, and prior to the more detailed study in Chapter 9, the following is an example of a typical program block for a three-axis continuous path-control operation:

N4, G2, X ± 43, Y ± 43, Z ± 43, I43, J43, K43, F7, S4, T2, M2, $.

In this specific case the meanings of each of the items in this program line (block) are:

N04:   Three-digit block number (sequence number). A whole program can be divided into program blocks from N00 to N9999. Some controllers only accept up to line N999.

G02:   Preparatory function—circular interpolation, clockwise *(Table 10–2) p. 142.*

X ± 4.3, Y ± 4.3, and Z ± 4.3:   This is path data. Normally four digits before and three digits after the decimal point are permitted. The decimal point is omitted, and generally leading zeros and positive signs are also omitted (in absolute value programming).

I4.3, J4.3, and K4.3:   These are auxiliary parameters of the circle center for the profile being cut. Only IJ, JK, or IK may occur in any one block as these correspond to planes XY, YZ, and XZ respectively.

F7:   Seven-digit feed rate, usually given in millimeters or inches/ minute.

S4:   Four-digit spindle speed, in rpm.

T02:   Two-digit tool identification number; up to eight digits are possible.

M02:   Miscellaneous function machine command, in this case indicating end of program *(Table 10–3) p. 143.*

$:   End-of-block code. Feasibly one block might contain all word addresses. However, each word address must only appear once in any one block, although some modern controllers do permit more than one G, M, or T address per block.

2.8.2   DIMENSIONS AND AUXILIARY FUNCTIONS

Before a machine tool can execute desired motions and produce a part, the appropriate geometrical and technological data must be entered into its controller. It is then processed, cutter path information is calculated, and all auxiliary and miscellaneous functions are suitably interpreted *(Fig. 2–10, p. 18).*

Geometrical data determines:

- Target positions to be achieved
- Feed-drive direction (or defines quadrant position, depending on sign)
- The program cycle, that is, the sequence of movements. This is determined by the order in which the data is presented.

(Addresses represented by the characters X, Y, Z, A, B, C, U, V, W, I, J, K, G, and R are used for geometrical-data input—see Table 10–1, *p. 137.*)

In addition to geometrical data, technological information must also be provided, as this makes it possible to call up the desired tooling, use the correct spindle speeds and direction of rotation, maintain suitable feed rates, and so on. Auxiliary functions are used for this purpose and the data is entered using the addresses F, H, M, S, and T. Addresses D, E, L, and P are freely programmable addresses, and are used by different controller suppliers for inputting various data specific to them.

FIGURE 2–10 Conversion of component specification and machining data into dimensional and auxiliary function information suitable for NC machine control.

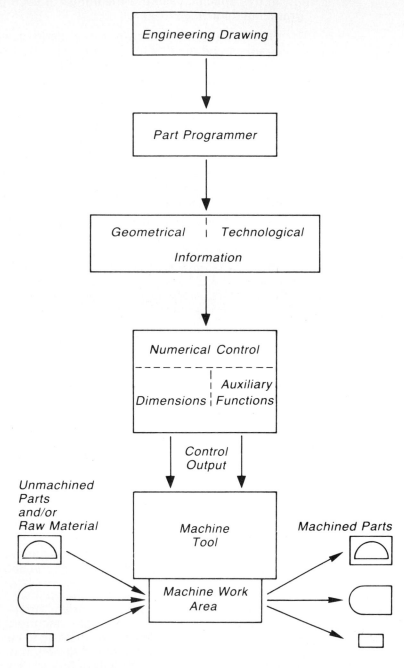

FIGURE 2–11   Dimensioning systems.

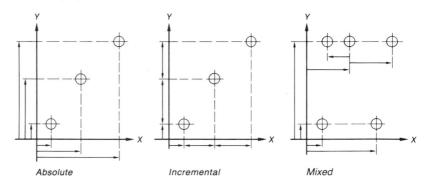

Absolute   *Incremental*   *Mixed*

2.8.3   ABSOLUTE AND INCREMENTAL DIMENSIONS

Geometrical data may be expressed in two ways—absolute and incremental *(Fig. 2–11)*, and both forms of dimensioning should be acceptable to most of today's controllers.

In the Cartesian coordinate geometry system, all points can be described as either absolute or incremental. An absolute measurement for each point is always taken from the same zero established for a given coordinate system. In incremental dimensioning, also called chain dimensioning, measurement for each point is expressed as the path differential from the preceding position (Fig. 2–11). In incremental programming the controller must therefore only store and process the additional path measurement. However modern NCs have the functions G90/G91 *(Table 10–2, p. 142)*, thereby enabling the programmer to switch at will from absolute to incremental dimensions (and vice versa), without losing the zero data point of the coordinate system in use.

A tool which is to traverse the seven positions in Fig. 2–12 and then return to zero will be presented with coordinate values as listed in Fig. 2–13 *(p. 20)*, depending on which dimensioning scheme is being employed.

The principal advantage of programming in absolute dimensions is that any point can be readily changed without affecting subsequent di-

FIGURE 2–12   Drilling pattern.

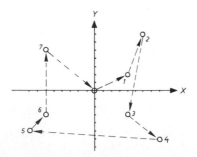

FIGURE 2–13 Drilling pattern programmed in both absolute and incremental systems.

Hole No.	Absolute Dimensioning		Incremental Dimensioning	
	x	y	x	y
1	4	2	+4	+2
2	6	7	+2	+5
3	4	−3	−2	−10
4	8	−6	+4	−3
5	−8	−5	−16	+1
6	−6	−3	+2	+2
7	−6	+5	0	+8
0	0	0	+6	−5
			$\Sigma = 0$	$\Sigma = 0$

mensions, unlike the situation that exists when incremental dimensioning is used. Thus, reentering a program after an interruption due to a power outage, for example, is much easier when the program is based on absolute dimensions.

Incremental programming does however have certain advantages, two of the most important being:

- The sum of both the X and Y dimensions must always equal zero when the start position is resumed at the end of a complete cycle *(Fig. 2–13)*. This makes it easy to check a program, but this is not possible, of course, when incremental and absolute dimensions are mixed.
- It is very simple to copy and transfer specific geometries such as drilling patterns, chamfers, fillets, and milling cycles when dimensions are incremental.

2.9 DATA INPUT DEVICES

There are various forms of data carriers used for program storage, but they must all have the ability to interface with machine controllers to enable them to readily download their stored information into the NC unit.

2.9.1 TAPE READER

One of the oldest data input devices is the punched-tape reader *(Fig. 2–14, p. 21)*, and it is still the most frequently used. Punched tape is scanned photoelectrically at reading speeds ranging from 150 to

FIGURE 2–14   Photoelectric tape reader with take-up reels.

300 characters per s. Reel diameters range from 4 to 10 in., and the length of tape *(L)* which a reel can hold may be calculated from:

$$L = 0.786 \frac{(D_2^2 - D_1^2)}{P}$$

where

D_1 = smallest reel diameter
D_2 = largest reel diameter
P = paper strength factor (determines tape thickness)

With CNC machines the complete part program, which may extend to a number of tapes, is entered into the programmer's memory store and retained there. This reduces wear on both the tape and the tape reader and makes the machining speed independent of the reading speed of the tape reader. Another advantage is that it is possible to start the next part quickly because it is not necessary to wait for the tape reader to rewind the tape(s) before it can read the program once more from the beginning.

On reading the tape a parity check is automatically performed on each punched-tape character for:

- Odd-numbered punch combinations in EIA code and/or even-numbered punch combinations in ISO code
- Logical character content in a given punch combination
- The correct order of characters, that is, first the address and then value and other data
- Correct addresses and correct block length
- Contradictory information

Error detection automatically stops the reading procedure and triggers an error-signal indicator lamp. Most controls repeat the reading of a block up to seven times before the error is definitely confirmed as a "wrong character," thus avoiding unnecessary machine downtime due to isolated misread errors. Wrongly entered data cannot be detected by the automatic check, but other checking procedures are available for this purpose.

2.9.2   KEYBOARD

With the ASCII keyboard, the user enters the program blocks word by word, and the CNC stores the program in its program memory. Errors are corrected in the same way with the aid of an editor. CNCs especially designed for shop-floor programming have between five and ten so-called "soft-keys" in addition to the normal keyboard keys. These soft-keys are programmable to offer regularly used special functions, their functions being displayed on the VDU screen.

2.9.3   MAGNETIC TAPE CASSETTES

Magnetic tape cassettes are convenient data carriers when large amounts of data are to be stored. Tape cassettes of two different sizes are currently available *(Fig. 2–15).*

FIGURE 2–15   Tape cassettes of different size and memory capacity.

Digital "magtape" equipment should have an adjustable transmission speed of between 110 and 19,600 characters per s to permit connection to a wide range of controllers.

There are five good reasons for the use of tape cassettes:

- Programs manually entered on the shop floor must be readily stored after use. This is simple with magnetic tape.
- It is possible to erase the data stored on magnetic tapes and reuse the tapes for the storage of new programs.
- Magnetic tape equipment may be used for both data input and output, and is cheaper than the punch and the reader needed for punch tapes.
- Tape cassettes are available in two different sizes: standard cassettes have a memory capacity of about 400 Kbytes and minicassettes hold about 64 Kbytes per side. (The storage of 200 Kbytes would require over 1500 ft of punch tape!)
- Mobile magtape equipment can be used at several machines and/or programming stations.

Despite these advantages there has been no breakthrough in the use of tape cassettes because of several major disadvantages:

- Data stored on magnetic tape is not visually controllable.
- Magtape is very sensitive to dirt and stray magnetic fields.

FIGURE 2–16   Data input and output devices for NC include a typewriter unit for paper tape punching and reading, magnetic tape readers for both standard and minicassettes, and floppy disks (5.25 and 3.5 inch).

- Magtape equipment does not produce a directly readable output.
- Rewinding the tape to find specific programs is time-consuming.

For these reasons magtape should only be used with controllers having a large program memory and a display which shows the data read into it so that a comparison with the program manuscript may be made.

2.9.4   FLOPPY DISKS

Floppy disks are similar in principle to magtapes, in that they are electro-magnetic reading media. Of the two common sizes, (5.25 in. and 3.5 in.), the 3.5 in. disks have the following advantages for shop-floor conditions:

- A sturdy plastic housing
- Protection of the sensitive disk coating by a metal cover, which automatically covers the reading window

- Memory capacity of up to 800 Kbytes
- Short access time to any location on the disk

Disk drives have standard interfaces, are sturdy and well protected against ingress of foreign matter, are very reliable, and are readily available in every computer shop.

It is surprising that disks are not used with NCs more frequently, especially in view of the recent drop in price of both disks and disk drives. Custom-made packages are even available offering a built-in disk drive, LCD display, ASCII keyboard, and a standard interface which allows connection to almost any type of NC controller.

2.9.5 DIRECT NUMERICAL CONTROL (DNC)

DNC computers are capable of handling a wider range of programs and much larger amounts of data than any other data input device. Such a computer consists of a central processing unit with a mass memory, which is directly linked to each NC unit in such a way as to permit bidirectional data transfer, that is, from the computer to any controller and vice versa.

DNC operation is considered in more detail in Chapter 17.

2.9.6 TEACH METHOD

The teach method consists basically of an experienced operator carrying out manually the functions and motions required to correctly produce the desired part. The machine's controller then memorizes the target values by operating a teach-in key. This process is particularly suited to the programming of robotic NC equipment.

2.9.7 INTERFACES

Interfaces are necessary for connecting data input devices to the NC unit. Typical interfaces to a modern CNC are shown in Fig. 2–17.

Several standard interface formats are available, but it is important to adjust voltage, current, transmission rate, and addresses to be compatible with the devices used. Fig. 2–18 *(p. 26)* lists basic transmission speeds of some typical interfaces.

2.10 VISUAL DISPLAYS

Because displays are the interface between controller and the user, good, informative displays are a vital prerequisite for error-free machine operation. Early NCs displayed only the current values of the individual axes, but the user was at least able to see, from almost any position, whether the axes were still moving or had already reached their target positions. This was a major improvement over the mechanical scales normal on machine tools at that time.

With the introduction of more advanced NCs the demand for greater operator information at the machine increased rapidly, and it is

FIGURE 2–17   Typical interfaces of a modern CNC.

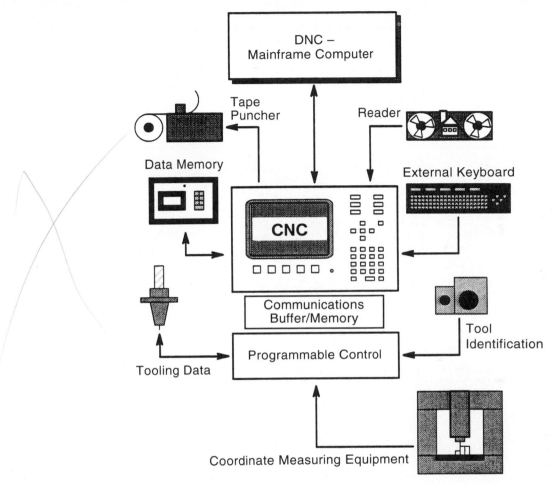

now possible to offer the user, at any time, a visual display of the following information:

- Program number, name, and occupied memory space
- Free memory space
- Correction factors for all tooling in the machine
- Zero point shifts
- Current feed rates, spindle speeds, and G and M functions
- Subroutines and "canned cycles" available
- Tool and piecepart administration status
- Error messages and information on the condition of the machine
- Machine parameters
- Input and simulation graphics

FIGURE 2–18   Interface transmission speeds.

INTERFACE	APPLICATION	TRANSMISSION SPEED	CONNECTIBLE DEVICES
BTR-input (8-bit parallel)	Data input for DNC operation (no output)	Maximum 500 characters/s	DNC computer
8-bit parallel	Data input via punch-tape reader or keyboard, suitable for short connecting lines only (no output)	maximum 500 characters/s	Punch tape reader keyboard
Bit-serial 20 mA line current (current-coupled)	Data input/output, appropriate for long connecting lines, undisturbed	up to 960 characters/s	Teletype, teleprinter, punch-tape reader
RS 232C (V24) voltage-coupled bit-serial	Data input/output, suited only for short connecting lines	up to 960 characters/s	terminal, printer, punch-tape reader
RS 422	Data input/output with safe transmission even through long connecting lines because of earth balanced data lines (2 sending and 2 receiving lines)	180 KBaud (about 18,000 characters/s)	Computer special operating fields (external station)

Additionally, text and graphics facilities for troubleshooting may also be required.

Of all the types of display devices available, the VDU screen display is generally the preferred choice in almost every case. Depending on the complexity of the controller, screens may be either large or small, and either monochromatic or in color. Some displays even allow the size of the characters displayed to be changed, so that positional values can be read easily from a distance, while normal character size is used for the display of programs and for data entry. It is occasionally helpful if a second or even a third screen is connected in parallel with the primary screen on large machines, so that a screen is always visible from any location.

2.11 THE COST OF (C)NC

If 1970 wage levels are used as a data baseline and by 1991 incomes have increased by over 300 percent while the prices of NC/CNC have dropped by 25–40 percent, depending on the number of control options offered.

For many companies this contramovement of prices and wages is a major reason for introducing NC machines, and there is no evidence to

FIGURE 2–19   The reduction in price of numerical controls (NC→CNC) compared with the increases in wages within the metal industry.

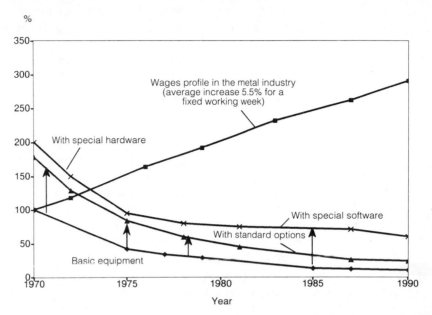

indicate that this trend will not continue for the foreseeable future.

The cost of numerical controls having comparable specification has dropped by almost half over the past 20 years *(Fig. 2–19)*. Most of this reduction occurred in the 1970s as since then, costs of color screens, the increase in the number of NC axes required, and the large expandible program memories now offered have broadly offset any further price reductions.

The attractive price pattern shown in Fig. 2–19 is mainly a result of the availability and use of modern, inexpensive standard microelectronics modules. It is indeed fortunate that electronic control and computer systems continue to develop rapidly, as today's CNC user is always looking for an ever increasing number of additional features on new controllers at no extra cost. Unfortunately extra facilities take up much free memory space which, in turn, reduces the controller's processing speed. Yet more microprocessors and memory have then to be provided.

QUESTIONS FOR CHAPTER 2

1. What is the fundamental difference between "NC and CNC?"
2. What are the principal constituents comprising a modern CNC system?
3. What is a "data carrier" as used for NC?
4. What is meant by the term "parity check?"
5. To what do the terms "technological and geometrical data" refer, and how do they differ?
6. Describe the various types of electronic modules used in NC controllers for memory storage.
7. What is an NC's operating system and what are its main functions?
8. Describe the four control modes used in NC.
9. What is meant by "interpolation" in the context of NC? Briefly describe at least three interpolation methods.
10. Give an example of a typical NC program block, explaining the meaning of each elemental word that you use.
11. What is the difference between absolute and incremental dimensioning; what are the principal advantages and limitations of each?
12. Why do you think floppy disks have not been as popular a medium for data storage as one might have expected?
13. What essential data would you require to be displayed on the VDU of a controller fitted to a modern turning center?
14. Why have machine controllers not continued to drop in price in recent years in the same way as they did in the 1970s?
15. Do you think that the pattern of wages versus controller costs that evolved in the 1980s is likely to continue in the 1990s? If so, why?

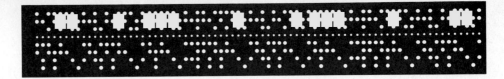

CHAPTER 3

CODED DATA FOR NUMERICALLY CONTROLLED SYSTEMS

After studying this chapter you should:

1. Understand the basis of the binary code.
2. Know why control data is frequently converted to binary format.
3. Be aware of the two most common forms of eight-track punched-tape codes.
4. Appreciate the advantages and disadvantages of punch tape as a binary data-carrying medium.
5. Understand how bar codes are formulated.

The digital encoding of data is essential if efficient storage, high-speed transmission, and automatic retrieval from the data carrier are to be achieved. Most coding systems are based on the binary code. This is described, as are the two most commonly used international code systems for data transmission in the field of numerical control. A brief insight is also provided into bar coding, and the use of magnetic cassettes as a data-storage medium.

3.1 BINARY CODE

As manufacturing professionals we all know that electronic devices and computers have no "intelligence" of their own, but merely perform predetermined tasks which people have "programmed" them to do. The "vocabulary" of electronic devices is limited to only two opposing concepts: ON and OFF, or, expressed differently, 1 and 0. Numerical control (NC) operates via electronic impulses; as a result the data entered into the control must also be represented by electronic impulses. There are only two possibilities:

- Impulse—current flowing (1)
- No impulse—no current flowing (0)

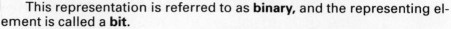

This representation is referred to as **binary**, and the representing element is called a **bit**.

How is it possible to express digits, numerals, characters, and letters with such a limited vocabulary?

Through the combination of several bits it is possible to express as many meanings as necessary. Representing certain characters with a bit-combination is called **absolute coding** and the rules governing such a conversion are called a **code**.

The best example of a binary system is the punch tape with two possible conditions that can occur in any one of eight signal tracks (8 bits): punched hole (1) and no punched hole (0).

3.2 THE BINARY NUMBERING SYSTEM

Our familiar numerical system, the decimal system, utilizes 10 digits: 0 1 2 3 4 5 6 7 8 9. In order to encode digits 0 through 9 in the 1/0 representation, 10 bits would have to be used—one bit for each digit from 0 through 9. See, for example, the number 5209 shown in Fig. 3–1.

FIGURE 3–1   Decimal code.

Track	Value	Code
1	1	
2	2	o
3	3	
4	4	
5	5	o
6	6	
7	7	
8	8	
9	9	o
10	0	o

5 2 0 9

Since even more bits would be necessary for letters and characters, this system would be very expensive. The binary numbering system is much simpler because it utilizes only two digits, 0 and 1. Therefore, binary numbers are only represented by digits 0 and 1. For example, 1101 = 13 and 111111100 = 508 *(Fig. 3–2)*.

FIGURE 3–2   Binary number 508.

256	128	64	32	16	8	4	2	1
1	1	1	1	1	1	1	0	0

$$256 + 128 + 64 + 32 + 16 + 8 + 4 + 0 + 0 = 508$$

With the decimal system, the order value of a digit is given by powers of 10. Thus 521 is expressed by:

$$10^0 \times 1 = 1$$
$$10^1 \times 2 = 20$$
$$10^2 \times 5 = \underline{500}$$
$$\underline{\underline{521}}$$

With the binary system, the order value is given by powers of 2. For example:

$$\mathbf{1101} = 2^0 \times 1 = 1$$
$$2^1 \times 0 = 0$$
$$2^2 \times 1 = 4$$
$$2^3 \times 1 = \underline{8}$$

Thus binary 1101 = $\underline{13}$

With the binary system, *n* bits (binary signals, tracks) can define two conditions or represent two characters *(Fig. 3–3)*.

FIGURE 3–3   Code table for binary-decimal conversion.

Bits			Number of Representable Characters
1	2^1	=	2
2	2^2	=	4
3	2^3	=	8
4	2^4	=	16
5	2^5	=	32
6	2^6	=	64
7	2^7	=	128
8	2^8	=	256
9	2^9	=	512
10	2^{10}	=	1 024
11	2^{11}	=	2 048
12	2^{12}	=	4 096
13	2^{13}	=	8 192
14	2^{14}	=	16 384
15	2^{15}	=	32 768
16	2^{16}	=	65 536
17	2^{17}	=	131 072
18	2^{18}	=	262 144
19	2^{19}	=	524 288
20	2^{20}	=	1 048 576
21	2^{21}	=	2 097 152
22	2^{22}	=	4 194 304
23	2^{23}	=	8 388 608

Applying a pure binary system would very quickly lead to difficulties because:

1. Only eight tracks (8 bits) are available on a standard punch tape.
2. Large decimal numbers are cumbersome to encode.

Therefore the decimal and binary systems have been combined to form the binary-coded decimal code (BCD).

3.3 THE BINARY-CODED DECIMAL CODE

In BCD, only the digits 0 through 9 are coded as binary *(Fig. 3–4),* and the decimal position is treated as it is in the decimal system. For example:

0001	0111	0100	0010	0011	0110	= 174 236
1	7	4	2	3	6	

With the BCD code it is thus possible to represent any desired numerical value since the number of positions is unlimited. The BCD-coded punch tape is therefore ideal for data storage and as input for NC.

FIGURE 3–4   Principle of punch-tape code (for demonstration purposes, only significant tracks are represented).

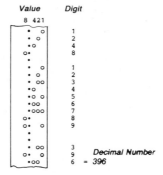

With the BCD code it is possible to easily represent any desired numerical value.

3.4 PUNCH-TAPE CODES

The 1-in. wide, 8-track punch tape *(Fig. 3–5)* offers an adequate supply of possible binary combinations and has become an internationally

FIGURE 3–5   8-track punch tape.

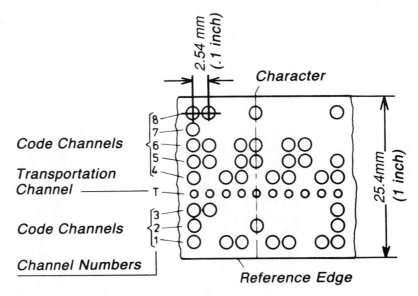

standardized format. The most common punch-tape codes are the EIA and the ISO forms.

3.4.1   EIA CODE

Tracks 1–4:   Binary-coded digits
Track 5:   Parity bit
Track 6:   Digit 0
Tracks 6 & 7: In combination with 1 and 4: letters and characters
Track 8:   End of block

Using a parity bit in track 5 always ensures an odd number of punch holes per character, thereby facilitating testing for simple punching errors. The system automatically punches a hole in track 5 when the sum of the data-punch holes is even.

3.4.2   ISO CODE

Tracks 1–4: In combination with 5–6:   Digits 0–9
Tracks 1–5: In combination with 7:   Letters A–Z
Track 8:   Parity bit
Tracks 1–4: In combination with 6:   Characters

The parity bit in track 8 provides an even number of holes per character. This representation enables the numerical controller to read the numerical values, addresses, and characters necessary for machine control directly from the punch tape.

FIGURES 3–6 AND 3–7 EIA code and ISO code.

TAPE CODE

EIA-Code (RS-244) | **ISO-Code (DIN 66024)**

EIA Symbol	Description	ISO Symbol
0	Numerical Value	0
1	Numerical Value	1
2	Numerical Value	2
3	Numerical Value	3
4	Numerical Value	4
5	Numerical Value	5
6	Numerical Value	6
7	Numerical Value	7
8	Numerical Value	8
9	Numerical Value	9
a	Address - Rotary Axis about x	A
b	Address - Rotary Axis about y	B
c	Address - Rotary Axis about z	C
d	Address - Path Compensation	D
e	Address - Reader Monitor	E
f	Address - Feedrate/Dwell	F
g	Address - Preparatory Functions	G
h	Address - Tool Length Compens.	H
i	Address - Interpolation Parameter	I
j	Address - Interpolation Parameter	J
k	Address - Interpolation Parameter	K
l	unassigned	L
m	Address - Machine Instructions	M
n	Address - Sequence Number	N
o	not used	O
p	Address - Dwell/Subprogram	P
q	Address - Subprogram	Q
r	Plane Reference/Radius	R
s	Address - Spindle Speed	S
t	Address - Tool/Offset	T
u	Address - Parallel Axis	U
v	Address - Parallel Axis	V
w	Address - Parallel Axis	W
x	Address - Main Axes	X
y	Address - Main Axes	Y
z	Address - Main Axes	Z
<‖	End of Block	LF
STOP	Program Start	%
/	Optional Block Delete	/
–	Negative Traversing Direction	–
	Operator Instruction ON	(
	Operator Instruction OFF	)
*		*
•	Decimal Point	•

Characters accepted but not processed

EIA Symbol	Description	ISO Symbol
+	Positive Traversing Direction	+
,	Comma	,
:	Colon	:
TAB	Tabulator	HT
IRR	Delete Character	DEL
ZWR	Space	SP
	Sprocket	NUL
RT	Back Space	BS
%	Percent	
–	Carriage Return	CR

Channel 5 is check channel (parity check) | **Channel 8 is check channel (parity check)**

Only listed characters can be used

An 8-bit unit is called 1 byte and 1 byte represents either:

- 1 letter
- 1 digit
- 1 character

Accordingly, words or numerals in the BCD code require as many bytes as they contain letters or digits. For example,

- The word John uses 4 bytes.
- The number 256 uses 3 bytes.
- The character / uses 1 byte.

On this basis, it is rather simple to use coded instructions in communicating with the numerical controller.

3.5 ADVANTAGES AND DISADVANTAGES OF PUNCH TAPE AS A DATA CARRIER

Advantages:

- Capacity of approximately 64,000 characters per roll (500 ft) is usually sufficient for most jobs.
- Data is permanently well stored.
- Data is visually controllable.
- Format is standardized.
- Reading speed is sufficiently high (standard 150–250 characters per s, up to a maximum of 1000 characters per s).
- Unlike punch cards, punch tapes are in no danger of being erroneously mixed.
- There is no danger of accidentally erasing information as there is with magnetic tapes.
- Punch tape is shop-floor suited, that is, insensitive to magnetic fields or oil contamination.

Disadvantages:

- Once a tape is punched, there is no way of correcting it.
- Storage density is low.
- Tapes are not erasable and then reusable.
- Tape readers are relatively sensitive to physical disturbances.
- Tape reader and punch are both necessary. With magnetic tapes the recorder fulfills both the record (input) and the replay (output) functions.
- If the paper-tape material used is reinforced with a plastic layer, the punch is subject to increased wear.
- Considerable organizational effort is necessary with increasing stocks of part programs.

Current trends are to use erasable and reusable data carriers with higher information density, higher reading speed and simpler administration. Storage devices used are floppy disks, magnetic tape cassettes, and bubble memories. Nevertheless, punch tape is still popular because it is handy to use and allows visual control of the punched information. In contrast, data stored on magnetic tape is visually controllable only after being read into a data storage and then displayed on a VDU screen or printer.

3.6 BAR CODES

The bar code has become well known because it is used for the identification of everyday products—in supermarkets for example. A bar code is made up of a band of narrow and wide stripes and gaps (Fig. 3–8).

There are several standard codes. With some of them, information is contained only in the bars and the gaps are of no significance, while other codes use both the bars and the gaps.

The ratio of the dimensions, narrow to wide, differs from code to code. It is thus difficult to visually read the bar code without a great deal of experience. This is why additional arabic numerals are normally printed adjacent to the code in most instances. However a bar code can be read quickly by special electronic devices without problems and with high reliability. Laser scanners even allow a distance of up to approximately 30 in. between the reading device and the printed code.

The necessary size of the bar code depends on the reading speed, the angle between the code and the scanner, and the number of signs and figures to be decoded.

With NC machines, bar codes are mainly employed for marking workpieces and tools and, instead of expensive, mechanical coding devices, cheap bar-code stickers can be used. This information is transferred from the electronic scanner to the NC or the mainframe computer where it is stored and processed. Thus the flow of material or tools in a manufacturing system can be followed electronically. This is why it is usually sufficient to read the code only once—when the part or tool enters the system. Thus the danger of reading errors due to dirty bar-code stickers is eliminated. Bar-code stickers can be produced economically and quickly with common matrix or laser printers.

3.7 MAGNETIC TAPE CASSETTES

Magnetic tape cassettes are suitable data carriers whenever large amounts of data are to be recorded and stored. To accommodate the length of the program to be stored two cassette sizes are available:

1. Minicassettes which can store about 32 Kbytes per side—equal to approximately 260 ft of punch paper tape.
2. Standard audio cassettes which have a storage capacity of about 200 Kbytes per side, depending on tape length—equal to approximately 1600 ft of punch tape.

FIGURE 3-8   Bar codes.

Code Table

Code No.	L1	L2	L3	L4	L5
1	1	0	0	0	1
2	0	1	0	0	1
3	1	1	0	0	0
4	0	0	1	0	1
5	1	0	1	0	0
6	0	1	1	0	0
7	0	0	0	1	1
8	1	0	0	1	0
9	0	1	0	1	0
0	0	0	1	1	0
Start	1	1	0		
End	1	0	1		

L1-L5=Line 1-5, 1=Thick Line, 0=Thin Line

EXAMPLES

A ' 1 ' 2 ' 3 ' 4 ' 5 ' 6 ' 7 ' 8 ' 9 ' 0 ' 5 ' E

   1234

A ' 1 ' 2 ' 3 ' 4 ' E

Ordinary tape recorders cannot be used. Only devices which have been specifically designed for NC applications should be used as they possess special functions that guarantee the required reliability for data reading and writing. Such functions are, for example:

- Microprocessor control for multifunction operation (read, write, start, stop, automatic, search for, and so on)
- Automatic self diagnosis after being switched on
- Automatic error correction during the procedure of writing data onto tapes
- Parallel and/or serial interfaces for connection to the NC's various programming systems
- Adjustable transmission rate (reading speed), from 110 to 9600 baud
- Ability to record in ISO code or binary code
- Input buffer storage to permit use in connection with simple programming devices instead of tape punches
- Shop-floor-quality enclosure case

The application of magnetic tape cassettes in preference to punch paper tapes has the following advantages:

- Easy program correction. Repeated writing and erasing of the tapes as necessary permits easy program correction.
- Economy. The tape recorder fulfills the tasks of both the punch and the tape reader required for production of punch tapes.

Special care must be exercised when handling cassettes on the shop floor. There is danger of accidental data erasure, if they are subjected to stray magnetic fields.

Despite their advantages the magnetic tape cassette may never become so popular a data-carrier medium as punch tape, because direct downloading of data from a host computer in the latest direct numerical control (DNC) systems is rapidly taking over the tasks of data storage and administration.

QUESTIONS FOR CHAPTER 3

1. Why is it necessary to code information processed by a data carrier?
2. How many characters are used in binary code?
3. Describe the BCD system, and transcribe the numbers 7, 11, and 16 into this format.
4. Convert the BCD code 00110110 into decimal form.
5. Which is the most commonly used tape coding system in NC equipment?
6. What is the length of an 8-track punch tape containing 1000 characters?

7. Is it feasible to edit punch-tape programs? If so, how?
8. What is the most significant difference between the EIA and ISO tape codes?
9. What advantages and disadvantages do magnetic-based-data carrier media have over punch tape?

CHAPTER 4

NC MACHINE-TOOL MEASURING SYSTEMS

After studying this chapter you should understand:

1. The need for accurate path-measuring systems to be fitted to NC machines.
2. The alternative basic principles on which linear path-measurement and radial-location devices operate.
3. The difference between direct and indirect measuring systems.
4. The difference between incremental and absolute path-measuring systems.
5. What the basic differences are between resolvers and encoders.
6. How rotary and linear inductosyns work.

The machine-tool builder selects, at the design stage, the path-measuring system best suited to the machine's fundamental characteristics. Major factors that are taken into consideration are typically the required operating path length, maximum traverse velocity, minimum incremental step required, accuracy level, repeatability, ease of fitting onto the machine tool, and overall system cost.

4.1 INTRODUCTION

Each axis of a NC machine tool requires its own path-measuring system which is capable of delivering electronic signals that are readily processable by the machine's NC unit. This can be accomplished in a number of ways but most of today's NCs are predominantly designed for use with incremental path-measuring systems.

The machine's design and its required accuracy determine whether a photoelectrically scanned scale or ball-screw monitoring is the preferred method. However the way in which target positional values are programmed does not depend on the measuring procedure used, and with modern controllers both absolute and/or incremental programming may be selected, independent of the measuring system employed.

FIGURE 4–1   Characteristics of path measurement.

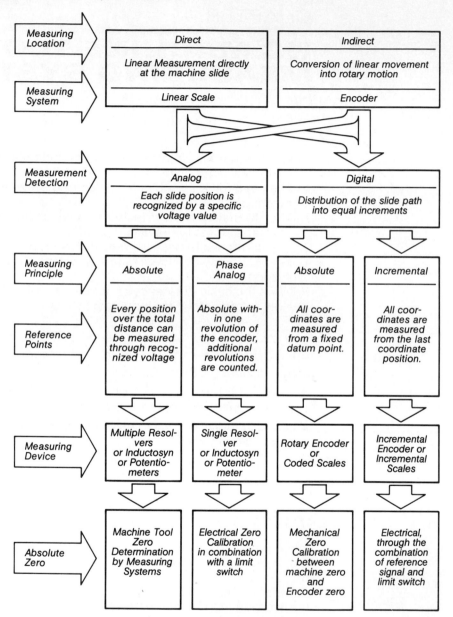

For satisfactory operation, the numerical control of machine tools requires a measuring system having an incremental step of 0.00005 in. or less. The pitch of all scales therefore always requires further subdivision, some measuring systems performing an electronic "interpolation" at the same time as the scale is scanned to achieve the required degree of subdivision.

4.2 AXIS MEASURING SYSTEMS

A wide variety of measuring systems is now available for NC machines, each employing its own measuring principles and related signal processing procedures.

4.2.1 THE MEASURING SYSTEM

All NC path-measuring systems have a constant pitch, the size of which is an important characteristic as it determines the system's resolution. Optoelectronic measuring systems have the highest resolution because their measuring principle permits extremely small "pitches." Photoelectric scale pitches typically go down to 0.0003 in. and they also have the advantage of being insensitive to dirt, thus requiring no housing or cover.

Scales incorporating permanent magnets have a pitch of 0.008 in., while inductosyn scales have a pitch of approximately 0.1 in. It should be remembered that the pitch of ball screws is identical to one rotation of the spindle (typically 0.25–0.5 in.), while rack-and-pinion systems have a pitch that is identical to the circumference of the pinion and is much larger—normally around 4 in.

For satisfactory operation, the numerical control of machine tools requires a measuring system having an incremental step of 0.00005 in. or less. The pitch of all scales therefore always requires further subdivision, some measuring systems performing an electronic "interpolation" at the same time as the scale is scanned to achieve the required degree of subdivision.

4.2.2 DIRECT AND INDIRECT MEASURING SYSTEMS

Photoelectric or inductive scales produce an electrical signal for direct input into the controller unit, whereas mechanical elements like ball screws or rack and pinions need a rotary encoder or resolver to produce an electrical signal. This is why measuring systems with a direct response feedback sensing device are called " direct measuring systems" (Fig. 4–2), and those with mechanical elements plus encoder or resolver are referred to as "indirect measuring systems" (Fig. 4–3, *p. 44*).

FIGURE 4–2a   Direct path measurement at the machine table.

FIGURE 4–2b   Principle of direct path measurement with reflecting scale.

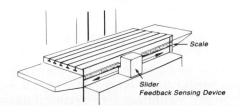

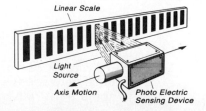

FIGURE 4–3   Indirect path measurement with ball screw/nut and rack/pinion mechanical devices.

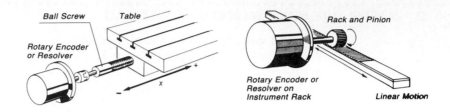

In some instances the desired resolution can only be achieved with a special mechanical amplification mechanism being installed between the mechanical elements and the resolver or encoder. The required ratio *(i)* is:

$$i = M \times \frac{n}{T}$$

where

    M = desired incremental step (resolution) (eg. 0.00005 in. for example)
    n = number of incremental steps per encoder revolution (10,000 for example)
    T = pitch or linear path per revolution

If such a mechanism is used, any transmission error adds to the inaccuracy of the mechanical elements (ball screw/nut or rack/pinion) and thus adversely influences overall measurement accuracy of the system. Also, because backlash can always be a source of serious measurement errors, most NCs have error compensation features incorporated to minimize such systematic deviations. Modern controllers also offer electronic compensation on each separate axis for nonsystematic errors.

4.2.3   ABSOLUTE AND INCREMENTAL PATH-MEASURING SYSTEMS

Movement of a machine axis may be measured in two ways—by difference between two measurements, both being taken from a fixed "machine zero" datum point, or simply by noting the start and finish points without reference to any absolute reference point at all; this is synonymous with the absolute and incremental programming methods referred to in Section 2.8.3. Hence the former measuring method is termed absolute measurement, while the latter is referred to as incremental measurement.

Incremental Measuring Systems

Every measuring scale has its entire path length divided into many incremental steps, and as the axis moves, an electronic counter summates all impulses from the resolver or encoder, adding them up to a value that corresponds to the path length traveled. With incremental measuring systems, zero shifts are not a problem because zero point can be freely selected. Machine zero point is marked on each axis of the machine by a reference mark on the scale or disk of the measuring system, and when the axis reaches the position of this data mark, a reference impulse is generated.

Absolute Path-Measuring Systems

Absolute measuring systems recognize the location of each machine axis immediately after the machine is switched on, the position of each axis being known to the control as an absolute value without the need to traverse a zero or reference point *(Figs. 4–4, 4–5, 4–6a & b)*. Each point on the traverse path is given via a unique signal and is thus identifiable without ambiguity.

FIGURE 4–4   Scanning principle of a rotary encoder.

FIGURE 4–5   Decimally encoded scale.

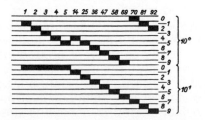

FIGURE 4–6a Straight binary encoded disk.

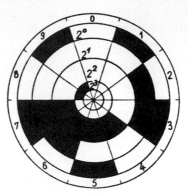

FIGURE 4–6b Binary-decimal encoded scale.

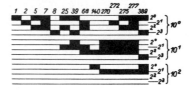

Absolute measuring systems are particularly attractive as it is unnecessary to move each axis back to its reference point to reestablish absolute position after, say, an interruption in the machining process. Unfortunately, direct absolute measuring systems are not currently available as they require much space, and their operating procedure is very sophisticated and hence expensive. However, there are hybrid measurement systems, such as using an inductosyn scale whose pitch period is identified by an absolute rotary encoder attached to the axis ball screw (pitch period interpolation is absolute). Because the whole path length of the axis requires many rotations of the ball screw, so-called multiturn encoders are necessary. Indirect absolute measuring systems are thus currently the norm, incorporating spindles with photoelectric multiturn encoders/resolvers.

Early controllers predominantly employed "cyclic-absolute" measuring systems using resolvers or inductosyn scales. The absolute position was detected only once per resolver revolution, and for longer distances an additional electronic counter monitored the number of resolver rotations. Thus the absolute position, relative to a reference point on the axis, was determined without ambiguity. Unfortunately, if the counter memory had been cleared due to power outage, the absolute distance from the reference point was no longer known, and the controller had to be reset to zero at the reference point. However, the introduction of an additional absolute resolver to log the number of rotations avoided this problem.

More recently the demand for low-cost absolute measuring systems has led to the development of new, cheaper devices which are best termed "pseudo-absolute."

4.3 DESIGN OF NC PATH-MEASURING SYSTEMS

A basic understanding of the elements comprising most path-measuring systems is helpful to more fully appreciate overall system function. The following subsections (4.3.1 and 4.3.2) provide this introduction for both the inductive path and photoelectric approaches.

4.3.1 INDUCTIVE PATH-MEASURING SYSTEM ELEMENTS

Resolvers, synchro and inductosyn scales all belong to this category. Any system which uses the inductive principle outputs two measuring voltages which are out of phase by 90°, both having the same frequency. One output is a reference voltage while the other is axis-position dependent.

The controller compares both phase position and amplitude of the measuring voltage to the fixed reference voltage, and is therefore able to electronically evaluate actual axis position at all times.

Resolvers

A resolver is intended to provide an accurate measure of angular position, its design being the same as that of an AC slip-ring motor, only smaller and more precise *(Fig. 4–7, p. 48)*. It consists of a solid steel housing (the stator frame) and a rotor running in high-precision bearings. The stator has two windings electrically out of phase by 90°, while the rotor winding is of single-phase construction, to which a transformer applies a voltage. Because no brushes are necessary, contact and arcing problems are avoided, thus making the resolver maintenance-free.

In operation the transformer applies a fixed-frequency sinusoidal voltage to the rotor coil, and rotation therefore produces inductive voltages in the two stator windings that are out of phase by 90°. The effective value, and the phase offset of one voltage relative to the other, depend on the position of the rotor (the angle between rotor and stator coils), and enable the generation of an angular position signal of 10 to 16 bit resolution, that is, each revolution of the rotor is subdivided into 1024 to 65,536 measuring steps.

In addition to 2-pole resolvers, there are also 10-pole units available. They have a stator with five windings so that one revolution of the rotor is equated to five times 360° of "electrical angle," that is, turning the rotor through 72° corresponds to an "electrical angle" of a full 360°.

FIGURE 4–7   Measurement resolvers.

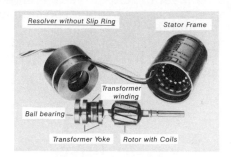

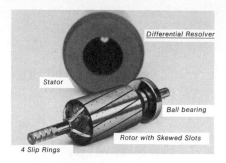

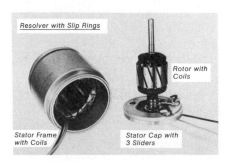

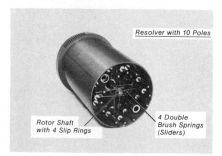

Rotary and Linear Inductosyns

The rotary inductosyn *(Fig. 4–8)* may be compared to a synchronous resolver with a very large number of poles and a surface-like measuring arrangement. Thus, for example, with a 2000-pole rotary inductosyn (with 1000 pole pairs), an electrical phase shift of 360° will result from only a 0.36° rotation of the rotary inductosyn.

The linear inductosyn *(Fig. 4–9)* is similar to a rotary unit except that its windings are laid out linearly—similar to a linear motor. The amplitude and phase shift of the induced voltage via the linear motion depends on the relative positions of the two elements, that is, the fixed scale windings corresponding to rotor windings, and the sliding scale windings corresponding to stator windings.

FIGURE 4–8   Rotary inductosyn.

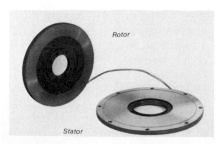

FIGURE 4–9   Linear inductosyn.

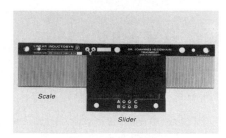

4.3.2   PHOTOELECTRIC SYSTEMS

Photoelectric path-measuring systems are of either the encoder or linear measuring scale format, while shaft encoders and scales are of either the incremental or absolute type.

Incremental Shaft Encoders

An encoder *(Fig. 4–10)* is a rotary transducer device which generates a preset number of evenly spaced electronic pulses every revolution. Shaft encoders come in standard sizes ranging from 1.5 to 7 in. in outside diameter, and with grid sensitivity ranges from 50 to 100,000 pulses per revolution. However, encoders with an outside diameter of 2.25 in. and a grid division of 5000 pulses per revolution have now become the main industrial standard.

Encoders are usually combined with electronic multiplier circuits to increase the number of encoder impulses per revolution. Four, five, ten, and even twenty-five times the grid division sensitivity are now common.

In addition to the grid index, the glass disk of the encoder also has a zero reference mark to provide a precise reference impulse point once every revolution. This is used to set the impulse counter to zero, as well as to control the encoder by arranging for an error-signal to be generated if the number of actual measuring impulses between the two reference impulses deviates by more than plus or minus one impulse from the set value.

FIGURE 4–10   Incremental shaft encoder.

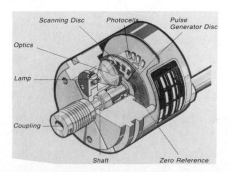

Incremental shaft encoders are frequently used because of the following advantages:

- High level of reliability
- High rate of maximum acceleration
- Possibility of high rotation speed
- High resolution
- Relatively low cost compared to the rest of the system
- Ease of installation

Incremental Measuring Scales

These systems work on the same principle as incremental shaft encoders: photoelectric scanning of a grid index consisting of alternating opaque and transparent areas of equal width engraved on either glass or reflecting steel tape *(Fig. 4–11)*.

Two sinusoidal wave signals are produced via relative motion between reference and sliding grid scales which have an electrical phase shift of 90°. The electronics of the measuring system converts these signals into direction-specific impulses, which are then counted to provide an indication of precise position.

When employed on machine tools, linear scales that are completely enclosed (encapsulated linear measuring systems) are used to avoid ingress of dirt, coolant, and so forth *(Fig. 4–12)*.

FIGURE 4–11   Design and operating principle of a linear path-measuring system. Photoelectric measuring systems and encoders normally operate on the principle of fine grid-index scanning. The grid index is made up of opaque and transparent sections of equal width. Parallel to the index is a reference mark to precisely define zero points.

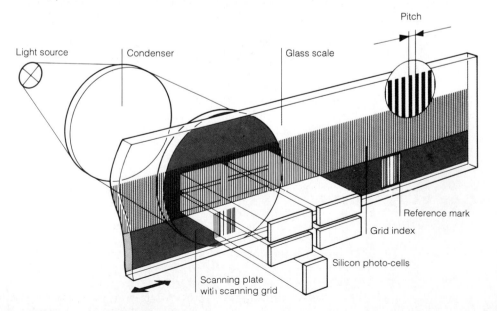

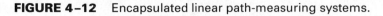

FIGURE 4–12   Encapsulated linear path-measuring systems.

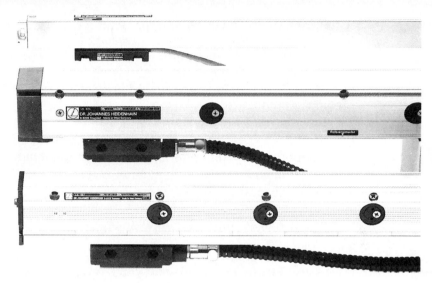

Absolute Shaft Encoders

The actual angular position of an encoder is computed via signals generated photoelectrically from incremental segments on the encoder disk. As with other "absolute" devices, absolute axis position is automatically established immediately after the machine tool is switched on.

Absolute shaft encoders are available in different pitch sizes, for example:

2^{10} = 1024 increments per revolution
    (approximately 1 per 21 min of arc)
2^{13} = 8192 increments per revolution
    (approximately 1 per 2.64 min of arc)
2^{17} = 131,072 increments per revolution
    (approximately 1 per 10 sec of arc)

4.4 SUMMARY

Various types of path-measuring systems are fitted to NC machines, and the measurement signal format produced differs widely. Therefore the controller used must have the appropriate interfacing to be able to accept and analyze the input-signal data. Processing of this input data in numerical controllers is always digital.

Most manufacturers of measuring systems offer electronic analyzer and amplifier units to match their systems, and these are best employed wherever possible to ensure optimum compatibility.

QUESTIONS FOR CHAPTER 4

1. What are the basic requirements of any measuring system fitted to NC machine tools?
2. What is the fundamental difference between a direct and an indirect measuring system?
3. What is the main advantage of a direct measuring system?
4. What is the principal attraction of fitting NC machine tools with an absolute measuring system?
5. What is backlash compensation? What is it used for?
6. What are the main differences between resolvers and encoders?
7. What enables an NC to find its zero reference point precisely?
8. Why do optoelectronic measuring systems have a higher resolution than other methods of NC axis measurement?
9. What makes an incremental shaft encoder a particularly attractive device?
10. What is the effect of fitting an absolute shaft encoder with a finer pitch size? Illustrate your answer with a numerical example.

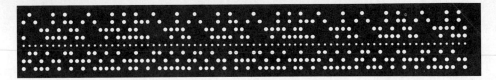

CHAPTER 5

PRINCIPLES OF NUMERICAL CONTROL AS APPLIED TO MACHINE TOOLS

After studying this chapter you should understand:

1. The main elements of a numerically-controlled machine tool.
2. The influence that NC has had on machine-tool design, cutting-tool development, machine-tool price, and on the industrial organization as a whole.
3. The principal advantages of NC in manufacturing.
4. What determines NC machine-tool accuracy, and how this can influence production.
5. The main safety features necessary on NC machine tools.
6. The importance of efficient maintenance and service provision when operating an NC shop.

The basic principle of controlling machine tools via numerical control has remained unchanged since its inception. However, the number of functions and tasks allocated to the controller has grown steadily over the years and now offers a high level of automation.

5.1 DEVELOPMENT OF THE NC MACHINE TOOL

A schematic diagram showing the basic constituent elements of a numerically controlled machine tool is shown in Figure 5–1. Such a machine tool differs considerably from a "conventional" machine, which is operated manually by a skilled worker who reads the part drawing and then applies the required machining parameters based on experience. Thus with conventional machines, machining quality and productivity depend to a great extent on the operator's skill, which explains

---

FIGURE 5–1   Schematic diagram of the basic elements comprising an NC machine tool.

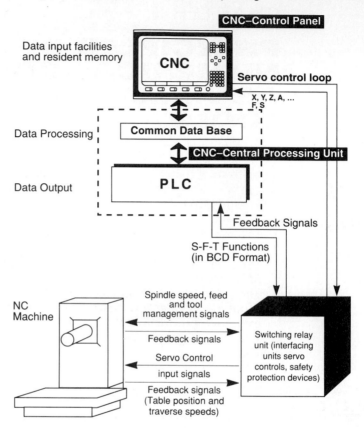

why quality of production varies from one worker to another and from day to day.

NC machines overcome this inconsistency because the control of the machine's functions is determined by a fixed program and is thus largely independent of the operator.

NC machines are freely programmable manufacturing devices and are exceptionally well suited to the automatic production of small- to medium-lot sizes. Their main advantages are their flexibility and the speed with which the machining programs can be changed with a minimum of manual interference, that is, with minimized set-up time.

NC machine flexibility is achieved because of:

- Repeatability in executing proven programs
- Ability to directly input part dimensions and tool-path data at the machine-tool level if desired (Chapter 8)
- Absence of mechanical path limiters such as cam rails, stops, or templates, which means that no mechanical adjustments are necessary

- Ability to input optimum technological values such as feed rate, spindle speed, and coolant on/off, which are then not normally alterable by the operator
- Computerized control of all additional machine functions, such as the automatic changeover of cutting tools and piecepart
- Programmable call-up of off-set values for both cutting tools and workpieces mounted on standardized pallets

5.2 THE NC MACHINE TOOL

A fundamental feature of any NC machine is its accurate, high resolution measuring system, which delivers electronically processible output signals that are then used to control the drive motor on each of the machine's axes (Chapter 4). These motors replace the handwheels and levers found on conventional machines, and in so doing offer fully mechanized operation.

Basically it is possible to control most types of machines digitally, and the underlying operating principle is the same; however, the details differ considerably from one machine type to another. This is why their control requirements vary, making it impossible to specify a standard control suitable for all broadly similar equipment.

5.3 THE IMPACT OF NC ON MANUFACTURING INDUSTRY

In all walks of life new developments often have far-reaching implications. The invention of numerical control is no exception, having had a major impact on the area of machine-tool design as well as on most other areas of the industrial organizational structure.

5.3.1   THE INFLUENCE OF NC ON MACHINE-TOOL DESIGN PHILOSOPHY

NC has led the design of machine tools in the direction of ensuring that they carry out as many machining operations as possible on a component during one set-up. Automatic pallet changers and automatic tool change, combined with quick-acting cutting tool clamping, all serve to increase the overall degree of machine automation. In the case of turning centers, special oblique and sloping bed designs allow for near perfect chip removal, and custom gearing and spindle mounting prevent precision loss due to thermal distortion of the machine. Also, all parts that can influence the accuracy of the machine tool (lead screws for example) are enclosed to protect them against the ingress of either coolant or chips. Dynamic and static rigidity have also been enhanced to withstand the much greater cutting and other operational forces encountered when running an NC machine to its design limits.

5.3.2 THE INFLUENCE OF NC ON CUTTING TOOL DEVELOPMENT

In addition to tooling which was designed originally for use on conventional machine tools and which can still be used on NC machines, a wide range of special tooling has now been developed specifically for NC machines. This topic is dealt with fully in Chapter 13, but in the context of this chapter, it is worth noting some special requirements which NC tooling is designed to fulfill:

- Positive interlocking of tools in the machine's spindle
- High level of precision and rigidity
- Coolant delivery through the tooling
- Presetting capability of tooling remote from the machine tool
- Manual and automatic tool changing capability
- Suitability for special gripper mechanism for automatic tool change
- Tooling capable of being automatically identified

It is vital that the user minimize the variety of tooling that must be stocked to meet machining requirements. To this end the major cutting-tool suppliers have now developed universal tooling systems suitable for use in both machining and turning centers. Furthermore, storage capacity of the machine's tooling magazines is limited, and as frequent tool exchanges to and from these magazines are both expensive and unproductive, tools should be kept to a minimum. Indeed, experienced NC users now distinguish between standard, batch, and special tooling, and associate each with its own specific manufacturing costs, thus providing a real incentive to use standard tooling wherever possible. Furthermore, users can expect to receive significant support from cutting-tool manufacturers in terms of both consultation and the provision of extensive technical literature.

5.3.3 THE INFLUENCE OF NC ON MACHINE TOOL DRIVE ELEMENTS

Because of the higher utilization and heavier loads expected of NC machine tools, drives, gearing, bedways, spindles, and bearings, they all have to be resized, and, where necessary, reinforced. Tapered lead screws have given way to recirculating ball-screw designs, and gear changers have yielded to variable speed drives. Even here changes are occurring in that current DC motor drives are increasingly being replaced in favor of brushless and maintenance-free servodrives.

As rapid traverse rates and accelerations become even greater, (up to 130 ft/s^2), the machine's elements have to be redesigned to absorb the effects of these larger operating forces without damage. It is also becoming increasingly common for axis drives to be fitted with safety couplings to minimize damage in the event of machine, workpiece, or tooling collision.

5.3.4   THE INFLUENCE OF NC ON MACHINE TOOL PRICE

The improved design and quality of NC machine tools, the need for superprecision measuring systems, and the necessity of more extensive predelivery and post-installation commissioning and training programs collectively contribute to making the cost of NC machines considerably higher than conventional ones. Therefore, prior to purchasing such machines, the potential user must conduct an economic analysis, taking into account profitability, machine utilization, workload projections, effects of multiple shift operation, and so on. This is the only way to justify the purchase of such high capital-cost equipment.

5.3.5   THE INFLUENCE OF NC ON THE INDUSTRIAL ORGANIZATION

The application of NC machine tools also influences the more generalized total manufacturing process from preliminary design—through process planning, production, and storage—to assembly. When properly employed, the advantages of NC machines can provide cost savings throughout the entire manufacturing process, assuming that an appropriate balance between the individual elements is achieved. To assist in this regard it is usual to introduce NC machines in the following three stages:

1. Replacement of one or two conventional machine tools by a single NC machine
2. Expansion of the NC facility by the purchase of additional NC machines and the systematic distribution of production over several machines
3. Integration and addition of various NC ancillaries to establish flexible manufacturing islands and/or systems, and employment of direct numerical control (DNC) operation. Chapters 17 and 18 deal with these aspects in detail.

Clearly the scope of the planning and preparation necessary will decrease with subsequent machine purchases due to the experience gained from installing the first machine.

5.3.6   THE INFLUENCE OF NC ON THE TOTAL CONCEPT OF PRODUCTION

Assuming that all relevant aspects influencing design and construction of NC machine tools have been taken into consideration, the purchaser and/or user of any NC equipment should have three basic expectations:

1. Absolute dependability of the total system is guaranteed.
2. Operational efficiency must be maintained over a prolonged period.
3. The system must be easy to operate, facilitating rapid training of workers.

To limit technological risk, purchasers frequently prefer tried and tested products which have a proven track record in practical application. However, progressive development, new designs, and differing customer requirements do not always permit such a simple, guaranteed solution. Therefore, in selecting a machine-tool/controller combination, the user should particularly focus on the elements that have the greatest impact on the machine tool's intended use. In addition to basic considerations one should also include an evaluation of the modular expansion and automation accessories offered by the manufacturer that may be subsequently purchased to increase or extend system performance.

Finally, the quality of the eventual manufacturing process is directly dependent on the software that has been prepared for it. Therefore it is extremely important to pay special attention to programming standards, and how one's production-planning department will cope with the complexities of piecepart programming.

5.4 PRIME ADVANTAGES OF NC IN MANUFACTURING

For medium- to small-lot sizes, NC machining often represents the most economical production method for the following reasons:

- Relative ease with which complex parts can be manufactured once a program is available
- Assurance of consistently reliable precision and accuracy
- Lower scrap rates
- Lower production-control costs
- Small optimum lot sizes
- Shorter throughput lead times
- Less money tied up in "work-in-progress"
- Shorter delivery times
- Multiple shift operation without affecting quality
- Multiple machine operation
- High level of flexibility
- High work-load factor
- More tightly self-disciplined organization
- Possibility of later integration into flexible manufacturing cells/islands/systems

These advantages are independent of the type of NC machine considered.

Many experienced users claim that shop-floor programming of machines saves time and offers a higher degree of flexibility. However, this is greatly influenced by the shop-floor staff—how readily they accept NC technology, their level of programming proficiency, and how capable they are of handling the machines and solving any minor problems that could cause downtime.

5.5 MACHINE TOOL ACCURACY

In many instances the absolute and repositioning accuracy achievable is a major deciding factor when considering whether or not to introduce NC machines. However, if acceptably high levels of consistent accuracy are possible, production-control costs, scrap rates, and so forth are dramatically reduced and a positive decision is much easier to justify.

In addition to the great rigidity of the machine tool's structure that is necessary if it is to maintain precision under dynamic and machining loads, a major factor in attaining high NC machining accuracy is its repeatable geometric precision over the entire length of each of the machine's axes *(Fig. 5–2)*.

FIGURE 5–2   Accuracy of an NC axis over its whole traverse path length.

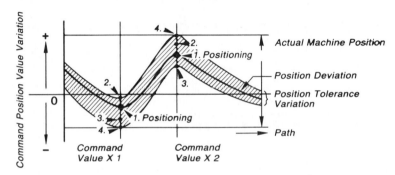

The dynamic performance of numerical controls also affects accuracy deviations, and high acceleration values of 30 ft/s^2 and above may cause dynamic deformation of the machine and its elements if the machine tool and controller are not well matched.

The measuring system, its method of installation, the quality of the drives used, and other factors induced by the inherent features of the machine's design all contribute to the final level of precision attainable.

5.6 SAFETY

A complex device such as a NC machine tool requires a high degree of inherent safety, not only for the protection of the operator, but also to prevent expensive damage to machine, workpiece, and tooling.

The NC and any fitted programmable logic controllers (Chapter 16) must together ensure safe operation by:

- Immediately recognizing dangerous operational errors and preventing their execution
- Detecting syntax and other program errors in advance of use on the machine tool

- Identifying any machine malfunction, turning the machine off, and displaying the cause of the malfunction
- Storing and displaying on demand all errors, and in the event of simultaneous errors or the creation of follow-up errors, displaying in the order of occurrence
- Detecting tool wear or breakage and taking immediate action to prevent the production of scrap

It is never possible to absolutely guarantee that all malfunctions will always be recognized and corrective action taken before machine damage occurs, but at least the most important and dangerous potential errors should be monitored effectively.

5.7 ASSESSING THE COST OF NC CONTROLS

Modern machines require modern controls to make full use of their capabilities, and a cheap controller, which has a limited range of functions, may not allow the use of certain specific features of the machine. Conversely, the most expensive and highly versatile controller does not guarantee increased profitability from the machine tool if the latter cannot take full advantage of the control's additional features.

If a supplier offers a standard control system, customers who insist on a different controller being integrated into their machines will generally pay a much higher price. Sometimes the price difference is even greater than any economic advantage of having one's first-choice controller fitted, even if it is already a company standard. Generally, different machine types require specially adapted controllers to make full use of their capabilities. If users decide against the optimized control system because they want to stay with a familiar system, they may have to accept decreased efficiency from the machine, as well as a significantly higher price for the controller.

5.8 MAINTENANCE AND SERVICE FACTORS

Substantial gains in productivity are not necessarily achieved by the use of rapid tool changers, high traverse speeds, and so forth; they are much more likely to be influenced by minimizing downtime.

NC machines are usually operated in two or three shifts, and as replacement machines or instant repair facilities are rarely available, machine downtime can never be totally avoided or lost production recovered. The possibility of repair time being necessary is often ignored by shop-floor loading personnel, and consequently each machine breakdown seriously disrupts the production schedule. This is why effective measures to minimize downtime must be introduced.

Regular maintenance is an obvious first preventive step, but one of the most effective measures that can be taken is to take out a maintenance/repair contract with the supplier, which guarantees agreed maximum delays in waiting for replacement parts or service personnel. It is of course possible to purchase and hold a replacement stock of parts, but there is no assurance that the part that malfunctions will be one of those held in stock!

Indeed, users should not rely solely on suppliers, but should ensure that their staff are also capable of solving minor problems themselves, having been trained by suppliers. Machine downtime is rarely caused by major malfunction, and in about 70 percent of all cases it is due to minor problems that are easily diagnosed and overcome by systematic analysis, requiring only basic system knowledge. Furthermore, to support the customer, modern controllers have excellent built-in self-diagnostic and troubleshooting features, and the user must only learn how to use them.

QUESTIONS FOR CHAPTER 5

1. Sketch the basic elements that comprise a NC machine tool. Briefly explain the main function of each element, and how this would have been carried out on a conventional machine tool of the same type.
2. What gives NC machines their inherent flexibility?
3. How has the introduction of NC influenced subsequent machine-tool design?
4. How has the introduction of NC influenced the development of modern cutting-tool systems?
5. Why are NC machine tools always significantly more expensive than their conventional counterparts? Where does most of this extra cost derive from?
6. What range of impacts does the introduction of NC technology have on the various departments directly concerned with a company's manufacturing activity?
7. List and explain the significance of the main advantages that NC brings to manufacturing.
8. How is the inherent accuracy of a NC machine tool established? What are the major factors influencing the level of accuracy achievable?
9. What is meant by the dynamic performance of a controller, and how does it influence the efficient operation of a NC machine tool?
10. List the principal features that one would expect to find included within any NC machine installation.
11. Why is buying the best controller that one can afford not necessarily a sound commercial or engineering decision?
12. Why is the avoidance of downtime so vital when operating a NC shop, and what steps can be taken to minimize the risk of it occurring?

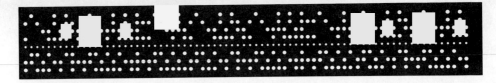

CHAPTER 6

COMPUTERS AND NC

After studying this chapter you should understand:

1. The functions of the five fundamental constituent parts of any computer system.
2. Why a computer is so well suited to the tasks of controlling NC machines.
3. How modern controllers differ from earlier versions.
4. The main functions of microcomputers in modern numerical-control applications.
5. The important relationship between NC hardware and software.

The first portion of this chapter deals with some basic aspects of computers and how they work. This may appear to be unnecessary with the general level of knowledge in this area today, but where technical applications and control of rapid operational sequences are concerned, the level of expertise is much lower.

Appreciation of such details as, for example, multicomputer operation, cycle timing, and movement control with feedback requires a high level of technical knowledge. For this reason, and to help clarify some of the more common expressions used when referring to the computer as applied to NC technology, this chapter has been included.

6.1 WHAT IS A COMPUTER?

It should be understood at the outset that a computer is not an "electronic brain" as it was often referred to in the early days of computer development. It is, in fact, only an electronic logic device which has the ability to handle data at extremely high speed. This speed characteristic is put to good use in most applications, and, in engineering, expensive and inflexible mechanical systems can often be replaced by much cheaper, more flexible electronic ones. A classic example of this is the application of computers to numerically controlled machine tools. This involves essentially the difficult and time-consuming task of continuously processing large amounts of digitized data—a function ideally suited to the modern computer.

Computers basically consist of five functional units:

- Input devices
- Controller ⎫ Central
- Memory store(s) ⎬ processing
- Processor unit ⎭ unit (CPU)
- Output devices

Any device that is used to enter data or programs into a computer is referred to as an input device. Keyboards, disk drives, magnetic tape based devices, and punch tape readers are all input devices *(Fig. 6–1)*. They all supply alphanumeric characters to the computer, in a digitized format, and at high speed. Because electronic input devices have both highest reading speed and reliability, they are now the most favored.

FIGURE 6–1   Typical computer data-input/output devices.

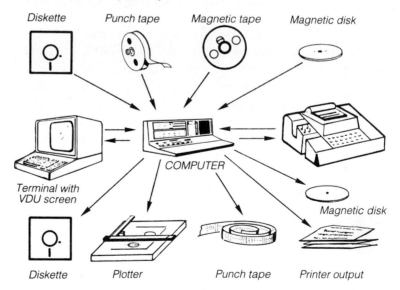

The controller, memory, and processor units together form the so-called "Central Processing Unit" (CPU). This physically consists of a printed circuit board with a microprocessor and several memory modules for data storage. Small computers usually have an internal memory storage capacity of a minimum of 640 Kbytes, while larger computers and workstations measure memory capacity in megabytes.

Apart from its volatile working memory, the computer also needs external memory capacity for permanent or long-term data storage, and this is usually achieved on small computers by using magnetic tapes or diskettes (floppy disks). Computers with internal permanent memories (hard disks) are now becoming commonplace and typically have a 40 MByte capacity.

The activities of data processing—performing calculations, for example—are all carried out by the computer's processor, which gets its input data from the main memory and returns the obtained results to the main memory. However, it is characteristic of computers used to control machine tools that they produce voluminous output data from only a small amount of input data. Consider, for example, the large number of generated path coordinates necessary to express a linear or circular motion in three simultaneous machine axes.

Output devices present data in a form which is readily understood by the user, with the most important device for text, illustrations, and graphics being the screen, or visual display unit (VDU). Printers are the next most common output device, especially where a permanent record is required *(Fig. 6–1)*.

The output from a computer dedicated to NC use is generally different from that produced by a standard computer in that output data is not only displayed to the user, but is usually also simultaneously transmitted directly to the control circuits of the machine tool.

The computer programmer writes programs to instruct the computer what it should do by using a set of predefined commands, placed in a certain order (the syntax). These command lists make up the programming language; typical examples are BASIC, FORTRAN and PASCAL. In NC technology, manufacturing-oriented programming languages, such as APT, EXAPT, and COMPACT II, have been developed, which are particularly suited to describing workpiece geometry and specifying technological information to machine-tool controllers (Chapters 9, 10, and 11).

6.2 COMPUTERS SPECIFICALLY FOR PROGRAMMING NC MACHINES

Microcomputers form the switching and processing portions of modern numerical controls. Their high operating speed suffices for meeting the performance of the many different, frequently concurrent, tasks required to control a machine tool. However, if one microcomputer is not capable of coping with all tasks in the available time, additional computers are used and the duties shared between them. Since the number of features offered and the tasks required of machine tool controllers is growing continuously, most modern units now tend to be of this multiprocessor type, with all functions being integrated within a few hardware modules controlled via powerful software packages.

More and more functions which once required the use of large mainframe computers can now be performed by the latest microcomputers, and this is making expensive programming systems and postprocessors gradually obsolete. Furthermore, controllers offering manual data-input facilities at the shop-floor level have now been developed, offering superb programming aids and graphic displays, and with the improvements in "computer intelligence" now available, the necessary programming effort for any given piecepart has been dramatically reduced. "Complex" and "simple" parts are no longer differentiated, and as the necessary intelligence is now integrated within the computer and its associated software, current powerful programming aids do not require extensive programming experience.

Modern graphics are the most important programming aid. Ideally a programmer should be able to observe the generation of a component while writing its program, no longer having to wait until the listing is complete before starting the checking and debugging exercise. Even cutting tools can now be displayed to scale, thereby permitting the immediate identification of any likely critical situations.

Also, complex and tedious calculations to establish accurate intersection points, contour transitions, chamfers, fillets, and so forth are now generally performed automatically by modern controllers provided with the necessary software. The programmer has only to enter the small amount of data that is given on the technical drawing, and the rest of the job is then carried out automatically by the controller.

Too, automatic error detection capability now helps to minimize programming mistakes by carrying out plausibility checks while the program is being written, and providing an error signal immediately on the detection of any programming fault.

6.3 FROM NC TO CNC

A commonly used formula for explaining the relationship between NC and Computer Numerical Control (CNC) is: CNC = (NC + Computer), but this is not entirely correct. It was perhaps more true for the first CNC systems developed, as they were actually made from NC systems linked to a standard microcomputer. However, today's CNCs differ totally from these prototypes in that they incorporate specifically designed processors and CPUs.

The growth from NC to CNC technology has been rapid. Only 40 years after Parsons developed the first NC for a machine tool, over 1000 different controllers are now developed worldwide every year. The major advances in microelectronics have contributed considerably to this situation. For example, a NC developed in 1968 embodied about 400 circuit boards, each bristling with transistors, whereas a modern CNC requires only one circuit board to perform the same tasks. Indeed, the physical size of a current CNC with medium functionality is basically determined by the size of the VDU screen and its operating panel, as the latter cannot be made any smaller without becoming user-unfriendly.

CNC development has also had a large impact on machine-tool design. The large and voluminous external controllers of the past have disappeared as much of the electronic circuitry is now integrated within the machine tool's structure. Cutting-tool and pallet changers have also now been introduced, as well as automatic loading and unloading of workstations, and the latest inspection systems and sensors now offer measurement dimensional checks within milliseconds. Thus there is little doubt that the enormous advances in computer design and their incorporation into modern CNCs have made a major contribution to the realization of highly efficient manufacturing at a reasonable cost.

6.4 HARDWARE AND SOFTWARE

When referring in general to a "computer," one has to distinguish between its two elemental parts:

- The hardware, consisting of the mechanical and electronic parts and the power supply unit and its peripheral equipment, such as the reader, printer, and any external memories
- The software, which determines the "intelligence" or capabilities of the computer and coordinates all the tasks to be performed by the individual hardware modules

This same distinction applies equally to CNC systems—see Chapter 2, Sections 2.3 and 2.4

The CNC software, which embodies the basic operating system of the microprocessor(s) used, contains much of the manufacturer's machine-tool-control know-how. The full potential of the whole system is thus only realized when used in conjunction with the appropriate hardware, and this is why hardware and software development are so closely interlinked.

The continuing trend towards miniaturizing the hardware elements of computers reduces physical space requirements but has had little effect on software complexity and capability.

Hardware costs have steadily decreased, but software is still relatively expensive. This implies a shift in development costs and effort from hardware to software, as shown in Fig. 6–2, and this trend offers the following advantages:

FIGURE 6–2 The shift in emphasis of development costs during the transition from NC to CNC.

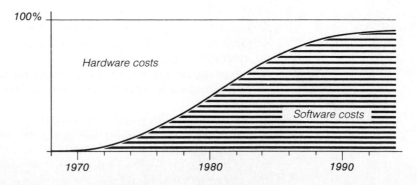

- Costs of copying software (legally!) and reusing it, suitably modi-fied, in enhanced systems are minimal.
- Software is not prone to wear and is maintenance free.
- It is possible to upgrade and improve software without having to make significant changes to the hardware.
- Various controller types can be produced using the same basic hardware, by simply modifying or changing the operating soft-ware involved.

The software determines the number of machine axes that are con-trolled, which features may be performed simultaneously, and which sequentially. Thus it is mainly the software which must be changed to enable a specific CNC system to be used to control different machine tools; the hardware can remain substantially the same.

6.5 THE FUTURE

Despite the development of computers and numerical controls having always been closely linked, full exploitation of computer technology in the manufacturing industry is still in its infancy. Computers will become increasingly integrated into complex networks, manufacturing fields which traditionally have been purely "mechanical" in nature will be-come more and more computer based, and areas where CNC is already well established will reach new levels of sophistication.

QUESTIONS FOR CHAPTER 6

1. Explain, in general terms, what you understand by the word "computer."
2. List and describe the basic functions of the principal elements comprising a modern computer system.
3. What is a CPU, and what are its prime functions?
4. Why is a computer so well suited to the tasks of controlling a modern machine tool?
5. What recent advances have been made to assist part program-ming, and what effects have they had in the production planning office?
6. In what ways do the computers used in machine-tool controllers differ from those used for more generalized commercial com-puting duties?
7. How have advances in modern CNC technology affected the de-sign of NC machine tools?

8. Define the terms "hardware" and "software," and briefly describe why their functions must be complementary.

9. Why has there been a positive shift in emphasis towards CNC software development at the expense of similar activity in the associated hardware area?

CHAPTER 7

COMPUTER NUMERICAL CONTROL (CNC)

After studying this chapter you should understand:

1. The differences between NC and CNC.
2. The most important parameters of a CNC controller.
3. The influence of the microcomputer on CNC controllers.
4. How to solve many of the common problems associated with the practical application of CNC to machine tools.

The integration of microcomputers into NC units to form CNCs has occurred for two main reasons: the computer's flexibility and speed of operation, and its ability to replace expensive hardware containing complex control wiring with cheaper and more flexible software. The use of micros has thus provided a relatively simple user-friendly CNC system, and has progressively been upgraded to the highly complex data-processing control with powerful function capabilities that it is today—and all at an increasingly attractive price.

7.1 FROM NC TO CNC

Figure 7–1, *p. 72* schematically represents the first step from NC to CNC, namely, the NC with additional memory. Between the data-input components (reader or manual-input keyboard) and the actual control, a large buffer memory was installed which was expandable in stages up to a memory capacity of approximately 32,000 characters—corresponding to about 250 ft of punch tape. This memory stored complete machining programs as well as tool compensation values and various other blocks of information. The remaining control logic for data processing, interpolation of axes, control of switching functions, and so on required no alteration.

FIGURE 7–1 Comparison between NC/CNC. In addition to pure control functions, CNC has expanded functional capabilities.

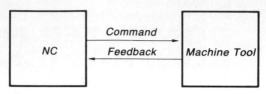

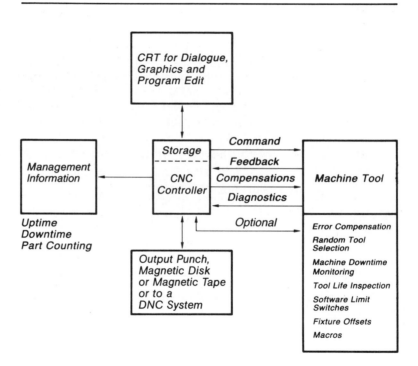

However, modern CNC is a totally new control concept *(Fig. 7–2).* All hard-wired controls have been converted to operating programs within the integral high-power computer, and input and output peripherals have been adapted and converted to operate in accordance with the "busline" system—see Chapter 16.

7.2 CONTROLLER DESIGN

When a CNC manufacturer develops a new control, the first and most important task is the division of functions between software and hardware in such a way as to achieve the best possible compromise between the following requirements:

- Low cost
- Compact design
- Flexibility
- High-speed processing
- Adaptability and expansion capability
- Ease of operation and maintenance

Of prime importance, however, is the achievement of maximum reliability.

FIGURE 7–2   Development from hardware controls to software controls.

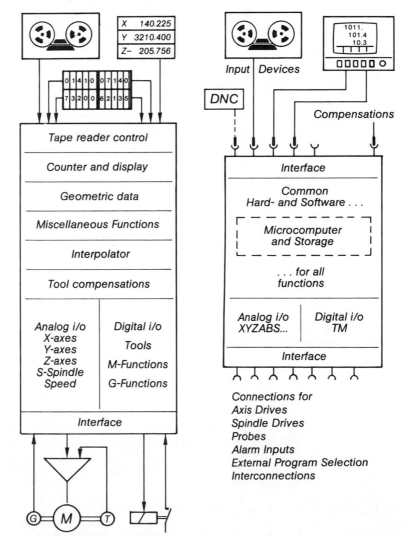

Depending on the importance assigned to the above concepts, two different CNC alternatives arise:

1. The inexpensive unified compact panel assembly CNC, produced in quantity, with limited expansion capability
2. The more expensive, expandable CNC system, to a large extent programmable without "external intelligence"

The concept of "universal CNC" lies in the fact that hardware components built in large quantities can be adapted to handle various special functions by corresponding software input. Additional functions, which the manufacturer offers as optional expansion stages, could similarly be combined without having to make basic changes in the hardware. Through data exchange via a common **busline**, wiring changes are eliminated, which is another one of the great technical and cost advantages of CNC.

In this manner, the functional scope of CNC can vary and a variety of new control functions for the many different types of machines can be easily realized.

Multiple electronic memory modules are available for storing CNC operating programs (the software):

- **EPROM**, with reusable memory components that are erasable via UV light.
- **RAM**, which loses its contents without power supply and must therefore be buffered.
- **ROM,** whose memory content is "burned-in" and cannot be altered.
- **Bubble Memory**, a memory component with high data density. The data are retained without a continuous power supply.

7.3 MICROCOMPUTERS AND NC

The introduction of numerical control was initially rather slow, whereas the development of microelectronics progressed at a rate which surpassed all expectations. In the course of only a few years, its modules became more and more compact, efficient, reliable, and inexpensive. This has created completely new possibilities for CNC manufacturing. Along with the classical task of controlling relative movement between tool and workpiece, the scope of operating functions has, in comparison to the NC pioneering efforts, expanded to include the following typical CNC attributes:

- Display screens for operation and diagnosis
- Program memory for several programs
- Program-editing possibilities at the machine-tool
- Program output to external memories
- Machine-tool operation via dialogue
- Increased security functions

These functions have been specifically designed to simplify the operation of the NC machine and to provide a clearer overall view of its operation.

Additional features have been introduced to ease programming. Examples include:

- Range of standard contour geometries for complex component programming
- Functional keyboard input
- Teach-in programming
- Subprogramming technology with assigned parameters
- Automatic determination of the number of roughing and finishing cuts needed
- Graphic display screens in full color

Additional functions, which were assigned to the CNC computer, followed rapidly, and within a short time CNC had not only changed the design of controls, but also had had a major impact on the design of machine tools and associated areas. These functions included:

- Compensation for lead-screw pitch and measurement errors
- Software limit switches
- Tool-location variability via coded tooling
- Tool-life monitoring
- Machine-parameter input
- Integrated adaptive control

The tendency toward increased machine-related intelligence (artificial intelligence) seems to continue as CNC technology is becoming increasingly commonplace. Data storage, computing, controlling, and correcting at the machine are becoming less and less expensive and therefore more attractive, even for small machines. The enormous **flexibility** of CNC is clearly demonstrated by the software—for example the computer programs, with which the control functions are generated and stored in the CNC computer. The hardware modules, on the other hand, are often the same among the individual control makes in spite of differing CNC specifications. However, methods of programming, instrumentation and other functions vary widely between different makes of controller.

7.4 SOLUTIONS TO TYPICAL CNC PROBLEMS

The experienced user will initially investigate where the application of CNC is likely to offer improved solutions to existing problems. These problem areas may relate to the technology, production, reliability or cost.

The tendency to replace expensive mechanical solutions with cheaper electronic alternatives has been greatly furthered by the drastic cost reduction of electronic components since the introduction of

FIGURE 7–3   Price development in numerical controls of approximately equal specifications as a result of innovations in the electronics sector.

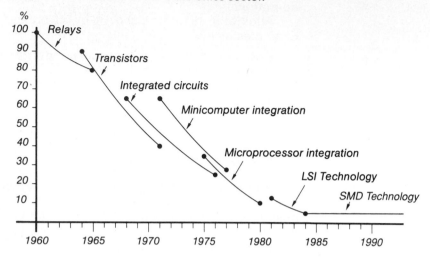

numerical controls. Fig. 7–3 illustrates how the price of controls has decreased over the years due to the application of new technology. Further cost reductions will result from the application of specialized NC Large Scale Integrated Units (LSIs) now under development, but a limit will be reached due to the physical constraints of mechanical components such as indicators, keyboards, transformers, and various other sundry hardware items.

A typical CNC solution is given for each of the common technical problems described below.

7.4.1   READ ERRORS

From a practical point of view, the most feared NC malfunctions are input errors caused by defective punch tapes or malfunctions of the punch-tape reader. Prompt recognition of read errors would significantly increase the operating safety of the machines and prevent expensive workpieces from being scrapped.

CNC Solution: Qualifying test of characters within each block *(Fig. 7–4).*

Each row of holes is binarily scanned and the total number of punched holes per block ascertained by the postprocessor. After each End of Block the postprocessor also punches an added address, E, for example, into the tape which is a three-digit position valuation. A fourth bit, possibly used for longer blocks of information, is usually suppressed without any negative consequences. The CNC computer executes the same evaluation for each block of information as it is being entered into the buffer memory; consequently, each block is tested for conformity to the value programmed. In the case of a match, an

FIGURE 7–4   Reliability check.

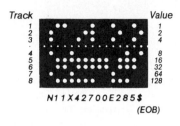

N11X42700E285$

(EOB)

Character	Value in ASCII-Code		
N	2+4+8+64	=	78
1	1+16+32+128	=	177
1	1+16+32+128	=	177
X	8+16+64+128	=	216
4	4+16+32+128	=	180
2	2+16+32+128	=	178
7	1+2+4+16+32+128	=	183
0	16+32	=	48
0	16+32	=	48

Checksum   1285
285

1 is suppressed

error-free input is virtually guaranteed, and the block is released for further processing. Should there be a deviation, an error warning will appear and processing will stop. The machine can be restarted only after corrective action has been executed by the operator.

By means of this test, incorrect characters, or characters entered too often or not at all, can be recognized safely. This is much more reliable than the usual parity-check test, which does not recognize repetitive errors.

Computer-aided part-programming and subsequent post processing in order to output the punch tape via a specialized postprocessor are also required.

7.4.2   INCORRECTLY PROGRAMMED PATH MEASUREMENTS

In all machining functions, especially in milling and turning large parts, there is a finite limit to the size of working envelopes. Erroneous input of larger path measurements could destroy workpieces, tools, and perhaps even the machine, through collision.

CNC Solution: Programmed work area limitation.

The allowable work envelope of the tool is limited by specialized programming, and the input of minimum and maximum limiting values is achieved via the punch tape or by manual input into the memory of the CNC. Example:

N 1234 G 25 X 100 Y 250 Z 70 $
N 1235 G 26 X 400 Y 300 Z 120 $

In the first block after G25 the minimum values of work envelope are entered, and the maximum values are entered in the second block. In this way, the operating area in the programmed axes is limited to the dimensions entered. The input of larger values triggers an error signal which leads to program stop. Dangerous input or programming errors are thus recognized before damage occurs.

The programmed work-area limit may be erased by programming G27, and a new work area then can be defined if required.

7.4.3 UNDERCUTS RESULTING FROM READ ERRORS

Undercuts on a workpiece result from stopping a machine tool while cutting, or can occur because of read errors, possibly leading to appearance flaws or scrap. These errors therefore are especially feared in the milling of expensive, complicated workpieces made of exotic materials.

CNC Solution: Multiblock buffer memory.

By selecting and using part of the computer capacity, a so-called multiblock buffer memory may be established in which, for example, 1000 or 2000 characters of punch tape program may be prestored, depending on the operating program. If an input error occurs, a minimum character supply of, say, 3×256 punch-tape characters will still be present. On average, this corresponds to about 6 ft of punch tape. Therefore, if there is an error signal, the operator still has enough time to stop the machine at a suitable point, or a program stop occurs automatically as soon as the tool is disengaged, for rapid traverse, tool changes, and so on. Because of the continuous input of program blocks with a minimum of 256 characters, the reading mechanism is also protected and in this way the service life and reliability of the reader are substantially increased.

7.4.4 FEED RATE TOO HIGH

Modern machine tools have a very large feed-rate range, which for example may extend from 0.001 in. to 150 ft/min. Erroneous input of too high a feed rate due to read error, false correction, or operating error can cause damage to the workpiece, tools, or both. Expensive rejects, tool breakage, or long changeover periods can result.

CNC Solution: By programming a feed-rate limit, the maximum permitted feed rate, with or without rapid traverse, can be limited as desired. Again the input of limit values is applied via punch tape or manual input into the CNC memory. Example: N128 G36 F40 $

If the feed rate limit has been set, say at 40 in./min, higher values will automatically be reduced to this maximum value. Furthermore, the control checks to see whether the maximum possible axis speed, for example in 3-D interpolation, has been exceeded in any axis and, if necessary, reduces the feed rate until the maximum permitted value is reached (G37 = limitation OFF).

7.4.5 AXIS EXCHANGE

Machining programs, which, for example, have been established for a milling machine with a vertical spindle, cannot be used on a machine tool with horizontal spindle and preset angular head, since the axis coordinates are not the same.

CNC Solution: Coordinate conversion.

With a manual or a limit switch the *Y* and *Z* axes are interchanged with the angular head fixed so that operating elements and indicators again agree with the axis assignment of the horizontal spindle *(Fig. 7–5).* The programs can be used without limitation as long as all other data agree. If this is not the case, corresponding conversion programs are necessary.

FIGURE 7–5   Axis exchange with preset angular head.

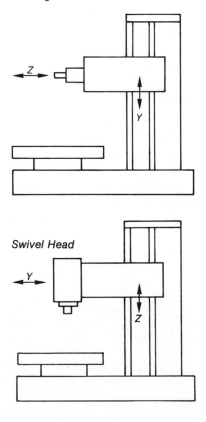

7.4.6　INPUT OF TOOL COMPENSATION VALUES

The possibility exists in CNC to use a part of the controller's memory for entering tool compensation values and thereby replacing the relevant decade switch with all its cumbersome wiring and assembly. With this the number of compensation values can be expanded as desired, permitting considerable programming simplification when dealing with complicated workpieces. The manual input of many compensation values is however very time consuming.

　　CNC Solution: Compensation value input via program tapes.

　　During tool presetting in the tool crib or during tool adjustment, the absolute or compensation values of tool lengths and radii are ascertained and suitably formatted for entering onto tape.

7.4.7　ACCURACY

Every measuring system used to measure axis position on machine tools is less than perfect. Positional deviations arising in even high-precision machines require corrective action from even more expensive measuring systems.

　　CNC Solution: Scale-error compensation *(Fig. 7–6).*

　　After the machine has been prepared for operation, an error curve $\Delta l = f(l)$ is plotted for each axis and corresponding compensation values at fixed distances of 0.1 in. are entered into the computer, stored, and later automatically recalled. In this way, great precision can be achieved over the whole scale length.

FIGURE 7–6　Scale-error compensation.

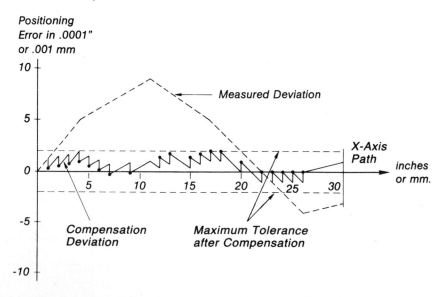

7.4.8   OPERATOR GUIDELINES

Occasionally it is necessary to give the machine operator instructions concerning any required manual intervention. For this purpose either single-sheet instructions, program printouts, or guideline lists are issued, but these do not always guarantee error-free execution of directives.

CNC Solution: Display of instruction on the screen *(Fig. 7–7)*.

Via programming, the data for machine control is displayed on the screen as guidelines for the operator. The advantages are as follows:

- Provides simple and reliable instructions for the operator
- Minimizes confusion
- Eliminates searching in program printouts
- Displays clearly written text which can be in various languages.

FIGURE 7–7   Programmed guidelines on the CNC display screen.

7.4.9   PROGRAM CORRECTION AND EDITING

The part programs prepared by the programming department are not always free of errors. They contain mostly simple errors, such as incorrectly punched holes, parity errors, or transposed characters. Others may contain incorrect feed rate or speed commands, or missing signals initiating miscellaneous functions, such as coolant supply or tool change. Such errors are particularly common in manual part programming. Since detail program verification would either take too long or is not feasible technically, these errors are discovered, at the earliest, during the first test run on the machine. In order to avoid long waiting periods for corrected programs, provision has to be made to correct such errors as soon as possible.

CNC Solution: Program correction at the CNC controller *(Fig. 7–8)*.

Correction and optimization of part programs at the machine-tool level are probably the best-known and most often mentioned CNC advantages. Characters, words, and blocks of information can be corrected in the punch-tape syntax by means of the manual input keyboard.

FIGURE 7–8 Program edit in CNC.

Program Edit –
long programs

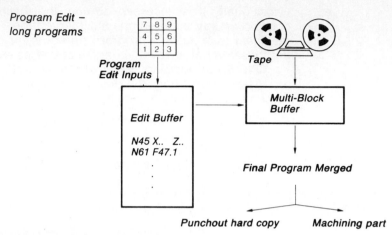

In the case of long part programs, only the corrections are stored.

Program Edit –
short programs

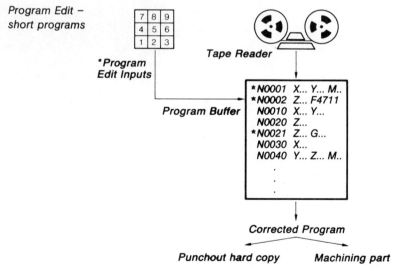

In the case of short programs, the part program is
corrected and then stored.

Incorrect characters are erased and corrected, or missing data are
added. Obviously, correction of geometrical data is also possible, but
should remain limited to simple cases. Complicated multiaxis movements or 3-D interpolations is better corrected using the computer with
the aid of the programming language and postprocessor. If the control
is equipped with a data input/output port, a portable tape punch or

magnetic tape device can be connected and the optimized program with all corrections can be quickly documented and stored for later repetition.

7.4.10 POCKET MILLING

In pocket milling, an overload on the tool may be generated when machining the corners of the pocket. This overload may damage the tool as well as the component. In order to avoid this, feed-rate deceleration may be programmed for each corner, but this leads to higher programming expense and longer program tapes.

CNC Solution: Automatic corner deceleration *(Fig. 7–9)*.

FIGURE 7– 9 Corner deceleration prevents tool overload, tool breakage, and component damage in pocket milling.

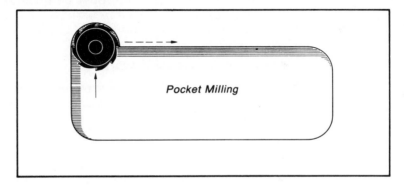

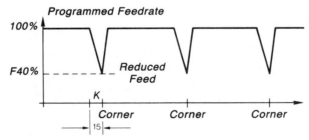

The feed rate can be constantly reduced to a programmable percentage *(F)* via the insertion of a modal operating *G* function into a single block, starting at a programmable distance *(K)* along the milling path of the tool. Example:

N 123 G 28 K 15 F 40

Explanation: 15 in. before each corner point, the feed rate is reduced by 60 percent. It is also possible to input the deceleration data manually via the keyboard, which would allow the control to add this data to an existing program tape not previously programmed for corner deceleration. The automatic corner deceleration is cancelled by using a *G* 29 function in most milling machine controllers.

7.4.11 BACKLASH COMPENSATION

In indirect path measurement, the backlash between transducer and axis movement is recorded as a position error when the direction of the spindle is reversed. In circular milling, concentricity errors and under-cuts at the quadrant transitions arise because of this.

CNC Solution: Backlash compensation.

When the traverse direction of an axis is reversed the preset back-lash compensation of the drive is carried out cumulatively before the transducer signals are used to determine position. The requirements are as follows:

- The backlash must be constant over the entire displacement path; otherwise only an average value can be compensated.
- All drive elements should accelerate gradually at start-up.
- The measuring system must be positively coupled to the drive motor (in a backlash-free manner) in order to clearly detect the compensation movement and to avoid control problems.

7.4.12 SCALE FACTOR

With numerically controlled flame-cutting machines, it sometimes be-comes necessary to produce programmed workpieces to a different scale.

CNC Solution: Scale factor, translation, and rotation *(p X, q X) (Fig. 7–10).*

FIGURE 7–10   Scale factor p X and q Y as well as angle of rotation.

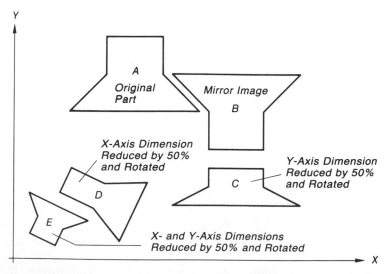

A = Original program   D = X dimension halved
B = Mirror about X-axis and translated   E = (X,Y) · 0.5 scale and rotating
C = Y dimension halved

All dimensions of a programmed workpiece can be scaled by any factor. In fact, each axis is handled individually. With this ability it is not only possible to produce geometrically similar parts, but these parts can also be compressed or stretched along any axis. In addition, some CNC systems also allow for the translation of a part program or the rotation of a part program about a selected axis.

7.4.13   RESTARTING A CUT ON JOB PROFILE

After tool breakage, tool change, or an emergency stop during cutting, it is necessary to return the tool to the exact cutting position on the profile geometry. Any newly entered tool compensation values must also be taken into consideration at this time.

CNC Solution: Automatic restarting at the profile *(Fig. 7–11).*

FIGURE 7–11   Automatic reentry cycle after milling tool breakage.

Figure 7–11a: Breakage and stop in same block

Figure 7–11b: Breakage and stop after several blocks.

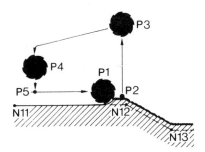

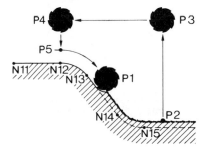

P1 = Breakage location
P2 = Stop point
P3 = Tool change point
P4 = Exit point for automatic
     re-entry cycle
P5 = Re-entry point in
     mid-point of milling path

By a shift of P4, P5 is also changed so that for a long path the re-entry point can be determined.

Here one should go back several blocks up to block 11, 12, or 13.

To accomplish this, the tool is first manually positioned back in the area of the desired reentry position. Upon the START command, restarting at the profile occurs automatically at the programmed feed rate and usually via a preprogrammed blend cycle to avoid dwell marks on the piecepart *(Fig. 7–11a).*

If the machine had already processed several blocks of information with a broken tool *(Fig. 7–11b)* before it was stopped and the tool replaced, one must go back an appropriate number of blocks in the program before operating the START command.

7.4.14 AUTOMATIC MEASUREMENT

Alignment errors due to inadequate clamping and/or fixturing are not uncommon, particularly if work-changing is automated. These errors must be determined, analyzed, and compensated for to achieve a high level of accuracy and to avoid errors on the machined part.

CNC Solution: Automatic measurement using inspection probing.

By means of inspection probes (usually touch trigger probes) inserted into the machine tool's spindle, it is possible to check mounting position as well as component dimensions and make any necessary corrections. In order to employ inspection probes, a CNC must be capable of automatically carrying out several measuring program subroutines or canned cycles. Initially the probe position in the X and Y axes must be calibrated with the aid of a calibrated bore of known diameter and X/Y position *(Fig. 7-12)*. By means of this calibration procedure the

FIGURE 7-12   Calibration of touch trigger probe by means of a hole of known diameter and X/Y position.

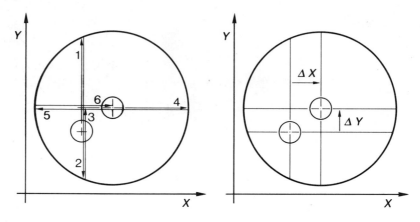

following data is obtained and employed when making all subsequent measurements:

- Probe offset in the X and Y axes
- Errors in the direction-dependent signal of the touch-trigger probe
- Precise positioning of the probe in the X/Y plane

Following calibration, in the case of hole checking measuring cycles carry out the following tasks automatically:

- Determination of the hole diameter
- Determination of hole center position
- Comparison with target values
- Calculation and feedback of tolerances actually being achieved

7.4.15   SUBDIVISION OF A TOOL-HOLDING MAGAZINE

Machine tools which have a coding system for specifying cutting tool positions employ the same T statement in every program for calling up tooling. This is why it is usually impossible to equip such a machine tool with a large tool magazine in order to store tools for two or more different part programs.

CNC Solution: Divide up the tool magazine into segments.

A number of tool positions are assigned to each of the programs stored in the CNC memory, each segment being specific to a particular program. Thus the correct tools can be called up by each program even though several tools in the magazine have the same code number *(Fig. 7–13).*

FIGURE 7–13   Segmentation of a cutting-tool magazine.

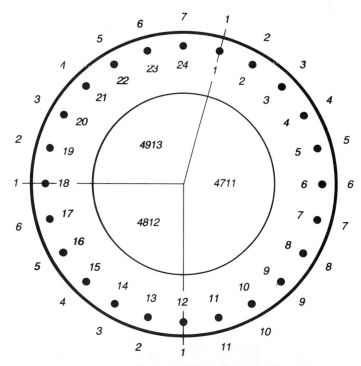

Program No	Tool No	Position No
4711	1	1
4812	1	12
4913	1	18

7.4.16 ADMINISTRATION OF SISTER TOOLING

A supply of spare tools at the CNC machine to replace those withdrawn from service due to excessive wear or fracture is a major prerequisite for fully automated operation. This means that several tools with the same code number must be stored in the magazine to enable a sister tool to be called up as soon as either fracture has been detected or tool service-life limit has been reached.

CNC Solution: Continuous monitoring and control of tool service life, and administration of sister tooling.

The program usually operates in the following manner:

- Tooling which is held in the machine's magazine but which has not yet been called into service cannot be activated. (These could be either sister tooling with the same code number or tooling yet to be employed)
- Activated tools that are in position can be loaded into the machine spindle immediately on demand
- Reject tools cannot be placed back in the machine spindle again

In the tool magazine only one tool of each type is released at a time. This is used until the tool-control system or the service-life control indicates its need for replacement, for example at the end of its service life. It is then withdrawn from service and is "blocked" in such a way that it cannot be used again, with a sister tool being called up to replace it. The new compensation data relating to the new sister tool must then be entered into the control unit, and this procedure is repeated until all tools of a given type have been used.

For tool management purposes, a clearly structured screen display is indispensable so that the following real-time information may be continuously monitored:

- Tool and position number and assignment
- Remaining service life of each tool
- Tool status: withdrawn from service, activated, or reserve

7.4.17 AUTOMATIC TOOL LENGTH DETERMINATION

Milling and drilling machines sometimes use tools of a nonpreset length, so that tool length compensation value has to be determined automatically at the machine tool itself.

CNC Solution: Automatic tool length measurement with the aid of a contact measuring device.

When a tool is inserted into the machine's spindle for the first time, an automatic measuring cycle is initiated. The absolute tool length is determined by measuring the path along which the spindle travels until the tool tip touches a measuring device, the data then being stored in the compensation value memory *(Fig. 7–14)*.

7.4.18 OVERLOADED CNC OPERATING PANEL

The continual extension of the range of available functions since the introduction of CNC technology has partly led to increasingly numerous

FIGURE 7–14   Automatic tool length measurement with contact measuring device.

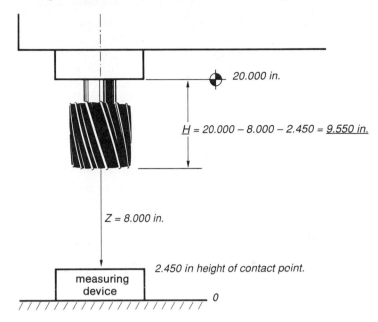

20.000 in.

$\underline{H} = 20.000 - 8.000 - 2.450 = \underline{9.550\ in.}$

$Z = 8.000\ in.$

2.450 in height of contact point.

measuring device

0

keys and operating elements. Such keyboards are no longer user-friendly, they are less well structured, and programming mistakes are consequently more likely. The overall dimensions of such panels have become too large, especially for manual data input controls with screen display. However, without sufficient spare keys further extension of the functions available will become impractical.

CNC Solution: Keys with changeable (nonfixed) function assignment—softkeys.

The basic principle of softkeys is that, for manual data input, only a limited number of keys are available for each input sequence. Consequently six or eight keys which the software can assign to various functions at the programmer's choice are sufficient, as long as each key's assignment is clearly displayed on the VDU screen. Data and complete statements can be entered progressively while the operator is guided through the whole input routine so that he knows exactly when to enter specific data and which keys to use in any given sequence. As soon as data input of one block has been completed and the information confirmed and stored in the memory, the next block can be dealt with, after reassigning functions to the softkeys if necessary.

A special cursor key allows the editing of those blocks which have already been confirmed and stored in the memory. Step by step they trace the programming routine executed to date, in reverse direction, until any errors are found; these can then easily be corrected. Hence softkeys avoid overly complex keyboard layout, reduce the amount of hardware required, and increase programming reliability.

7.4.19 PROGRAMMING WITH THE ASSISTANCE OF DISPLAY SCREENS

Manual programming without screen display does not require many sophisticated devices, but it is time consuming and very prone to error. Allowing for labor costs, it can therefore be an expensive process. For computer-assisted programming a considerable number of special devices are necessary, such as computer, printer, punch, processor, and postprocessor software. Usually such devices can be employed universally, but they do require a minimum knowledge of a programming language, and computing in general. Thus neither of these two methods of programming is considered to be ideal.

CNC Solution: Interactive graphical NC programming.

Interactive graphical NC programming allows the user to graphically create the workpiece on a VDU screen and simulate the machining process before actually operating the machine tool, i.e. before starting the actual metal-cutting process. The system offers dynamic analysis of the machining sequences and the programming efficiency of the tool paths. Sometimes different colors are employed to graphically illustrate different elements of an NC program: workpiece geometry, tool paths, cutting tools, and clamping devices. Zoom functions make it possible to enlarge or reduce the scale to which workpieces or simulated machining procedures can be displayed. Graphic NC programming requires a knowledge of machining technology but not of a programming language, as the system deals automatically with all necessary calculations.

There are three different methods of graphic NC programming:

1. Machine-related programming at the CNC
2. Separate machine-related programming
3. Centralized, computerized programming with the aid of CAD systems

7.4.20 ERROR DETECTION AND ANALYSIS

Often it is difficult to find the actual reason for breakdown, disruption, or failure of a machine tool. In most cases service technicians must analyze problems on their own because either the operators genuinely do not know what went wrong, or they may be reluctant to say because of a sense of guilt for having made an error.

CNC Solution: Automatic recording log-book.

Comparable to an aircraft log-book, a continuous record of all instructions, data, and functions entered or changed, is automatically logged by the CNC. Thus, in cases of breakdown, the last events which were recorded up to the point that breakdown was indicated or emergency stop initiated can be used to chronologically trace back the error and, it is hoped, diagnose the cause. Special measures can be taken to prevent deletion of such data in case of breakdown, to guarantee that it is available to the service technicians.

7.4.21   MACHINING OF SLOPING SURFACES

Sometimes the surfaces to be machined are neither parallel nor vertical to the workholding plane. Although a swiveling spindle head may be used for such machining tasks to achieve adjustment of the cutting tool direction to the required angle, when the tool is in such a tilted position, neither tool compensation nor canned cycles are of any use for controlling the machining process. For example, to drill a hole on a sloping surface, complex calculations, involving linear interpolation in up to three axes, are required to position the tool on the centerline of the hole.

CNC Solution: A sufficiently powerful controller, capable of accommodating the specific kinematics of the swivel head used.

With modern controllers the user is only required to program the angle of the sloping surface, and the CNC then automatically calculates the resulting movements of the individual axes for feed, depth of cut, tool compensation, and so on.

7.4.22   SUPPLEMENTARY NC AXES CONTROL

In addition to their main axes, CNC machines are often equipped with supplementary or auxiliary axes. However, their control must be controllable completely independent of the machine's main axes, as they are used, for example, to transport tooling (robotic axes) or for tool changing on turning centers.

CNC Solution: A channel structure capable of controlling synchronous or asynchronous axes via the CNC independent of the machine's main controls.

In contrast to the main axes *(X, Y, Z, A, B),* which can be interpolated simultaneously during the cutting operation, auxiliary axes *(U, V, W)* move under the direction of a separate program and with totally independent timing. The target position for tool-handling axes is not programmed but determined automatically by the CNC, with the data needed for this purpose, such as tool identification number and magazine position, being stored in a file and updated after each tool change.

7.4.23   DATA BLOCK CYCLE TIME

To achieve both precision and good surface finish, a machine's CNC must execute its commands rapidly and then transmit the resulting data to the machine's axes without delay. All calculations, including cutter compensations, zero shifts, and subroutines, must all be performed rapidly enough to permit uninterrupted tool-feed movement. If the time to execute a command is less than the time required to calculate the parameters for the next command, cutting will be temporarily interrupted, possibly leaving dwell marks on the workpiece. To prevent this, if the CNC is given the ability to calculate at ultra high speed, its cost then becomes very high.

CNC Solution: A dynamic buffer memory store *(Fig. 7–15, p. 92).*

The above problem can usually be inexpensively solved by the use of a buffer store, which is capable of transmitting stored program blocks to the CNC's working memory at high speed. The buffer memory

FIGURE 7–15   Dynamic buffer memory with short transmission time to avoid interruption of the cutting process.

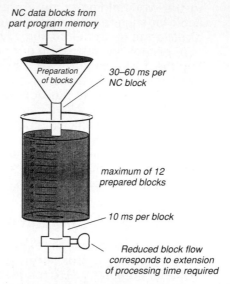

NC data blocks from part program memory

Preparation of blocks

30–60 ms per NC block

maximum of 12 prepared blocks

10 ms per block

Reduced block flow corresponds to extension of processing time required

is continuously filled with program blocks awaiting execution, with the number of blocks that can be stored depending on buffer size. This is adjusted to suit the particular CNC/machine tool combination to guarantee uninterrupted cutting at all times. If this simple solution does not solve the problem, the machine's feed rate must be temporarily reduced until the critical problem cutting area has been passed.

QUESTIONS FOR CHAPTER 7

1. What characterizes the difference between NC and CNC?
2. Why has CNC now totally superseded NC on machine tools?
3. What are the principal requirements of a well-designed CNC unit?
4. What are the main electronic memory modules generally used for CNC data storage?
5. Briefly describe methods of checking programs for data input errors.
6. What is tool compensation?
7. What is sister tooling, and how are minor differences allowed for?
8. How are the effects of inherent variations in a machine tool's measuring system eliminated?
9. What steps can be taken to minimize CNC operator error?

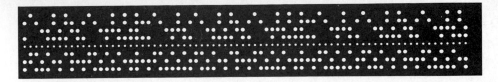

CHAPTER 8

MANUAL DATA INPUT AT THE MACHINE TOOL

After studying this chapter you should understand:

1. How machine tools are programmed at the shop-floor level.
2. The main advantages and disadvantages of shop-floor programming.
3. How to make a quantified analysis of the most economic programming procedure for any given installation.
4. The different uses of NC machine graphics screens.
5. The principal requirements of shop-floor programming systems.

Despite doubts concerning their economics, NC machine tools with manual data input developed rapidly—far more quickly than they were accepted by production engineers. Many of these machine tools now have integrated programming aids which make them extremely efficient, yet easy to use.

8.1 INTRODUCTION

The process of manual data input (MDI) is not new; it has always been possible to enter NC data into numerical controls manually instead of via punch or magnetic tape. Initially, decade switches were used to switch from one function to another when entering data, and this was adequate for rapid switching between cutting operations, calling up spindle speeds, adjusting feed rates, and switching to miscellaneous functions.

Because there was no means of storage for the manually entered data, the whole process had to be carried out laboriously step-by-step each time, with consequent interruption of machining during data input. This was obviously unsatisfactory, but it was just an early stage in the development of NC data-input techniques which led, in due course, to punch paper-tape data input and storage. It rapidly became

FIGURE 8–1 The changes in control panels used for manual data input and external programming, covering four different generations of control systems.

The input and display elements could only fulfill the requirements of the specific generation of control systems for which they were designed. The first, still purely alphanumeric display screens, were rejected because of the dangerously high voltages needed for the cathode ray tube. However, today graphic displays are considered as a prerequisite for all good programming and NC machine operation.

The number of necessary elements was reduced despite an enlarged range of functions, thus simplifying control-system operation. Microelectronics has influenced control-system development and resulted in recent advances: powerful microprocessors, large electronic data stores, and, above all, acceptable prices.

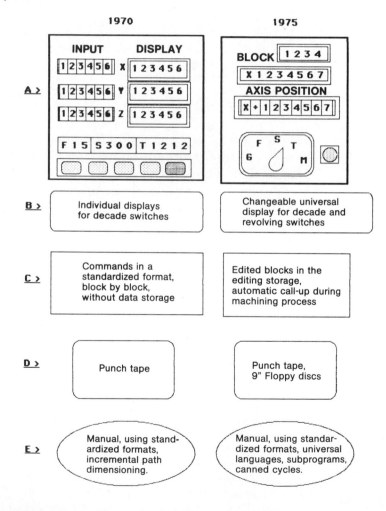

A>Panel Design, B>Main operating features,
C>Possibility of Manual Data Input, D>Data Storage,
E>External Programming.

relegated to merely a stop-gap process used to maintain a machine tool in operation in such situations as, for example, where a new tape contained errors, and the operator was awaiting production of the corrected tape.

The introduction of the alphanumeric keyboard and data-storage hardware made it possible to manually type complete programs into the NC unit and the geometrical and technological complexity of the data necessary to produce a given component determined just how cumbersome this data-input procedure became. However, even simple items required a process that was still tedious, time-consuming, and costly because the machine tool could not be operated during the data-inputting process, the control only being capable of either processing input data or controlling the machine tool.

The next natural development was to provide the facility to program while the machine tool was still operating. Unfortunately, howev-

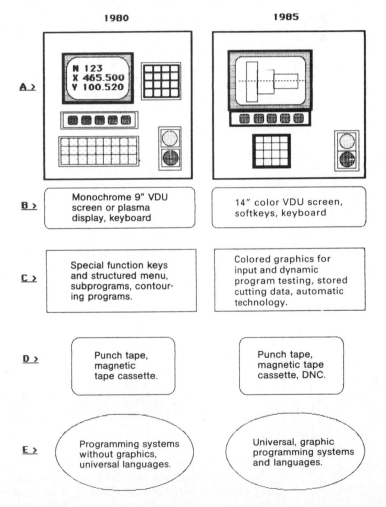

er, this meant that there was no opportunity to pretest any new programs created. Again the machine tool was required for a noncutting purpose—program proof testing—and the data-entering procedure could only be simplified, shortened, and made safer by the support of a powerful unit for performing any necessary geometric calculations.

It was not until the introduction of graphics screens that most of the above limitations and disadvantages were eliminated. Fortunately, the price for a CNC with a graphics-display unit for the entering and testing of programs has been kept within the limits that users are prepared to pay.

NC manual data input is nowadays usually associated with CNC having an integrated programming system and a 14-in. color screen, each programming step's resulting geometry being displayed on this VDU screen. After program input is complete, the cutting tools, their motions, and the cutting process itself are all simulated without recourse to the machine tool's NC control unit.

Data no longer needs to be entered using the formats and addresses *X, Z, G, F, S, T,* and *M,* but by means of special symbol or function keys and a menu; thus a highly "user-friendly" direct dialogue between the human operator and the machine tool is provided. Using relatively little input data, control systems can now automatically calculate intersections, transitions, lands, and radii, as well as specify entire machining cycles, including selecting the tools, number of cuts, spindle speeds, feed rates, and so on. Programs, once written, may then be recorded and later reloaded in the event of repeat orders, via a DNC link or a tape

FIGURE 8–2   Manual data input—CNC for lathes with graphic display of the programmed workpiece. Data for dimensioning individual graphic elements is entered with the aid of five softkeys situated below the display screen and the numeric keyboard.

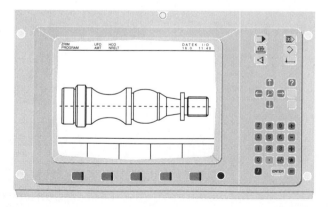

recorder if magnetic tapes are used as the data storage medium.

It is the development of the above user-friendly type of programming controls which have contributed most to NC machines being accepted so readily on the shop floor after only a short period of operational experience. Today it is no longer a question of long, tedious

FIGURE 8-3   Manual data input CNC for milling machines with 3-dimensional display of the workpiece. The graphics can be displayed in various attitudes by tilting or turning the workpiece display on the screen.

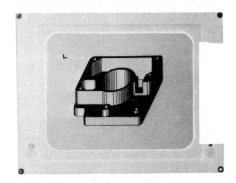

inputting of manual data as was once the case, thanks to the modern multiprocessor systems with ever growing capability. As microprocessors have become more versatile and faster and as larger data stores are provided, more and more complex workpieces can be programmed at the machine-tool level. Indeed, if the programmer becomes really adept at manually inputting data, almost any workpiece can be programmed at this level, regardless of its complexity.

Despite the current ease of at-the-machine programming, the disadvantages of machine-related programming should not be overlooked. Machine tools with sophisticated local programming capability are expensive, each one requiring the full range of ancillaries such as display screen, data storage, and software, as well as needing the services of a skilled programmer/operator. Clearly with ordinary CNC machine tools being much less expensive, and with off-line, preproven programs being downloaded directly from a host computer, a multimachine installation, with each machine having full local programming facilities, is not generally the most economic proposition.

8.2 WHY PROGRAM AT THE MACHINE-TOOL LEVEL?

The user's desire to enter NC control data directly at the machine tool, step-by-step, rather than programming remotely in a process-planning office, can probably be traced back to the beginnings of NC technology. Even today, those who do not yet use NC are intuitively convinced that at-the-machine program input, with instant visual monitoring as workpiece machining proceeds, is more suitable in practical terms, and is faster than (remote) office programming. Even playback or "teach-in" appears to be more acceptable than any type of office programming, because the machine tool itself is at least involved in the programming procedure!

Local programming today does, however, enable data entry while another operation is being completed. For example, often the machining of one hole takes sufficient time to allow data entry for the position of the next bore to be entered while cutting is proceeding. But this technique can rarely be applied to lathes or milling machines because the single machining sequences are usually too short. For these, machine programs have to be available in a complete, edited form before they can be started. For this reason a programming system must be used which is capable of writing the next part program while a workpiece is still being machined; there are no problems in doing this with modern CNCs. More experienced NC users still like the facility of local programming at the machine tool, but for different reasons. Since for them, the shop floor has always been totally responsible for production, why not leave the responsibility at a proven location, to experienced supervisors and a skilled workforce? This at least gives staff the opportunity of utilizing their knowledge and practical skills.

Clearly, production management has its own views regarding programming at the machine-tool level, in that it does not welcome the high extra costs of duplicating programming systems or the additional numbers of workers that are required for the operation and application of manual programming procedures. On the other hand, it becomes more attractive from the economic point of view to use the workforce more fully and profitably once automatic loading and unloading of parts has been installed. This can be achieved by retaining programming on the shop floor, which, in turn, can constitute part of a total reevaluation of the job function of CNC machine-tool operation. It could even contribute to the creation of decentralized "programming islands," thereby reducing the workload of the programming department.

Finally, reluctance to learn abstract programming languages is particularly evident in medium- and small-sized companies. Once a certain programming system has been installed, the initial capital and training costs alone establish a long-term commitment to that system. Also, the physical separation of the programming office from the NC workshop can foster doubts about workload, flexibility, and essential information feedback. Every user of machine tools with MDI will agree that such machines do allow a more flexible response to customers' requests to change or postpone orders than is possible using indirect programming. With so many objective arguments in favor of shop-floor programming, it is unwise to belittle the advantages by suggesting that the CNC machine is a more expensive programming station. This is no longer true when all relevant factors are taken into account. Furthermore, MDI controls have one major advantage: they can be specially designed for a specific machine tool and can therefore utilize all the programming facilities and methods which are provided to maximize the possibilities and design characteristics of the particular machine. This explains why lathes with 2×2 axes are now equipped with MDI controls; not long ago this was considered impossible. Such a control is capable of preventing collisions and delegating tasks faster than any untrained programmer.

8.3 SHOP-FLOOR OPINIONS AND ATTITUDES

In addition to technical and economic considerations, one important factor of shop-floor programming should not be neglected, and that is its psychological and motivational effect on workshop personnel. Skilled workers who felt themselves demoted to the level of "button pushers" with the introduction of the NC machine tool, and who were frequently angered by what they considered to be the planning-office programmer's "incompetence," see themselves once again in their rightful position of having full control over the machine tool. Shop-floor programming gives them the chance to apply their knowledge and skills, and it enables them to demonstrate a positive attitude towards "at-the-machine" programming. Experience indicates that they enjoy the challenging work and are motivated to operate NC machines as economically and, efficiently as possible. This implies that skilled workers should be given an opportunity to contribute to the total programming effort equaling that of the computer-aided programming offices. Motivated workers are much more efficient than those who are not, and in the long run, this motivation will have a positive influence on overall installation profitability.

8.4 GRAPHICS SCREENS

MDI controls with graphics screens are particularly well suited to engineering technicians who are learning the art of NC programming. However, caution must be exercised when selecting systems, since great differences exist between the various graphics units available. The major difference lies in the objectives of the graphics system, that is, the distinction between input graphics for entering data (such as menu graphics and programming graphics) and test graphics such as simulation graphics, and simultaneous graphics which have been designed principally to display programmed sequences while the machine tool is operating.

8.4.1   INPUT GRAPHICS

Menu graphics *(Fig. 8–5, p.100)* enable a subroutine, a cycle, or a contour to be called up, and a suitable sketch displayed which indicates the parameter values being entered. Various areas are illuminated successively, demanding the input of specific data which is automatically checked for logical and technical feasibility via an internal logic system. Once all values have been entered, some systems then display real graphics (to scale) on the screen. The programmer checks and confirms the programmed procedure which, if correct, is then stored by the control system.

Programming graphics *(Fig. 8–6, p. 101)* are much more useful, as they allow a graphic buildup of the profile of the part being programmed, that is, step-by-step, individual portions of the contour are

FIGURE 8-4   Screen display of an MDI control for nibbling and punching machines. The programmed workpiece covers most of the screen and is scaled automatically. Additionally, the control system deals with the technology; that is, it structures the cutting sequences if the operator does not give any overriding special commands.

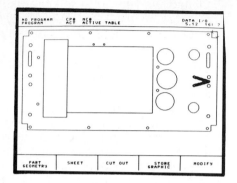

entered and finally fit together to form the complete outline of the workpiece. Any data-input errors can be immediately observed and corrected. Experienced, skilled operator/programmers prefer this form of graphics-assisted input because, in many ways, it is akin to actual shop-floor practice. The process of visually controlling the structure of a program step-by-step is identical to the operation of a conventional machine tool, where it is possible, although time-consuming, to compare the actual workpiece dimensions with the drawing at any time. The programmer is guided and feels confident throughout the programming procedure. This is essential for very complex part programs.

The value of graphics-assistance is best appreciated when it comes to the input of contours with complex dimensions. The programming system not only calculates all intersection and transition values, but it also displays graphically one or more possible solutions. The programmer selects the preferred one and can then be confident that this con-

FIGURE 8-5   Graphics menu display of a programmed pitch circle (to scale).

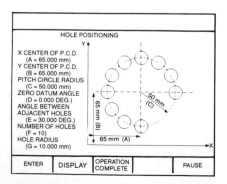

FIGURE 8–6   Programming graphics, the external contour being created by combining four basic graphic elements: cylinder; cone; tundish; sphere.
Four additional elements may also be used: body recess; relief turning; chamfers; radii, with tangential transitions to the contour. (The latter elements are not illustrated in this figure.)

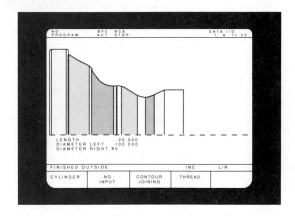

tour will be correctly reproduced on the actual workpiece. This interactive technique contributes significantly to faster programming because the programmer can proceed with confidence even when dealing with complex shapes. The graphic display is a help in understanding the most complicated machining sequences with the computer logic driving the display, rapidly calculating and indicating correct geometry profiles, and even selecting cutting and other technological data *(Figs. 8–7 and 8–8, p.102).*

Color graphics do not necessarily imply higher technical capability, and the possibility of utilizing various colors leads many software writers into overloading displays with information, making them less easily read than the alternative monochromatic screen graphics. However, if colors are carefully employed and logically selected, with similar information always located in the same position, they can be very useful indeed and a great help to anyone working with the system regularly. This is especially true where the user is able to select a choice of colors. Unfortunately such systems are much more expensive than monochromatic graphics displays.

8.4.2   TEST GRAPHICS

The simplest way of visually displaying what paths the cutting tool(s) will follow is with simultaneous graphics; when using them the operator completes the programming, then runs the simulation, noting any errors and correcting them before actually using the program to cut metal *(Fig. 8–9, p. 103).* In the case of "real-time" simulation the operating time can be measured, but this procedure is often too slow and is thus rarely used.

FIGURE 8–7   Simulation of the motion of the tool tip: dotted line = rapid traverse; full line = cutting profile; vertical line = body recess or radial feed. Experienced programmers are able to judge a machining operation solely on the basis of such a display, and need no additional animated graphics simulation.

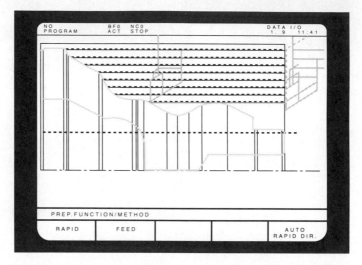

FIGURE 8–8   Close-up of component shown in Figure 8-7, enlarged with the aid of an electronic magnifier. By this means particularly crucial details of the machining operation, such as nonlinear transitions, can be examined closely. It is also possible to edit the close-up.

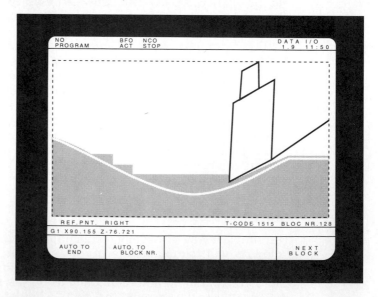

FIGURE 8-9   Animated graphic simulation of a machining procedure with the display of the cutting tools employed. (a) internal boring; (b) external machining.

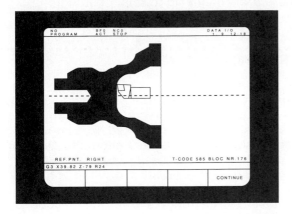 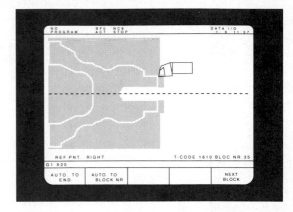

Simultaneous simulation, which is carried out while the machine is cutting, allows continuous monitoring throughout the machining process—an advantage that would otherwise be visually impossible if, for example, coolant obscured the view. Lathe-control systems typically display the individual tools to the same scale as the workpiece for both internal and external machining. The observer can see how the part changes shape, if there is the danger of collision, and if each cut is performed correctly. This facility is a prerequisite if tool data and profile are freely entered by the individual operator *(Fig. 8-10)*.

FIGURE 8-10   Graphic table of the programmed tooling. Each cutting tool can be programmed and displayed to scale by the individual user of the control. In order to carry out an animated graphic simulation, the CNC calls up the required programmed tool graphics.

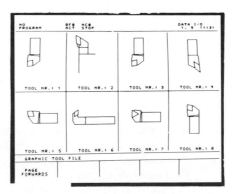

Test graphics are of no assistance in the initial programming procedure but are undoubtedly an essential safety device. Collisions between cutting tool, workpiece, and clamping devices, as well as geometric errors, are easily detectable and may be corrected before damage occurs or incorrect items are produced. This is a great advantage, especially when dealing with large, single workpieces or expensive materials. Graphic simulation is therefore a major aid to safer operation.

8.5 CRITERIA FOR USING SHOP-FLOOR PROGRAMMING

Many NC users prefer to carry out programming on the shop floor, especially if the numerical controls have an integrated programming unit. About 90 percent of all workpieces to be machined on a lathe are simple, belong to a family of parts with similar 2-D geometry, and can be considered as routine items, which can easily be dealt with by any shop-floor programmer/operator. This justifies on-the-spot programming and explains why many experienced NC users do not store simple part programs but just rewrite them if they are needed again. Because considerable effort in documentation, storage, and administration is avoided, this method often proves to be cheaper and quicker than looking for old, rarely used programs.

A particular company may, after careful consideration, conclude that manual data input is particularly advantageous if it:

- Does not yet have NC machines and wants to enter NC manufacturing gradually.
- Has only a very few NC machines and a special programming department would have insufficient workload.
- Wants to avoid high startup costs, incurred, for example, by computer-aided programming, programmer training, and tool cataloguing and presetting facilities.
- Wishes to supply workpieces at short notice to key departments, such as research and development, assembly shop, or customer service, where short lead times and flexibility outweigh other economic considerations.
- Is engaged in the manufacture of small batch sizes or even single parts where optimal programming is not a factor, and the time spent in programming would be more costly than the projected savings because of the short machining time involved.
- Is engaged in the manufacture of a large number of items where the machine tool can continuously operate with the aid of just a few optimized programs.
- Wants to replace conventional machine tools with NC machines, provided this does not require major changes in its internal organization.
- Is a large company and intends to become more flexible by distributing risks and responsibilities to smaller workshop units capable of providing their own part programs.

Shop-floor programming requires highly skilled workers who have also been trained in NC. It is their task to fully control the machining cycle and to enter corrections into the system when necessary, even when using computer programming aids.

Shop-floor programming appears to be inappropriate in the following situations:

- If CNC machines have more than four NC axes. Because of increased risk of collisions and calculation complexity, these complex machine tools can be more efficiently manipulated by means of suitable postprocessors.
- If CNC machines have automatic tool and workpiece changers. Productivity is the most important factor with such machine tools, and all production times are best planned by the production engineering office.
- If NC machine tools form part of a linked flexible production system. In this case, shop-floor programming would be totally inappropriate, because the distribution of machining cycles to two or more corresponding machine tools requires central programming by the programming department.
- If machines are required to perform predominantly continuous-path tasks, including 3-D interpolation. Such programs can be prepared much more effectively with the aid of efficient programming systems and languages (APT for example).

One disadvantage of machine tools fitted with MDI controls is that, with the purchase of further machine tools, the variety of different programming methods might be increased. Not only does this inhibit the interchange of programs between machine tools, but it also restricts workers to those machines that they have been trained to program.

8.6 REQUIREMENTS OF PROGRAMMING SYSTEMS SUITABLE FOR THE SHOP FLOOR

In summary, a programming system suitable for the shop floor should meet the requirements outlined below.

8.6.1 DISPLAYS

- The screen display forms the center-point of the system, as far as data transfer to the programmer/operator is concerned. It provides information on component geometry, tooling, zero-point shifts, correction values, program flow, and active functions during both the programming procedure and actual machine tool operation *(Fig. 8–11, p. 106)*.
- The programmer must be supported interactively during the programming procedure, that is, the entered geometry has to appear on the screen immediately in order to confirm the input data.
- A color graphics screen should greatly assist input and testing of programs.
- Identical information should always appear in the same position on the screen and in the same color. Error codes and warning signs are best flashed in red.

FIGURE 8–11   The display screen serves as the information center for operation and programming. Dependent on the mode chosen, the display can be switched to different graphics. This illustration shows maintenance instructions indicating the positions of lubricating points.

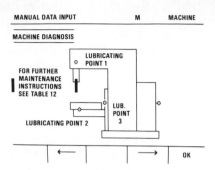

- Each display page must be clearly structured and must be easy to scan; the amount of information shown should not be too great.
- Simulation graphics must simulate the cutting process, including indication of the tooling, sufficiently well for the programmer to assess the accuracy of the part program without recourse to the machine tool.
- The dimensions of the machine tool's working envelope should be programmable and graphically displayed, including such obstacles as clamps, tailstock, and steadies, so that traverse limits can be controlled and collisions avoided.
- Position coordinate displays should be as large as possible, and it should be easy to switch the display from actual values to target values, or to path movement yet to be covered.

8.6.2   INPUT

- Foil keyboards must be splashproof. However, ordinary keyboards with buttons are generally preferred because they are more user-friendly and positive.
- Softkeys should be situated immediately below the screen showing the menu display to which they refer, and not on the left- or right-hand side. Usually the number of softkeys should not exceed approximately eight because the buttons will become too small to be easily pushed by "shop-floor fingers" more used to handling heavy workpieces.
- All symbols employed should conform to international standards and be easy to understand, permanently wear-resistant, and large enough for easy readability (*Fig. 8–12, p. 107*).

8.6.3   MANUAL OPERATION

- Each axis should be operated via its own key so that simultaneous movement along two axes is feasible.

FIGURE 8–12   MDI with large format display for easy viewing in a shop-floor environment. The star behind the coordinate values indicates that the programmed positions have been reached.

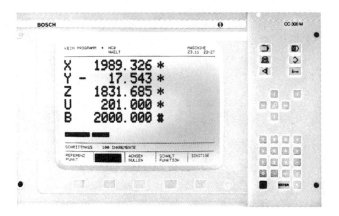

- Most users require one or two electronic servo override controls for precise operation of the machine tool along the axes, although most machines allow incremental feed-in and offer a large variety of steps, at 1/10/100/ 1000/10,000 increments, for example.
- The method of "teach-in" programming used for cutter-path and function commands, or for overwriting of dimensions, can be a great help and is considered extremely useful.
- Programming can often be facilitated if entered path dimensions and commands can be immediately checked on the machine tool.

8.6.4 PART PROGRAMMING

- It should be possible to perform programming in a sitting position to avoid physical strain on the programmer's posture.
- The programming unit and CNC must be built as separate units and should be capable of operating independently of one another, the secret of success being that NC machine-tool downtime must not occur because of programming activities.
- Step-by-step program input analogous to manual operations, which follows the drawing logically and provides operator guidance through dialogue, must be possible.
- It should be possible to enter chain dimensions as well as relative dimensions randomly, starting from either left or right of the workpiece. Special workpiece dimensioning specifically to aid programming should not be necessary.
- Instead of a complex programming language having first to be learned, a logical combination of symbol and function keys, in combination with the display screen, should be all that is necessary to commence programming.

- Data to be entered must be limited to an absolute minimum. Calculations of tangential transitions or intersections should be carried out within the system. The use of pocket calculators at the machine-tool level should be unnecessary.
- Operator guidance requesting all necessary data via keyboard and monitors should be possible through dialogue in the language spoken in the country where the machine is being used.
- Automatic cutting tool technology, as well as computer-aided geometry calculations, should be provided so that no time is wasted checking cutting data tables. This will ensure full utilization of machine-tool power and maximization of tool-cutting efficiency.
- Apart from input graphics, good test graphics for geometry and dynamic simulation of the machining process are highly desirable.
- It is essential that the system establish error-free programs from error-free input data, because machine downtime caused by prolonged CNC program correction must be avoided.
- External programming and external loading of programs should be possible, and the feasibility of program interchangeability between machine tools should be checked.
- It should be possible to program without operator guidance or at least with greatly reduced computer assistance, thereby allowing experienced programmers to input data at a rate limited only by their personal abilities.
- Some control systems are capable of creating individual graphics which are especially designed for those who wish to have the assignment of parameters and the program flow visually displayed. The keyboard of the control system should be suitable for such special tasks, thereby avoiding the necessity for expensive ancillary devices.

8.6.5 PROGRAM TESTING FACILITIES

- Once the input data is entered, it should be possible to compare and check several contours on the display screen, for example, before and after machining, selection of the number of cuts, the geometry of each cutting tool, and so on.
- Everything should be to scale, and all internal and external cutting should be clearly visible with a zoom-function to obtain close-ups of crucial details which cannot be observed when viewed at the general-scale size *(Fig. 8–8, p. 102)*.

8.6.6 REQUIREMENTS FOR EFFICIENT PROGRAM OPERATION

- It should be possible to start from any block in the program after selecting the appropriate data block number.
- Program must have the ability to continue cutting a contour after interruption—after tool failure and/or tool change, for example.
- Real-time simulation, simultaneous with the machining process, must be possible, thus allowing continuous monitoring of every

stage of machining. This is especially valuable if coolant prevents direct observation of the workpiece during cutting.

■ Rapid-motion simulation reduces program test time and is preferred to real-time simulation by experienced programmers.

■ Manual data input and DNC must not conflict with each other! Therefore it is essential that the DNC has an interface allowing for manual data input and output if and when required.

8.6.7   OPERATIONAL SAFETY

■ Limit zones should be predefined by the operator as this helps avoid damage if the program is not error-free, and helps to detect potential collision situations. The more advanced systems provide for this type of collision detection automatically.

■ Error codes should not be displayed in the form of code numbers, but explanatory remarks should allow the programmer to quickly identify and rectify errors.

■ Automatic withdrawal of the cutting tool, followed by the ability to resume cutting at the point of interruption, is necessary to prevent component scrap in the event of tool failure or other emergency.

■ Automatic monitoring of input data and checks on its logical feasibility are essential to avoid inputting incorrect or incomplete data.

8.6.8   DOCUMENTATION FOR SYSTEM LEARNING

■ It is vital that the system manual be comprehensive and easy to read and understand.

■ Demonstration video tapes may aid programmers to become quickly familiar with new programming systems, and help them learn how to operate the systems efficiently by working through special examples.

■ So-called HELP routines are very useful because they offer background information on how to enter data or complete programs. They can be called up at any time by the operator, who will then get the explanatory remarks displayed on the VDU screen.

8.7 COST COMPARISON

For some time lack of economy was a well-established argument against manual data input programming. This method was considered expensive because programming time meant machine-tool downtime. However, modern CNC machines now allow shop-floor programming to proceed while the machine tool is still operating. Despite this, many users remained unconvinced regarding profitability until the first machine tool allowing simultaneous programming was actually installed and operating.

Experience has shown that MDI programming systems can be used for two or even three shifts per day, whereas equipment in programming offices will probably only be used eight hours per day. Also if programming, testing, and editing are performed by the same person, the preparation time calculated per workpiece has been found to be reduced by a factor of 25 percent. Figure 8–13 *(p. 111)* illustrates an example of the difference in costs between the following four different programming methods.

- Manual programming in the planning office but editing at the CNC machine tool (without graphics). The programming procedure takes an enormous amount of time ($A + C = 0.6$ h), as do the corrections carried out in the office ($B = 0.2$ h), because there is no computer assistance; all values must be calculated manually. Due to the high risk of error, considerable time is again spent in editing the program on the shop floor ($B + C = 0.4$ h).
- Computer-assisted programming in the planning office but editing at the CNC machine tool. Programming and testing prove to be far less time-consuming ($A + B + C = 0.4$ h), but are more expensive due to the higher hourly rate of $40/h. Error probability is greatly reduced, resulting in less time being needed for test and correction both in the office ($B + C = 0.1$ h) and at the machine tool ($B + C = 0.2$ h).
- Manual input at the CNC machine tool during downtime (without graphics). External preparation time *(D)* is reduced to 0.2 h, but due to shop-floor programming without graphics assistance, the entire time taken for programming, testing, correction, and waiting is higher by a factor of 25 percent compared to the previous option. This is the most expensive way of programming because machine-tool downtime causes extra costs of $80/h (= full hourly machine-tool rate).
- Manual data input (with graphics), with programming unit separate from the CNC control. This method requires only 0.4 h for programming and testing, and external preparation time is reduced to 0.1 h. Indeed, this method will still be the second most economical even if the high, full hourly machine-tool rate is added to the cost, since the time saved greatly offsets the high hourly machine rate.

Computer-assisted programming in the planning office, with editing at the machine tool, is the most economical method for the example chosen. This cost comparison exercise should be repeated for different workpieces, especially if the machining time for one workpiece is shorter than the programming time for the next workpiece, as this will cause machine tool downtime once again. Clearly, the time spent on specific programming sequences varies with the workpiece concerned.

FIGURE 8–13   Comparison between programming costs of four different programming methods **for a specific workpiece.**

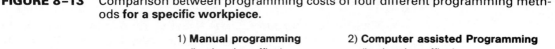

1) **Manual programming**
(in planning office)

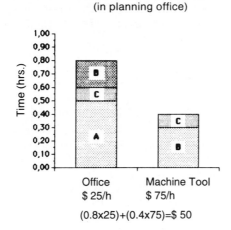

Office
$ 25/h

Machine Tool
$ 75/h

(0.8x25)+(0.4x75)=$ 50

2) **Computer assisted Programming**
(in planning office)

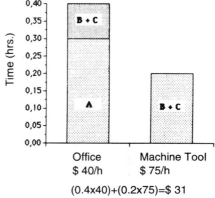

Office
$ 40/h

Machine Tool
$ 75/h

(0.4x40)+(0.2x75)=$ 31

3) **Manual Data Input without Graphics**

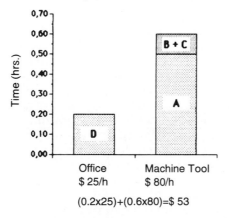

Office
$ 25/h

Machine Tool
$ 80/h

(0.2x25)+(0.6x80)=$ 53

4) **Manual Data Input with Graphics**

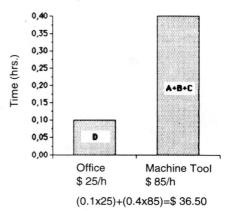

Office
$ 25/h

Machine Tool
$ 85/h

(0.1x25)+(0.4x85)=$ 36.50

A=Programming Time;   B=Testing and Editing Time;
C=Waiting Time;   D=External Preparation Time.

Assumed average costs/hr.:

Manual programming	$ 25
Computer assisted programming	$ 40
Machine Tool with NC	$ 75
Machine Tool without graphics display	$ 80
Machine Tool with programming graphics	$ 85

••
8.8 CONCLUSIONS

- Manual programming at the machine tool, that is, typing columns of data into the CNC unit manually while the machine is on standby awaiting data entry, goes against the fundamental principles of NC technology. Those favoring this method claim greater flexibility but often neglect the economic aspects of the more expensive NC machine tool's programming units. They value short lead times for small batch sizes more than a general productivity increase from the complete machining installation.

- Preparing programs in the planning office with subsequent supplementary manual input into the machine-tool is no solution either, as this method combines the disadvantages of both procedures. Under such circumstances computer-aided manual input controls should not really exist at the machine tool level.

- The development of efficient, computer-aided, "away-from-the-machine" programming helps create a viable alternative to machine-tool/shop-floor programming. It allows programs to be written simply, reliably, and in a practical manner without creating problems for the skilled worker at the machine tool. Operator program checking and monitoring through display screen dialogue and graphic display avoids the operator's need to use the machine tool as an input-control medium. Such units are more economical than the large, universal programming systems, because they are specifically designed for a particular machine tool.

- For complex workpieces, it is usually more economical and better in terms of manufacturing control to turn NC programming over to an efficient, well-equipped programming office, and to install the necessary equipment there. This is inevitable in the case of units involving large numbers of NC machines, for NC machines with more than three or four axes, and for interconnected machines, since none of them could be programmed without adversely affecting overall productivity, operational flexibility, and profitability.

- MDI can be considered an alternative to a centralized programming office, but only if the latter is likely to cause bottlenecks in the manufacturing process.

- Despite the most sophisticated programming aids, error-free programs cannot be guaranteed by any programming method. However, CNC machines with a manual input facility in standardized formats do provide for efficient editing and error correction.

- MDI does not necessarily imply a direct step towards increased automation. For this purpose additional controls are required which provide for a higher "level of intelligence" for overall process control, such as in-process gauging with automatic feedback correction or automatic correction of clamping tolerances. Many manual-input CNC systems now offer these additional options.

- Manual input controls with a high degree of intelligence are now available, which provide for programming while the machine tool is actually operating. Unfortunately purchasing policies are frequently based solely on price and thus the cheaper control systems are often bought, leaving shop-floor staff to struggle with the less than ideal new equipment. One solution to this problem could be either to make purchasers program or programmers purchase!

• •
8.9 INFLUENCE OF MDI ON FUTURE PROGRAMMING PLANS

Modern electronics make equipment available which enables the most efficient shop-floor programming to be carried out with comparative ease. MDI controls with the highest levels of versatility are feasible, thanks to increasingly sophisticated software automatically calculating intersections, storing tool data and cutting technology tables, providing graphic displays, and having a limited automatic process planning capability. All such features should be utilized if programming is to be wholly or partially carried out on the shop floor. Thus workshop staff are able to employ their practical know-how to the fullest, creating well planned programs, and thereby operating their machine tools in the most flexible manner.

However, it is impossible to assess precisely whether, in general, shop-floor programming is both sensible and profitable, as this depends on too many factors. Thus every user should carry out a thorough comparison of all methods and systems available to him, and if he comes to the conclusion that shop-based programming is the preferred solution he should not hesitate to install it. He is not making an irrevocable decision, and there is no better way of gaining experience with CNC than by employing the shop-floor programming technique.

The purchase of NC machine tools with MDI control by no means restricts future options. Regardless of the number of CNC machines already in use or planned, MDI control does not restrict the variety of programming methods that may be employed: that is, MDI at the machine tool; shop-floor programming with the aid of a separate programming system; programming in a planning office, either manually or with computer assistance; or CAD-assisted programming, where the CAD system supplies all necessary geometrical data, although the actual process plan is developed at the machine tool.

Thus MDI is not a dead-end street. Rather MDI is a positive learning step towards ultimately developing a full computer-integrated manufacturing system.

QUESTIONS FOR CHAPTER 8

1. Briefly describe what is meant by MDI?
2. What alternatives to MDI operation are there?
3. Why do many companies prefer MDI to alternative options?
4. What advantages and disadvantages are associated with all part programming being carried out in a central programming office?

5. How does a machine tool's input graphics differ from its test graphics?
6. What features would you look for in a shop-floor programming system to ensure optimum operational safety?
7. If MDI is selected initially, how will this decision influence any future assessments of workshop programming operation? Does your answer apply equally to the selection of a programming language?

FIGURE 8–14   The Four Principles of Programming.
A. Conventional programming—drawing is sent to the process planning department where the part program is written and tape produced.
B. Shop-floor programming—drawing is sent directly to the shop floor where the machine tool is programmed with the assistance of an MDI control unit.
C. Computer-aided design—all data on the part drawing is contained in an internal computer model. The geometric data can be transferred through a DNC system to the MDI control of the machine tool, where the operator programs in the technological machining data and finally effects the machining process.
D. Computer-aided design and programming with automatic creation of NC programs in the CAD computer. The complete program is handled by the DNC computer and transferred to the CNC unit of whichever machine tool calls it up. The operator no longer performs the programming task but only applies any necessary corrections. To date this method is feasible in only a few specialized cases, but it will become more common as increasing amounts of empirical planning data are committed to software.

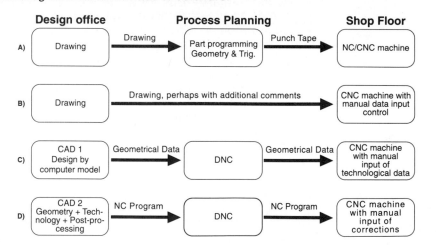

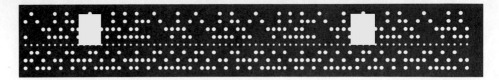

CHAPTER 9

PROGRAMS AND PROGRAMMING

After studying this chapter you should understand:

1. How an NC program is constructed.
2. The various ways of programming an NC machine tool.
3. How modern computer-aided part programming is carried out and the benefits that it offers programmers.
4. The functions of processors and postprocessors in NC technology.
5. Factors that should be taken into account when selecting an NC programming language system.

The economics of NC machine tools depend largely on the programming system used to generate the control data. The easier and quicker that "bug-free" programs are produced and made available at the machine tool, the more cost effective and flexible becomes the NC manufacturing process.

9.1 DEFINITIONS

A program is made up of a sequence of instructions which cause a computer or NC machine to carry out a definite machining task. For NC machines, this task is the manufacture of a certain workpiece by relative motion between tool and component, with dimensional inputs expressed in inches or millimeters. Such an NC part program contains all the necessary path information as well as the switching information and miscellaneous commands necessary for completely unmanned manufacture of the component.

The process of establishing sequences of directions for the tools from the part drawing and tool catalogues, together with developing specific programming instructions, and then transferring all this information onto a data carrier, which is especially coded for an NC system which can read it automatically, is called programming.

There are various formats which describe the general sequence and arrangement of information that must be on the data carrier depending on the machine-tool/controller combination. The most common type of tape format is the word address format standardized by the Electronics Industries Association which uses letters to identify each word within a sentence or block of information. The block length and the word length within a block of information depend on the design of the individual control.

9.2 DESIGN AND CONTENT OF NC PROGRAMS

Figure 9–1 illustrates the basic design of an NC part program for input into the NC. The program contents are made up of a number of blocks, which describe the operating sequence of the machine by steps or "sentences." Each block represents a geometrical machining step and/or a certain machine function. The individual blocks are numbered consecutively and separated from each other by the end-of-block code ($).

FIGURE 9–1   An example of a word address format.

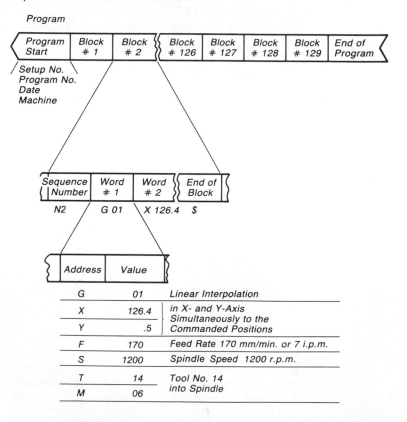

Address	Value	
G	01	Linear Interpolation
X	126.4	in X- and Y-Axis
Y	.5	Simultaneously to the Commanded Positions
F	170	Feed Rate 170 mm/min. or 7 i.p.m.
S	1200	Spindle Speed 1200 r.p.m.
T	14	Tool No. 14
M	06	into Spindle

Each block is made up of one or more words which are usually composed of alphanumeric characters, with the alpha character addressing the numerical values that cause specific machine motions and switching functions.

A block can contain different instructions. Distinctions are made among the following types of instructions:

- Geometric instructions that control the relative motions between tool and workpiece (addresses X, Y, Z, A, B, C, U, V, W, P, R, and so on)
- Technological instructions that specify feed rate (F), spindle rpm (S), and tools (T)
- Travel instructions that determine the type of motion (G), as, for example, rapid movement, linear interpolation, or circular interpolation
- Switching commands that select the tools (T); miscellaneous functions (M), representing such items as coolant supply on/off, spindle on/off, and spindle directional rotation; and correction commands that compensate for tool length, cutter radius, tool nose radius, and zero offsets (G)
- Cycle or subprogram commands that recall frequently recurring program sections

The address is usually a predetermined alpha character which specifies where the numerical value that follows is to be stored, that is, within which block of information. Each address can appear only once in each block. For purposes of clarity, double addresses per block should never be used, even with controls that allow several G or M commands per block.

Decimal-point programming represents numerical path data with the decimal point handled by "leading" or "trailing" zeros, depending on the word length and resolution of the control *(Table 9–1)*.

To determine the true value of a number with controls that do not express their values in decimal format, the leading or trailing zeros must be written in accordance with the special instructions that apply to the controller used. For example, if the X dimension word is limited to six characters in length by the control builder and the resolution of

TABLE 9–1   Drawing dimensions converted to various programming data formats.

DRAWING DIMENSION IN.	LEADING ZEROS*	TRAILING ZEROS**	DECIMAL POINT
1.500	X 0015	X 1500	X 1.5
.400	X 0004	X 400	X .4
.002	X 000002	X 2	X .002
1.942	X 001942	X 1942	X 1.942

*LEADING ZEROS = Trailing zero suppression

**TRAILING ZEROS = Leading zero suppression

the machine tool is limited to 0.001 in., then Table 9–1 is representative of leading and trailing zeros as well as decimal programming.

Finally, the following distinction is made between main blocks and subordinate blocks.

- Main blocks contain any address with numerical values that facilitate reentry into the interrupted program sequence on long programs. To mark main blocks, either a colon is written before the N address, or all blocks with even 100 or 1000 numbers are simply made into main blocks.
- Subordinate blocks include only blocks whose values change. The programming instructions of respective NC machines give information on these and other specific rules of the program.

9.3 PROGRAMMING PROCEDURES

Figure 9–2 *(p. 119)* shows possible programming procedures. Distinction is essentially based on:

- Programming location
- Degree of automation available
- Type of computer used
- Programming aids available
- Control and checking aids

In addition to manual part programming, various other computer-assisted NC programming schemes are now considered.

9.3.1 MANUAL PROGRAMMING

In manual part programming, a programmer completes the programming task without any computer assistance. The only aids used are data tables, a pocket calculator, the programming instructions for the specific machine-tool/controller combination, a tape-preparation device, and experience!

Programmers should always begin and conclude their training by manual part programming, since it is essential that they be able to readily understand, read, and modify part programs. A programmer must feel confident to correct programs both at the CNC machine and in the office.

Figure 9–3 *(p. 120)* shows the manual programming procedure, which is basically as follows.

After selecting the most appropriate NC machine based on the geometrical complexity of the piecepart configuration, the programmer outlines the machining sequence in a program manuscript.

The second step is to determine, with the aid of a tool data file, the number, type, and sequence of the cutting tools necessary, and whether any individual fixtures or holding devices are needed to clamp

FIGURE 9–2   Breakdown of programming methods and systems.

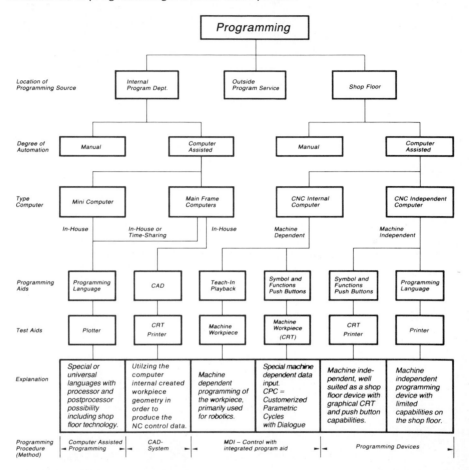

the job. Depending on the material to be machined, spindle speeds and feed rates are also selected at this time.

Following these two preliminary steps, work with the geometrical data from the drawing begins. When programming the relative motion between tool and component, additional geometrical calculations are usually necessary to determine cutting points, equidistant cutter centerlines, and intersection points, depending on the computing capabilities of the controller to be used and the complexity of the workpiece. Also, precise calculation of all motions is necessary to ensure that collisions between tools, parts, fixtures, or chuck are avoided. All these tasks must be carried out within the rules specified in the programming instructions that apply to the machine controller involved.

A good manual programmer should ideally have the following qualifications:

- A detailed knowledge of the machine-tool/controller system
- A familiarity with the axes nomenclature of the machine tool

FIGURE 9–3   Information flow in manual part programming.

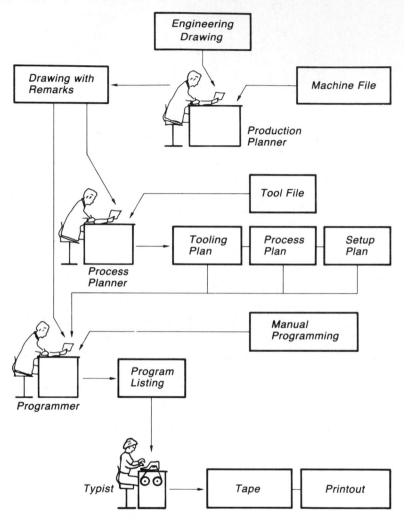

- The ability to operate equipment to produce a clean punch tape
- A precise knowledge of programming system instructions, such as format details in terms of maximum word and block lengths permissible
- Mastery of the coding of the individual machine functions and familiarity with their operational capabilities
- A knowledge of the interpolations available (linear, circular, parabolic, 2½-D, and 3-D, for example) and of their proper application
- The ability to recognize the limitations of the system
- The ability to accurately calculate tool paths
- A precise knowledge of any peculiarities of the controls, and any other factors that might influence programming

Experience suggests that a programmer can manually program reliably, at the most, four different NC machine types.

Finally, a tape must be made as the information carrier, particularly when the program is very large or when the programmed part is intended to be machined regularly. The data carrier is usually in the form of either punch-paper or magnetic tape. Data are transcribed block-by-block from the handwritten manuscript onto the data carrier via an alphanumeric keyboard connected to either a punch tape or a magnetic recorder.

The 8-track punch tape used with most controls has already been described in Chapter 3. Paper tape is usually employed for the first trial tape, but tapes that are to be used frequently must be more wear resistant and are usually made of a plastic-coated material.

Manual programming requires many routine calculations and has to be executed with great care. Fortunately, any mistakes that do occur are usually recognized or eliminated by an automatic checking system and serious consequences are thereby avoided.

9.3.2 COMPUTER-AIDED PROGRAMMING

In computer-assisted part programming, the programmer describes the component to the computer in a programming language that the computer understands. This so-called "source program" may be entered in either of the two following ways:

- Off-line. The source program is entered into the computer via a data carrier. Punch cards are an example of an off-line data carrier. The data is punched on the cards which are read sequentially into the computer via a device not connected directly to the computer.
- On-line. Data is input directly into the computer via a terminal, using a suitable programming language.

It is the task of the programming language to aid in the description of the component, that is, the motion between cutting tool and part, so that the required shape can be machined on any NC machine that is equipped for the task.

Clearly, the expression "language" is not meant literally here since it is not spoken but is only a means of communication between a person and a computer using symbolic characters. The number of symbolic characters varies with the language and/or its subsets. APT, for example, uses about 300 symbols, whereas ADAPT uses only about 175. Using these characters the programmer is able to describe most pieceparts, and also the necessary machining sequences. See Section 9.4 for a detailed discussion of programming language development.

The performance of the individual programming language varies considerably, and is often tailored to a certain machine type or manufacturer.

There is a distinction between machine-tool dependent languages that refer only to a specific machine controller or machine-tool type, and machine-tool independent languages that are, in general, universally applicable to most NC machines.

The ideal programming language must fulfill various requirements:

- It must not be tailored to a specific NC machine, but should be universal.
- It must be operable in every computer facility.
- It must have only a moderate number of words to facilitate quick learning.
- It must be clearly laid out and well documented.
- It should be split into two parts: technological and geometric.

Furthermore the language supplier should be able to furnish any necessary postprocessor software, should offer training courses, and should maintain the language, furnishing regular updates.

Figure 9–4 *(p. 123)* illustrates the information flow of computer-aided programming and Fig. 9–5 *(p. 124)* shows the activities of a part programmer.

NC programs are usually generated in two separate computer passes. During the first pass a language processor establishes a standardized program. In the second pass, via a postprocessor, this interim result is transcribed into a final part program that is fully readable by the selected NC controller/machine tool. This division of final data processing is described in detail in Section 9.3.6.

9.3.3 INTEGRATION WITH COMPUTER-AIDED DESIGN (CAD) SYSTEMS

In due course one will have to consider NC part programming as being logically linked to CAD. The timescale in going from part design through preparation of all manufacturing documentation (including NC programs) to the finished machined part could be considerably shortened if a fully integrated system existed linking CAD with CAM. For example, during the design process the component geometry is created and captured digitally at the CAD workstation. Because this same information is required for the geometrical data part of the corresponding NC program, a common data base could be used. This would result in a significant reduction in part programming effort and risk of errors. *(See also Chapter 24.)*

Because of high investment costs, integrated CAD/CAM systems that are truly flexible are, to date, rare indeed. However, in certain specialized areas, such as the design and subsequent manufacture of printed circuit boards, this type of link is being increasingly used.

9.3.4 MANUAL DATA INPUT CONTROLS

With modern CNC systems sophisticated control of an NC machine tool is now possible even when data is input manually at the machine controller on the shopfloor. Manual data input controls are now normal on every modern controller, and they provide a convenient way to establish a user-friendly dialogue with the machine via dedicated "softkeys," and subroutine canned cycles. Because of input-error monitoring facilities and the calculation of tool-path data locally within

FIGURE 9–4 Information flow in computer-assisted part programming.

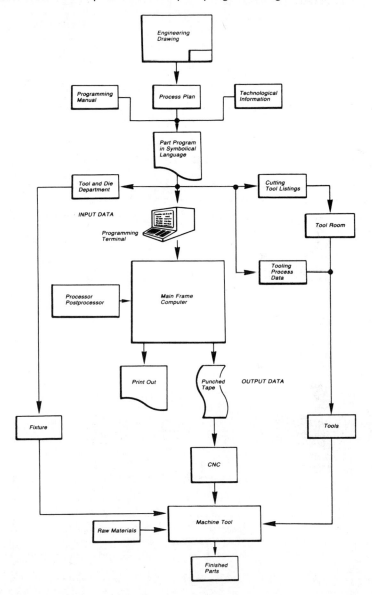

the CNC, the necessary amount of input data is now significantly small-er than it was when programming was done manually in the planning office.

This important area has, however, been dealt with fully in Chapter 8, and will therefore not be discussed further here.

FIGURE 9–5 Computer-assisted part programming.

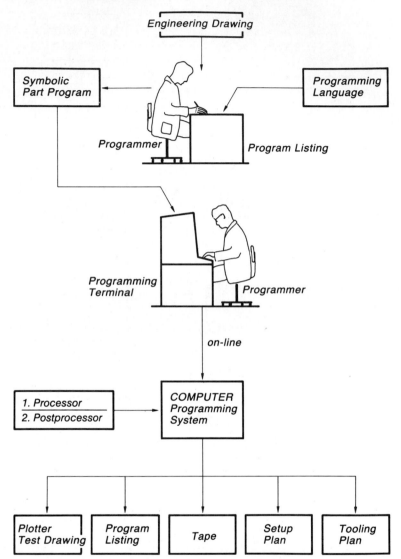

9.3.5 PORTABLE PROGRAMMING EQUIPMENT

NC portable programming is normally taken to imply either computer-aided programming equipment that has been built into the NC machine (thanks to miniaturization and its ability to function independently) or it can refer to a truly "stand-alone" portable package. In either case portable programming allows computer-aided programming at the machine-tool level, as well as the use of established part programs on several NC machines.

The transfer of programs from the programming device into the CNC is done either by data carrier or directly by cable link. The programming comfort and visual surveillance of the data produced via high-resolution dynamic screen displays ensures great reliability and gives the programmer added confidence.

The use of modern microcomputers and improved software has enormously increased the performance of portable programming equipment. Special-function and symbol keyboards, as well as interactive screen operation, raise this type of equipment to a class of performance that was, until recently, reserved for medium to large computer-based systems.

9.3.6 PROCESSORS AND POSTPROCESSORS

The information entered into a computer (input) is represented by a symbolic language and is processed by the computer to produce information (output) which will eventually drive a given machine-tool/controller combination. Before the symbolic language can be entered, however, a special computer program must be installed into the computer, allowing for computer-assisted part programming. This conversion program, the so-called processor (sometimes incorrectly referred to as the compiler), translates the symbolic language into the machine language of the computer and carries out the following operations:

- Analysis and encoding of the symbolic language words
- Interpretation of macro instructions into individual computer instructions
- Establishment of needed subprograms
- Management of interim results
- Calculation of the cutting-tool centerline data

Such a processor consists of numerous subprograms which are called on at various times during the processing of the part program. The processor is also designed to detect programming errors which may have been entered by the part programmer. These errors are detected by the system and sent to the display medium as an error message. All error diagnostics are handled by the processor generally, that is, in a manner that is not specific to a particular machine-tool/controller combination. Therefore, most error diagnostics deal with the syntax of the processor language and the geometry describing the workpiece. Only the postprocessor will fit the program to a specific NC machine/controller combination and consequently deal with errors that concern the NC system.

The postprocessor is a computer program that further processes the cutter centerline data from the processor into instruction sets designed for a specific NC machine-tool/controller combination. Any special machine-tool features are taken into consideration by the post-processor and converted into the language of that specific machine-tool controller. The postprocessor takes into consideration the input format required by the respective control unit of the machine, and assigns finite codes to individual speeds, feed rates, and control information, according to the respective characteristics of the machine tool involved.

Each postprocessor consists of five essential elements *(Fig. 9–6)*:

- Input
- Motions (geometry and dynamics)
- Miscellaneous functions
- Output
- Data-flow monitoring

FIGURE 9–6   The five basic elements of a postprocessor.

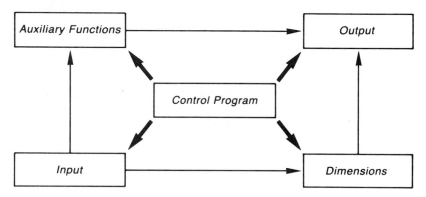

Input

The input element of the postprocessor contains the information on tool position and other technological information that was downloaded via the processor. Checks are made and a diagnosis is given if the furnished information is not correct. With this routine, the data input is processed in such a way that subsequent processing is performed by the postprocessor without difficulty.

Motions

This portion of the postprocessor deals with the adjustment of the feed rates to the dynamic conditions of the machine-tool/controller combination as demanded by the part programmer. It may, for example, reduce the feed rate in order to machine around corners, making machining in these areas possible within the specified tolerances.

Besides dynamic monitoring, mechanical limitation values are also checked. This is necessary to ensure that the equipment is not mechanically overloaded and that the cutting tool is not lifted unintentionally or does not collide with the machine or fixtures. Checks are also made to ensure that tolerances with regard to the tool path are observed during combined linear and rotary machining. This is called "linearization."

Miscellaneous Functions

This part of the postprocessor deals with assigning machine-tool dependent data, such as coolant ON and spindle ON, as functions to be executed by the controller. The postprocessor inserts the required codes into the appropriate places in the control instruction.

Output

This section receives data from the "motion" part of the postprocessor and transfers it to the required output code; now direct-tape production can take place. The same is true for machine function as well as preparatory functions. Furthermore, the postprocessor can provide a listing containing all the information that has been provided on tape as well as other comments pertinent to the operation of the machine tool if required.

Data-Flow Monitoring (Control)

This element of the postprocessor is responsible for the flawless internal information flow within the postprocessor program, as well as for the monitoring of its subsequent execution.

9.4 DEVELOPMENT OF COMPUTER-AIDED PROGRAMMING

As the first NC machine tools were developed it became clear that the programming of even relatively simple controllers was a complex task. The controllers at that time were only capable of linear interpolation, and it was therefore impossible to write part programs for complicated pieceparts of the type required by the aircraft industry. It was obvious that extensive computations were impossible without the aid of a computer, and this resulted in the development of computer-aided programming.

Massachusetts Institute of Technology (MIT) was awarded a contract for the development of this programming aid, which was financed by the U.S. Air Force. The USAF had previously sponsored the successful development of the first NC machine tool at MIT.

As a result of this project a programming language, called Automatically Programmed Tool (APT), was developed. It has since become the basis of almost all subsequent programming languages used in NC technology, having passed on to them most of its main features. APT has been subject to continual development and the current version is APT IV.

APT deals exclusively with geometric problems, and is very powerful in this field. It can be used to write programs which require the simultaneous interpolation of up to five axes, but it can run only on computers with a working memory of at least 256 Kbytes.

As the use of NC machine tools in general production engineering expanded, the number of part programs required increased rapidly, but most of the parts needed were not highly complex, and APT proved to be too cumbersome and too expensive for these simpler tasks. As a consequence, many less comprehensive programming languages were derived from APT, such as AUTOSPOT, AUTOMAP, AUTOPROMPT (IBM), COMPAC (Bendix), SPLIT (Sunstrand), and COMPACT II. However, all these languages were still able to solve only geometric problems.

For components requiring simple geometry, the computation of the technological parameters formed a major part of the programming effort. Programming languages were therefore devised with this bias, and the first such language which incorporated technological calculations was AUTOPIT (Pittler 1964). Based on this, EXAPT was developed in 1967, in West Germany.

The continuous development of software and the growing power of available hardware, has made it possible to develop programming languages which are nearly as user-friendly as those developed for general commercial data processing, but which are specifically tailored to the needs of part programming in the manufacturing industry. Today, as mentioned in Section 9.3.5, even portable computer-aided programming systems suitable for shop-floor programming are available. They use microprocessors and graphics screen displays and have simple function/symbolic keys.

An independent development in the field of mainframe computers has led to programming languages which are group-technology based, such as MITURN. See Chapter 23. The elements described with these languages are not geometric, but are based on elements of form and function. The amount of input work is thus reduced dramatically. However, not all parts can be described with these "comfortable" languages; their application is still limited to turning work.

9.5 SELECTION OF PROGRAMMING SYSTEM

Error-free part programs are a prime requisite for the cost-efficient use of NC machines, and the major aim must always be to produce error-free programs at the lowest possible cost.

Most NC users find it difficult to select the optimum programming system because each one has its own specific advantages and limitations. There are four main areas that must be considered when faced with this dilemma.

1. Variety of parts involved

- Complexity of component geometry
- Geometry of the raw material
- Effort necessary to determine technological data
- Degree of workpiece similarity

2. The NC machines

- Number of NC machines available
- Variety of NC machine types in use
- Manufacturing processes employed
- Range of numerical controllers in use

3. Production flow parameters

- Number of new NC part programs required per year
- Number of NC part programs stored in archives
- Frequency of part repetition
- Normal lot sizes

4. Background information

■ Availability of computing power
■ Qualifications of staff
■ NC experience of operators and programmers

Factors which make computer-aided programming systems essential are:

■ Complex parts requiring extensive geometrical and/or technological computations
■ A large variety of machine and controller types in use
■ Machines with a high level of automation
■ A large number of new NC part programs per year with minimal repetition rate
■ Staff inexperienced in the application of NC technology

Table 9–2 *(p. 130)* gives a brief resumé of the main programming systems currently available.

Selecting a programming language is much more difficult than selecting an NC machine tool, which still has features comparable to a conventional machine tool. Nevertheless, the system ultimately chosen must be made as programmer-friendly as possible. This is why investments in NC technology should be primarily looked at from the programmer's point of view. Postprocessors, terminals, the use of computers, and the necessary peripheral equipment are expensive and require well trained staff in order to pay off, but the rewards in efficient operation can be great.

The evaluation of the required power of a proposed NC programming system can also present problems because it depends on current and future priorities and shop-floor loadings. In no way does the decision to introduce computer-aided programming imply the necessity to purchase expensive software for mainframe computers. On the contrary, a number of simple but powerful programming systems based on microprocessors are now available, and these are easy to install in a network and to link into a mainframe system if required. This approach is widespread in the United States, and Europe is moving in the same direction.

It is worth remembering that it is possible to employ computer-aided and manual programming methods simultaneously, so that for each specific task the optimum programming method may be used, to keep programming costs to a minimum.

9.6 ADVANTAGES OF COMPUTER-AIDED PROGRAMMING

The use of computer facilities or computer-aided programming equipment significantly reduces the workload of the part programmer. The computer receives and analyzes the respective data, checks for input errors, carries out all necessary calculations, arranges the results in the optimum format, and locks the data into a logical sequence—all with-

TABLE 9–2 Classification of programming systems.

PROGRAMMING SYSTEM	METHOD CHARACTERISTICS
Integrated CAD/CAM Systems	Utilization of internal geometric data to automatically generate input for the CNC Controller.
Computer-Assisted Programming Systems	Machine tool independent computer-assisted part programming to generate geometric and technological data for the CNC Controller.
Portable Programming Devices	Machine tool dependent programming device suitable for the shop floor. Using symbolic function keyboard and CRT as an input-output device.
Manual Data Input Controllers	Machine-tool dependent programming capabilities with geometric and technological assist through CNC internal computer and software.
Manual Programming	Machine-dependent programming via punch tape input without computer assistance.
Teach-in Programming	Manual positional scanning with the machine and then digitally storing these positions' coordinates in the CNC (predominately used with robots).

out human intervention. The part programmer has only to formulate the machining problem, use the engineering drawing to establish a work plan, and then program in a user-friendly symbolic language.

The resulting advantages of this approach are:

- Use of a relatively easy symbolic language, that is, a symbol keyboard, to represent geometrical and technological data
- Considerable timesaving when describing the component and the necessary machining sequence
- Reduction in number of mistakes when establishing the parts program because of reduced data input, little or no computing outside the computer, and computer-based plausibility checks
- Considerable reductions in time and cost compared to conventional work-preparation methods
- Use of a common programming language
- Graphic display of the programmed part's geometry and graphic-dynamic simulation of the cutting procedure, including, in some cases, tool simulation

The best technical support that can be offered to a programmer is a programming system with integrated graphics. The programmer can control his input step by step, can edit the data while writing the program, and can finally check the program by graphic simulation. This gives the programmer considerable confidence and positively influences both programming speed and ability.

QUESTIONS FOR CHAPTER 9

1. What is an NC program? Why are NC programs subdivided into words and blocks?
2. What is the difference between a main and a subordinate block?
3. What are technological and geometric data? Where does the programmer acquire each type of data for any given job?
4. Explain, using a numerical example, the meaning of leading and trailing zeros in the context of NC part programming.
5. What are the principal advantages and disadvantages of manual part programming?
6. Discuss, in detail, some of the many advantages offered by computer-aided programming.
7. How can a part programmer be best helped in daily programming work?
8. Explain the difference between a processor and a postprocessor by describing the principal functions of each.
9. What is APT, and what is its significance today, bearing in mind that it is not now in common use?
10. List as many factors as possible that you would take into account when considering whether to install a new programming system in your company.
11. How many programming systems are presently available, and what are their main characteristics?
12. What is the current trend in the distribution of computing facilities in modern NC programming offices and workshops?

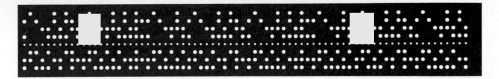

CHAPTER 10

PART PROGRAMMING OF NC MACHINE TOOLS

After studying this chapter you should understand:

1. The basic principles of manual part programming, including the use of G and M codes.
2. The significance of canned cycles.
3. The importance of various zero datum and reference points available to the part programmer.
4. The use of transformation when programming NC turning centers.
5. How cutting-tool length and diameter variations are catered for.
6. That computers may be used to assist the programmer task.

A knowledge of basic programming is essential if any programmer is to understand, write, or edit NC machining programs. However, in some instances, manual programming is by no means the most economic programming method, despite the use of canned cycles and G and M functions.

10.1 DEFINITIONS

Manual off-line programming of NC machines may be defined as the creation of NC part programs, which are completely coded and ready for direct entry into a specific NC machine tool without the assistance of a computer or a computer language.

Step by step, the programmer describes the machining task as per the component drawings, using a code which is directly understood by the NC machine without going through a processor. The only aids are usually data tables (indicating cutting data), a pocket calculator, specific instructions to the machine-tool/controller combination, and a tape-preparation device.

Computer-assisted part programming is the act of employing computer facilities to speed up the generation and processing of program data that the programmer would otherwise have to perform manually. An example of such a program is the subject of Chapter 11.

It should be clearly understood that the term "part program" does not refer to an incomplete part or a portion of an NC program! Although component or piecepart program would be a more descriptive term, part program has gained such universal acceptance that its use will be perpetuated here.

10.2 TRAINING

Anyone familiar with the operation of a specific type of machine tool can learn to program manually.

There is ample evidence to prove that skilled workers who have shop-floor experience working with conventional machine tools are particularly well suited for training as programmers. They have no difficulties in:

- Reading technical drawings and deciding on the required machining processes
- Planning the operations required in their correct sequence
- Correctly applying the appropriate know-how concerning cutting tools, materials, clamping devices, cutting speed, feed data, and so on

Additionally, knowledge of the following topics is necessary:

- The machine-tool/control system combination
- The programming instructions specific to the machine tool in question
- The structure of programs and the significance of various blocks of data
- The axis nomenclature and traverse instructions
- The position and significance of reference datum points

Basically manual programming is not difficult, provided that no sophisticated mathematical skills are necessary to calculate coordinate values, auxiliary points, or angles specified on the drawing. Fortunately, owing to the increasing use of dedicated microelectronics in programming and control systems, even complex calculations can be easily carried out without the need for significant mathematical skills on the part of the programmer.

Furthermore, computerized NC machines with integral programming aids, automatic tool compensation and calculation routines, and versatile computer-aided programming equipment can significantly reduce the demands on programmers. They thus become more accurate, faster, and therefore more efficient than the most highly skilled workers using pocket calculators.

Nevertheless, programming often becomes a time-consuming process of solving trigonometric problems, despite the fact that its real objective is to outline the necessary machining sequence of operations.

This is a problem that could for the most part be solved in the design office if engineering design drawings were to indicate the additional coordinate and other miscellaneous values needed in subsequent programming. Designers should be actively encouraged to provide all such additional data necessary for subsequent part programming as a matter of course. However, this is seldom the case and additional workpiece dimensions, included specifically to aid the programmer, still have to be calculated—a task that generally could be performed more efficiently by a designer than by a production planning engineer.

10.3 DELEGATED INTELLIGENCE

All users of NC are well aware that the operating efficiency of NC machines depends mainly on the quality and availability of NC part programs. It is generally accepted that the degree of difficulty in writing a part program is purely dependent on the complexity of the component itself and not on the type of machine tool used. The more complex the shape of the workpiece, the greater the programming skills required, and hence the greater the justification for some form of delegated intelligence.

Basically, there are three areas into which programming efforts can be delegated and it is up to the NC user to decide where to place the emphasis and how to distribute the programming tasks.

These three areas are:

1. With the programmer
2. In the programming equipment
3. In the numerical-control system

(See Fig. 10–1 p. 136.)
Each option has its own advantages as well as its technological and economic limitations.

Because a programmer must be free to concentrate on the sequence-planning activity, any calculations required only serve to reduce efficiency and decrease the number of blocks programmed per unit time. As soon as a programmer's effective output becomes inadequate to meet the demands of the workshop, the only option is to engage additional programmers to cope with the workload.

On the other hand, a large amount of capital may be invested in CNC machines with integrated programming aids, graphics-display units, and so on, and additional costs will still arise if the variety of machine-tool types is increased since the integrated programming systems will not normally be compatible. In other words, a wide variety of machine tools demands many programming systems which may then result in the installation being no longer cost effective.

For these reasons it is preferable to employ a mix of skilled programmers and programming systems that is suitable for the specific tasks required.

FIGURE 10–1   The principle of delegated intelligence (capability) for the solution of programming problems. A + B + C = 100 percent.

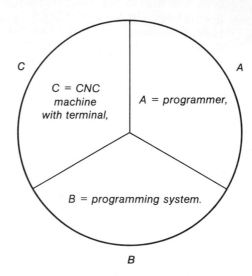

In any case, the training of every programmer should start and conclude with manual part-programming, since the ability to understand, read, and change part programs in local control language is vital. Only then can a programmer appreciate how to correct manual as well as computer-assisted programs on CNC machines. This ability demands a basic knowledge of mathematics, especially in the Pythagorean theorem and in fundamental trigonometric functions, although no programmer should have to be continuously engaged in such calculations.

10.4 FUNDAMENTALS OF PART PROGRAMMING

What follows is not a comprehensive course in manual part programming. Such a course could naturally be specific to no more than one machine-tool type. Only the basics of manual programming are explained with the aid of some examples. If a more detailed knowledge is required, one of the many NC programming courses offered by machine-tool manufacturers, educational establishments, or independent programming offices is recommended.

As each specific machine-tool type requires relevant specific knowledge, caution must be applied in selecting a course to ensure that its emphasis is actually in the area of special interest.

The proportion of time spent on both theoretical and practical training should be approximately equal to allow for comprehensive case studies on the shop floor. However most specialized courses do assume a basic knowledge of programming.

TABLE 10-1   Address arrangement according to EIA (Electronic Industries Association) Standard RS 274 B.

CHARACTER	ADDRESS FOR
A	Angular dimension around X axis
B	Angular dimension around Y axis
C	Angular dimension around Z axis
D	Angular dimension around special axis or third feed function*
E	Angular dimension around special axis or second feed function*
F	Feed function
G	Preparatory function
H	Unassigned
I	Distance to arc center or thread lead parallel to X
J	Distance to arc center or thread lead parallel to Y
K	Distance to arc center or thread lead parallel to Z
L	Do not use
M	Miscellaneous function
N	Sequence number
O	Reference rewind stop
P	Third rapid traverse dimension or tertiary motion dimension parallel to X*
Q	Second rapid traverse dimension or tertiary motion dimension parallel to Y*
R	First rapid traverse dimension or tertiary motion dimension parallel to Z*
S	Spindle speed function
T	Tool function
U	Secondary motion dimension parallel to X*
V	Secondary motion dimension parallel to Y*
W	Secondary motion dimension parallel to Z*
X	Primary X motion dimension
Y	Primary Y motion dimension
Z	Primary Z motion dimension

* Where D, E, P, Q, R, U, V, and W are not used as indicated, they may be used elsewhere.

10.4.1   SWITCHING COMMANDS

An NC machine has no switches for switching the various operating functions on and off—every command has to be programmed. This is done with the aid of machine commands which can have the following addresses:

- **S**   for spindle speed
- **T**   for tool identification number
- **M**   for miscellaneous functions
- **F**   for feed rate

The following blocks give some examples:

N 10 S 1460 M 13 $. This indicates Step 10: spindle speed 1460 rev/min, clockwise rotation, and coolant on.

N 60 G 95 F0 15 $. This indicates Step 60: feed rate 0.15 mm/rev.

N 140 T 17 M 06 $. This indicates Step 140: tool number 17 into spindle.

N 320 M 00 $. This indicates Step 320: program stop and wait for new START signal.

N 410 M 30 $. This indicates Step 410: end of program, spindle stop and coolant off, rewind punch tape to the beginning of the program.

Switching instructions are dealt with as if the functions performed had actually been switched on via an ordinary switch. They can be changed or switched off by overwriting. If logical and feasible, several instructions may be combined in one block of information.

When using M-functions, it must be borne in mind that some of them become effective as soon as the beginning of the block is read, whereas others remain ineffective until the complete block has been performed. Programming manuals related to specific machine-tool types provide more information about such peculiarities.

A comprehensive listing of G and M codes are shown in Tables 10–2 *(p. 142)* and 10–3 *(p. 143)*.

10.4.2   PREPARATORY AND TRAVERSE INSTRUCTIONS

The preparatory function path code, which consists of the letter G and two digits (assigned to various functions), and the path information data (X, Y, Z, R, A, and so on) operate together. G-functions determine how the path information that follows is to be calculated and/or processed. The path code defines the type of motion and the path information indicates where the motion is to be performed. In most cases several G-functions are needed to prepare a numerical control system for the significance of the succeeding path information. This is why these codes are referred to as "preparatory path codes."

Normally it is necessary for several G-functions to be stored and maintained active, but whether one block may contain several G-functions or whether G-functions have to be quoted in successive blocks will depend on the particular control system.

In order to avoid confusion, distinction is made between three types of G-functions. Only one G-function in each group can be effective at any one time. The following illustrates the use of the three types of path codes and some of the G-functions and their designations. Those printed in boldface type indicate the state of a function being switched on, and with most machine tools there is no need for these to be programmed. The reader will find it helpful to refer to Tables 10–2 and 10–3.

1. Modal G-functions effective in all subsequent blocks until cancelled.

Interpolation method:
G00, G01, G02, G03, G06

Plane selection:
G17, G18, G19

Tool compensation:
G40, G41, G42, G43, G44

Zero point shift:
G92, **G53**-G59

Starting conditions (acceleration, deceleration, positioning, etc.):
G08, G09, G60, G61, G62

Fixed (canned) cycle:
G80-G89

Dimensions input:
G90, G91

Feed rate:
G93, **G94**, G95

Spindle speed:
G96, G97

2. G-functions effective only during one block (non-modal)

Dwell:
G04 (combined with F indicating a time period)

Acceleration, deceleration:
G08, G09

Threading:
G63

Reference point shift:
G92

3. Unassigned G-functions

Although various organizations in the United States and in Europe have proposed standards for G and M codes, no universal assignment standard has yet been adopted. Nevertheless, with minor exceptions, Tables 10–2 and 10–3 provide a list of the generally accepted codes that have been adopted by most machine-tool builders worldwide.

FIGURE 10–2 Example of the "G41" function.

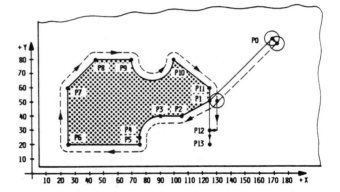

• N010	G17				
N020	G41	D2			
N030	G1	X125	Y50	F3000	➤ P1
N040		X105	Y40		➤ P2
N050		X90			➤ P3
N060	G3	X75	Y25	J-15	➤ P4
N070	G1	Y20			➤ P5
N080		X25			➤ P6
N090		Y60			➤ P7
N100		X45	Y80		➤ P8
N110		X70			➤ P9
N120	G3	X100	I15		➤ P10
N130	G1	X125	Y60		➤ P11
N140		Y50			➤ P1
N150		Y30			➤ P12
N160	G40	Y20	M30		➤ P13

Examples:

N10 G81 $

From step 10 onward the following command is valid: Drilling cycle G81 is called up, that is, all values of Z are relative values, rapid feed advance in the X and Y axes, drilling feed rate in in./min.

N40 G02 G17 X460 Y125 I116 J84 $

Block No. 40: perform clockwise circular interpolation to final position X460, Y125.

N70 G04 F10 $

Block No. 70: dwell for 10 s, that is, spindle keeps rotating while feed is interrupted for 10 s.

N100 G17 G41 H11 T11 $

Block No. 100 onward: cutter compensation value, stored under address H11, is called up and becomes effective in the X-Y plane, causing an offset to the left of the tool path.

N160 G54 $

Block No. 160: call for zero point shift on all axes.

FIGURE 10–3   Examples of G-coded functions, G00, 01, 02 and 03.

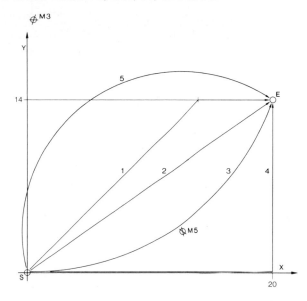

Examples of G-coded Functions G00, 01, 02 and 03 usage. There are several paths leading from the starting point S to the final point E. *(See Fig. 10–3.)* The choice is determined by the appropriate G-functions, as shown in the following:

Path 1:
N100 G00 X20 Y14 $
Rapid traverse from S to E: 14 in. at an angle of 45° the remaining traverse parallel to the X axis to the final point E.

Path 2:
N200 G01 X20 Y14 F40 $
Along a straight line from S to E (linear interpolation), with a feed rate of 40 in./min.

Path 3:
N300 G03 G17 X20 Y14 R20 F20 $
Circular interpolation counterclockwise around the center M3, with a radius of 20 in., and feed rate of 20 in./min.

Path 4:
N400 G00 X20 $
N401 Y14 $
Rapid traverse from S to E, first along the X axis, then parallel to the Y axis.

Path 5:
N500 G02 X20 Y14 R13 $
Circular interpolation clockwise around the center M5, with a radius of 13 in.

TABLE 10–2 Preparatory functions (G codes).

CODE	FUNCTION
G00	Point-to-point positioning, rapid traverse
G01	Linear interpolation
G02	Circular interpolation, clockwise (CW)
G03	Circular interpolation, anti-clockwise (CCW)
G04	Dwell
G05	Hold/Delay
G06	Parabolic interpolation
G07	Unassigned
G08	Acceleration of feed rate
G09	Deceleration of feed rate
G10	Linear interpolation for "long dimensions" (10 inches–100 inches
G11	Linear interpolation for "short dimensions" (up to 10 inches)
G12	Unassigned
G13-G16	Axis designation
G17	XY plane designation
G18	ZX plane designation
G19	YZ plane designation
G20	Circular interpolation, CW for "long dimensions"
G21	Circular interpolation, CW for "short dimensions"
G22-G29	Unassigned
G30	Circular interpolation, CCW for "long dimensions"
G31	Circular interpolation, CCW for "short dimensions"
G32	Unassigned
G33	Thread cutting, constant lead
G34	Thread cutting, linearly increasing lead
G35	Thread cutting, linearly decreasing lead
G36-G39	Unassigned
G40	Cutter compensation-cancels to zero
G41	Cutter radius compensation-offset left
G42	Cutter radius compensation-offset right
G43	Cutter compensation-positive
G44	Cutter compensation-negative
G45-G52	Unassigned
G53	Deletion of zero offset
G54-G59	Datum point/zero shift
G60	Target value, positioning tolerance 1
G61	Target value, positioning tolerance 2, or loop cycle
G62	Rapid traverse positioning
G63	Tapping cycle
G64	Change in feed rate or speed
G65-G69	Unassigned
G70	Dimensioning in inch units
G71	Dimensioning in metric units
G72-G79	Unassigned
G80	Canned cycle cancelled
G81-G89	Canned drilling and boring cycles
G90	Specifies absolute input dimensions
G91	Specifies incremental input dimensions
G92	Programmed reference point shift
G93	Unassigned
G94	Feed rate/min (inch units when combined with G70)
G95	Feed rate/rev (metric units when combined with G71)
G96	Spindle feed rate for constant surface feed
G97-G99	Unassigned

TABLE 10-3   Miscellaneous functions (M codes).

CODE	FUNCTION
M00	Program stop, spindle and coolant off
M01	Optional programmable stop
M02	End of program-often interchangeable with M30
M03	Spindle on, CW
M04	Spindle on, CCW
M05	Spindle stop
M06	Tool change
M07	Coolant supply No. 1 on
M08	Coolant supply No. 2 on
M09	Coolant off
M10	Clamp
M11	Unclamp
M12	Unassigned
M13	Spindle on, CW + coolant on
M14	Spindle on, CCW + coolant on
M15	Rapid traverse in + direction
M16	Rapid traverse in – direction
M17-M18	Unassigned
M19	Spindle stop at specified angular position
M20-M29	Unassigned
M30	Program stop at end of tape + tape rewind
M31	Interlock by-pass
M32-M35	Constant cutting velocity
M36-M39	Unassigned
M40-M45	Gear changes; otherwise unassigned
M46-M49	Unassigned
M50	Coolant supply No. 3 on
M51	Coolant supply No. 4 on
M52-M54	Unassigned
M55	Linear cutter offset No. 1 shift
M56	Linear cutter offset No. 2 shift
M57-M59	Unassigned
M60	Piecepart change
M61	Linear piecepart shift, location1
M62	Linear piecepart shift, location 2
M63-M67	Unassigned
M68	Clamp piecepart
M69	Unclamp piecepart
M70	Unassigned
M71	Angular piecepart shift, location 1
M72	Angular piecepart shift, location 2
M73-M77	Unassigned
M78	Clamp non-activated machine bed-ways
M79	Unclamp non-activated machine bed-ways
M80-M99	Unassigned

10.4.3   CANNED CYCLES

In situations where frequently recurring cycles exist, most numerical control systems have fixed ("canned") cycles programmed in the form of subroutines. Their existence simplifies and shortens programming in that, when required, any given fixed cycle may be immediately called up with only the specific parameters needing to be specified in the program.

Distinction is made between the following types of cycle:

Drilling: for drilling, reaming, countersinking, tapping (G80-G89).

Milling: for milling key-ways, contour milling, down-cut milling, profile milling, pocket milling, and so on. These are not standardized and individually assigned dependent on the controller type.

FIGURE 10–4   Drilling cycles.

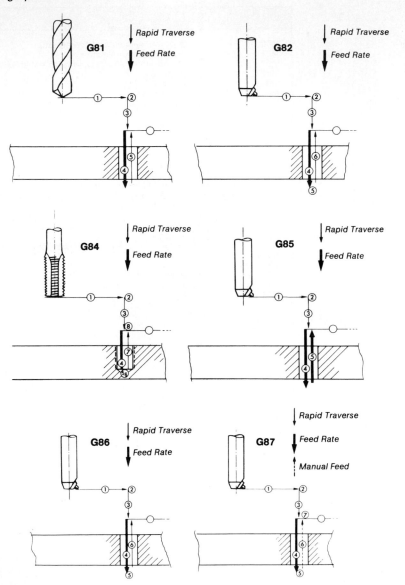

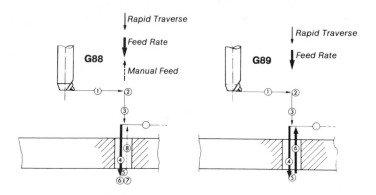

TABLE 10–4   Canned cycles for drilling, boring, and tapping operations.

FIXED CYCLE NO.	FEED FROM SURFACE	DWELL	AT PROGRAMMED DEPTH (FEED ENDPOINT)		EXAMPLE
			SPINDLE SPEED	SPINDLE RETURN MOTION	
G 80	Off	-	Stop	-	cancellation
G 81	const.	-	-	rapid	drilling centering
G 82	const.	yes	-	rapid	drilling countersinking
G 83	intermitt	-	-	rapid	deep hole drilling
G 84	const.	-	reverse	feed	tapping
G 85	const.	-	-	feed	boring
G 86	const.	-	Stop	rapid	recessing
G 87	const.	-	Stop	manually	multiple boring
G 88	const.	yes	Stop	manually	boring
G 98	const.	yes	-	feed	boring

All G-functions are modal instructions

Turning: for longitudinal cutting, facing, thread cutting (parallel to axis or conical) with automatic feed, as well as cycles for infeed with automatic choice of the number of cuts. Turning cycles are not standardized and their assignment depends on the controller type *(Fig. 10–5).*

User Assignable Cycles: certain "sub-programs", are individually assigned for each machine type: for example, the tool changing cycle M06, or geometric cycles such as gun drilling, the milling of segments of circles, and so on.

FIGURE 10–5 Turning cycle "rough turning with cut distribution."

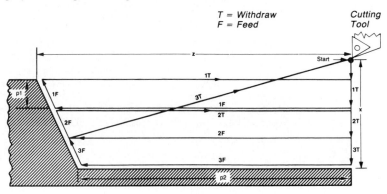

FIGURE 10–6 Example of the "G81" function.

```
● N10  G90  S1000  M42
  N20  G81  X85  Y45   Z 25   R 55  F300    M3
  N30       X45  Y30   Z 15   R 40
  N40       X25
  N50  G80  Z 60  H0
  N60  G0   X150 Y0    M30
```

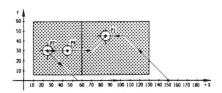

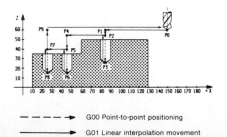

- - - - ▶   G00 Point-to-point positioning

───────▶   G01 Linear interpolation movement

● ●

10.5 ZERO POINTS AND REFERENCE POINTS

On each NC machine tool, zero points and reference points are defined, and component programming dimensions are usually specified relative to these points *(Fig. 10–7).*

10.5.1 MACHINE ZERO POINT (M)

The machine zero point is at the origin of the machine's coordinate measuring system. It is fixed and cannot be shifted. In practice this zero point should be quickly approached after the machine is turned on. Ideally, the control can approach this zero position automatically in each axis, the command for this being triggered either by activating a key or by the program itself.

This zero point must be located within an accuracy of ±1 path increment. In case of shaft encoding and inductosyn scales, one of the electrical zero crossovers of the measuring systems is used for this. As a result, the measuring system must be adjusted accordingly at the time the machine is installed; see Chapter 4.

10.5.2 MACHINE REFERENCE POINT (R)

Sometimes the machine reference point cannot be approached, as is the case in the following examples:

- Gantry-type milling machines where the spindle head cannot be displaced across the whole work-holding surface
- Very big machines were it would be time-consuming to approach the zero point repeatedly
- Cases where the zero point cannot be approached due to a clamped workpiece or a fixture causing obstruction
- Machines with adapted rotational tables or indexing clamping devices

In the above cases, it is recommended that a more convenient point be adopted as the machine's reference point. Instead of setting the axis position to zero, the position value would then correspond to the difference between true machine zero point and the newly adopted reference point.

FIGURE 10–7 Zero points.

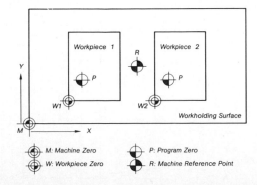

In practice, no strict distinction is made between the zero-point and reference-point concept. For example, on machines that must return to a fixed point for tool or pallet change, the point of return is also referred to as a "reference point."

10.5.3   PIECEPART ZERO POINT (W) AND PROGRAM ZERO POINT (P)

The origin of the piecepart coordinate system is the part's zero reference point which is freely selected by the programmer. However, on turning machines it lies at the rotary axis intersection with the longitudinal dimension reference edge *(Fig. 10–8).* Axis designation and positive axis direction are selected to conform with the machine's coordinate system, and will depend on the type of machine used.

Coordinate values, defined according to the machine zero point, are usually not suitable for programming, since they do not relate the piecepart zero position to the machine reference zero point in multi-axis machines. For this reason, the programmer determines a program zero point as it applies to the piecepart; relating the geometrical values to that point so that start and pickup can follow quickly after the piecepart has been clamped onto the machine. The axes are then set at zero, that is, the zero point is shifted from machine zero point to program zero point.

FIGURE 10–8   Zero and datum reference points for lathes.
M = Machine-tool zero point.
A = Blocking point. Can be identical with piecepart zero point.
W = Piecepart zero point = program zero point.
C = Control zero point. May be shifted to equal the piecepart zero point.
B = Start point, to be determined in the program. This is from where the first tool starts the machining procedure.
R = Reference point of the machine tool. Its position is determined by cams and the measuring system. It is essential to know the distance between R and M in order to relate the position of the axis to that of the reference point.

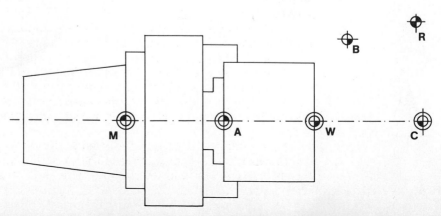

10.5.4 ZERO-POINT SHIFTING

Zero-point shifting facilitates the programmer's job, especially when the program zero point is also programmable and may be shifted by any value on each axis. This is known as a floating zero. Thus fixed drilling patterns, for example, may be transferred to any position while still maintaining the established pattern of coordinate values. For machine tools with pallet change, the programmer uses zero-point shift, together with a compensating value which may be changed manually to correct for the inevitable clamping variations.

10.6 TRANSFORMATION

The shifting of coordinates, or of the origin of a coordinate system, is termed transformation. It can be effected either manually or by program (G54–G59). This can greatly facilitate programming; for example, initially different machine-tool and workpiece zero points can be shifted to achieve coincidence. Alternatively the operator determines a reference point for the tips of all cutting tools so that the distance between each of them and the workpiece zero point is the same.

A major advantage of this is that the programmer can write a program without considering to know individual tool lengths.

10.7 COMPENSATING CORRECTIONS

The need for compensating corrections during machining remains even if the part programs, accessories, machine tools, and other aids involved in the process are prepared free of errors. Often this becomes evident only after initiating machining or on inspection of chip formation or workpiece geometry. Compensating correction possibilities vary according to machine type and control facilities.

Tool-length compensation *(Fig. 10–9 p. 150)* allows for correction between preset and actual tool length, or the adjustment necessary after the tool has been reground. The differential measurement or absolute length is then set via a group of decade switches or entered via a keyboard into the tool compensation value memory of the control. Recall takes place via address H or D and the desired memory location number.

The same is true for milling cutter radius compensation. Compensation direction is determined via preparatory functions G43 and G44 independent of the quadrant from which machining is referenced *(Fig. 10–10)*.

The function of tool path compensation is to establish the necessary tool center path for each workpiece profile programmed. This applies to turning as well as milling. The tool must follow the profile exactly, including around inconsistent profile transitions such as chamfers and radii *(Figures. 10–12 to 10–14).*

In the early days of NC, path compensations required additional programming of auxiliary parameters and change-over radii. Modern, efficient controls feature path compensations requiring only the tool radius and information as to tool location in relation to the component *(Figs. 10–11 to 10–14).*

Machines with pallet changers usually require an offset parallel to the axes of the individual workpieces for adjustment. Rotating a circular indexing table causes deviations in relation to the zero point position which must be corrected as shown in Figure 10–15 *(p. 153).*

FIGURE 10–9   Tool-length compensation.

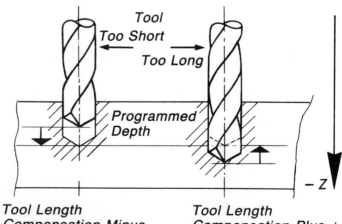

Tool
Too Short
Too Long
Programmed Depth
$-z$

Tool Length Compensation-Minus –   *Tool Length Compensation-Plus +*

FIGURE 10–10   Milling offset in inside and outside milling.
G43 positive offset. G44 negative offset.

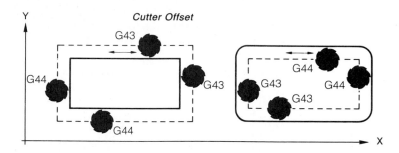

FIGURE 10–11   Milling path compensation.
G41 workpiece to the right of the milling path (offset to the left).
G42 workpiece to the left of the milling path (offset to the right).

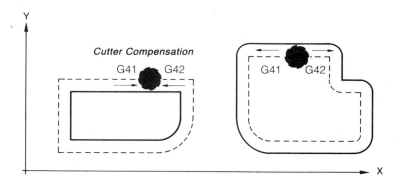

FIGURE 10–12   Profile defects occurring at cutting-tool radius without equidistant path compensation. Contour errors occur when the path of point P is programmed but the profiling tangents of the cutter do not run through P; that is, the profile produced does not agree with the required profile.

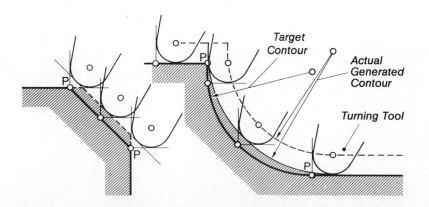

FIGURE 10–13 Equidistants with automatic transition circle at α.

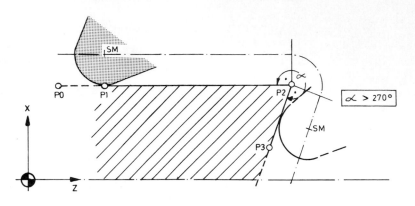

FIGURE 10–14 Differences between (A) tool nose compensation and (B) cutter radius compensation. Profile geometry is programmed. The CNC automatically generates transition radii and equidistant compensation. For turning, tool-nose compensation is necessary because the tool-nose point S is not coincident with the cutting edge T. Tool-nose compensation ensures that the tool zero point S travels along the programmed path at a constant distance normal to the target contour of the workpiece at all times. Milling cutter radius compensation is different from tool-nose compensation in turning, although the principle of ensuring a constant distance normal to the required profile (equal to cutter radius) still applies.

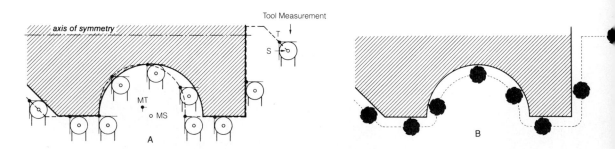

FIGURE 10–15   Zero point offset ΔX and ΔY of a workpiece as it rotates by $3 \times 90°$.

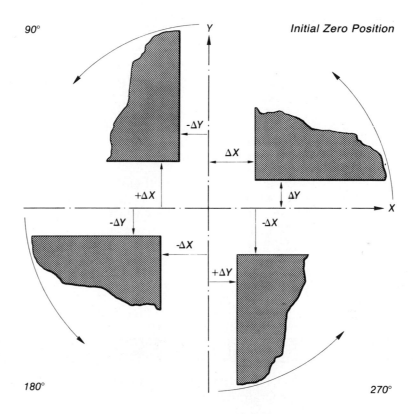

Fixture Offset Values		
Table Position	X-Axis	Y-Axis
0°	ΔX	ΔY
90°	$-\Delta Y$	$+\Delta X$
180°	$-\Delta X$	$-\Delta Y$
270°	$+\Delta Y$	$-\Delta X$

•••
10.8 SUMMARY

The most common addresses used in NC programming are: N G X Y Z R F S T and M.

Whereas a familiarity with how they work and a knowledge of how to employ them will allow just about anyone to run virtually any NC machine tool, these are only the most basic fundamentals of programming. Not only must a large range of additional, specific address details be mastered, but programming will also differ according to the type of machine tool or control system involved.

Differences typically exist with regard to:

- Automatic choice in the number and depths of cuts for turning cycles
- How to program zero point shifts
- Repetition and omission of program sequence cycles
- How to command automatic control of tool service life and tool fracture monitoring

The programming of these and other functions can only be learned when related to a specific type of machine controller, and practical training on the shop floor must constitute a major part of the overall training period.

Only one who receives such training and who gains experience in manual programming before embarking on more advanced programming using computer assisting facilities can be considered a thoroughly trained NC programmer.

QUESTIONS FOR CHAPTER 10

1. Why do experienced production engineers usually make the best NC programmers?
2. What is the basic difference between manual part programming and NC part programming?
3. What is meant by switching commands?
4. What are G and M functions; why are they so useful to both programmer and machine-tool operator?
5. What is a canned cycle? Give an example applicable to both turning and milling operations.
6. Explain the difference between machine data point and program zero point.
7. Explain the terms "tool compensation" and "zero offset."
8. Explain the meaning of the following line taken from an NC part program:
   N25 G01 G17 G42 G91 X47 Y98 F14 S1250 T1416 M13 $

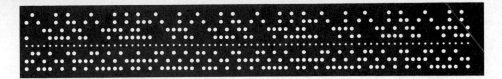

CHAPTER 11

EXAMPLE OF COMPUTER-ASSISTED PROGRAMMING

After studying this chapter you should:

1. Know the four basic types of instruction contained in a computer-aided program.
2. Understand how a program in COMPACT II is constructed.
3. Recognize the form of a part program after it has been processed through a typical compiler.

There are many computer-aided programming systems, and most of them are based on the automatically programmed tool (APT) language developed in the United States in the 1960s. One of the most popular of these derived programming languages, COMPACT II, is illustrated here as an example of how logical such APT-based, computer-assisted programming systems generally are for the user.

11.1 DEFINITIONS

The component chosen to illustrate the use of COMPACT II is the one shown in Figure 11–1, *p. 156.*

When using COMPACT II style language, the program will consist of four types of instructions:

1. Machine-related instructions; given at the beginning of a program
2. Geometric data (definition of required shape)
3. Technological data (description of tooling and specification of speeds and feeds to be used)
4. Definitions of tool paths

FIGURE 11–1   Component to be produced. (All dimensions are in mm.)

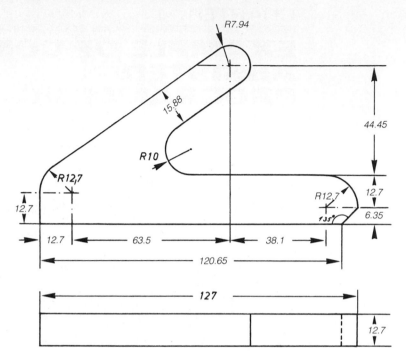

The COMPACT II language is almost free of formats, which means that, apart from (1) above, all the other types of instructions may be mixed, and the order in which data relating to the part is given within single instructions can be chosen at random.

11.2 MACHINE-RELATED INSTRUCTIONS

The first line of a COMPACT II program must contain an identification of the machine tool upon which the component is to be machined. For example: MACHIN, MILLING-MACHINE, and so on.

The second line can be used to name the workpiece, identify the part number, or give any other information that permits the tape to be produced and to be always identifiable. For example: IDENT, ANGLE-SHAPED, and so on.

Next follows a SETUP instruction determining the cutting-tool position relative to the absolute zero point of the machine tool. The following coordinates are the relevant data for our imaginary machine tool's tool change position: X axis = 0 mm, Y axis = 85 mm. In order to ensure a safe distance from the workholding data surface, the position in the Z axis is made 250 mm. Consequently the third line in the program is:

SETUP, 0LX, 85LY, 250LZ.

•••

11.3　GEOMETRICAL-DATA INPUT

Before the geometric description of the workpiece may be stated, it is necessary to define the workpiece zero point. As the dimensions in the technical drawing all refer to the bottom left-hand corner, it will be defined as the origin of the part geometry using the following instructions: BASE, 25.4XA, 25.4YA, 0ZA.

The statements XA, YA, and ZA indicate the coordinates, and the numbers in front of them denote the distance between workpiece and the machine's imaginary absolute zero point. These dimensions have to be taken into account when clamping the workpiece. Now the description of the part geometry can be given, on the basis of the dimensions shown in Figure 11–1, *p. 156.*

The bottom edge of the workpiece is termed line 1 *(see Fig. 11–2).* It lies on the X axis and is defined in COMPACT II by: DLN1, YB. (Where DLN1 stands for "define line 1" and YB indicates that the line intersects the Y axis at zero). Since no value for X is given, it is automatically assumed that the line is parallel to the X axis, that is, in this particular case identical to it.

Line 2 is defined next, intersecting line 1 at a distance of 120.65 mm from the base point, and at an angle of 135° *(Fig. 11–3).*

The definition of angles in COMPACT II is indicated in Figure 11–4, *p. 158.* Generally, a horizontal line between P and any point to the right of P is considered to be at the angle of 0°. Starting from this line, angles

FIGURE 11–2

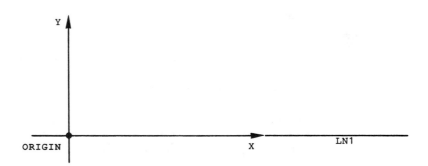

FIGURE 11–3

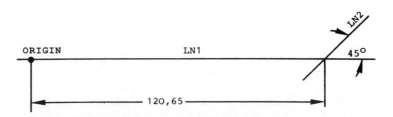

FIGURE 11–4

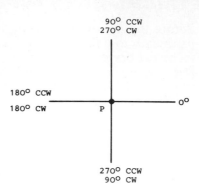

can either be measured in a clockwise (CW) or counterclockwise (CCW) direction. In a program, both ways of describing angles can be used, simply by adding the corresponding letter code, CW or CCW. Applying this definition, line 2 intersects line 1 at an angle of 45° CCW, and therefore the instruction needed to define line 2 is:

DLN2, 120.65XB, YB, 45 CCW.

Following the contour of the workpiece, the next geometric element must be a circle with a radius of 12.7 mm *(Fig. 11–5)*. The position of its center point (termed point 1), that is, the coordinates giving the distance from the origin point, may be given in terms of the sum dimensions of each axis if more convenient to the programmer. This avoids any additional calculations having to be carried out by the programmer. In this example the coordinate value of the X axis is not given explicitly, therefore, for the sake of convenience, the sum indicated in the drawing can be programmed without being summated, that is, 12.7 + 63.5 + 38.1.

The coordinate values of the Y and Z axes are 6.35 mm and 0 mm respectively. The Z value is arbitrary since point 1 only serves as an auxiliary point for positioning the circle; thus this coordinate is irrelevant to the part geometry. Point 1 is consequently defined by the following statement:

DPT1, 12.7 + 63.5 + 38.1XB, 6.35YB, ZB, where DPT1 stands for "define point 1."

FIGURE 11–5

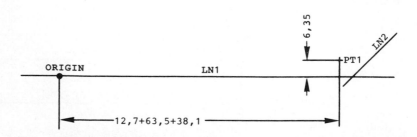

Referring to point 1 as the center point, the circle itself can be described by programming its radius in the form of:

DCIR1, PT1, 12.7R, where DCIR stands for "define circle," PT1 for "point 1," and 12.7R for "12.7 mm radius" *(See Fig. 11–6).*

FIGURE 11–6

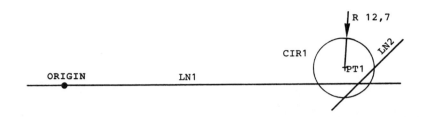

Having given both the position and the radius of the circle, the intersection which is to be used for continuing the contour of the workpiece must now be defined *(Fig. 11–7).* This can be done by defining an offset line to the X axis at the distance of 12.7 + 6.35 mm measured in the positive direction of the Y axis: DLN3, 19.05YB.

FIGURE 11–7

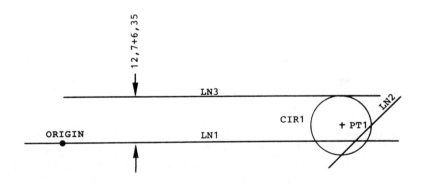

Continuing to follow the outline shown in Figure 11–1, *p. 156* the next geometric element to be defined would again be a portion of a circle to link line 3 to the next horizontal line.

However, as the diameter of the milling cutter to be used is 20 mm and the radius of the curve to be machined is 10 mm, there is no necessity to explicitly describe the radial profiling as it will automatically be cut by the tool following its defined path, that is, parallel to the required contour.

Before defining any further lines, it is easier to program two more circles as they can then be used for positioning the lines without having to calculate the angle at which they intersect line 3.

As it is also possible to combine the position and radius of a circle in one instruction, this is done for circle 2 *(Fig. 11–8, p. 160)* by the statement:

DCIR2, 12.7 + 63.5XB, 6.35 + 12.7 + 44.45YB, 7.94R.

FIGURE 11–8

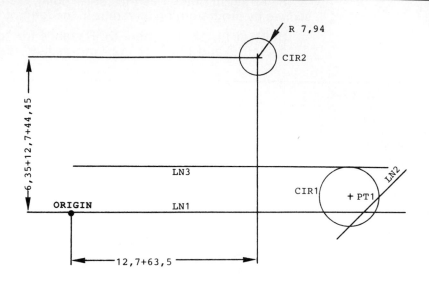

The third circle *(Fig. 11–9)* can be defined in the same manner:

DCIR3, 12.7XB, 12.7YB, 12.7R

It is now no longer a problem to program the remaining parts of the contour since line 4 *(Fig. 11–10)* is a tangent to the circles 2 and 3. The corresponding instruction is thus: DLN4, CIR2, CIR3.

However, as there are two different possibilities of linking both circles by a tangent (LN4 and the dotted line in Figure 11–10, *p. 161)*, the program must state which of them is to be followed. This can be done by giving a relative coordinate value of the point at which the line touches circle 3. It is sufficient to say that the touching point of the line desired has a Y value larger than the other point, and the code for this is simply YL. Thus the complete statement is: DLN4, CIR2, YL, CIR3.

FIGURE 11–9

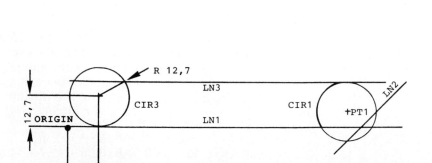

FIGURE 11–10

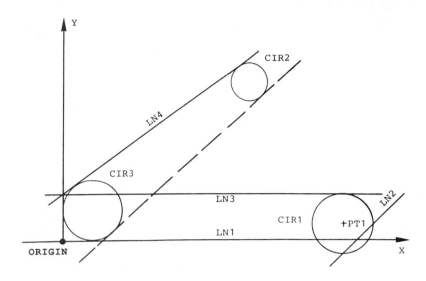

Since the other side of the contour is parallel to line 4, *(Fig. 11–11, p.162),* it is sufficient to define it as an offset line at a distance of 15.88 mm. Again, there are two lines possible, this time the desired line intersects the X axis at a larger value than the other possible line; the code therefore is XL, standing for "X larger." Line 5 is thus defined as: DLN5, LN4/15.88XL.

Finally the outline of the workpiece can be completed by line 6 *(Fig. 11–12, p.162),* which lies on the Y axis and can be defined by: DLN6, XB.

All geometric elements of the workpiece are hence now defined. Apart from the various methods of describing points, lines, and circles explained in this example, COMPACT II offers many more ways of defining part geometry.

11.4 TECHNOLOGICAL-DATA INPUT

The next step in this program is to specify the technological information, and this commences by calling up instructions for the milling cutter tool:

ATCHG, TOOL1, GL200, TD20, 900RPM, 230MMPM, CON. where ATCHG is the abbreviation for automatic tool change,
TOOL 1 for "tool number 1,"
GL200 for "gage length 200 mm,"
TD20 for "tool diameter 20 mm,"
900RPM for "speed of 900 rev/min,"
230MMPM for "feed rate of 230 mm/min,"
CON for "coolant on."

FIGURE 11–11

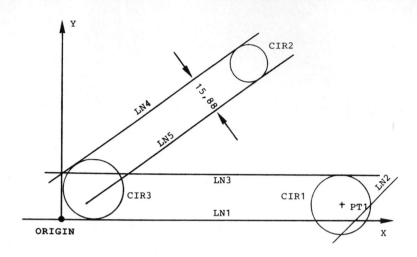

The command ATCHG initiates automatic tool change, calling up the tool named, which is then inserted into the machine tool's spindle. By means of the instruction GL200 the computer is told the gage length of the tool; this dimension is allowed for in all motions along the Z axis. Having determined the tool diameter via TD20, the tool path can be described in terms of the part contour already defined, and the computer then automatically calculates the path along which the center point of the cutter travels, that is, tangential to the contour of the component, at

FIGURE 11–12

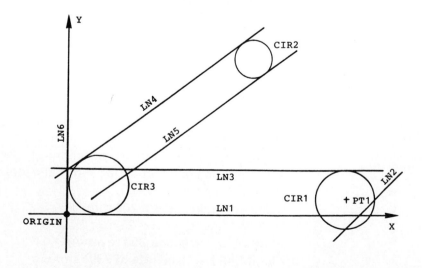

a distance of 10 mm—the cutter radius.

Cutting data is given by 900RPM and 230MMPM, and coolant is switched on via the command CON.

•••
11.5 DEFINITION OF TOOL PATHS

The tool described above has to travel rapidly from its initial position to where the milling process starts *(Fig. 11–13);* this movement is generated by:

MOVE, OFFLN1/YS, OFFLN6/5XS, 10ZB,

where MOVE indicates rapid traverse from the tool-changing position to the next position. The movement along the Y axis must stop when the cutter reaches line 1; OFFLN1 means "off line 1." In order to define at which side of line 1 the tool is to dwell, the code YS is used, meaning the side where the Y value of the actual position of the tool center is smallest. Having determined the final position on the Y axis, the one on the X axis can be defined.

The cutter will approach line 6 from the direction where the X value of the actual tool position is smaller. In order to avoid the cutter touching the workpiece, motion along the X axis must stop at a distance of 5 mm from line 6—specified by OFFLN6/5XS. Finally in-feed along the Z axis has to be defined; allowing for the height of the workpiece, the milling cutter moves to within 10 mm of the workholding surface: 10ZB.

FIGURE 11–13

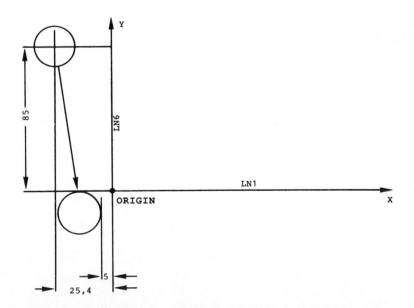

Having determined the target values of the rapid traverse, the actual cutting path can now be described.

First, the tool must move along line 1 until it has crossed line 2 *(Fig. 11–14),* for which the corresponding command in COMPACT II language is:

CUT, PARLN1, PASTLN2,

FIGURE 11–14

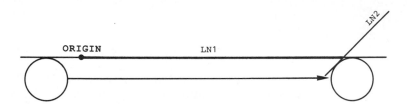

where CUT initiates movement in accordance with the above entered cutting data, the path must be parallel to line 1 (PARLN1), and the final position is reached as soon as the cutter has passed line 2 (PASTLN2).

The second path is parallel to line 2 leading to a position outside circle 1. However, as shown in Figure 11–15, line 2 intersects circle 1 at two points. This is why an additional statement is necessary to specify which intersection is meant to be the target value. In this case it is the one with a larger coordinate value on the Y axis.

Thus the instruction is:

CUT, PARLN2, OUTCIR1, YL.

FIGURE 11–15

The next path is along the contour of circle 1 *(Fig. 11–16, p. 165),* which is termed "out CONtouring" (OCON) in COMPACT II. The rotating movement is to be counterclockwise (CCW), and is to start at the location where the last motion ended S(LOC). The target position, where the motion finishes, is the point where line 3 touches circle 1: F(TANLN3). The command is therefore:

FIGURE 11–16

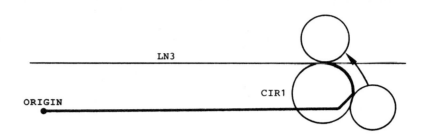

OCON, CIR1, CCW, S(LOC), F(TANLN3).

The cutter movement is now again parallel to line LN5 is reached *(Fig. 11–17).* As the cutter radius and the radius of the rounded edge are identical, this part of the contour is produced automatically; no specification is necessary: CUT, PARLN3, TOLN 5.

FIGURE 11–17

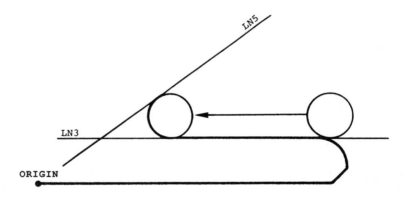

Next, motion parallel to LN5 is required until the contour of CIR2 is touched, which is then followed until the path intersects LN4 *(Fig. 11–18, p. 166).* It is possible to specify these two sequences in one line in COMPACT II because they can be combined into one outcontouring instruction (OCON). Although outcontouring of CIR3 in counterclockwise direction does not start until the tangent point with LN5 is reached, the cutter travels automatically to this point, parallel to LN5. End position is the tangent point with LN4, so the command can be written as follows:

OCON, CIR2, CCW, S(TANLN5), F(TANLN4).

The outcontouring procedure along CIR3 *(Fig. 11–19 p. 166)* can be specified in the same manner:

OCON, CIR3, CCW, S(TANLN4), F(TANLN6).

FIGURE 11–18

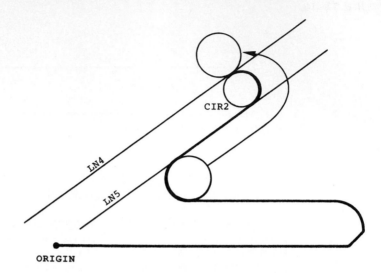

Finally cutter movement parallel to LN6 until LN1 has been passed *(Fig. 11–20, p. 167)* is necessary to complete the outline of the workpiece:
CUT, PASTLN1.
The end of the COMPACT II program is simply indicated by the instruction:
END.

FIGURE 11–19

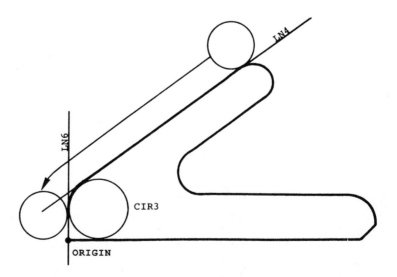

FIGURE 11–20

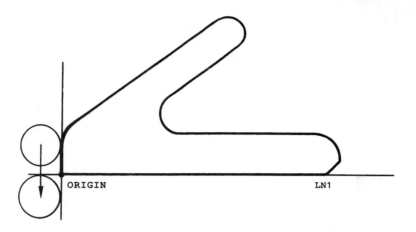

ORIGIN   LN1

11.6 COMPLETE PROGRAM LISTING

The complete part program which has been created is therefore:

```
MACHIN, MILLING MACHINE
IDENT, ANGLE-SHAPED EXAMPLE
SETUP, OLX, 85LY, 250LZ
BASE, 25.4XA, 25.4YA, 0ZA
DLN1, YB
DLN2, 120.65XB, YB, 45CCW
DPT1, 12.7 + 63.5 + 38.1XB, 6.35YB, ZB
DCIR1, PT1, 12.7R
DLN3, 19.05YB
DCIR2, 12.7 + 63.5XB, 6.35 + 12.7 + 44.45YB, 7.94R
DCIR3, 12.7XB, 12.7YB, 12.7R
DLN4, CIR2, YL, CIR3
DLN5, LN4/15.88XL
DLN6, XB
ATCHG, TOOL1, GL200, TD20, 900RPM,
230MMPM, CON
MOVE, OFFLN1/YS, OFFLN6/5XS, 10ZB
CUT, PARLN1, PASTLN2
CUT, PARLN2, OUTCIR1, YL
OCON, CIR1, CCW, S(LOC), F(TANLN3)
CUT, PARLN3, TOLN5
OCON, CIR2, CCW, S(TANLN5),
F(TANLN4)
OCON, CIR3, CCW, S(TANLN4),
F(TANLN6)
CUT, PASTLN1
END
```

The above program, which has been explained in detail, is quite elaborate and therefore unlikely to be written in such a way by any experienced programmer. In order to illustrate how instructions could have been abbreviated, a shortened version of the same part program is now given, so that a comparison between the two alternative programs is possible.

```
MACHINE, MILLING MACHINE
IDENT, ANGLE-SHAPED EXAMPLE
SETUP, LX, 85LY, 25LZ
BASE, 25.4XA, 25.4YA, ZA
DCIR1, 76.2XB, 63.5YB, 7.94R
DPB1, RPT, XB, YB, 10ZB, CR;
SPT1, −15XB, −10YB, 10ZB;
YB, S(LN(XB));
LN(120.65XB,YB,45CCW);
CIR(114.3XB,6.35YB,12.7R),
CCW,S(YL); 19.05YB; 10R;
LN(CIR1,XL,30CCW);
CIR1, CCW; LN(CIR1,XS,30CCW);
12.7R; XB, F(LN(−10YB)),
NOMORE
ATCHG, TOOL1, TD20, GL200, 900RPM,
230MMPM, CON
MOVE, PB11/3SPT1
CUT, PB1
END
```

Both programs lead to exactly the same result, that is, identical tapes are created.

> N.B. Due to the input accuracy of
> 0.05 mm (0.002 in.), coordinate
> values are likely to be rounded up.

11.7 COMPILER-PROCESSED PROGRAM

The program, when processed by the compiler into the code understood by a typical control system, appears as follows:

```
N1G80G40G00T0150
N2T0150M06
N3G80M08
N4G90
N5G00X10400Y15400S79M03
N6Z210000
N7G01G62X150192F230
N8X161926Y27134
N9G03G91X474Y4616I22226J4616
N10X-22700Y22700I22700
```

```
N11G01G90X83895
N12X111937Y74287
N13G03G91X7563
     Y14613I10337J14613
N14X-17900Y17900I17900
N15X-10337Y-3287J17900
N16G01G90X24990Y56632
N17G03G91X-9590Y-
     18532I13110J18532
N18G01G90Y15400
N19G00Z250000T00M05
N20X000Y85000
N21T00M06
N22M30
```

QUESTIONS FOR CHAPTER 11

1. From what language are many computer-assisted programming languages derived?

2. What are the four main constituent parts of most computer-assisted part programs, and in what order must they be specified?

3. What is the most striking feature of programming languages such as COMPACT II?

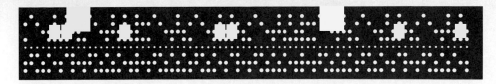

CHAPTER 12

NC MACHINE TOOLS USED IN INDUSTRY

After studying this chapter you should understand:

1. The fundamental changes in machine-tool design philosophy brought about by the introduction of numerical control.
2. How to determine the correct designation of the various axes of any NC machine tool.
3. How NC has been applied to a wide range of machine tools and the effects this has had on their operating efficiency.
4. An appreciation of the types of ancillary NC equipment commonly married to NC machines to enhance system efficiency.
5. How NC technology has been applied to inspection of components, and the resulting impact on production quality.

The effect of the increasing application of numerical control to conventional machine tools over the past 25 to 30 years has led to totally new concepts in machine-tool design and operation. Today the NC machine tool has become the core element in flexibly automated manufacturing installations.

12.1 INTRODUCTION

Machine tools available in the early days of NC development were not really suited to NC technology. Indeed, the special requirements of NC were not even known at that stage. Therefore the first numerical controllers were attached to machine tools designed for operating with conventional controls. Typical examples of such machines were jig borers and lathes fitted with cam or tracer controls.

The experience gained within a few years resulted in a completely new generation of specially designed machine tools, which have continued to be refined and extended. Typical characteristics of this new generation of machine tools, and the more important related equipment, are now briefly examined as a general introduction to this chapter.

12.2 MACHINE DESIGN OVERVIEW

To meet the demand for consistently higher accuracy, machine-tool structures required both improved rigidity and better vibration damping characteristics. Bearings and spindles needed virtually zero play; drive systems, spindles, and so forth were all required to be dynamically balanced; and linear slideway bearing surfaces demanded the lowest possible friction levels to avoid "stick-slip" problems.

Traditional thread-type leadscrews have been entirely replaced by the recirculating ball/screw system, which has very low friction and zero backlash. Their mechanical efficiency now reaches around 98 percent, which results in minimal heat generation and consistently high-pitch accuracy, and enables them to transmit significantly higher loads than threaded leadscrews of comparable size.

Long leadscrews are of large diameter to provide high torsional rigidity, and as their moment of inertia is high, it is the nut that is generally driven rather than the leadscrew. When traverse lengths exceed about 15 ft, the rack-and-pinion configuration of leadscrew is generally preferred to the recirculating ball/screw type. Backlash and play are eliminated by so-called tandem drives which consist of two drives with two pinion wheels engaging with the same rack.

12.3 FEED AND MAIN SPINDLE DRIVES

This area of NC machine-tool design is dealt with in considerable detail in Chapter 14. However an initial overview is included here by way of a general introduction.

12.3.1 FEED DRIVES

Initially the slideways of NC machines were powered by a single, central three-phase motor, whose gearing permitted the selection of just three or four speed ratios. However this principle was superseded many years ago in favor of highly responsive servodrives offering a wide speed range and a high level of rigidity.

Traverse path (feed) controls require separate servodrives for each axis, and modern drives, which are integrated into the positional control circuitry of modern CNCs, offer variable feed rates up to 50 ft/min in 0.00005 in. steps without the need for any gear ratio change.

Cheaper electrical or electrohydraulic stepping motors are rarely used today, and are only employed when neither control requirements, dynamic behavior nor speed range are critical.

When stepping motors are used, they are generally operated in the open-loop control mode, which requires neither a feedback path measuring system, tachos, nor resolvers. They have a major disadvantage in that overload can cause uncontrolled positional errors, and this is why open-loop control is normally only employed for valve actuation and for small, non-critical, linear movements.

The drive systems of nibbling and punching machines are rather specialized as they must be highly dynamic and have good thermal dissipation characteristics because of the high stroke frequency, and the need to be absolutely stationary momentarily twice every cutting stroke.

The development of powerful electronic circuits has now made it possible to employ dc drives for almost any application, although the trend is in the direction of frequency-controlled, brushless servodrives.

12.3.2   MAIN SPINDLE DRIVES

The first NC spindle drives consisting of predominantly simple three-phase motors, coupled via extensive gearing to permit the selection of a limited number of speeds, gave way to variable-speed dc drives many years ago. Today frequency converters are readily available for both asynchronous and synchronous motors, making ac drives increasingly attractive once again.

In addition to speed control, main spindle drives require a sensing device for detection of the spindle's radial orientation when stationary. This is important for the collision-free retraction of asymmetrical cutting tools. Automatic tool change also requires a well defined orientation of tooling to permit the correct operation of grippers and tool magazines.

12.4 ANCILLARY MACHINE COMPONENTS

The aforementioned modifications to conventional machine-tool design do little to satisfy the needs of automation. For example, a basic NC machine tool still requires manual tool changing, and this has resulted in the invention of the tool magazine and the automatic tool changer. Piecepart automatic transfer and transportation of standardized pallets by either automatically guided vehicles or rail-guided or gantry loading systems are other examples of the use of NC technology to enhance the performance of NC machines via automation.

The first autochange tool systems were very similar to those already in use at the time on capstan and turret lathes, and held six or eight tools. The turret was fitted with a separate indexing drive, and each of the stations on the turret was marked with a special coding. It was thus possible to call up the tools independently of their order in the turret. Turning centers still have this turret-type tool-change system because the turrets do not require expensive tool-change mechanisms, and such systems are therefore cheaper than tool magazines. The most frequently used types are the disk-turret and cross-turret formats.

The number of different cutting tools required when operating machining centers is much greater than is necessary with turning centers, and is far too high to permit the application of turret-type tool systems. Chain, disk, or rotary type magazines are therefore used, most of which are depicted in various diagrams in this chapter.

Some of these systems permit the storage of over 200 tools per machine. The size of the magazine, however, has a negative effect: the longer the chain or the larger the diameter of the disk, the longer it takes to locate an individual tool. To overcome this problem, further development led to the splitting of the very large capacity tool magazines into two separate half-size units, one half on either side of the machine; with ring-type magazines, the tools are arranged in two concentric circles.

12.5 AXIS DESIGNATION CONVENTIONS

Axis designation for each type of machine tool is suggested in the EIA (Electronic Industries Association) RS 274-B standard; this conforms to ISO Recommendation R 841.

The nomenclature of the three main axes (X, Y, and Z) is based on the "right-hand rule," involving the middle and index fingers and the thumb of the right hand *(Fig. 12–1)*. The thumb indicates the orientation of the X axis, the index finger indicates the Y axis, and the middle finger points in the direction of the Z axis.

To define the axes of an NC machine tool via this rule, one first imagines one's middle finger is "in" the main spindle of the machine. This is the Z axis and its positive direction is away from the component, that is, in the direction of tool retraction. Next turn the hand such that the thumb points in the direction of the longer of the two remaining main axes: this is the X axis. The index finger now points in the positive direction of the Y axis.

Designation of each rotational axis is based on the linear axis about which rotation occurs: A is rotation about the X axis, B is rotation about the Y axis, and C is rotation about the Z axis *(Fig. 12–2)*. When looking along a main axis in the + direction, clockwise rotation is positive.

Other useful secondary linear axis designations are:

U is parallel to the X axis
V is parallel to the Y axis
W is parallel to the Z axis

FIGURE 12–1   Right-hand rule for machine tool axis designation.

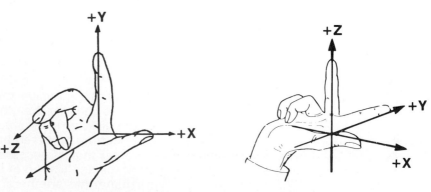

Axis designation for horizontal Z   Axis designation for vertical Z

FIGURE 12–2 Cartesian coordinate system for designating main axes of NC machine tools.

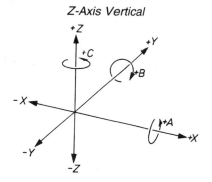

Z-Axis Vertical

The letters P, Q, and R are designations for further axes which are usually parallel to the main axes. The letter R is commonly used as the address of the reference plane of a piecepart in boring cycles, that is, the plane where the Z axis motion changes from rapid-traverse speed to the cutting-feed rate. P and Q are similar axes relative to the X and Y axes respectively.

Occasionally designations like X1/X2 and Y1/Y2 are used. They refer to gantry axes which have separate drives on each side of the gantry to permit the exact positioning of the gantry under asymmetric loads. These axes are not independent of each other, and their path is programmed using the same X and/or Y designation.

Designating the positive direction of an axis is based on the principle that the tool moves and the workpiece remains stationary. Also, for safety reasons, positive axis direction is always when the tool moves away from the component.

When a workpiece is moved on, say, a rotary table as well as horizontally traversing along the bed of the machine, axis direction and the direction of motion may oppose each other; for example, the bed may move to the right, the tool making a relative movement to the left. In this case the actual axis direction is used but the designation is marked by an apostrophe: +X', +Y', +Z', +A', +B', and +C'. This convention has the advantage that the programmer can write part programs independently of machine configuration, and the desired relative motion between tool and piecepart will always be performed in the correct direction, whether it is the tool or the piecepart that actually moves.

12.6 DRILLING MACHINES

All NC drills, from the simplest to the most complicated, have the following common design features:

- A spindle head which picks up the tool and performs the rotating movement

- A table to which the part is clamped and which can move in coordinates X and Y
- Feed mechanisms which control and feed the tool into the workpiece (Z coordinate)

However, there are several possible variations to this. For instance, the table can be stationary and the spindle head can move in the coordinate axes, a workpiece can be machined by one or more spindles, tool change systems can be added, and at times even light milling operations may be carried out.

In its simplest form the drilling machine has only one numerically controlled coordinate workholding surface, the drilling depth being predetermined by preset stops or cam rails. After final positioning in machines of this type, the drilling cycle is initiated by a "workholding surface in position" signal, and the cycle then proceeds mechanically or electrically without NC influence. At the end of the drilling process, another repeater signal, "spindle up," is applied to the NC, and the next positioning command begins. In order to increase positioning accuracy, point-to-point controls can almost always "loop the loop" *(Fig. 12–3)*, that is, all positions are always approached from a specific direction, preferably from the direction of the machine zero point. This is completely independent of how the actual movement direction occurs in the positioning process. In simple milling operations, this unidirectional startup control is automatically switched off.

FIGURE 12–3 Positioning with backlash compensation.

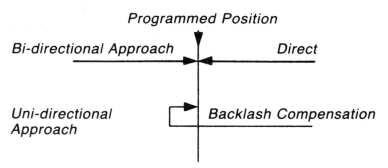

For simple drilling machines, because of cost factors, the selection of optional control equipment is usually limited to block readouts, position readouts, and manual input.

In addition to NC control of X and Y axes, for more complex drilling operations drilling machines also offer NC control of the Z axis.

Not only the end point of the movement (that is, the drilling depth) is programmed in the Z direction, but also the transition point, which causes the drilling spindle to switch from rapid traverse to machining feed rate shortly before the tool reaches the surface to be drilled.

A further expansion stage possible is automatic tool change capability. This requires additional mechanization, but it is only in this stage that the operator's activity is limited to a purely monitoring function, and that true automatic machining is approximated.

The following additional expansion stages may also be considered:

- In order to further avoid manual intervention and optimize the cutting process, the option for programmable selection of spindle speed and feed rate can be included.

    As soon as extensive milling is required, particularly on profiles, continuous path control (2½-D is generally sufficient for most jobs of this type) must replace point-to-point control.

- Mirror imaging can facilitate the manipulation of drilling patterns *(Fig. 12–4)*. It is possible to machine workpieces which repeat themselves by a mirror image in another quadrant by reflecting the pattern about the X and Y, or the X or Y axes. The switch used for this purpose is referred to as a mirror switch, and make it only necessary to program a quarter of the total program in order to machine the entire drilling pattern. After machining has been completed in one quadrant, the tape is rewound to the beginning of the program, the mirror switch set to mirror imaging about the X axis, for example, and the machining is repeated, this time in the second quadrant. The tape is again rewound to the beginning of the program, switched to mirror imaging about Y, and finally to mirror imaging about X and Y.

- Fixed machining cycles, also known as drilling cycles, are usually part of the basic equipment of drilling machines. They represent a type of "canned cycle" subprogram that can be called up via the appropriate G code and carried out automatically when each new X, Y position is reached.

- Tool-length compensation is another useful option for drilling machines. It permits the use of tools whose actual length does not correspond to the nominal length provided for in the program. This principle was illustrated earlier but for convenience, is again illustrated here in Fig. *12–5, p. 178*.

FIGURE 12–4   Mirror imaging.

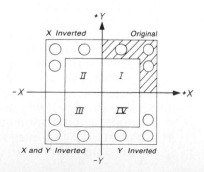

FIGURE 12–5   Tool-length compensation.

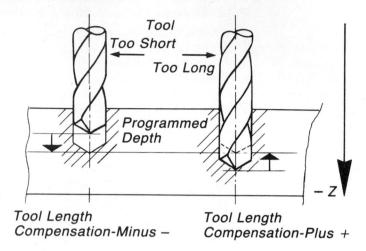

12.6.1   DRILLING MACHINES FOR PRINTED CIRCUIT BOARDS (PCBs)

A specialized group of drilling machines has been developed to machine PCBs for the electronics industry. Several similar circuit boards are stacked on top of each other on the workholding surface and then simultaneously drilled using several drilling spindles simultaneously.

The drilling spindles attached to a traverse column have a speed range from 15,000 to 60,000 rev/min and features automatic tool changing in some cases. Pickup and deposit of tools occur at a tool-change position located at either the back or front of the machine's workholding surface. Here all spindles pick up and/or deposit their tools at the same time. In this manner, PC board drilling, as well as the subsequent milling of cutouts and borders, takes place in a single setup. However, this type of application cannot effectively be utilized without specialized functions, such as:

- Control of two axes (X, Y) in fast positioning (rapid traverse) and feed-rate controlled path operation for milling. Spindle action takes place after the desired position has been reached. The top and bottom limits of the drill spindle movement (Z axis) are preset manually during setup and are not part of the program.
- Programmable call-up of individual spindles or spindle groups so that the programmer can select various spindles to remain in the retracted position at any time.
- Programming with the teach-in method, that is, by setting the individual drilling positions via manual displacement of the workholding surface using an optical system, followed by sequential storage of the position values so established.
- Scale factor input in order to take into account variations in PC board design parameters.

- Subprogram technique for drilling patterns of rows of holes and bolt hole circles so that only one fixed location point need be programmed for ICs, LSIs, switches, and other components with standardized connector dimensions.
- Rotation of a hole pattern about any programmable angle.
- The possibility of programming and storing client-tailored cycles and drilling or milling patterns—character milling, for example, for labeling the PC board with model designation, serial numbers, date, and so on. This requires a special character generator so that any text can be directly entered and engraved without laborious programming.
- NC control of the following machine functions:

    Spindle selection and speed
    Feed rate selection for drilling (Z) and milling (X, Y)
    Automatic tool changing
    Drilling ON/OFF
    Milling ON/OFF

These functions are controlled via freely assignable M functions as specified by the controller manufacturer.

The control needs a suitably large program memory in which several programs can be stored for immediate call-up, and which has the facility to carry out corrections and necessary improvements quickly and without difficulty. Since PC board drilling machines operate at an enormously fast cycle rate of up to 10 strokes/s, the processing and output speed of the NC must be correspondingly high to avoid even short waiting times due to internal NC data processing.

12.7 TURNING MACHINES

With few exceptions, numerical control of a lathe or turning center contains only the X and Z axes *(Fig. 12–6, p. 180)*. As long as no profiles, conical parts, or threads have to be produced, the application of linear path control is adequate to complete much of the turning work carried out. Even the most basic turning machines require a certain NC standard which contains, in most cases, linear path-control capability. Almost every turning machine will also have functions for spindle speed, feed, and tool change. Linear and circular interpolation are adequate for most profiling, but the thread-cutting option requires an impulse transmitter (encoder) to report spindle speed to the control. Additionally, this specialized shaft encoder provides a reference impulse once per revolution to ensure that the threading tool always engages with the workpiece at a very specific main spindle radial position during each thread-cutting pass.

Turning machines are provided with tool-offset compensation as opposed to tool-length compensation. In turning, correction in both axes is

FIGURE 12–6 Axis designations for turning machines.

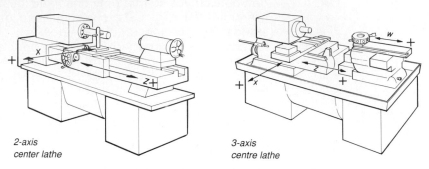

2-axis
center lathe

3-axis
centre lathe

necessary to compensate for different tool-wear rates in each axis, the corrective values being input via paired decade switching circuits or via keyboard into the tool-compensation value memory of the controller.

Tool compensation values are not permanently assigned but can be freely coordinated through the program. Occasionally, dual-axis path correction is necessary in order to eliminate form defects in the programming of component profiles resulting from the cutting radius of the tool. However, in most cases this option is unnecessary.

12.7.1 TURRET-HEAD TURNING MACHINES

Turret-head turning machines are always equipped with linear path controls because of their variety of machining capabilities, and all the options discussed for the normal NC lathe are equally applicable here. Beyond that, there are no special requirements *(Fig. 12–7)*.

12.7.2 VERTICAL TURNING MACHINES WITH TWO HEADS

Turning machines with 2×2 axes are capable of using controls with 2×2 NC axes or a separate two axes control for each head *(Fig. 12–8, p. 182)*. Handling, operation, and programming are therefore very different. When two separate controls are used as a dual control, the following advantages result:

- Two standard controls for every two axes are cheaper than special two-axis controls.

- Programming is simpler.

- There are separate tapes for each head. As a result, program changes or correction of programming errors is simplified.

- If there is a mechanical or electrical malfunction of one head, the other head may remain fully operational. Depending on machine design, a program exchange may even be possible in order to machine the programmed workpiece on the malfunctioning head on the head which is still operative.

- Operation is clear and simplified, as a separate NC is dedicated to each head.

FIGURE 12–7   Two-axis vertical lathe.

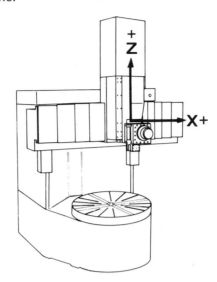

Because of their programming complexities, turning machine controls with built-in 2 × 2 axes can therefore only be recommended if additional program memory deemed necessary can be provided for each head.

12.8   BORING MACHINES

In its simplest form, a boring mill equipped with just actual position open loop readout in only the X and Y axes is adequate *(Fig. 12–9, p. 183).* This view is based on the fact that boring mills have only a small amount of nonproductive time. Therefore focusing on further reduction of this "idle" time in many applications would have no significant economic impact.

If a higher degree of automation is required, and if the error related to open loop position readout is to be reduced, then full closed loop axes positioning control, must be provided. Jig-boring mills and profile mills ordinarily use three- and four-axis position controls, and large profile boring mills have up to seven continuous-path-controlled axes.

Selection of the correct control is principally dependent on the profile geometry of the workpiece to be machined and not on the type of machine tool. If provision for internal profiles, conical machining, or milling functions is not required, the application of a simple two- or three-axis positioning control is wholly sufficient. Otherwise continuous path controls are essential.

Readouts are used for block numbers, miscellaneous functions, and axis positions, with switching between target and actual positions as required. Tool selection, tool length compensation, and mirror switches

FIGURE 12–8   Multiple axis vertical and horizontal turning machines.

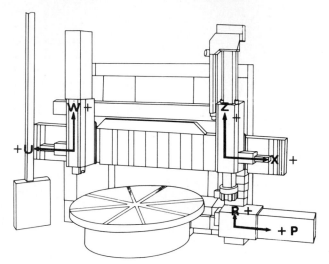

3 x 2 axis vertical lathe.

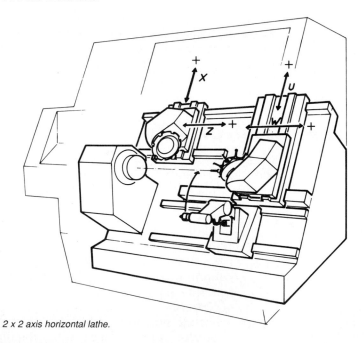

2 x 2 axis horizontal lathe.

often find interesting application possibilities for mirror-imaging. To the extent that they are justified by their proposed use, linear and circular interpolation are useful facilities. In this way the generation of holes or the cutting of internal or external threads is possible. Because of higher precision requirements, boring mills are usually equipped with direct linear measuring systems (see 4.2.2).

FIGURE 12–9   Three-axis boring mill.   Four-axis boring mill.

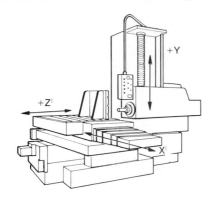
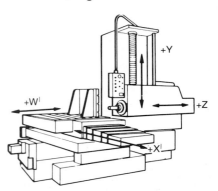

•••
12.9 MILLING MACHINES

With the exception of machining centers, milling machines are probably the most versatile machine tools. Several well-known types are briefly described here; they are grouped into horizontal and vertical milling machines based on the position of the milling spindle. These machines are always equipped with continuous path controls and have at least three, and often five or more axes under control, as well as spatial interpolation capabilities in most cases. Since milling machines must also perform boring and drilling operations, it is advantageous if the controls also contain preprogrammed drilling cycles. If programming of this machine type is done with the aid of a computer, it is then easy to call up any required drilling cycles contained in a series of individual blocks as and when required.

Milling machines rarely have automatic tool changers available and they can therefore be eliminated as an option unless one wishes to indicate to the operator, via digital readout, the identification number of the next tool and perhaps block further machining until the end of the tool change. With respect to tool compensation, tool radius compensation and/or milling path compensation is desirable.

For large milling machines, differential shaft encoders or similar manual override possibilities are advantageous since they allow simplified alignment and trouble-free restarting after tool breakage or other cutting interruptions.

12.9.1 MOVING GANTRY MILLING MACHINES

This type of machine *(Fig. 12–10, p. 184)* is preferred under the following conditions:

- Piecepart: Flat or similar, long components
- Plant: Limited floor space for the placement of machines
- Operation: Convenient machine operation especially in the vicinity of the spindle.
- Design: Possibility of elongating the machine at a later time

FIGURE 12–10 Three-axis gantry-type milling machine with three vertical spindle heads.

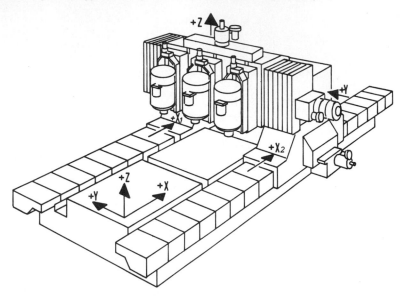

These conditions are mostly called for in the production of aircraft parts. Once a certain machine size is reached, two feed drives are required to move the gantry along the X axis, and this also requires two measuring systems (one on each side) to monitor position, thus preventing the gantry from "crabbing." Through the same or opposing movements (mirror imaging) in the Y and X axes, it becomes possible to produce two identical or two mirror like components simultaneously.

In some designs, the reverse side of the gantry is also equipped with milling heads so that two component groups can be clamped onto the workholding surface behind each other and machined simultaneously. With machines of this size, a mobile control device is essential during setup of the machine. The largest and most expensive 3-D continuous path controls with all the available options, such as parallel axes and gantry-position monitoring, are used in this type of machine. Because of the high-data volume requirements with four and five axes, high-speed readers of at least 250 characters/s with large winding reels are needed. Programming for such installations is difficult and expensive and can therefore only be carried out with computer-assisted part programming and corresponding postprocessors.

12.9.2 FIVE-AXIS MILLING MACHINES

Five-axis milling machines *(Figs. 12–11, p. 185 and 12–12, p. 186)* can position the end of the tool at any point on a three-dimensional workpiece, thereby permitting any desired tool-axis position. This universal relative motion between tool and workpiece can be achieved in the following three ways:

FIGURE 12–11   Five-axis vertical spindle milling machine with swivel head and rotary table.

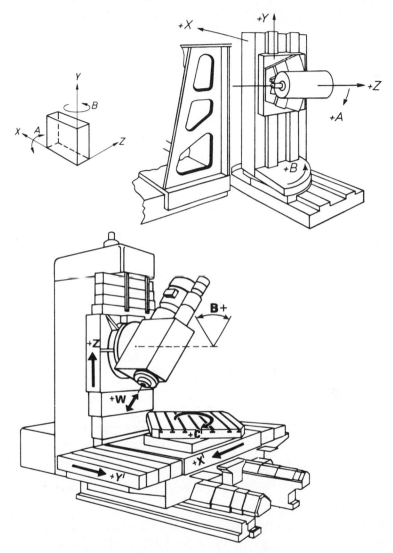

1. With stationary tool axis and dual pivoting motion of the work-piece, for example, via two combined rotary tables or a swiveling rotary table

2. With pivoting motion of the tool axis and workpiece where the axes are at 90° angles to each other

3. With a stationary workpiece and two tool swivel axes *(Fig. 12–13, p.186)*

Geometrically complicated parts can be manufactured with these machines, including curved surfaces, using inserted-tooth-cutter-heads for higher chip removal rates than is possible with the usual flat-bottom

FIGURE 12–12 Five-axis milling machine with four swivel spindle heads.

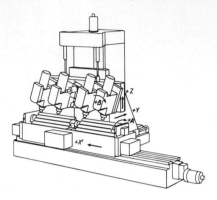

or ball-nose cutters. Preparation of the control program for a five-axis machine is generally only possible with computer-assisted part programming and the postprocessor will then determine the final movement of

FIGURE 12–13 Tool swivel head.

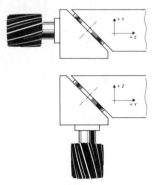

the tool during its rotational swing. It is also assumed that the actual length and diameter of the tool agrees with the values specified in the initial part program, since neither tool length nor cutter radius compensation of the NC can compensate for the workpiece defects which would otherwise arise. In the case of multispindle machines with automatic tool changers, either adjustable holders or standardized tool boxes provide for the exact and unified tool-length adjustment of all tools used.

12.10 MACHINING CENTERS

The machining center is now the most common of all NC machine tools but it only came into existence with the development of advanced digital-control technology.

Its typical characteristics are:

- Prismatic components can be machined in one setup on four, or even five, sides. To this end four or five axes are numerically controlled *(Figs. 12–14 and 12–15, p. 188).*

FIGURE 12–14   Four-axis machining center with horizontal rotary axis (B).

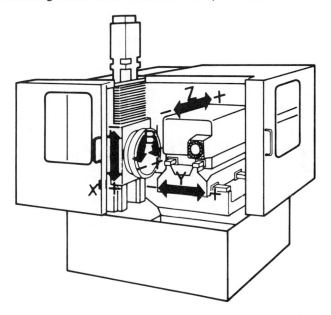

- All types of machining can be carried out, such as face milling, drilling, reaming, boring, and thread cutting, and with further expansion complex profiling and drilling is possible. Spindle speed and feed rates are, of course, also numerically controlled.
- The required tool is automatically located via the program and placed into the operating spindle. The number of stored tools is theoretically unlimited, but it is generally between 60 and 120, depending on the type of magazine used.
- Automatic component loading and unloading equipment shortens the setup time by permitting release of one component while another is still being machined *(Fig. 12–16, p. 189).*

The three numerically-controlled linear main axes (X, Y, and Z) of machining centers follow the Cartesian coordinate system. Further axes may be added for more complex designs involving rotary tables, pivoting motions of the spindle or workholding surface, or additional secondary or tertiary axes parallel to the main axes.

The versatility of machining centers is only fully realized with 3-D continuous path control, although in many cases a 2½-D control is sufficient. However, recallable compensation values for tool length, tool diameter, and zero-shift are mandatory because of the large number of tools used.

FIGURE 12–15   Five-axis machining center.

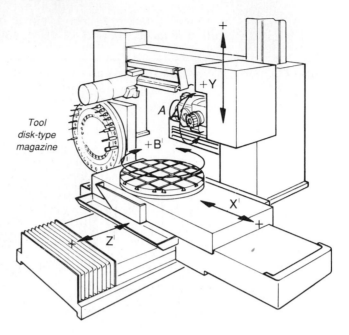

12.10.1   AUTOMATIC TOOL CHANGERS

Machine tools performing cutting operations require to be supplied with tooling in a preset sequence as specified by the work cycle. The tool turret performed this function prior to the introduction of NC, especially on drilling and turning machines. The number of tools which could be accommodated in the turrets was limited to six to eight, since most turret dimensions increase as the number of tools is increased, finally causing interference between the tools themselves. For this reason, some turning machines use two disk turrets. With significant engineering effort it is possible to store up to 16 tools per turret, but the number of tools required is often much greater—sometimes 200 or more. As a result, the following types of magazines have been developed:

- Longitudinal magazine, where the tools are lined up in a row within the magazine
- Disk-type magazine, which, depending on machine design, is arranged above, behind, or to one side of the machining spindle *(Fig. 12–15)*
- Ring-type magazine, where the tools are arranged in two concentric rings
- Chain-type magazine, having the largest carrying capacity, is arranged on the side or above the machine and can be enlarged as needed *(Fig. 12–16)*

FIGURE 12–16   Three-axis machining center with four spindles and automatic tool changer.

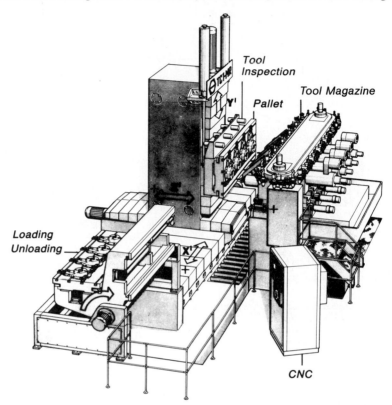

- Rotary-type magazine, developed for automatic, simultaneous tool changing in multispindle milling machines
- Automatic drill-head changer, designed to aid the changing of large/very large boring heads

Depending on their design, the tool magazine and exchanging mechanism may be part of the machine-tool unit, or it may form a machine-independent unit which is placed near the NC machine and connected to it.

The automatic tool-change cycle involves using single or double grippers. A direct exchange of tools from the magazine into the spindle can take place without additional exchange arms, and although this process is the simplest in design, it takes the greatest amount of time.

A typical tool-exchange cycle basically consists of the following steps *(see Fig. 12–17, p. 190):*

1. Locate the next tool to be used in the magazine.
2. Remove the used tool from the spindle.
3. Insert the new tool into the machining spindle.
4. Return the used tool back to the magazine.

FIGURE 12–17   Automatic tool changer with dual gripper.

1

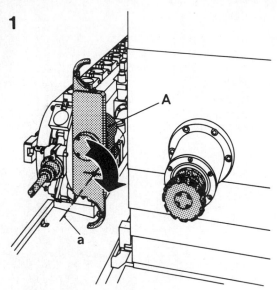

Gripper rotates toward magazine
matrix and spindle 90°.
Simultaneously, the gripper
clamps both tools.

2

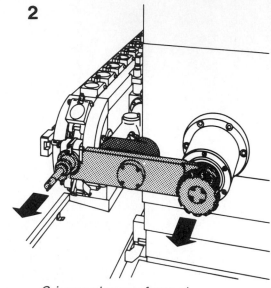

Gripper advances forward
removing both new tool from
the magazine matrix and old
tool from spindle.

3

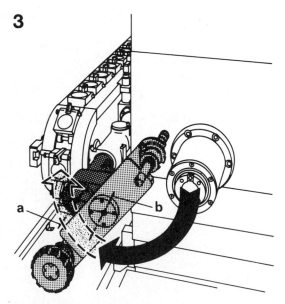

In the extended forward position,
the gripper rotates 180° to
position b.

4

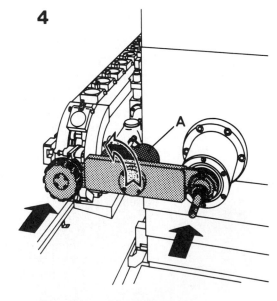

Retraction of the gripper
inserts the new tool into the
spindle and the old tool into
the magazine.

Since this exchange operation interrupts the machining time, which in turn decreases the productivity of the machine, several problems must be solved as magazines become larger:

- Locating, preparing, and returning the tools must occur during production time and must not be allowed to interrupt machining.
- The tool-change cycle must be easy to program (MO6), with all required axes and gripper movements running in sequence like a subprogram and with only a brief machining interruption.
- The operator must be able to find individual tools in the magazine quickly and be able to exchange them manually, if necessary.
- The operator should be able to manually enter into the NC the necessary tool-compensation values for length, diameter, and tool nose radius, either automatically through measuring devices or semiautomatically via the data carrier.

Another important matter is the manner and system of tool encoding. Various, different methods are employed:

1. Direct magazine, where the tools are called up consecutively in a fixed sequence having been prearranged in the magazine.

Advantages:

- This is the simplest and least expensive method.
- No encoding is necessary.

Disadvantages:

- Multiple callup of individual tools is not possible (unless by repeated through-cycling of the magazine).
- Frequently needed tools must be available by duplication.
- Empty places must be skipped as specified by the program.
- Usually the magazine has only one cycle direction.

2. Fixed location encoding, where individual magazine locations are encoded from 1 to *n* and the stored tools within these locations are called up by number. After use, each tool is returned to its assigned location in the magazine.

Advantages:

- The shortest location search is shorter than it is with other encoding systems.
- Relatively long identification cams result in high-speed magazine displacement and dynamic, easy location recognition.
- Oversized tools may be arranged at random, minimizing the danger of their colliding with neighboring tools by arranging unoccupied places to the right and left of each one.

Disadvantages:

- When changing programs written on the basis of random tool-location assignment, the entire set of tools must be resorted and/or exchanged to the sequence established by the programmer. (A partial solution is to assign fixed locations to standard tools.)

- Problems arise in the case of random-sequence machining of different workpieces if identical locations are programmed for different tools in each program. When loading the magazine, the operator must ensure that each tool is placed in its correct location.

3. Tool encoding, whereby each tool is fitted with encoding rings on its cylindrical shaft as its unique identification *(Fig. 12–18)*. However, this is increasingly being achieved by including this information on an inbuilt EPROM microchip embodied within the tool holder (see also 13.4).

FIGURE 12–18   Tool adapter with tool–encoding rings.

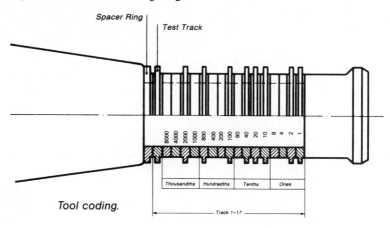

Tool coding.

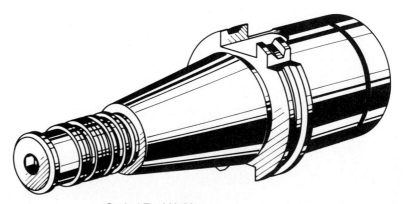

Coded Tool Holder

Advantages:

- The tools in the magazine are randomly arranged.
- The tool number is programmed.
- Random sequencing of tools is possible.
- Tools may be presorted in the magazine as desired.
- Exchange time is shortened through use of dual grippers.

Disadvantages:

- Time is wasted and there is a possibility of error when the encoding rings are assembled. (This is not a problem with the "chip" identification method).
- Tool holders with an encoding device are expensive.
- Dynamic, more difficult tool recognition in comparison with location encoding, results in limited location speed of the magazine.
- Search time is prolonged since the shortest route is not known (unless the tools are arranged in ascending number sequence and retain their locations).

4. Variable location encoding, or random tool selection, a method which utilizes most of the essential advantages of the procedures discussed above.

Advantages:

- Uncoded tools may be used.
- Location encoding is reliable.
- The tool number is in the program.
- Search takes place via the shortest route.
- Exchange time is short through dual grippers, each time exchanging magazine and spindle location of two tools.

A precondition for variable location encoding is that the NC must have a special logic which remembers the location of each tool within the magazine and makes updates after each tool exchange. A tabular readout of the actual status of the tools in the magazine is therefore part of this option.

Disadvantages:

- Errors occur during initial tooling line-up in the magazine (line-up and tabular input must be in agreement).
- The random tool arrangement in the magazine, which changes after each tool exchange, makes manual location and replacement of certain tools difficult, especially if no clear tool position readout is available.
- Problems arise when using large tools, such as plate-shaped cutters or multispindle heads. Because of the oversized tools, the right and left neighboring magazine locations must not be occupied.

12.10.2   WORKCHANGERS

Machine tool downtime due to the aligning, clamping, loading, and unloading of workpieces can be largely avoided by means of automatic workchanging equipment, since these tasks can be performed away from the machine without interruption of the machining process.

Generally pallet-changing systems are used, pallets being work-storing platforms which provide special seating faces and other features to allow for accurate location and clamping to the work-holding surfaces of the machine tool *(Figs. 12–19 and 12–21, p. 196)*. Pallet changing installations automatically carry the pallets from holding buffer stations to the machine-tool work area and back again after machining has been completed. Thus workpieces can be exchanged within seconds. With the aid of additional pallet stores or closed-loop systems, automatic workchange is feasible within the machine tool's local buffer store area during periods of prolonged machining of the component actually being worked on. Furthermore, automatic workchanging is an indispensable prerequisite for the integration of machining centers into cells *(Fig. 12-20, p. 195)*, islands or complete flexible manufacturing systems *(Fig. 18-10, p. 305)*. Pallets employed for such applications must be equipped with automatic read and write code-identification systems, so that, for example, specific workpieces and machine tools can be programmed for any required machining sequence.

These codes also have to enable the user to trace back and establish the machine within the flexible machining installation to which any

---

FIGURE 12–19   Load/unload side pallet changer for a machining center.

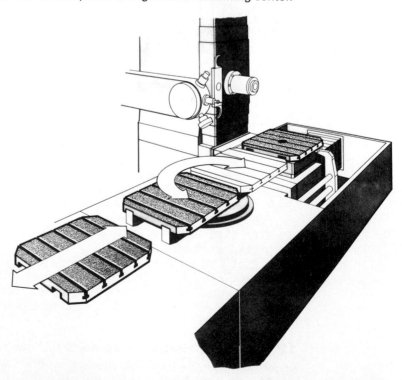

FIGURE 12–20   Flexible machining cell with eight pallet stations and two load/unload pallets.

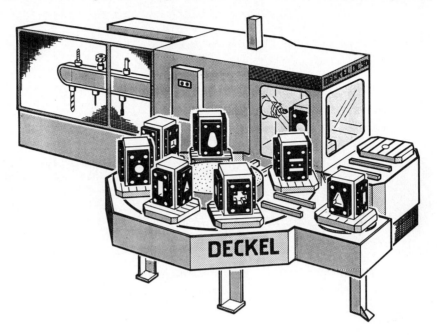

specific pallet has been presented during a whole manufacturing cycle. This helps in the detection of defective machines or cutting tools responsible for any particular machining errors, exceeded tolerances, or scrap production.

12.11 PUNCHING AND NIBBLING MACHINES

This type of machine is now considered to be an ideal application for NC technology *(Fig. 12–22, p. 197)*. Increased productivity is achieved through the reduction of nonproductive time for positioning and profile nibbling. Compared to conventional machines and considering the profile complexity of the workpiece geometry, total machining time is reduced by 70-90 percent.

There are three reasons for this:

1. The very high positioning speeds of 120 to 150 ft/min in each axis.
2. The elimination of much preparatory and refinishing work.
3. The high degree of automation compared to conventional types of control.

These reasons account for the large number of machines already equipped with NC. Adding automatic tool change and material handling capabilities saves only a small amount of time but greatly increases the degree of automation *(Fig. 12–23, p. 197)*.

FIGURE 12–21   Five-axes machining center with automatic pallet and toolhead changer.

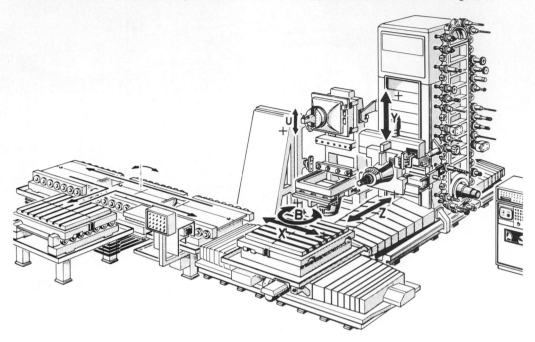

While a positioning control is sufficient for punching operations, profile nibbling operations require a two-axis continuous path control. Nibbling process technology imposes several very specific requirements on the NC, namely, the programming of the feed rate in in. per stroke, maintaining a minimum feed rate/stroke, as well as taking into consideration the various thicknesses of the sheet-metal being punched. As a result, standard type controls without these facilities cannot be used. Therefore, the advantages of joint development between the machine and NC manufacturers are obvious.

In most cases, similar parts are produced from a single sheet-metal plate. For this reason, program memories in combination with programmable repetitions are advantageous, since they reduce programming effort and the possibility of errors, and eliminate the waiting periods arising from punch-tape rewinding. Controls without program memories should thus have fast rewinding tape readers at their disposal, capable of handling tape at about 450 ft per min.

FIGURE 12–22   Two-axis punching and nibbling machine.

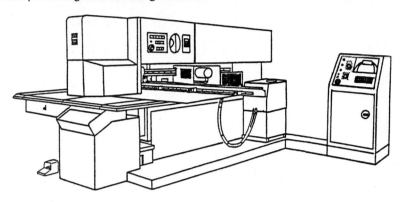

FIGURE 12–23   Sheet-metal NC machine with material handling system.

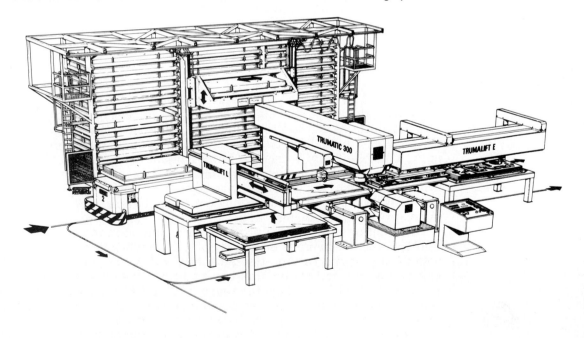

12.12 SPOT-WELDING MACHINES

Numerically-controlled spot-welding installations are now in operation in the automobile industry. They have been used, for example, where lot sizes were too small to justify welding transfer lines and multispot welding machines. In such cases spot welding had been performed manually. Here NC must meet exacting demands and, because of the complicated geometry of many welded parts, programming of the first part is done via the teach-in procedure described elsewhere in this book. In this manner substantial coordinate calculations are eliminated which would otherwise be necessary for simultaneous positioning of the electrode tongs in as many as six axes.

Generally, several machines of this type are linked to form an automatic NC welding line. Call-up of required welding programs from the memory of each control occurs manually or automatically via appropriate pallet encoding.

12.13 SPARK-ERODE MACHINING (ELECTRODISCHARGE MACHINING)

Electrodischarge machining (EDM) using wire electrodes had its first industrial applications through NC technology. In contrast to conventional countersunk spark erosion, machining is not performed with a sectional electrode but rather with a continuously running copper or tungsten wire or "universal electrode." The desired part form geometry is achieved via NC continuous path control of the wire electrode *(see Figure 12-24, p. 199)*. The precise setting of the spark gap necessary in EDM depends on variable electrical parameters, which is why a specialized NC must provide control data on a continuous basis. A return memory facility permits the repetition of the last controlled path distance of approximately 0.1 in. in case of process malfunction or machine stoppage. Also, it is customary to manually input path offsets up to ±0.04 in. from the center of the wire electrode so that dimensions for various tool components may be corrected. In this way press tools, dieplates, centering plates, or carrier plates can be cut with the same program tape.

In addition to the NC control, a spark generator, the machine tool, and a dielectric fluid are all part of an EDM installation. The machine tool itself must be very precise and rigid so that the fine spark or discharge gap needed for erosion can be kept constant and accurate results can be achieved. For this reason, advanced machine designs of this type incorporate electronic positional compensation devices. They process laser-scanned, stored compensation values and guarantee simultaneous compensation of regulating and linearity errors in both axes as well as in the working height.

The drive and guidance system of the wire electrode is also of great significance in achieving precise machining results since machining must be done with as constant a tensile stress in the wire as possible.

Through adjustable tilting of the upper wire guide or electronic control of a semiaxis, conical cuts can also be achieved, such as those needed for cutting dies or the convex forms of injection molding and die-casting tools. As with all erosion techniques, even sintered materials can be machined via EDM, and as hardly any mechanical forces occur in the piecepart, difficult geometrical profiles can be precisely produced.

FIGURE 12–24   Five-axis wire erosion machine.

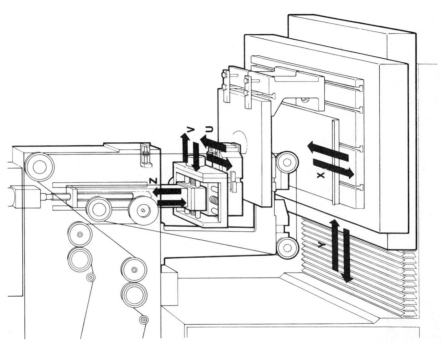

•••
12.14 ELECTRON BEAM MACHINING

Electron beam machines (EBM) are used predominantly for welding, but they are also used for drilling, quenching, remelt converting, and engraving.

In all electron beam machines, the "tool" used is an energized, narrow, sharply focused beam of high-velocity electrons.

Generation of this beam is similar to the process occurring in the neck of a television picture tube, but the radiation outputs are higher by many powers of ten. The acceleration voltages lie between 30 kV and 150 kV, outputs being between 1 kW and 100 kW. These outputs are converted into a concentrated beam and focused onto the workpiece in a spot between 0.005 and 0.1 in. in diameter, giving very high output power densities of 10^7 to 10^{10} W/in.^{2} *(Fig. 12–25).*

FIGURE 12–25 Electron beam welding machine.

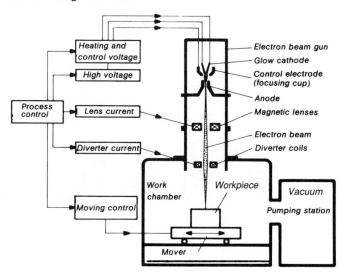

When such electron beams encounter the surface of a workpiece, the electrons come to an abrupt halt, and their kinetic energy is almost completely converted into heat at the impact spot. Depending on how spatial and timely the control of the beam is (continuous beam, pulse mode operation, beam deflection), various machining processes can be performed, such as welding or drilling. Therefore, the practically in-ertia-free electron beam tool is often coupled to an NC system for ease of control.

Beam generation and machining process must take place in a vacuum because, at atmospheric pressure, the electron beam is so highly dispersed by air molecules that the required output concentration and controllability would be lost. Electron beam machines for production applications therefore consist of the following subassemblies:

- Electron beam guns with electric power supply
- Work chamber with vacuum pumping unit
- Clamping and moving equipment for the workpiece
- Process controller

The process controls used may vary from simple switching functions to multiaxis CNC systems. With these systems, the most diverse machining functions can be carried out simply by writing suitable software.

Examples of EBM's capabilities are the drilling of gas turbine components such as blades, flame chamber rings, and mixer cowls for cooling purposes. This particular area of application requires extremely complicated three-dimensional electron beam path techniques. The drilling channels often lie at very small angles, up to about 20° from the surface, which in itself has a complicated shape. Over 3700 holes with position tolerances of approximately 0.004 in. have to be drilled into the mixing cowl shown in Figure 12–26. The total cycle time (including loading and unloading, orientation, evacuation of the work chamber, and fully automatic drilling) takes only 40 min, which is a small fraction of the time required for any other drilling process.

FIGURE 12–26   Part of a helicopter turbine; holes "drilled" by electron beam.

12.15 LASER MACHINING

Laser cutting may be considered to be a type of fine flame cutting where the material is brought to its melting point by an invisible beam of light, and by making use of exothermic reaction with the cutting gas (oxygen). Cuts through sheets up to 0.25 in. in thickness can be executed.

Laser cutting has the following advantages over the usual flame-cutting technique:

- Very narrow cutting seams of between 0.008 to 0.015 in.
- Small heat affected zone of about 0.004 in.
- No edge radius at the top of the sheet
- No burr on the underside of the sheet
- Minimal roughness of parallel cutting seam (groove) edges
- Problem-free application with thin sheets

Laser cutting also has big advantages compared to mechanical machining processes such as stamping and nibbling:

- No tool necessary; hence no tool wear
- No cutting forces involved
- No force-related impairment of the component
- Ability to produce narrow slots and webs
- Ability to produce tapered notches
- Higher cutting speed than with nibbling
- Fewer rough edges than with nibbling
- Quieter than nibbling operation

In contrast to electron beam machining, no vacuum is necessary in laser machining.

Since no tool is necessary for laser cutting, not only are acquisition costs for tools eliminated, but the total organizational expenses involved in purchasing, preparation, tool changing, and so on are avoided. This tool independence leads to greater production flexibility, which in turn is important in meeting deadlines for product delivery. The sample workpiece *(Fig. 12–27, p. 203)* exemplifies the cutting capabilities of a laser. The unit time of 1.1 min for a workpiece with steel sheet thickness of 0.04 in. illustrates the high productivity rate of this technique.

When NC is applied to laser cutting its main function is to control the movement of the workpiece material, which occurs in one plane, necessitating only a biaxial control of the type developed from the controllers for drilling and milling machines. Continuous path control is necessary, with linear and circular interpolation, only if profiling capabilities are required.

In contrast to stamping and nibbling, in laser cutting large movements occur during machining. With a laser output of 500 W the feed rate in laser cutting can be as high as 30 ft/min, although most cutting speeds lie between 3 and 10 ft/min. These cutting speeds can be managed easily by NC even where radii are tight. If one wishes to cut workpieces of standard sheet thickness with a preset laser output, burr-free and with the least possible edge roughness, then the optimum cutting speed must be used. The operator can, however, modify the cutting speed specified by the programmer via a potentiometer and in this way it is possible to cut differing sheet thicknesses at their respective optimal speeds.

FIGURE 12–27   Laser cutting technique.

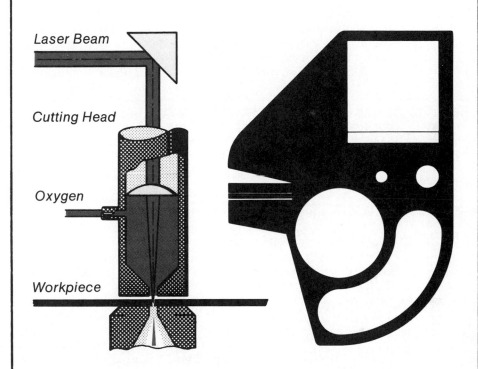

Laser Cutting Technique

Laser Beam

Cutting Head

Oxygen

Workpiece

The laser beam is reflected by mirrors through three tubes to a focusing lens and onto the surface of the workpiece. Vaporized material generated by the laser cut is blown away by pressurized air. The efficiency of the laser cut can be improved in certain materials by the use of oxygen instead of air.

Workpiece Size:
11" x 8"

Sheet Thickness: 0.04"

Number of Punched Holes: 0
(no punches therefore required)

Laser Path: 90°

Machine Run Time: 1.1 minutes

12.16 GRINDING MACHINES

Whether grinding flat, cylindrical, or relieved surfaces, grinding technology is invariably associated with precision, high quality surface finish, and accuracy. For this reason grinding is a technology which is especially suited to the application of NC, but surprisingly it is only in recent years that it has been fully applied to this group of machine tools.

A considerable period elapsed before NC manufacturers succeeded in solving the special problems associated with NC grinding, with the result that a number of grinding machine manufacturers developed their own NC systems.

A typical CNC grinding system is illustrated in Figure 12–28.

FIGURE 12–28   CNC grinding machine installation. (a) Slant bed, (b) Grinding wheel, (c) Component holding/rotating unit, (d) Saddle, (e) Automatic grinding wheel changeover mechanism, (f) Automatic wheel dressing device, (g) Automatic workpiece load/unload mechanism, (h) Electronic measuring system, (i) CNC console.

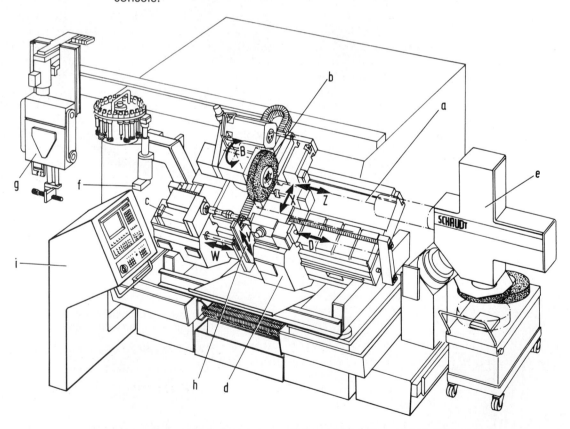

Standard controls designed for lathes and milling machines are generally inapplicable to grinding machines, since control systems for the latter have to meet totally different requirements, such as:

- Greater accuracy and resolution, sometimes to 0.00005 in.
- Particularly high feed-rate ranges, from 0.001 in./min up to 200 ft/min
- Availability of specific canned grinding cycles and subroutines— for example, gradual infeed, dwell, oscillation, and wheel sharpening routines
- Automatic "tool" compensation after dressing the grinding wheel
- Linear and circular interpolation without deceleration, that is, zero following error, to avoid any contour deviation when automatically dressing relief grinding wheels
- Simple input and editing of the program to allow input of test cut values by the operator

The differences between the various types of grinders are considerably greater than between the various types of lathes for example. Grinders do not require tool compensation to allow for continuous wear as do single and multipoint cutting tools. Automatic correction is necessary only after redressing the grinding wheel. This procedure is not regularly required as it is with other tooling; its frequency depends more on actual wear rate of the wheel and the accuracy demanded. Wheels without relief are redressed by moving a diamond across the cutting surface one or more times, and the amount by which wheel size is reduced must be automatically compensated for by the NC unit.

Cylindrical grinding machines usually have two axes and their design is similar in this respect to lathes. Flat (surface) grinders mainly have three axes and thus more closely resemble milling machines. Longitudinal movement (X axis) is performed by the workholding surface; infeed (Z axis) and traverse movements (Y axis) are carried out by the spindle which holds the grinding wheel.

Tool-cutter grinders can have up to five numerically controlled axes, with special-purpose machines being equipped with as many as ten NC axes!

12.17 PIPE-BENDING MACHINES

Pipes with multiple bends are needed for many different purposes. Some examples are given below:

- In the aircraft industry, for support of various components within the wings, power units, control surfaces, and brakes
- In the machine tool industry, for hydraulic and compressed air systems and heat exchangers

- In the automobile industry, for exhaust systems, fuel tanks, seat frames, and bicycle and motorcycle handlebars
- In the appliance industry, for cooling systems and heating coils
- In industries producing sporting equipment, tools, and outdoor furniture

Pipes normally require a precision of ± 0.1° for bending and torsion angles as well as approximately 0.005 in. tolerance for the distance between individual curves. In order to fulfill these requirements, the ability to input additional compensating values is required for longitudinal position as well as for bend and torsion angles. These parameters are not functionally interdependent, and therefore relatively simple numerical linear path controls for three axes without interpolation are sufficient.

Hydraulic cylinders or DC servodrives are used as axis drives. Input of the bending program into the memory of the NC takes place either by keyboard, punch tape, or magnetic tape cassette.

A bending program can be prepared in various ways:

- On the basis of a bent-parts drawing containing the bending data
- With a bent sample or a bending caliper to which the bent pipe is matched
- By using a digitizing pipe-measuring machine which computes and then produces the completed pipe-bending program based on the measurement of a pipe or wire model *(Fig. 12–29)*.

FIGURE 12–29   Programming system for a tube-bending machine.

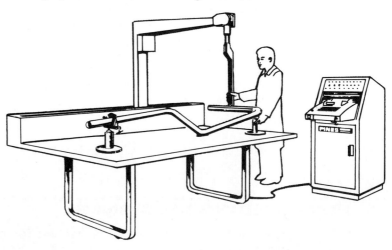

Generally such a 3-axis pipe measuring machine consists of:

- A computer with connected teleprinter
- A dial gauge caliper which is fastened to a movable arm with various joints
- A support table on which the pipe or wire model to be measured can be secured

In order to prepare a program, the geometry of the model is manually scanned, using a dial gauge caliper. The computer then automatically digitally computes the necessary bending data which can appear as a printout or on a punch tape. If a direct link exists between bending machine and pipe measuring machine, the prepared program can also be directly transferred into the control of the bending machine *(Fig. 12–30).*

The first bent pipe is measured on the pipe measuring machine and the computer compares the actual values with the target values of the model. Any deviations can then be entered as compensation values into the NC of the pipe-bending machine.

NC pipe-bending machines fulfill the requirements for precision, fast correction capability, and quick changeover. For fully automatic production, they are also provided with magazine feed, welding seam positioning, and auto-ejection of the finished pipe so that multiple machine operation can take place.

FIGURE 12–30   Three-axis tube-bending machine.

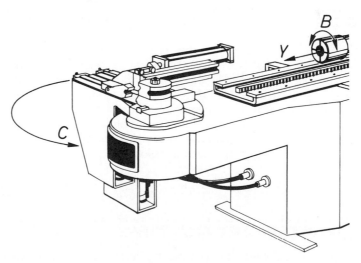

12.18 FLOW TURNING

Flow turning is anything but a new metal forming process. In the Middle Ages spinning techniques were employed, forming hollow shapes in the form of utensils from sheets of copper or tin.

Gradually the strength of the materials used increased as new alloys were developed, as did the wall thickness of the shapes produced to further increase component stiffness. These developments gave rise to the demand for machine-assisted production as human force was no longer sufficient to effect the forming process.

Continuous development has led to the special flow-turning machines which are currently in use. In some respects, these are similar to lathes, despite the fact that the cutting tool is replaced by a forming tool (usually a roller), which actually performs the metal deformation.

The technique of flow turning (or shear spinning as it is sometimes known) can be briefly described as follows.

Lateral pressure is applied to a revolving blank on a lathe so that the metal assumes the shape of a former which is rotating adjacent to it. Deformation is effected by a combination of bending and stretching, pressure being exerted by means of a forming roller. Thus thick-gauge material is caused to flow plastically (shear formed) by the pressure roller in the direction of the roller traverse.

NC machines have now made it possible to replace the revolving solid former with a computer reaction roller exerting an equal and opposite counterforce to the force of the forming roller as it moves along the outer surface of the workpiece. Such machines can be employed very flexibly and permit multipurpose operation. Although the machine illustrated in Fig. 12–31, *p. 209* has only four NC axes, the number of NC axes which have to be controlled simultaneously may be increased from four to six.

Both inside and outside rollers must be controlled in such a way that they both travel at an accurately defined angle to the axis of rotation and with a constant distance between them to ensure uniform wall thickness of the component. Only with the assistance of computer-aided programming would it be feasible to meet this requirement.

Although the principle of this technique of sheet-metal work is not new, few designers are familiar with it and it has yet to find application in general production.

12.19 WATER-JET CUTTING

Water has proven to be a medium well suited for cutting materials such as plastics, reinforced composites, leather, paper, and even sheet metal up to a thickness of 0.05 in. Cutting speed ranges achievable are from 3 in./min to 40 in./min, with a water pressure of between 4000 and 9000 bars, and a jet diameter of only 0.005 in. Cutting speed depends of course on the material being cut and its thickness, but it should generally not exceed 0.625 in. if cut faces and edges are to be clean and free of burrs.

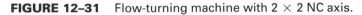

FIGURE 12–31   Flow-turning machine with 2 × 2 NC axis.

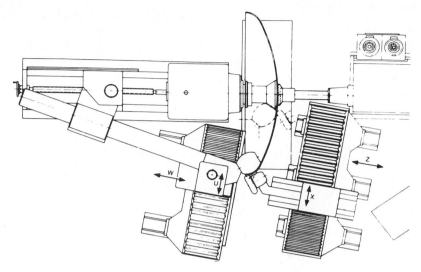

Approximately 0.3 gal of water is used per min, due to the very high jet emission velocity of 3000 ft/s—about three times the speed of sound. The water is cleaned by microfilters, which have a porosity of about 5 to 10 μ, whence it can be reintroduced back into the system and used once again.

Water-jet cutting has the following advantages:

- The production of dust, which can impair the cutting process, is avoided.
- No feed forces are imposed on the workpiece.
- Workpieces cannot become electrically charged, which is important if, for example, printed-circuit boards are being cut.

The design of water-jet cutting machines is similar to that of gantry-type robots and contains an adjustable water-jet nozzle fitted to a swinging arm with two axes of motion *(Fig. 12–32, p. 210)*. With such machine tools, it is even possible to cut three-dimensional workpieces from plastic without difficulty.

12.20 COORDINATE MEASURING MACHINES

The installation of NC machine tools almost always requires extensive modifications in quality control to cope with a constantly changing range of simple and complicated workpieces that must be tested to exacting quality standards. Increasingly a coordinate measuring machine (CMM) *(Fig. 12–33, p. 210)* is used to distinguish between good and bad

FIGURE 12–32 Water-jet cutting.

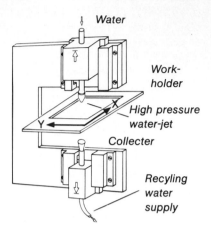

components, or, in other cases, to provide correction data back to the manufacturing process.

Depending on the part's geometry, the measuring time can often amount to about 30–100 percent of machining time. The necessity to measure mainly three-dimensional workpieces initially led to the development of hand-operated 3-D measuring machines. The measuring speed, however, was greatly increased when time-consuming alignment and calculation work was eliminated through computer assis-

FIGURE 12–33 Three-axis coordinate measuring machine.

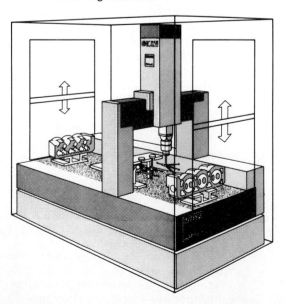

tance. Next followed automation of the CMM's traverse functions via the use of servomotors. Typically, servodrives place a spherical-ended probe *(Fig. 12–34)* into the X and Y axes to the approximate point above a hole to be measured, and the probe is then lowered along the Z axis. The probe is centered in the hole, *(Fig. 12–35a, p. 213),* and the final values achieved are noted by the computer, stored, and then assessed against target values.

In 1970-71 probes that were sensitive only in the Z direction were replaced by probes which also reacted to lateral deflection. However, since this electronic "feeler" only provided precise measuring values in one (later two) measuring direction, the Z axis also had to be rotational. In this way a very flexible and efficient probing system was achieved but considerable programming effort for 3-D parts was still required.

FIGURE 12–34   Inspection probe.

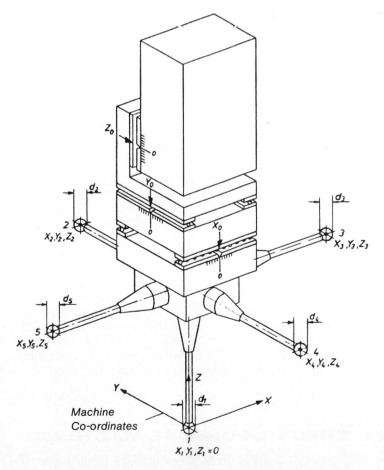

Machine Co-ordinates

Only through the use of specially developed programming languages (FOCAL and CMAP) and corresponding special programs is the user in a position to fully exploit the potential of the CMM. Moreover, only NC measuring machines, equipped with the necessary options for specialized measuring functions can fulfill the following important requirements:

- Universal measuring feeler for multiple axes response
- No significant delay in reloading measuring programs
- High measuring speed, that is, displacement speed of up to 10 ft/min, precise positioning, and rapid collection of the coordinate values when contact is made between part and probe
- Minimal uncertainty, high measurement accuracy and repeatability
- Excessive number of data points not necessary to increase measurement precision
- Quick changeover from one component to another
- Measurement data output which makes possible a rapid judgment of component accuracy and its constituent elements, such as ellipses, circles, straight lines, and intersecting points *(Fig. 12–35f, p. 213)*
- Correlation of a series of measured points to establish the accuracy of the feature(s) of the component being examined, for example distance, angle, and symmetry *(Fig. 12–35g, p. 213)*

The NC of a measuring machine differs from the NC of a machine tool in a few small, but important details. The machining process for a machine tool presumes that the tool and machine geometry agree with the programmed values. The measuring machine must therefore determine:

- How large the actual/target deviations on the component are
- Whether the holes drilled or bored into surfaces are perpendicular to one another
- Whether a hole/bevel/flat surface is present at all
- If, when, and how a compensation value should enter the process in order to maintain tolerances
- Whether the production process should be stopped immediately, since increasing deviations will lead to machine-tool shutdown.

In order to convert the measuring machine to measuring or programming duties, the operating program must be exchangeable, the control must have a sufficiently large data memory at its disposal, and the computing speed must be high enough to carry out the many computing operations in the shortest time possible.

12.21 SPECIAL-PURPOSE MACHINES

In addition to the machine tools discussed in this chapter, numerical control can be meaningfully applied to many other types of machines,

FIGURE 12–35   Measuring cycles using probing: (a) Measuring cycle to locate the center of a hole; (b) Measuring cycle to locate the center of a cylindrical shaft; (c) Measuring cycle to locate the geometric center of a pocket; (d) Measuring cycle to locate the geometric center of a spigot; (e) Measuring cycle for surface location; (f) Measuring cycle for angular measurement; (g) Measuring cycle for establishing a series of coordinate points relative to a given axis.

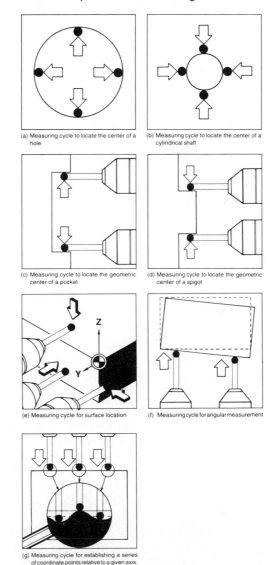

(a) Measuring cycle to locate the center of a hole

(b) Measuring cycle to locate the center of a cylindrical shaft

(c) Measuring cycle to locate the geometric center of a pocket

(d) Measuring cycle to locate the geometric center of a spigot

(e) Measuring cycle for surface location

(f) Measuring cycle for angular measurement

(g) Measuring cycle for establishing a series of coordinate points relative to a given axis.

for example, automatic wire-wrapping machines, drafting installations, and flame cutting machines, and plotters *(Fig. 12-36, p. 214).*

Because of the specialized functions and the control versions needed for any given special-purpose machine, specification of the type of NC needed in any particular case must be determined individually.

FIGURE 12–36 Two-axis plotter.

1. Briefly explain the reasons for the most important changes in machine-tool design that were found to be necessary before they would operate satisfactorily under numerical control.

2. Suggest ways in which an NC machine tool's performance and productivity can be enhanced without large additional expenditure.

3. Explain the "right-hand rule" for determining the designation of NC machine axes. Show how it is applied to a five-axes machining center. How many axes can an NC machine have?

4. What is "mirror-imaging", and what is it used for in NC machining?

5. What is the difference between a turning center and a machining center?

6. What is the biggest single difference in tooling management on an NC machine compared to a conventional machine?

7. What is a tool magazine? Describe at least three types, listing the main advantages and disadvantages of each.

8. What item of equipment had to be invented to enable NC machines to be automatically loaded and unloaded with components?

9. What are gantry-type NC machines, and what are their main advantages?

10. Why are NC punching and nibbling machines so popular in the sheet-metal industry, especially in the area of aircraft component production?

11. Explain the differences between EDM and EBM. What are the main attractions for applying NC to both of these machining processes?

12. What are the particular advantages of laser machining, and why is NC control advantageous?

13. Why is water-jet machining similar, in certain respects, to laser machining?

14. What is a CMM, and why has it assumed such importance in most modern NC machine shops?

15. Explain, using simple sketches, how a probing system establishes its spatial data. How would it determine the center of a pocket in a component both in isolation, and with reference to other data on the component?

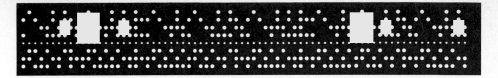

CHAPTER 13

CUTTING-TOOL SYSTEMS FOR NC MACHINE TOOLS

After studying this chapter you should understand:

1. The special requirements of tooling dedicated to CNC machines.
2. The differences between tooling for machining centers and turning centers.
3. The benefits of employing power tooling on CNC lathes.
4. The importance of a separate tool presetting area.

To take full advantage of the efficient operating potential of NC machine tools, it is essential that an appropriate cutting-tool system be selected which will embrace the whole NC operation. The system chosen must be universal, flexible, and able to cope with all chip-removal tasks, must incorporate a high degree of tool rigidity, and must lend itself to high chip-removal rates while remaining within acceptable cost limits.

13.1 INTRODUCTION

The performance, capability, and reliability of the cutting tools themselves are essential factors in determining the productivity of any NC machine tool. Performance has to be seen in terms of available empirical cutting-tool data, including cutting speeds and feed rates, chip cross-sectional area and volume, tool life, tool productivity, and the material being cut. Cutting-tool reliability has both a technological and a geometrical aspect and both are of critical importance for economical machining.

Technological reliability is related to the degree to which tool performance output data are repeatable, that is, it must be possible to know in advance what cutting data form the limits within which tool insert fracture will not occur, and what output can be achieved between tool changes without detriment to product quality.

Geometrical repeatability of tooling in the context of NC machine tool movements is achieved by the desired tool geometrical dimensions being "processed" by the CNC control in exactly the same way as the desired workpiece dimensions. If actual tool dimensions deviate from the desired dimensions stored in the CNC memory, the result is likely to be the production of scrap. It follows that any tooling system for NC machine tools must therefore ensure that the position of the tool determining the final dimensions must not shift in use, and that even after a tool change, the set position must be restored to a high degree of precision. Computer tool correction, itself easily achievable with modern control systems, at all times, presupposes checking actual tool dimensions. However, for this to be carried out while machining is in progress is both costly and time-consuming; it should therefore be limited to areas having critical tolerances.

For many users of machining centers, tool system flexibility is a third important factor which must be added to "geometrical" and "technological" reliability. Particularly in the case of smaller jobbing shop operators, it is frequently necessary to be able to change from one form of workpiece to another rapidly—and to have the necessary special tooling available immediately. The logical answer to this problem is provided by a modular tool system, which makes it possible for the user to assemble a wide variety of tool configurations from the standard components which make up the system.

Despite enhanced tool performance and reliability, it may still not be possible to maximize the advantages of NC technology, (rapid response to changing machining requirements, for example), without the use of a tool-handling system. In theory at least, tools should relate to the workpieces being machined. In practice this is not always so, which is significant as the tool's cutting edge is a major determinant of efficiency, and hence of the economy with which the system—consisting of the machine tool, control unit, and cutting tool—can produce the workpiece.

13.2 TOOLING SYSTEMS

Tool systems form the essential link between the cutting edge which produces the chip, and on which the three principal cutting forces act, and the machine tool which absorbs these forces, while simultaneously guiding the movements taking place between cutting tool and workpiece.

Tool system design must above all be adapted to the machining process (drilling, milling, and turning, for example) and to the basic design features of the machine tool itself.

13.2.1 TOOLING SYSTEMS FOR MACHINING CENTERS

The development of the NC machining center evolved from the manual drilling and milling machine coupled up to a machine control unit. The notable new feature is that tool changing has become an automated process. Even if manual tool changing is still used in some cases to minimize capital expenditure, it is important to ensure that the relevant components can be converted to fully automatic operation at a later stage if required.

The essential system components are:

- The tool holder that secures the tool into the drive spindle
- The cutting tool itself coupled to its adapter unit (the whole assembly usually being preset prior to delivery to the machine tool)
- The tool magazine in which the various tools needed for machining are stored
- A tool-changing mechanism for transferring tool and adapter between machine spindle and tool magazine

Chapter 12, "NC Machine Tools used in Industry," includes illustrations of typical automatic tool changers and tooling facilities.

The tool adapter is the most important component in any tooling system. Despite efforts made on an international level to achieve standardization, various noncompatible systems are still in use, particularly in the areas of gripper slots in the tool holder for automatic tool changing, and in the automatic device to insert the tool assembly into the machine's spindle. In the latter case adapters are available with either drawbolt or a collet. The taper on adapters has been standardized by the American National Standard Institute (ANSI B5.18, 1972), and the taper angle is reflected in numerical values such as 30, 40, 45, 50, and 60 (the ISO standard uses the same nomenclature—ISO 40, ISO 50, and so on). The end of the taper, that is, the pilot diameter and the clearance hole for the draw-in bolt may vary, based on the design of the specific draw mechanism, but often tapers are interchangeable. Figure 13–1, *p. 219* shows a number of tool holders, as used by various machining center manufacturers, and Figure 13–2, *p. 220* gives the essential dimensions of a typical ISO tool holder for machining centers.

FIGURE 13–1   Tool holders for NC machining centers.

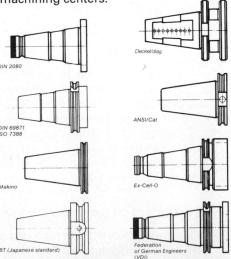

DIN 2080

Deckel/diag.

DIN 69871
ISO 7388

ANSI/Cat

Makino

Ex-Cell-O

BT (Japanese standard)

Federation
of German Engineers
(VDI)

FIGURE 13–2 Principal dimensions of ISO standard tool holder.

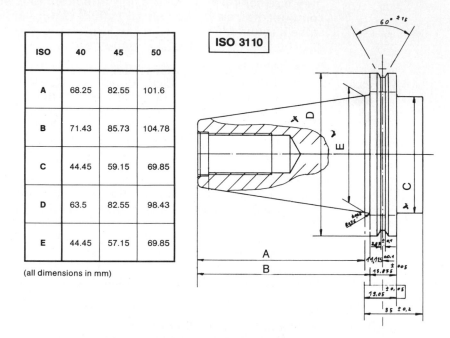

ISO	40	45	50
A	68.25	82.55	101.6
B	71.43	85.73	104.78
C	44.45	59.15	69.85
D	63.5	82.55	98.43
E	44.45	57.15	69.85

(all dimensions in mm)

If tool changing is to be fast and reliable, it is essential that the same type of tool adapter be used for every tool. Tool adapter design depends mainly on:

- The machine-tool spindle taper
- The gripper grooves matched to the automatic tool changer, including data reference marks for tool radial orientation
- The type of clamping system used for positive tool adapter location in the spindle, thereby ensuring reliable transmission of cutting forces

In order to minimize costs when a number of different machining centers are used, tool holders should ideally be standardized for all cutting tools used.

There is clear evidence of a trend towards standardization of taper and gripper design at the international level. The German DIN standard, for example, is being used as the starting point for the ISO standard currently in preparation.

Figure 13–3 illustrates possible combinations of cutting tools and attachments for horizontal/vertical CNC machining centers, while Figure 13–4, *p. 222* shows a typical boring tool system using replaceable inserts.

13.2.2 TOOLING SYSTEMS FOR TURNING CENTERS

NC turning centers may be used with two basically different tool systems (the difference being in the tool carrier):

FIGURE 13–3   Milling tool system for NC gantry-type machining centers.

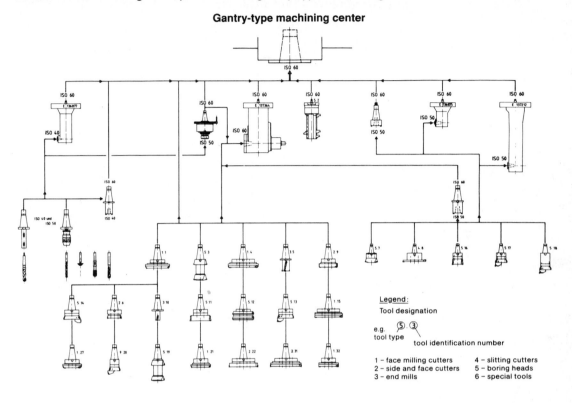

- Indexing tool turrets
- Tool magazines in combination with a tool changer attachment

Both systems offer certain advantages. Tool turrets permit rapid tool changing because of short indexing times. Tool magazines enable a greater number of tools to be stored without the risk of collision within the working area of the NC turning center.

In both cases tool shanks are usually clamped in tool blocks held at indexed positions on the tool carrier. The tool blocks correspond to tool holders on machining centers and are once again standardized into two formats: *(Fig. 13–5 p. 222)*

- With cylindrical shank
- With a prismatic pattern

As in the case of NC machining centers, there is also no internationally accepted standard for turning center tooling systems.

FIGURE 13–4   Boring tool system for NC machine tools.

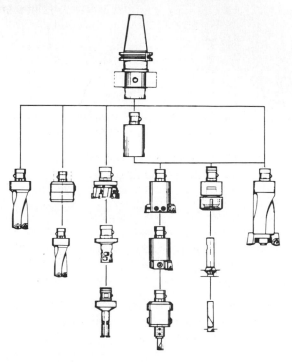

FIGURE 13–5   Tool holders for NC turning centers.

Tool Turret Designs

In addition to a number of standard turret designs, many NC lathe manufacturers have developed systems that are especially adapted to the working area and to the overall concept of their machine tools. Standard designs include:

- Cross-type turrets
- Disk turrets
- Drum turrets

Most machine-specific tool turret designs are in fact similar to the tool layout illustrated in Figure 13–6.

Tool Magazines for NC Lathes

Tool magazines are used less frequently than turrets with NC turning centers because the tool changer will usually be more expensive than the indexing mechanism of a turret. The decisive reason, therefore, for preference to be given to a magazine layout will be the reduced risk of collision, coupled with a capability for using a greater number of tools automatically without any need for manual intervention. The use of magazines on NC lathes, however, has been given a new impetus by tooling system developments whereby only the head of the tool with the insert is changed, rather than the entire tool block. A design of this kind will allow a greater number of inserts to be stored within a relatively small space and, with an appropriate automatic tool-changing mechanism, held in readiness over extended machining periods.

Power Tooling Attachments for NC Lathes

Many turned parts require additional machining operations that cannot normally be carried out on a lathe. Such operations include

---

FIGURE 13–6   Tool turrets for NC lathes: (a) Disk turret; (b) Cross-type turret (universal turret).

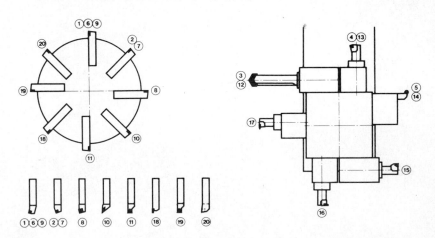

eccentric, axial, or radial drilling, milling of transverse or longitudinal grooves, axial or radial boring, and polygon section milling (Fig. 13-7).

Modern CNC lathes, however, can be used for such purposes if they have a numerically-controlled main spindle (C axis), and the tooling is powered at the turret head. Depending on the tools and drives fitted, a turning attachment of this type will be capable of turning, drilling, grinding (not recommended), countersinking, milling, or thread cutting.

For these tasks a number of tool manufacturers offer axial and radial tool heads connected to the drive in the turret through a special power takeoff coupling. For CNC it is not sufficient to provide a third axis for the spindle. Special programming is also necessary. For drilling work the spindle should be programmable by inputting polar coordinates (degrees/minutes), but milling operations, on the other hand, call for programming in Cartesian coordinates, as with an NC milling machine:

- Z/C for peripheral work
- X/C for face work

The complex interpolation of axis moves in relation to diameter is carried out by special CNC software.

FIGURE 13–7   End milling using a turret head power attachment on an NC lathe.

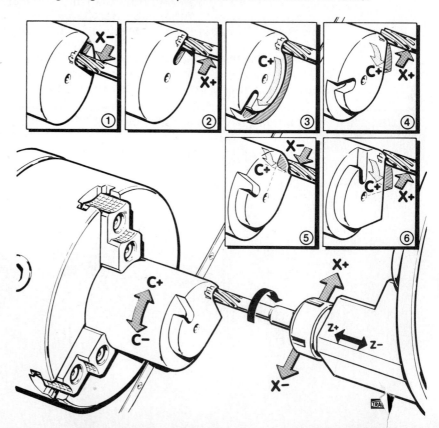

13.3 CUTTING-TOOL SELECTION

CNC machine tools offer a whole new range of possibilities for machining operations. These include the possibility of completely machining a component in a single setup, and with fewer cutting operations than with conventional production systems. Hence tool selection must be oriented accordingly, that is, NC equipment calls for multipurpose tooling. This entails an increase in the number of tools per workstation. Numerical control can, however, handle a larger geometric part spectrum because all slides are controlled by the machine control unit. Therefore form tooling is completely eliminated, which in turn reduces the number of tools normally necessary to form contours.

The correct choice of NC cutting tools is determined by the overall part configuration, rather than by individual section contours. A reduced number of higher-quality tools for more flexible tasks will always be a better choice than a large number of special-purpose tools. Technological optimization, however, is of great importance, since the use of replaceable inserts makes it easy to adapt cutting materials and insert geometry to the workpiece materials being cut. Particular attention must be paid to chip flow in this environment, since higher cutting performance and complex multidirectional movements of the cutting tool itself require the provision of an efficient, rapid, chip-removal system frequently in the form of a chip-conveyor system, although internal coolant feed, or coolant lines and connections integrated into tool blocks and adapters, will frequently minimize such problems without interfering with automatic tool-changing operations. All cutting-tool manufacturers are anxious to see their products used on NC machine tools, and this has prompted them to significantly expand their efforts to provide more comprehensive information and guidance concerning their products. For specific machine-tool types and component formats, special computerized catalogues recommending appropriate tooling packages and options are now freely available. Such data sources should be used at an early stage, and certainly at the time that the NC machine tool is selected.

FIGURE 13–8   Systems for lathes with interchangeable insert holders: (a) Block tools (Sandvik Coromant); (b) Multiflex (Krupp Widia); (c) FTS (Hertel).

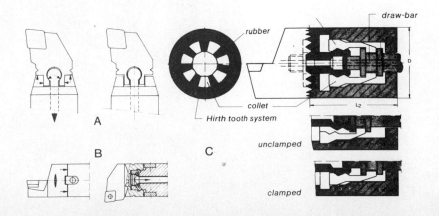

13.4 TOOL PRESETTING

NC machine tools are production machines, and if put to any use other than machining, their operation will become highly unproductive. This is equally true during the downtimes when tool setting is taking place at the machine. Consequently, almost all NC tooling systems are designed to ensure that the tool insert positions can be preset remotely from the machine tool. For this purpose use is made of setting devices with appropriate adapters which simulate the actual machine tool's location datum points. The position of the inserts is checked optically, using a microscope with optical screen or similar fixture, or by means of contact probes *(see Fig. 13–9)*, and the relevant tool offsets are then noted for downloading into the control unit of the appropriate machine tool or into a central tool data register if one exists.

In addition to vertical setting devices for boring tools, there are horizontal devices for turning centers on the market. For some time however universal units have been obtainable which can be used for both types of tooling. Tool setting is essentially concerned with adjusting both main and secondary metal-cutting edge profiles as accurately as possible in relation to a fixed datum point on the tool carrier in accordance with setting table data *(Fig. 13–10)*. This calls for appropriate setting facilities for the tool. Tool setting is, for example, necessary on NC machines devoid of tool path compensation, or when workpieces are processed with predetermined tool settings and dimensions. Boring

---

FIGURE 13–9   Universal tool measuring and setting device with interface to a computer and printer for tool data output.

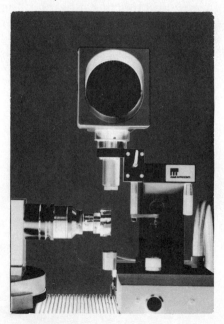

FIGURE 13–10   Adjustable tools.

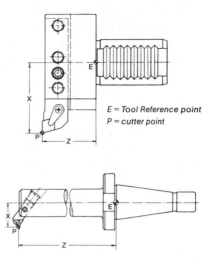

E = Tool Reference point
P = cutter point

bars require accurate diametral presetting, while tool length can be compensated for at the machine tool.

The purpose of tool measuring operations is the precise measurement of the given distance between the tool's cutting edge and a fixed datum point on the tool body *(Fig. 13–11)*. Tool measurement is necessary in order to make it possible with NC turning, milling, and drilling machines to input the absolute dimensions or correction values of tools into the CNC tool correction value register prior to tool usage. However, multispindle milling machines require tools with identical tool dimensions in all spindles because only one tool compensation can be ac-

FIGURE 13–11   Tool data to be measured; fixed tools.

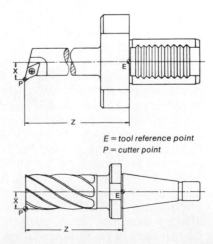

E = tool reference point
P = cutter point

commodated. Depending on convenience, or the degree to which the setting device is automated, actual values can be read from a scale or digital display, or automatically captured on a data carrier such as punched tape or a magnetic tape cassette. It is also possible to link printers that produce self-adhesive labels, showing tool designation, setting dimensions, and tool offset data. These labels are attached directly to the cutting tool and the data they contain is entered into the machine-tool computer when the tool is required for service. The latest tool holders incorporate an inbuilt EPROM micro-chip which contains both tool identification and setting data. This permits automatic tool data transfer to the CNC tool register both quickly and devoid of human error. With the more sophisticated production systems, measured tool data can be transmitted to the CNC tool data register directly—via the existing DNC system, for example. When choosing a tool presetting device for current NC machine-tool use, requirements for any new NC equipment that is likely to be acquired in the foreseeable future should also be taken into account. The criteria for selection will also be influenced by the overall tooling setup within the factory, with tools being issued from a central tool crib or assigned to either individual or groups of NC machine tools. With so many technical, organizational, and economic factors to take into account, it is advisable to compare methods used by other companies for solving this problem and to profit from their experience before making a final choice. Although grass-roots experience gained under operational conditions will often be of more value than general theorizing, it will never be possible to eliminate systematic planning of NC tooling systems and the need for presetting facilities.

13.5 IN-HOUSE TOOL CATALOGUES

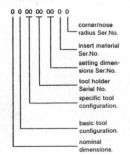

0 0 00 00 00 0 0
corner/nose radius Ser.No.
insert material Ser.No.
setting dimensions Ser.No.
tool holder Serial No.
specific tool configuration.
basic tool configuration.
nominal dimensions.

Control dimensions and other technical data relating to cutting tools used with NC equipment are incorporated into NC part programs. Standardization aimed at making it possible to perform similar tasks with similar tools presupposes systematic control of tools and their application. This can best be achieved by means of company-specific tool "catalogues," preferably using standardized file data forms. Apart from the general tool assembly layout, file data should also cover tool components, setting dimensions, and recommended cutting data. For computer-aided programming, the data should be recorded in a fixed format, a requirement which also applies to tool data input into tool data registers.

For a maximum understanding of tool systems and appropriate tool combinations, a classification and coding system is recommended, covering for example, the machining process, NC machine and tool-holder type, tool-holder block design, and tool-insert specification and geometry. A numerical key system of this sort must primarily be compatible with the existing in-house numbering/coding system. The following example of a system for lathes and related tools should therefore only be regarded as typical.

13.6 CNC TOOL MANAGEMENT

Any program, whether written manually or computer assisted, will be based on tools of given dimensions. Where actual tool data differ from the programmed values, the result can be anything from part dimensional variations to rejects. It follows therefore, that very special attention must be given to tooling and to the input and management of related correction data.

CNC managed and processed tool data include:

- Tool-length compensation to allow for the difference between desired and actual length (along the Z axis)
- Tool diameter compensation, also referred to as milling radius compensation, which automatically computes cutter center-line path; (With non-tangential transitions this logic will compute the appropriate transition radii for corners on external contours and the points of intersection for internal contours.) (It was only with the development of "true" cutting path correction that workpiece dimensions could be utilized as program data.)
- Tool-wear compensation to compensate automatically or manually for tool-tip wear without changing the initially programmed offset data

Earlier generations of numerical control systems incorporated all these correction capabilities and they are therefore well known. Later CNC versions offer additional, less widely known functions and facilities which, with flexible production units and systems, have made fully automatic operation feasible for the first time. One of these features which is assuming increasing importance is tool-life monitoring, which means continuously monitoring the usage of each individual tool in the magazine/system and comparing the findings with each tool's permitted cutting life. When tool life has expired, replacement tools are called up. For this contingency, sister-tooling is held in readiness by the automatic tool management facility. The logic system manages up to nine identical replacements for each tool in use, all with identical tool numbers, each of which is fed sequentially into service upon expiration of its predecessor's permitted service life.

Used tools, once returned to the magazine and/or tool crib, are electronically decoded, which in turn activates the request for replacements when they are next called up in a subsequent NC program.

The condition of every tool in any machine's magazine can be monitored on a VDU screen at any time. The limited number of tool locations in magazines leads to a further management problem, namely the time required to change used tooling without interrupting machine-tool operation (tool changing "on the fly"). This is the purpose of tool management software, which recognizes prolonged program sections devoid of programmed tool changes, and during such periods initiates the magazine for either manual or automatic tool release. As soon as the next programmed tool change approaches, the above procedure is interrupted in ample time to free the magazine for the next scheduled spindle-tool change.

Recent machine-tool designs make use of independently programmable equipment, including commercially available robots, for tool changing. However, with the new tools all tool-correction and tool-life data must once again be automatically input, stored in the correct location, and then automatically captured—a complex task indeed!

13.7 OVERALL REQUIREMENTS

Cutting tools for use with NC equipment form integral parts of machine tool/workpiece/numerical-control unit systems. They must be precision-manufactured to ensure interchangeability, and their optimum performance characteristics, that is, cutting characteristics and tool-life values, must all be reliably predictable. Finally, it must be possible, due to process demands and/or reasons of wear, to change tooling both quickly and accurately.

However, these hallmarks of good NC tool system management will have their full effect only if tool selection and preparation are carried out systematically and with care. The prerequisites here are tool presetting remote from the machine-tool area and efficient cataloguing. In cases of doubt, or where there is a lack of appropriate experience, it is essential to seek advice from reputable cutting tool manufacturers as well as experienced users.

QUESTIONS FOR CHAPTER 13

1. What is meant by a tooling system, as applied to CNC machine tools?
2. Explain how you would ensure the best conditions for accurate and consistent tool presetting in a plant that contains a wide range of CNC machine tools.
3. What is the difference between indexing turrets and a tool magazine with tool changer systems?
4. What is a tool file?
5. Briefly describe the most important benefits to be gained by using CNC lathes fitted with power tooling.
6. What is meant by "sister tooling"?
7. Describe three of the most important factors that must be controlled in an efficient CNC tool-management system.
8. What is meant by tool changing "on the fly," and why is it often incorporated into the design of CNC machine tools?

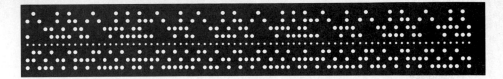

CHAPTER 14

MODERN SERVO AND SPINDLE DRIVE SYSTEMS

After studying this chapter you should understand:

1. The fundamental differences between servo feed and main spindle drives.
2. The various types of motors used for main spindle and feed duties.
3. The operating characteristics of both externally excited dc motors and asynchronous motors.
4. The significance of hydraulic feed-drive systems.
5. The main requirements of digital interfaces between numerical-controller unit and machine-tool drive elements.

Servodrives are vitally important components in every NC machine tool, and their behavioral characteristics have a particular influence on workpiece quality and the machine's operating speed. Hence the technical specifications for servodrive systems are very demanding.

Main spindle drives also have stringent specification requirements and in this area dc drives have predominated until recently. However, they are now gradually being replaced by ac drives, as these have many technical advantages.

14.1 SCOPE

Today, modern NC machine tools have servomotor drives fitted as standard equipment, and they provide infinitely variable feed and speed rates to both the machine axes and the main spindle. Usually such a servodrive comprises the following components (*Fig. 14–1 p. 232*):

FIGURE 14–1a   Schematic circuit diagram of a feed drive.

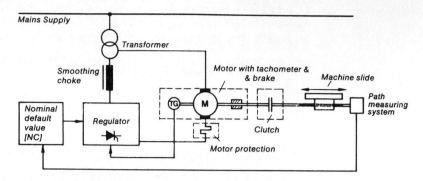

FIGURE 14–1b   Schematic circuit diagram of a main spindle drive.

 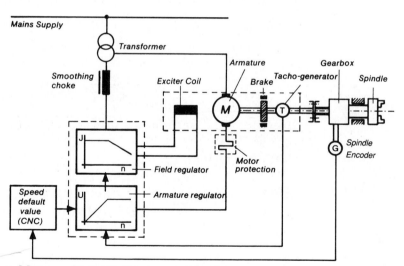

- Motor with tachometer and brake
- Control unit with power amplifier—for spindle drives with integrated field controller
- Mains transformer and smoothing choke
- Mechanical clutch, with overload protection
- Motor protection unit guarding against current overload or excess temperature
- A measuring element flanged directly onto the drive shaft: a path-measuring system for feed drives, and an angle-measuring system for spindle drives
- For spindle drives, a gearbox with fixed or variable gearing, to achieve fine adjustment of the motor speed in order to more precisely match speed and torque requirements at the spindle

It is the task of feed drives to accurately position each individual axis of a machine tool and to precisely control all movements, so that workpieces with fine tolerances can be machined. The required accuracy demands a strict adherence to the NC programmed position. With simultaneous motion of several axes, the relative motion between the tool and workpiece creates what is termed three-dimensional motion. Therefore dynamic behavior is the main criterion for the selection of a feed drive. All programmed movement must be executed with the minimum possible deceleration or overshoot, independent of other factors such as cutting-power fluctuations or varying frictional losses.

The cutting-tool spindle drive has to supply the power needed for the cutting process. The requirements of such a drive are dependent upon the machining method involved (that is, turning, milling, or grinding) as each method demands specific values of power, speed range, and torque behavior from the motor at minimum and maximum speeds. Load fluctuations have to be compensated for instantly to avoid any measurable speed variation—a prerequisite if long tool service life and optimum surface finish are to be achieved. Additionally, both feed and main spindle drives have to fulfill certain criteria regarding maintenance, wear, noise, vibration, heating, space requirements, and cost. Figure 14–1, *p. 232* shows the circuit diagrams for both feed and main spindle-drive units, and Table 14–1 lists the different requirements which each of these two drive systems have to meet.

TABLE 14–1   Differing requirements of feed and main spindle drive systems.

FEED DRIVES	MAIN SPINDLE DRIVES
Constant torque over whole speed range	Constant torque over a wide speed range
Rapid traverse speeds of up to 6,000 rev/min	Maximum speed up to 12,000 rev/min.
High peak torque of up to four times nominal torque	Peak torque of up to twice nominal torque
Nominal power up to 15kW	Nominal power up to 100 kW

14.2 FEED DRIVES

The feed motions of the axes of an NC machine tool have to be very precise, with as little deceleration and as high a repeatability as possible, in order to fulfill the accuracy requirements demanded. All motions must be independent of any counteracting forces such as those resulting from cutting, friction, or inertia. Positioning speeds should be as fast as possible to avoid any lags in arriving at the programmed parameters.

Development over the past few years has made it possible to meet all of these requirements (*Table 14–2a, p. 234*).

TABLE 14–2a   Improvement in machine tool performance over last 30 years.

YEAR	1960	65	70	75	80	85	90
Rapid traverse speed (ft/min)	8	13	32	65	130	200	300
Changeable gear ratios	1	4	0	0	0	0	0
Rapid traverse time (secs)	25	10	2	1	0.6	0.3	0.2
Positioning time (secs)	20	6	0.3	0.2	0.15	0.1	0.05
Total Time to Traverse 8" (secs)	45	16	2.3	1.2	0.75	0.4	0.3

Another important characteristic is uniformity and smoothness of motion—jumps or oscillations being totally unacceptable! In hydraulic motors, such effects are caused, typically, by their pistons, and although less severe, similar effects can also occur in dc motors, emanating from the grooving effect of the rotor, fluctuations in the contact resistance at the commutator, or the application of thyristor amplifiers. Even the slightest buzzing noise or any resonance of the motor will impair the surface finish of the machined workpiece to a point where it may be rejected. This is why motors with finely balanced rotors are usually employed—particularly in grinding machine servodrives.

In a continuous-path control system, each of the controlled axes requires its own drive so that any type of profile may be produced. The central drives (single-motor drives) with individual clutches and brakes for each axis that were employed in the past are no longer used, even for machines with typical point-to-point operations such as drilling and punching machines.

Once a location has been reached, it must be maintained with great security, with mechanical locking devices often employed for this purpose. Mechanical brakes are not normally adequate for this exacting

TABLE 14–2b   Positioning times of a punch and nibbling machine (measured with an acceleration of 30 ft/s^2, and a maximum feed rate of 300 ft/min).

RAPID TRAVERSE DISTANCE (IN.)	POSITIONING TIME (MSEC)
2	168
4	216
8	312
10	(300 ft/min reached)
12	360

task, and although some motors do have integral brakes, they are only suitable for stopping the motor in cases of power failure or emergency stop.

Another criterion for evaluating feed drives is their dynamic behavior, that is, the response of a drive to programmed speed changes which must be performed with as little deceleration or overshoot as possible. This characteristic is termed "reaction speed."

14.2.1   DC FEED DRIVES

This kind of drive is well proven and various models are available. Thanks to advances in the field of magnetic materials, permanently energized dc motors with four, six, or eight poles are now exclusively used (*Fig. 14–2a*).

FIGURE 14–2a   DC feed drive with built-in brake and tachogenerator.

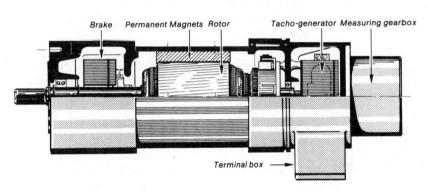

FIGURE 14–2b   Servodrive without brushes, developed from a three-phase synchronous motor, with built-in commutation controller.

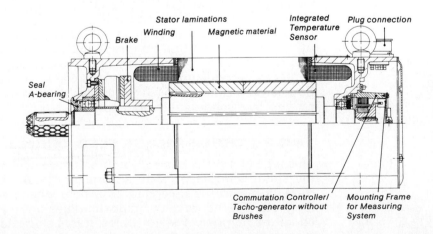

Speed changes are achieved by varying the armature voltage, speed being directly proportional to armature voltage, exciter field remaining constant. The current regulator compensates for the natural behavior of the motor, that is, speed drop due to static or dynamic loads, results in an appropriate increase in armature voltage. This is achieved by sensing even the smallest of decelerations, and speed fluctuations during the variations in load on the motor are therefore virtually eliminated.

The effective peak torque reduces with increasing speed due to the commutation limit. The protection of the collector, that is, a current limitation to avoid overheating, is also important at very low speeds, especially during standstill/stall conditions. This implies that the motor cannot offer the full torque under zero speed conditions. Current regulation ensures that the current limit is not exceeded; otherwise excessive arcing at the commutator's carbon brushes might destroy the commutator. For this reason, the usable speed of dc feed drives decreases with increasing torque requirements and motor size, but in an attempt to minimize this effect, dc feed drives have a bigger commutator diameter and more commutator segments than ordinary dc motors (*Fig. 14–3, p. 237*).

Another type of dc drive commonly used is the rotary disk motor. Its characteristic is that the current conductors are fixed to a disk made of insulating material which rotates between the exciter magnets *(Fig. 14–3).* The time constant of such a motor is very small, that is, its acceleration response ability is good, since the armature is not composed of iron and its inertial mass is therefore small. On the other hand, the thermal limits of disk rotor motors are very low, and if they are subjected to overload for any length of time, there is a serious danger of their burning out due to excess current. The achievable power or the maximum torque is therefore restricted to about 4.5 kW and 15 Nm respectively. If higher torques are required, motors are equipped with double or treble rotors. Disk rotor motors are mainly used in robot or other mechanical handling device applications.

The best final control elements for dc motors are of the pulsed transistor type. Their power limit is reached at mean currents of about 90 A, (peak currents of 180 A), and voltages up to 200 V. The voltage impulses, pulsed at a frequency of several kHz, are filtered by the inductance of the armature, so that no torque pulsation occurs, and thus the average reaction time is measured in microseconds. Due to certain disadvantages in regulation, thyristor amplifiers employed in the past have now largely been replaced by transistor amplifiers or, for high power ranges, by dischargeable thyristors.

14.2.2   THREE-PHASE FEED DRIVES

This type of drive is basically a three-phase synchronous motor, that is, the stator is equipped with an ordinary three-phase winding and the rotor (armature) is designed as a pole wheel, employing permanent magnets. The number of magnetic poles arranged on the rotor must equal the number of stator poles. It is a characteristic of synchronous motors that rotor speed equals the rotational frequency of the magnetic field of the stator (rotating field). It is therefore essential that rotor

FIGURE 14–3   Motor types.

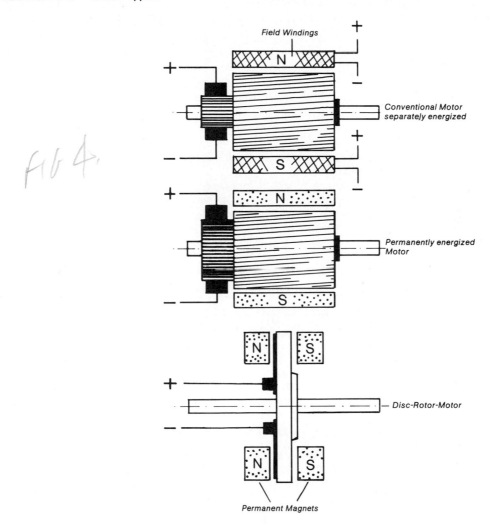

speed and the rotating speed of the magnetic field are always in synchronization for the required torque to be delivered. Only by controlling
the frequency of the rotating field can motor speed be regulated, and
this task is performed by a frequency converter—an electronic device
which employs a special armature angle measuring instrument for syn-
chronizing the rotation of the current within the motor winding with
rotor speed. When these motors were being developed, it was unclear
whether to call them "dc motors without brushes" or "frequency controlled synchronous motors," but the term "three-phase servodrives"
has now been generally accepted.

Compared with dc servodrives this type of motor has several advantages. For example:

- No commutator or carbon brushes are necessary, therefore practically no maintenance is required since there are no components subject to wear, apart from the bearings.
- There is no commutation limit, thus a higher speed of operation is possible which is not reduced with increased motor size.
- Speed-dependent losses are greatly reduced.
- Full torque is available during standstill/stall.
- There is no pollution caused by carbon dust.
- Torque is higher than with dc motors of the same physical size due to lower thermal resistance between windings and operating environment.
- There are thermal losses from the stator. Heavy cooling from an external source (a fan, for example), is essential if full protection is to be assured, but it is not necessary to duct cooling air through the motor as it often is with dc motors.
- Acceleration ability is increased because of a favorable torque-to-rotor inertia ratio.
- Power-to-weight ratio is considerably higher (by a factor of up to five) thanks to higher torques and greater speed range availability.

AC units require greater power than dc drives as far as their electronic servo-amplifiers are concerned. However leading manufacturers are now offering much simpler adjustment features and integrated diagnosis equipment for ac motors, and they are therefore becoming increasingly popular.

14.2.3   STEPPING MOTOR DRIVES

Stepping motors would appear to be particularly well suited to NC machine tools because they are able to directly convert digital-path data into actual mechanical displacement of axes. They need no analog intermediate equipment, no feedback from tachogenerators, and no path-measuring systems. Additionally, they require practically no maintenance, are fully enclosed, and are relatively economical.

But despite these important advantages, stepping motions are now rarely used in machine tools for the following reasons:

- Stepping frequencies and consequently, possible feed rates are too low.
- Maximum available torques are relatively low, that is, acceleration characteristics are poor.
- Even short-term overloads can cause "dropping out of step."
- Resolution (that is, the number of steps per revolution) is insufficient so that even at a resolution of 0.0004 in. per step, the rapid traverse speeds achievable are too low.

For these reasons stepping motors no longer assume any significance in modern machine tools, and will thus not be discussed further.

14.2.4   HYDRAULIC FEED DRIVES

While hydraulic drives for NC machines were replaced long ago by electrical drives, new developments could make hydraulic cylinder actuation (with electrical control valves and stroke lengths of up to 16 in.) attractive once again. Several applications have been tried and have given an excellent performance, providing high accuracy and feed steps of 0.0001 in. at various loads.

The employment of servocontrolled hydraulic cylinders has the following advantages:

- Light weight
- Compactness
- High load-bearing capability
- Direct linear motion without the need for lead-screws
- High level of inherent rigidity
- The low power requirements of the electronic control equipment

Additionally, since most NC machines already have a hydraulic power supply for other functions, the return to hydraulic feed drives is quite possible.

14.3   MAIN SPINDLE DRIVES

The spindle drive of a machine tool has the task of supplying the power needed for the cutting process, as well as overcoming all frictional losses that occur within the mechanical power transmission system. Furthermore, turning centers require a continuously variable spindle-speed capability to maintain the optimum cutting speed in instances where piecepart diameter is continually reducing during machining.

The requirement for precisely controlled spindle acceleration and deceleration, at the time of tool changing for instance, makes it essential that the drive used have accurate, reliably-controlled, dynamic behavioral characteristics.

Speed range ratios that are necessary depend on the machine tool type, but typically are between 40 and 60 for turning centers, 30 and 50 for milling machines, and 50 and 70 for machining centers.

14.3.1   DC MAIN DRIVES

In contrast to feed drives, separately excited motors with reversing poles and external ventilation are normally employed for main drives. Two operating speed ranges are hence possible: one for the armature control region, giving constant torque, and one for the field-control region, giving constant power.

A speed range ratio of approximately 20 to 30 is normal in the armature control region, but in the field-control region the normal ratio is only 3 to 4.

As the motor can be adjusted either in the armature or the field-control mode, special current converters have to be used. These make it possible, (during acceleration, for example) to run through the armature-control region with maximum field strength (maximum torque), and to start reducing the field current only after armature control has been established. The same procedure can be performed in reverse for deceleration, but it is important that the maximum current rating is not exceeded at any time.

The quality of the commutator of a motor influences the maximum acceptable values for both speed and armature current, and it becomes more critical with increasing speed. The commutation limit chart of a motor indicates the degree that armature voltage must be reduced with increasing speed, if arcing at the commutator brushes is to be kept within acceptable limits. For the same reason, commutation limits must also be considered when dealing with dc servodrives.

FIGURE 14–4   Characteristics of externally excited dc motors.
n_1: maximum rev/min at constant power
n_2: maximum rev/min at reduced power due to commutation limit

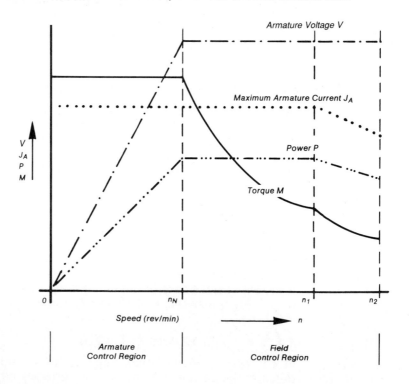

Externally-excited dc motors with field attenuation and speed control are generally the type employed as main drives for NC machine tools. The advantages of this technology are the simple control principles due to the separation of armature and field controls, and the relatively inexpensive thyristor control required. The disadvantages of dc motors are mainly due to the mechanical nature of the commutator. They are:

- Maintenance required as a result of mechanical wear of brushes and collector of both motor and tacho
- Limited current at low speeds, especially during stall conditions, to protect the collector
- Limited current at high speeds due to the commutation limit
- Possible problems concerning thyristor control
- High price in comparison with asynchronous drives

On balance, therefore, for any motor to be considered a realistic alternative drive to a dc motor it must offer significant technical advantages and fulfill the following requirements:

- Low maintenance
- High level of reliability
- Diagnostic features for status analysis and troubleshooting
- High level of dynamic performance, that is, a high overload capacity with a low moment of inertia
- Compact design (certainly no larger than comparable dc motors)
- Additional functions such as spindle orientation and measurement features (see Section 14.4 *p. 243*)
- A minimum cost for the complete drive system

14.3.2   THREE-PHASE MAIN SPINDLE DRIVES

For many years three-phase asynchronous (squirrel-cage) motors with short-circuited rotors, were mainly employed as the prime movers for main spindle drives. Because the power transfer to the rotor is via induction, this type of motor needs no collector—the most sensitive component in ordinary motors.

The robust, simple design of the short-circuited armature has many advantages with respect to maintenance and service life, and the only disadvantage of three-phase asynchronous motors has been that precise regulation of their speed was a major problem. Large gearboxes or pole changing motors were previously used to at least partially offset this difficulty. Now however modern frequency converters can virtually eliminate the problem.

Some of the more important characteristics of such controllers are examined below.

An off-load three-phase asynchronous motor operates at a speed (n_0) near to the nominal synchronous speed, as determined by the mains frequency (f), and the number of pole pairs (p):

$$n_0 = f \times p$$

When on-load the rotor speed drops from synchronous speed to an on-load speed (n_1), and the ratio of the difference between the two speeds (slip) is given by:

$$\text{Slip } (s) = \frac{n_0 - n_1}{n_0} \times 100 \ (\%).$$

If the mains frequency is constant, slip can be increased by reducing the mains voltage. However, this method of control causes considerable losses and is not applicable because the motor tends to stall when armature voltage is decreased by any appreciable amount. To maintain constant torque, the electromagnetic flux within the motor must also be kept constant. This requires a constant voltage-to-frequency ratio if excessive heat generation is to be avoided, and it is the frequency converter which fulfills this control function.

When operating a motor with a frequency converter, two speed-control operating ranges have to be again considered. As with dc motors, these ranges are termed "armature" and "field" control regions (*Fig. 14–5*).

FIGURE 14–5   Characteristics of asynchronous motors with converter supply.

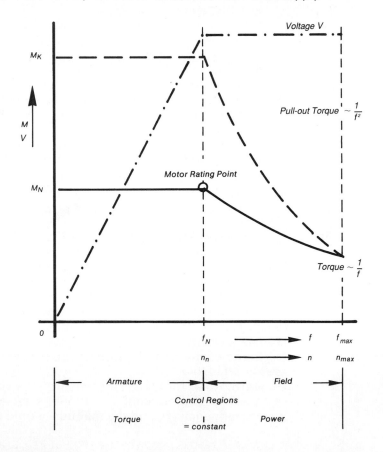

If mains current and torque are constant in the armature control region, the increase in power varies linearly with frequency. However, if the rated voltage is reached and frequency exceeds its rated value, the machine's power drops, the torque decreasing as the square of the frequency. Thus an increase in speed by a factor of two would cause the rated torque to decrease by a factor of four. Motors which are designed in such a manner retain their overload capacity but they become very large. However, with a modified design it is possible to achieve a hyperbolic torque response, that is, with increasing frequency (f), the torque only decreases by a factor of $(1/f)$. This gives a constant power characteristic as found in dc motors, but it does affect overload capacity.

The speed ratio that can be achieved with three-phase asynchronous motors with frequency conversion is about 1:100. Also, maximum speed is higher than the rated speed when operating at mains supply frequency, due to the enhanced frequency delivered by the frequency converter.

14.4 ADDITIONAL FUNCTIONS

14.4.1 SPINDLE ORIENTATION

The main spindle ideally needs an additional encoder, assisted by the numerical controller, to enhance its positioning efficiency. For this purpose, the spindle receives an analog target value to make it move to the programmed position while a special microcomputer (triggered by the command M19 = spindle positioning) calculates the deceleration profile necessary for accurate positioning, based on drive speed and allowable deceleration values.

14.4.2 SPINDLE AS A C AXIS (ROTATIONAL ABOUT THE Z AXIS)

Turning centers with power tooling require the ability to position the main spindle as though it were the C axis on a machining center, and to move it via simultaneous interpolation in the X and/or Z axis. This operation is comparable to that of a numerically controlled rotary table used on a machining center.

Interpolated motion of the C axis in coordination with the X or Z axis permits additional machining operations on parts without the necessity to reclamp them, thus eliminating the need for some, or even all, further machining operations.

14.4.3 MEASUREMENT SIGNAL OUTPUT

Some drives offer "characteristic measurement" output signal values, characteristic parameters typically being current, speed, power, and percentage of the maximum load employed. An electronic monitoring device permits the supervision of these parameters and triggers a signal or message if any parameter exceeds its preset limits.

14.5 DIGITAL INTERFACES

Transmission of signals from the (C)NC to the drives of an NC machine tool (and vice versa), are generally in analog format. Maximum motor speed, for example, normally corresponds to a nominal voltage of 10 V, and so with a typical control ratio of 1:10,000, the smallest nominal voltage can be as low as 1 microvolt. This is one of the major drawbacks of analog-control circuit interfaces.

Some manufacturers offer a bidirectional, serial, digital interface. This meets all the requirements for automatic data transfer and offers the facility to subsequently add new functions to increase the level of automation. Indeed, the digital coupling of CNC and drives permits a significant expansion of features, such as:

- Input and display of drive parameters via CNC keyboard and screen
- Simple checking and correction of drive parameters during servicing
- Improved diagnostics due to a continuous flow of drive parameter data to the CNC or master computer
- Reduced wiring complexity, despite the increased communication available when a fiber optic cable is used
- Considerable improvement in control characteristics and accuracy, especially at the lower end of the speed range

Standardization of digital interfaces and their acceptance by all manufacturers, however, is of major importance if CNCs and drives from different suppliers are to communicate and interact satisfactorily.

14.6 SAFETY EQUIPMENT

It is common that servomotors and main spindle-drive motors are loaded up to their full design capacity. This is why it is important to have reliable controls so that operating limits are not exceeded.

Load limits on a motor are determined by the following factors:

- Temperature of the windings and other motor parts, such as the bearings
- Commutation limit (arcing at the brushes) in dc motors
- Demagnetization limit for permanently energized motors
- Centrifugal forces in the case of motor overspeed

If insufficient protection against overload is not provided, a motor can suffer from severe damage after only a short operating period. Although built-in thermal cutouts and bimetallic relays can be installed within the armature windings to help control the temperature of the motor, it is essential to install motors in such a way that good air circulation is assured, thereby achieving the greatest heat dissipation.

An efficient current limiter is necessary to avoid dangerous overcurrent and arcing at the commutator brushes. It must also fulfill the task of limiting a short-circuit current and tripping out the power supply immediately in case of a motor stalling. Overspeed can be avoided by means of a governor, or more simply, by controlling the voltage of the tachogenerator.

QUESTIONS FOR CHAPTER 14

1. Why is it so important to use high quality servodrives on NC machine tools?
2. Compare and contrast the basic differences between servodrives employed for machine axis and main spindle-control duties.
3. Discuss the most important features necessary for any feed drive that is fitted to an NC machine tool.
4. How is speed change achieved in dc feed motors?
5. What is a rotary disk motor, and what are its principal advantages and limitations? Where are they most commonly used?
6. Describe at least six advantages offered by three-phase motor drives compared to the dc servodrive.
7. Why have stepping motors now been virtually eliminated from NC machine tools as devices for establishing accurate angular position? What method is now more commonly used?
8. Why does the future of hydraulic feed drives look increasingly attractive?
9. What advantages are offered by ac servodrives that make them an increasingly popular alternative to dc drives?
10. What are "characteristic parameters," and how is their monitoring used to improve modern NC machine-tool control?
11. Why is it so valuable for turning centers to have the ability to radially control component motion/location in the C axis as an auxiliary function?
12. What is the main drawback of analog-control circuit interfacing, and what is now offered as the preferred alternative?
13. Why is it so vital to provide the best possible mechanical and electrical protection devices on all types of servodrives? Discuss typical safeguards used.

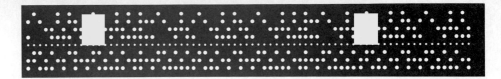

CHAPTER 15

ADAPTIVE CONTROL APPLIED TO NC MACHINE TOOLS

After studying this chapter you should understand:

1. What is meant by the term adaptive control (A/C).
2. The difference in the two main forms of A/C.
3. The principal objectives of A/C.
4. The main advantages offered by A/C.

With A/C the maximum possible metal removal rate, within the constraints of the machine tool, is usually the operational limiting factor and not, for example, a programmed parameter such as feed rate. Thus machine tools equipped with A/C are able to work nearer to their design limits, and achieve a higher productivity rate without risk of machine or cutter overload or increasing programming complexity.

15.1 MACHINING REQUIREMENTS

In recent years considerable interest has been generated in adaptive control (A/C) systems for machining. A/C is a concept that has commanded the attention of many engineers worldwide for over 20 years, and although it is not limited to one particular field, the metalworking industry usually thinks of A/C only as it applies to improving the machining process.

The primary objective of A/C is to produce a control system capable of sensing cutting conditions and thus to provide an automatic means of continually adjusting the speed and feed of the machine tool so that an acceptably machined part is produced at the lowest possible cost. In order to better understand the purpose and functioning of A/C, a brief look at NC, as it has been noted earlier in this book, may be helpful.

Usually the NC obtains its geometrical and technological data from either punch or magnetic tapes. The positions, feed rates, spindle rpm, and so on, are recorded on these tapes and cannot be easily changed. The input data have been established by the programmer "with a comfortable safety margin" so that they can be used for machining even under difficult conditions. If the programmer assumes optimal cutting parameters, malfunctions may arise during machining which cannot be predicted beforehand because of such variables as:

- Tool wear
- Nonhomogeneous materials
- Variation in dimensions of rough stock

Because of these variability factors, the programmer bases his calculations of cutting speed, feed rate, rpm, and cutting depth on a worst-case situation or on a practice-based median value. Casting variability is not taken into consideration, and, for the sake of simplicity, small air gaps are traversed with normal feed rate and not in rapid traverse. The resulting inadequate machine utilization for the normal situation therefore reduces the return on investment of expensive NC machines.

The program tape provides fixed data, and the NC guarantees the required repetition, precision, and speed independent of changing machining conditions. But only an A/C device makes automatic adaptation to changing machining conditions possible. Whereas NC basically only shortens nonproductive time and setup time, cutting time can now also be shortened by A/C. Instead of the "safety margin" built in by the programmer, A/C allows operation at maximum machining parameters at all times.

To this end, A/C systems have been divided into two groups each having different objectives:

- Adaptive Control Constraint (A/CC) With A/CC, feed rate and rpm can be changed so that machining can take place using maximum possible cutting force or cutting power.
- Adaptive Control Optimization (A/CO) With A/CO, an economically significant parameter, such as machining cost per part, is optimized by varying feed rate and rpm.

The A/C systems in operation today primarily belong to the A/CC group (*see Fig. 15–1, p. 249*).

15.2 DESIGN

With A/C it is necessary to measure different variables precisely and without interruption throughout the machining process. The machine itself presents the first problem. To measure torque, cutting power, and motor temperature, suitable detecting sensors must be installed on the machine (*Fig. 15–2*). As a rule, these sensors should be situated as close to the machining zone as possible in order to ensure rapid

FIGURE 15–1   Adaptive control concepts and objectives.

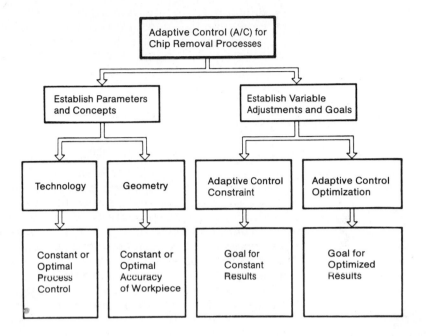

FIGURE 15–2   Numerical control with A/C option.

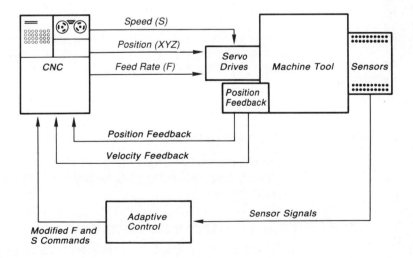

response, although this requirement presents difficulties in:

- Bringing out the instrumentation leads
- Protecting the measuring components from mechanical damage, oil, coolant, dirt, vibration and so on.
- Accessibility for adjustment and maintenance

15.3 A/C STRATEGY

The principal objectives of A/C are:

- Protection of the main spindle motor from overload
- Prevention of cutter or workpiece damage
- A steady, optimal metal removal rate
- Optimization of tool service life by maintaining constant cutting power and cutting or feed force
- Fastest possible travel in cutting unpredictable air gaps
- Elimination of the differences in technical knowledge required by programmer and NC operator
- No overshoot of permissible cutting power during reentry into material and under irregular cutting conditions

To achieve these objectives, the following changes during the machining process must be identified by the A/C:

- Increase or decrease in cutting depth
- Changes in workpiece hardness
- Air cuts
- Wear of tool cutting edges

Therefore the prime function of A/C logic is to quickly recognize changing machining conditions and immediately compensate for these changes by adjusting feed rate and/or rpm.

15.4 EXAMPLE: TURNING

When used on a CNC lathe (*Fig. 15–3, p. 251*) the A/C must automatically identify the following parameters and hence optimally alter the machining process:

15.4.1   CUTTING TOOL LOAD

In rough turning, the allowable tool loadings (feed force, end thrust force, tangential force, or cutting power) are programmed instead of the feed rate value. The A/C then controls the feed rate in such a way that the measured load parameter does not exceed the programmed value. Test runs to determine optimal feed rate values are therefore not necessary.

FIGURE 15–3   Adaptive control option on a CNC lathe.

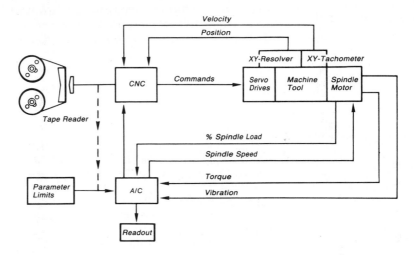

15.4.2   AIR CUTS, INTERRUPTED CUTS

The A/C logic constantly ascertains in what operational manner the machine is running:

- Air cut, that is, no tool load for more than one spindle revolution
- Interrupted cut, that is, multiple loading and unloading of the tool during one revolution
- Constant cutting at a value at which the programmed cutting force of the tool is achieved

15.4.3   SPINDLE DRIVE LOAD

Sometimes the maximum cutting output is limited by the spindle motor. The A/C prevents safety switch activation via the motor protection switch by monitoring motor current and motor temperature. If, for example, the temperature sensor detects that motor temperature has risen to just below a maximum allowable value, the A/C then reduces the motor current to a smaller value by reducing the feed rate and thereby the cutting power. When the motor cools, maximum output is resumed.

Motor load control by A/C is especially advantageous for heavy cuts on large diameters where the allowable torque limit is quickly reached.

Various cutting depths caused by large tolerances of unmachined parts (castings, forgings, and so on) or the hardness of different materials are automatically compensated for. This automatic load control thus permits heavy rough turning cuts so that the machine power available is always fully utilized.

15.4.4 CHATTER

On occasion machine or workpiece vibrations can occur which require a reduction in feed rate and/or spindle speed. The vibrations are measured with an accelerometer coupled to the machine structure.

15.5 ADVANTAGES OF A/C

To summarize, numerical controls with A/C attachment have the following advantages, depending on objective:

- Optimization of the cutting process
- Prevention of machine, cutter, or workpiece damage due to overload
- Optimization of tool life through uniform cutting forces or cutting power
- Prevention of operator override in the automatic mode
- Reduction of time loss in air cuts
- Maintenance of the highest possible material removal rate
- Simplified programming via automatic monitoring of the continuously changing machining process

15.6 DISADVANTAGES OF A/C

Despite its many attractions A/C has two significant disadvantages:

- It is difficult to achieve the necessary sensitivity over a large working range of torque/power in any given controller.
- As increasingly sophisticated machine controllers have become available at reduced costs, A/C has become relatively more expensive.

15.7 SUMMARY

Typical time savings possible using A/C when cutting common engineering metals are illustrated in Figure 15–4, *p. 253*.

However, because of the disadvantages given above, it is frequently difficult to justify the extra cost of A/C, and, despite its many attractions, until the cost question is addressed more vigorously, continued use of A/C in industrial applications seems in doubt.

FIGURE 15–4   Unit cutting times for NC machines with and without A/C.

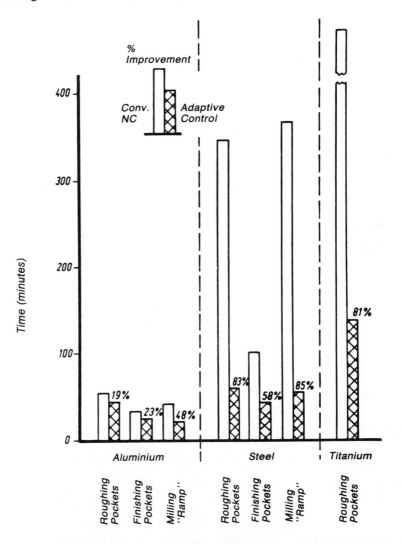

QUESTIONS FOR CHAPTER 15

1. What are the principal objectives of A/C?
2. Explain why driving an automobile is a specific example of A/C.
3. Is A/C also feasible without NC?
4. Why is A/C not standardly fitted to every CNC machine tool?
5. What changes during a cutting operation must be monitored by an A/C?
6. Why do savings offered by A/C vary widely depending upon both material being cut and the cutting operation being undertaken?

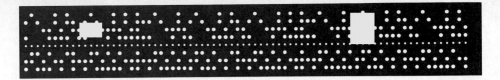

CHAPTER 16

PROGRAMMABLE LOGIC CONTROLLERS (PLCs)

After studying this chapter you should understand:

1. The capabilities of a PLC.
2. The constituent parts of a modern PLC.
3. How a busline works.
4. The principal reasons for using PLCs.
5. The comparative economics of PLCs and their alternatives.

The importance of programmable logic controllers (PLCs) has increased sharply in recent years. They now not only replace the earlier relay controls, but have taken over many additional control functions, diagnostics, and so on. They are effective with stand-alone machine tools and are even more effective with complex flexible manufacturing systems.

16.1 INTRODUCTION

In the past, there were only two categories of control technology: mechanical and electronic, the control elements being typically relays and semiconductors respectively. Today more detailed criteria are necessary to distinguish between the various control types because now whole systems are involved instead of single elements.

The development of PLCs has brought increased facilities. The word "programmable" indicates a close relationship to computers, for which programming languages such as FORTRAN, COBOL, and PASCAL are used. A capability of solving mathematical and technological problems is also implied. "Control" implies the objective of a PLC's industrial application, that is, to produce, send, and receive signals for the purpose of controlled activation or to stop specific functions of machines and/or complete installations.

PLCs were developed from computer technology in the 1968–70 period, and have gradually evolved to meet the requirements of the industry. The programming procedure was initially planned to be carried out in the electronics workshop where technical equipment and expertise could be readily combined. Recent developments, however, demand no knowledge of electronics, and the mechanical designer of a machine tool, who best knows its requirements, is able to program the control system via a suitably chosen programming device.

The degree of programmability is also an important criterion for classifying control systems. Distinction is made between controls which are alterable by the user and those which are not, that is, hardwired controls (*Fig. 16–1*).

FIGURE 16–1 Programming characteristics of different controls.

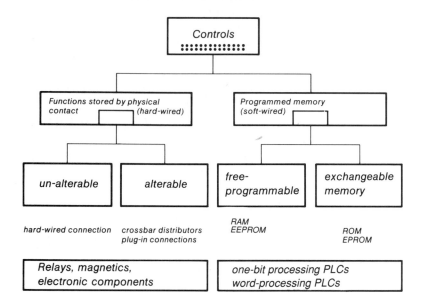

Relays are not the only controls to be considered hard-wired and hence unalterable, many controls composed of electronic components also fall into this category. If the function of a control is determined by the "hard-wired" inter-connection of the individual elements, then it is limited to an unalterable or fixed function control, and alterations can only be made by rearranging the wiring or exchanging certain components. Those inflexible controls that contain crossbar distributors, punch tape readers, or other plug-in connections, are reprogrammable, but only within certain very restricted limits.

Flexible controls can either be programmed directly or by exchanging memories; they are referred to as "free programmable" and "exchange memories" respectively. The former type of control consists of a random access memory (RAM), which allows data or commands to be changed or added to without mechanical operation. If read only memories (ROMs) are employed in a control, some of their components have to be changed when a program is edited or modified, e.g. "exchangeable memory" controllers. In contrast to ROMs, which can be programmed only once, erasable programmable read only memories (EPROMs) allow the information to be wiped clean from the EPROM chip, and therefore make it reprogrammable, but as this is only possible with special UV erasure devices, EPROMs are also considered as exchangeable memory units.

As the structure of a PLC is based on the same principles as those employed in computer architecture, it is not only capable of performing switching tasks, but also of performing other applications such as counting, calculating, comparing, or even the processing of analog signals of particular interest, for example, in process engineering. However, in this chapter only the application of PLCs to machine tools is considered, as a more general treatment of the wide-ranging utilization of PLCs would be inappropriate here.

16.2 THE ELEMENTS OF A PLC

The hardware design of a PLC, as illustrated in Fig. 16–2, comprises the following elements:

- General power supply for all modules
- Central processing unit (CPU)
- Program memory
- Input cards
- Output cards
- Interface cards
- Auxiliary functions
- Mechanical framework for housing the modules and connecting them to both the power supply and the busline

---

FIGURE 16–2   Hardware components of a programmable logic controller.

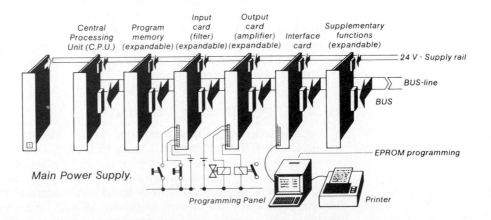

Central Processing Unit (C.P.U.) Program memory (expandable) Input card (filter) (expandable) Output card (amplifier) (expandable) Interface card Supplementary functions (expandable)

24 V - Supply rail
BUS-line
BUS

Main Power Supply.

EPROM programming

Programming Panel   Printer

A brief description of these modules now follows.

16.2.1 CPU

A processor appears only once in a PLC, and it can either be a one-bit or a word processor. Processors of the first type are adequate for dealing with logic operations, but as the processing time for a single signal is quite long, complex tasks cannot be carried out without timing problems. This is where word processors become attractive, as they are much more suited to fast processing of numerical information. The reason for their speed is that they do not process single bits but words, which can consist of up to 16 bits. However, word processing is more complex, and hence more expensive, which is why both types of processors are employed, depending on the application involved.

PLCs with word processors are used where processing text and numerical data, calculations, gaging, controlling, and recording as well as the simple processing of signals in binary code, are required.

The principle of operation of a CPU can be briefly described as follows:

The instructions stored in the program memory are called up sequentially, as controlled by the program counter contained within the processing unit. The processor links the individual signals according to this protocol and derives from them the resulting output commands. This serial operation of the program results in a delay while the program counter makes one complete cyclic pass and then starts all over again. This time period is referred to as "scan time," and it is directly dependent on the size of the memory.

Often scan time for a 1-Kbyte program is measured, and then used as a criterion for comparison between different types of PLCs. For many devices this delay can be as long as 20 milliseconds or more depending on memory-expansion size. In practice, this means that a limit switch, for example, could only be called up every 20 milliseconds. If this causes problems, special measures have to be taken, such as the repetition of specific call-ups during one scan, or control transfer instructions to omit call-ups of minor importance in cases where the scan time becomes unacceptably long. If no such solution is satisfactory then a faster PLC with a scan time of, say, 1 millisecond per Kbyte may be necessary. Thus, it is clear that it is the processor that determines the capabilities and functioning of a PLC; (*Fig. 16–3, p. 259*) compares one-bit and word CPU characteristics.

16.2.2 PROGRAM MEMORY

The actual control program is held within electronic storage components, such as the RAMs, PROMs, or EPROMs, in the program memory. The program is created with the assistance of a special programming unit, downloaded into the program memory, which is then plugged into the PLC frame. A backup battery supply is essential for the RAM to retain its program in the event of power failure. The memory is modular in design to permit easy adaptation to control functions of different sizes, and hence expansion is achieved through insertion of additional

---

FIGURE 16-3   Comparative characteristics of programmable logic controllers with Bit and word processors.

One-Bit Processor	Word Processor
Direct processing of input and output signals (singly addressable)	Input and output signals only addressable via words (extract through masks)
Smaller supply of commands; as a rule, only a YES/NO decision	Extensive command supply requires knowledge of micro-computing
Simple input language without computing knowledge, partly symbol keys	Complicated input language with extensive command supply
Limited capability of processing digital data (e. g. no mathematical or logic functions)	Gathering and processing of digital data
Serial program run without interruption, thereby relatively lengthy cycle times	Time-critical processes addressable through interrupt commands or emergency control transfer
Only simple computer interfaces	Interfaces for main-frame computers or systems
Limited processing of analog signals	Input/Output processing of analog signals

memory cards into the PLC frame. The program memory design is dealt with in more detail in Section 16.6.

16.2.3   INPUT CARDS

The input card serves to prepare external signals coming into the PLC and contains filters and power level adaptors for this purpose. So-called opto-interfaces separate the internal circuits from the external ones galvanically. As a rule, an input card is designed to receive several inputs (8–16–24–32, for example) and further input cards can simply be inserted if more inputs are required. Failure diagnosis can be greatly facilitated if each input is equipped with a light-emitting diode (LED), so that visual indication of the presence of input voltages is provided.

16.2.4   OUTPUT CARDS

Output cards are of similar design to input cards. They send output signals from the PLC directly to the servoactuators of the machine tool. This is why output cards that are compatible with a variety of output interfaces are offered.

LEDs can also help monitor output voltages. The possibility of visual control is even more important for devices with supplementary output fuses and a central LED can be of considerable additional help. The number of outputs that can be switched on at any one time depends on the type of device and it may be restricted for thermal and/or electronic reasons.

Usually output cards do not comprise power supply units and power is supplied externally via a simple dc supply with no special requirements needed for either stabilization or smoothing.

16.2.5 INTERFACE CARDS

Interface cards are used for the connection of external equipment, such as displays, programming devices, or expansion frames, to the PLC. Further supplementary functions are necessary along with pure logic functions, and they can be incorporated, in part, within the basic PLC design or they can be created by adding specialized supplementary logic cards which contain several, usually similar, supplementary functions.

16.2.6 AUXILIARY FUNCTIONS

Supplementary functions are, typically:

- Latching memories which have the same function as latching relays, that is, to store signals during power failure. When power is restored, the switching position of this memory is at the last position occupied prior to power loss.
- Timers which correspond to ON-delay or OFF-delay relays. The preset timings are programmed or even regulated externally.
- Counters which are either programmed by means of elementary logic commands or through supplementary cards. The counter presetting takes place through programming or via decade switching.
- Registers which correspond to step-switching mechanisms. The next step is released either by time emitters or via machine-dependent transfer circuit impulses.
- Arithmetic functions which are designed primarily to carry out the four basic arithmetic functions (addition, subtraction, multiplication, and division) and the comparison functions (greater than, less than, equal to, not equal to). The availability of arithmetic functions expands the PLC's scope of application considerably. Functions can thus be carried out for which a process computer would otherwise have been necessary.
- NC-modules for discrete axes which can be used for carrying out single, numerically controlled movements that are not interactive—the palletizing and stacking programs needed for component handling devices, for example.

PLCs with special auxiliary functions are only appropriate if they are intended to fulfill functions other than just replacing a simple relay control. If such additional functions cannot be fully utilized it is better to employ PLCs without these facilities.

16.3 THE BUSLINE

All the modules of a PLC are interconnected by a busline (bus), which consists of several parallel link circuits leading to each module. The complete data and signal exchange between modules takes place via these circuits, which can also provide external connections—to the CNC, for example. The following is a brief description of the bus, as it is frequently misunderstood. (*See Fig. 16–4.*)

FIGURE 16–4   Comparison between hard-wired and busline connection.

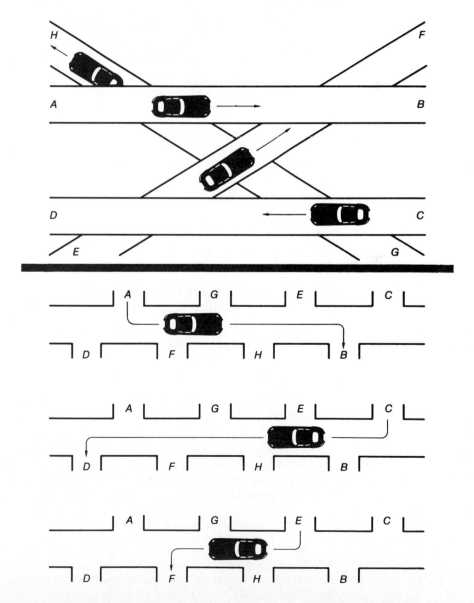

The expression "busline" derives from "businessline," a highway interchange system around cities. Vehicle drivers unfamiliar with a city and who are looking for a specific destination stay on the route marked "busline" until they reach the correct exit for their destination. Their return journey is accomplished by the same process effected in reverse.

The analogy is thus:

- The highway system corresponds to the "busline."
- The destination corresponds to the "address."
- The vehicle corresponds to the "data."

Various vehicles travel along the busline, one after another, in both directions, originating from different points, and having different destinations—typical traffic on any ordinary highway network.

If one extends this analogy to permanently wired logic:

- Each vehicle, from start to destination, would use a road built exclusively for it and specific for each direction.
- Points of origin and destination would be permanently connected by a "one-way street" and would, depending on the circumstances, be seldom used (low data density).
- Detours or changes in destination would require an alteration to the network or additional connections.

This analogy clearly illustrates that permanently programmed circuits are highly uneconomical!

16.4 PLC FUNCTION AND APPLICATION

Basically, the function of PLCs is the same as that of controls designed using relays or electronic components (*Fig. 16–5*), that is:

- To receive input and feedback commands
- To link these commands and branch or latch them in accordance with the program
- To issue the control commands derived

Two different applications of PLCs to machine tools can be specified on the basis of the above:

- Program controls that operate to a specific program of their own
- Adaptive controls, which form the link between an NC and a machine tool and allow the transfer of commands from the NC to the machine only if neither the human operator nor the machine or workpiece is endangered. This refers to ancillary equipment relevant to a mechanized process where all the procedures are centrally controlled by the PLC program—automatic tool or pallet changers, for example.

The input and output (I/O) devices of a PLC-controlled machine tool are connected to the input and output stages of the PLC—(*see Fig. 16–5, p. 263.*)

FIGURE 16-5   Principal PLC functions.

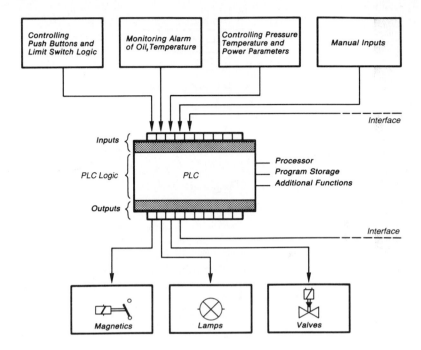

The number of I/Os depends on the requirements of the user, but as the I/Os increase, so does the required memory size for the program and in most devices the cycle or scan time also increases.

16.5 PROGRAMMING AND DOCUMENTATION

The facilities available at programming panels have a major influence on whether a PLC can be economically employed. In contrast to numerical controls, programmable controls can be used only if a suitable programming panel is available. Thus the purchase of a PLC also requires the purchase of the appropriate programming panel, usually from the same manufacturer. Even if input commands are standardized, the problem of each PLC having different, specific output commands remains.

The main difference between programmable controls and relay or semiconductor technology is the technique by which the control program is entered into the controller (*Fig. 16–6*). In relay controls, the switching control mechanically comprises individual modules in accordance with the circuit program, and the control sequence is controlled manually through wire connections; hence the term—"hard-wired" controls. In contrast to this, the input of a control sequence into a PLC is carried out via a programming panel and a program outline which indicates all possible methods and procedures of entering the logic into the

FIGURE 16–6   Differences in Formation/Preparation of a hard-wired control and a PLC.

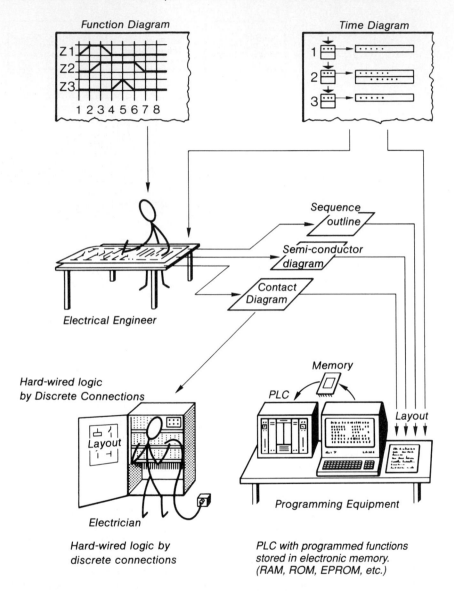

Hard-wired logic by discrete connections

PLC with programmed functions stored in electronic memory. (RAM, ROM, EPROM, etc.)

electronic storage components. The following models can be used for programming, as illustrated in Fig. 16–7, *p. 265*:

- Sequence format
- Function format
- Wiring diagram or contact circuit diagram
- Logic format

Which of the above models is appropriate depends on the type of PLC, and it is therefore important for the user to select a PLC system

FIGURE 16–7   The flow of data via various PLC programming methods.

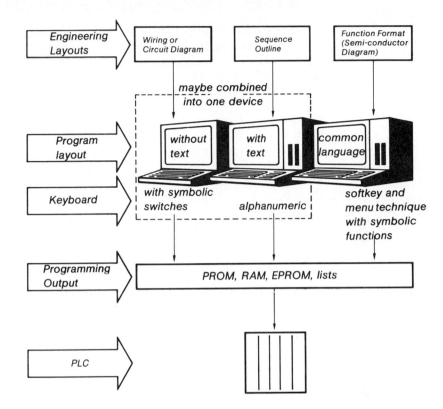

that allows data interchange without difficulty or unnecessary expense. Most of the devices currently on the market employ the sequence outline or a wiring diagram. More sophisticated devices allow the user to switch from one input method to the other even during the input procedure, because independent of the method used, the other format is created simultaneously. Experience has shown that programming with symbol and function keys causes few problems if programmers are familiar with relay controls, and if the contact circuit diagram displayed on the screen during the programming procedure accurately resembles the circuit plans employed in the relay technique. On the other hand, users who already have a basic knowledge of programming languages find it much easier to use the sequence format model. The mnemonic abbreviations used in this technique have the advantage that they do not restrict the capabilities of the PLC. Due to the variety of requirements to be met by programming equipment, most manufacturers offer several devices with varying capabilities. The simplest models are suitable as test devices for the start-up phase of an installation and maintenance, and for correcting the program at the machine tool level. They comprise the following basic functions:

- Programming and editing of sequence formats (even on-line)
- The search for and display of program steps, commands, and addresses

■ Signal displays for I/Os and results
■ Deletion, alteration, and programming of EPROMs

More advanced devices usually incorporate a screen display and interfaces for cassette tape recorders, tape printers, and internal and external disk drives. Even more sophisticated equipment is available, comprising a comfortable programming station, offering operator guidance, and automatic program documentation, and allowing direct input of commands and data without the use of any programming language. For these purposes it is also possible to employ personal computers if they are equipped with the necessary software and hardware options such as an EPROM programming option, function keys, and on-line connection to the PLC for monitor operation and program editing if RAMs are used.

FIGURE 16-8a   Semiconductor diagram (function format).

00022	4	U	E	0.0	S0	START
00023		UN	E	0.1	S1	LIFT
00024		(				
00025		U	E	0.2	S2	HOLD
00026		U	E	0.3	S3	STOP
00027		UN	E	0.4	S4	UP
00028		O	E	0.5	S5	DOWN
00029		)				
00030		U	E	0.6	S6	DRIVE
00031		(				
00032		U	E	0.7	S7	LEFT
00033		UN	E	1.0	S8	BEND
00034		O	E	1.1	S9	PRESS
00035		)				
00036		=	A	2.4	Y4	ON
00037		PE				

Once the program has been created, other tasks have to be carried out by the programming device, such as (*Fig. 16–8a & 16–8b*):

■ Printout of the sequence format with comments and names of devices controlled
■ Printout of reference lists indicating the connections of auxiliary memories, timers, and the controller to internal and external modules
■ Printout of address lists giving the details of which addresses are assigned to what input, output, auxiliary memory, timer, and so on
■ Printout of a contact circuit diagram showing the configuration and codes of the contacts, plus any additional information

The design and operation of programming devices varies from manufacturer to manufacturer. Staff with no PLC experience usually require two or three weeks to become accustomed to a new programming panel and to understand how it works. Even for experienced operators it takes approximately one week's training to be able to work with a new type of PLC with confidence.

FIGURE 16–8b   Sequence format.

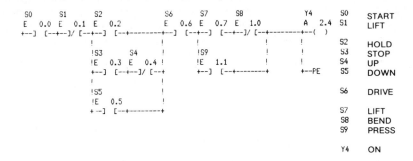

16.6 PROGRAM MEMORY DESIGN

It is only through the computer program that the PLC becomes functional and fulfills the tasks for which it is designed. Most program memories currently in use are semiconductor storages, and Fig. 16–9 lists the main characteristics of the four most commonly used types.

Depending on whether program alterations are carried out by exchanging memory components or by direct reprogramming, a distinction is made between exchangeable and free programmable memories. Controls employing the first programming technique mainly use memories which can be erased by UV light (EPROMs). After the erasure a waiting time of one hour is necessary before new data can be entered.

FIGURE 16–9   Characteristics of various memory formats.

Storage Type	On-line changes possible	Loss of Storage Memory due to Power Failure	Security against undesired Program Changes
RAM	Yes	Yes (without battery)	No
ROM	No	No	Yes
EPROM	No	No	Yes
EEPROM	Yes	No	No

Free programmable controls usually contain RAMs with a buffering battery to save the program in the event of power failure. Most recently developed CMOS (complementary metal oxide semiconductor) storage components have such a low energy consumption that even small batteries can sustain buffer storage power for more than a year. If the buffering time is exceeded or the battery is near exhaustion, an electronic control system will indicate this and prevent the program from starting when the machine or equipment is switched on until the battery has been replaced or the latest program reloaded. PLCs are also benefiting from the falling prices of electronic storage components, and when creating or editing a program it is no longer important to minimize the program length, as was the case in the past when limited storage capacity was a major problem. Instead other programming criteria have assumed importance:

- Clear program structure to avoid confusion
- Ease of program alteration/editing
- Predominant use of subroutines
- Ease of error detection

This last point has assumed special significance in order to keep machine downtimes to a minimum. In addition to the control program itself, special diagnostic programs are now available for:

- Machine tool control
- Observation of machine cycle times
- Comparison between programmed and actual procedures
- Creation of flow charts
- Decoding error messages
- Indication of any required corrections

One of the main requirements of diagnostic programs is assistance in the elimination of breakdowns of I/O modules and their connections. Special diagnosis components for program flow control have been developed which can be used even if the control program, or its data flow, are unknown. They are autodidactic, that is, the correct flow of the working program is memorized by the device, and in case of failure the program step at which the correct flow was interrupted is displayed on the VDU screen or the line display.

The advantages of such options are:

- They do not need programming.
- They do not influence the storage capacity of the PLC.
- Diagnostic assistance is available before the editing of a program is complete, that is, at the machine testing stage.

16.7 REASONS FOR USING PLCs

In the past PLCs were relatively expensive and limited in their capabilities and their programming procedure was complex. For these reasons, they were used only for special machine tools or installations where major changes of design were likely during commissioning and proving phases. However, continuously falling prices, accompanied by increasing PLC capabilities, have resulted in a considerable increase in the application of PLCs, and they are now available for a wide range of equipment (*Fig. 16–10, p. 269*).

Compact devices with up to 24 input and 16 output channels are suitable for simple standard machines, load/unload systems, and interconnecting installations. Automatic documentation is not necessary for PLCs

FIGURE 16–10   Application of programmable logic controls.

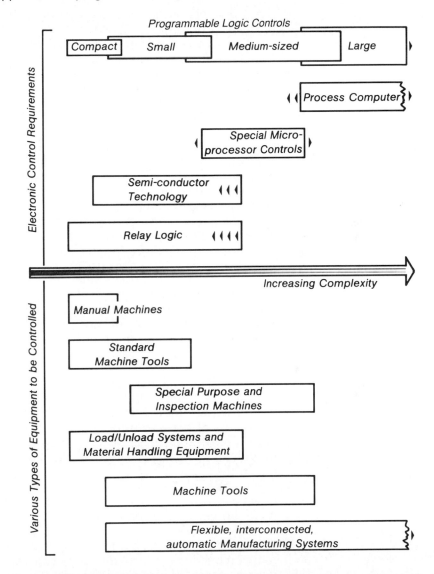

on standard machines because they are unlikely to be subject to any changes; therefore standard circuit diagrams are sufficient as documentation. The commercial attractiveness of PLCs can be confirmed for such simple applications because they are more reliable, take up less space, and obviate the need for wiring and assembly of relays and timers.

As PLCs with various capabilities and options are now employed for more complex tasks, it is desirable to have a whole range of PLCs that are programmable via a common panel format, and that use the same programming procedures.

The application of PLCs has many advantages for both the machine installation engineer and the end user.

Those most frequently quoted are:

- Quick delivery. Modular design permits simple adaptation to any given control function. Since controls and sub-assemblies can be held in stock as a matter of course, they can be immediately available. Furthermore, they can be reused later for other applications.
- Increased reliability. Electronic components have a much longer service life than electromechanical devices. The reliability of a PLC is therefore increased and service life is much longer. Also regularly scheduled maintenance, which is often necessary with relay controls, is eliminated with PLCs.
- Ease of program alteration/editing. Changes required either at start-up or subsequently can be easily carried out without any hard-wiring work. Any program alterations that prove necessary are automatically documented so that a record of all such changes is maintained.
- Simplified estimation of requirements. If the appropriate number of inputs and outputs required is known, the maximum required memory size (program length) can be estimated. It is therefore possible to select the type of PLC required, leaving the wiring of selected input and output stages and terminal selection until delivery and installation.
- Documentation. In many PLCs documentation occurs automatically, making the electronic design significantly simpler.
- Space saving. PLCs require less space than corresponding relay controls; in most cases space is reduced because separate boards are eliminated.
- Reproducibility. Using PLCs with identical control specifications means labor costs that are considerably lower than those incurred with relay controls; this results from the elimination of a large part of the assembly labor. Therefore, PLCs are attractive, not only for application to prototype equipment that is liable to modification during commissioning, but also for use on standard machines.
- Modifications. Controls with only minor differences in the sequence of functions can be reproduced by simply copying, modifying, and/or adding new parts. Those parts of a program which are already available can be reemployed without change. Compared to the relay technique, total assembly time can be greatly reduced because control functions can be programmed before or during assembly of the switchboard.
- Larger range of functions. PLCs are frequently employed for flexible automation because they offer the facilities of counting, comparing, correlating values, changing programs, and changing parameters, and because they are readily connected to a mainframe computer.

16.8 ECONOMICS OF PLCs

Whether it makes sense to install PLCs for given tasks cannot be determined by a simple price comparison of relays/electronic components and PLCs. Certainly there is no economic risk in employing PLCs; their prices are falling due to the steadily declining costs of electronic components, the development of cheaper designs, and the increasing number of applications of PLCs in all fields. However, when comparing costs, the costs of one or more programming panels, printers, tape recorders, and staff training must all be taken into consideration. Fig. 16–11 illustrates graphically a typical qualitative cost comparison.

FIGURE 16–11   Cost comparison between relay and programmable logic controls.

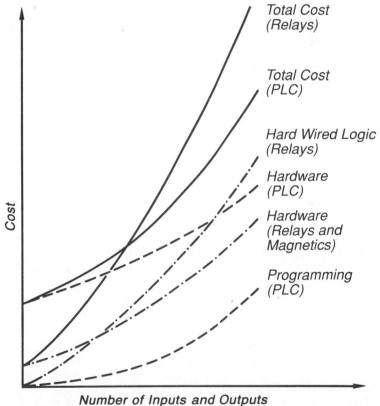

It is of major importance to employ skilled staff with good software knowledge for the planning and programming of PLCs because special purpose software is extremely expensive. Although much has been made feasible by means of software, software has not become cheap! Some PLC manufacturers offer complete, tested, software packages but inevitably changes and/or additions are still necessary and this demands certain software skills. If software is to be created externally in, say, a software company, it is even more vital that all anticipated requirements be precisely defined and clearly written down at the outset.

A typical cost breakdown for a prototype PLC installation is:

- 50 percent for hardware for the PLC
- 10 percent for design of the program format
- 15 percent for programming
- 20 percent for testing and editing
- 5 percent for documentation

PLCs with identical control specifications will hence cost approximately half as much as the initial prototype since only hardware costs must be incurred. This means that the price of PLCs is now comparable to that of relay controls, and with their much greater capabilities PLCs are actually cheaper than the more complex relay-type controls.

However, for profitable application, the relatively high costs of good programming panels and necessary staff training must be justified by a sufficiently large number of controls that require programming each year.

It is disadvantageous to machine tool manufacturers to be forced to employ different types of PLCs in order to comply with their customer's existing programming devices. This creates extra costs which have to be passed on via increased machine-tool prices. On the other hand, it is possible to rent programming devices if they are not to be employed full time, and this may be a less expensive solution.

The table in Figure 16–12, *p. 273* compares different types of control systems.

16.9 EVALUATION CRITERIA

The number of companies offering PLCs is vast, but only a few offer a full range of PLC types, from the very simple to sophisticated devices that have wide ranging capabilities and functions comparable to process computers. The inexperienced PLC user may find it helpful to profit from the studies that large-scale operators, such as the automobile industry, carry out every two to three years. They test the most attractive products on the market and select from two to five types for their production requirements in order to limit the costs of staff training, programming equipment, and spares.

With specific reference to CNC machine tools, other criteria for the selection of PLCs may be of significance (*Fig. 16–13, p. 274*). The integration of PLC functions into a CNC in terms of software and hardware is the only solution if minimum cost and maximum range of functions are to be achieved, and recent developments on CNC machines ensure provision of standard bus-connected PLCs. If both the CNC and the PLC are designed with the same bus structure, and if the software allows data transfer, no additional I/O components will be needed. A PLC which is integrated into the CNC operating program, in terms of software, will also not require a processor of its own. Yet the software

FIGURE 16–12   Comparison between electromechanical, contactless, and programmable logic controls.

Control designed from electro-magnetic components (relays, protective aids)	Control built up from contactless components	Programmable Logic controls
Advantages: • known and reliable for a long time • known dependability • standardized components • very insensitive to interference • most economical of small systems **Disadvantages:** • development and production time-intensive (wiring) • alterations difficult (wiring alterations) • extensive systems difficult to oversee • wear occurs so maintenance is necessary • large space requirements	**Advantages:** • reliable after initial breakdowns subside • easily exchangeable via plug-in technology • less space needed **Disadvantages:** • development and production time-intensive (wiring) • alterations difficult (wiring changes) • extensive systems are difficult to oversee • frequent breakdown in start-up phase	**Advantages:** • high reliability through use of contactless elements • easily exchangeable via plug-in technology • simple installation • control alterations can be carried out quickly without alteration of hardware • smaller space needs • connectable to a computer **Disadvantages:** • high acquisition cost • programming device often expensive • due to cyclical machining slower than parallel logic

structure of such a system is very complex and difficult to change; its application is therefore best restricted to standardized machine tools that are made in significant numbers. For this reason it is essential that CNC integrated PLCs be programmable, or that they allow program changes via the ASCII keyboard and display screen of the CNC.

16.10   TO INTEGRATE THE PLC OR NOT?

Programmable controls have only been used on NC machine tools comparatively recently. As the demand for flexible reprogrammability and automation increases, control tasks will become far too complex for relay systems.

However it has not yet been established whether total integration of PLC functions into the CNC of machine tools is sensible and economical or whether separate PLCs with a busline connection is more appropriate.

FIGURE 16–13a   CNC with separate PLC, communication via I/O components.

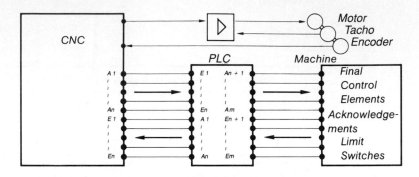

FIGURE 16–13b   CNC with bus-connected PLC, direct communication via bus, without I/O components.

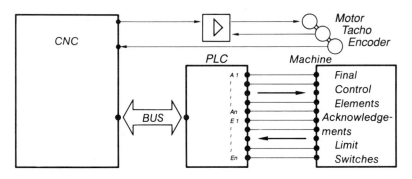

FIGURE 16–13c   CNC with software-integrated PLC: communication takes place within the CNC/PLC operating software.

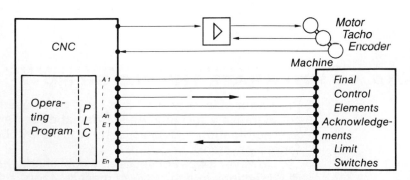

1. What type of control is a PLC? Describe its constituent parts.
2. What are the principal reasons for using PLCs in conjunction with CNC machines?
3. Where is a PLC's program stored?
4. Can the operation of a PLC be in any way compared with the function of a stepping switch?
5. Define the term "cycle time" as applied to a PLC.
6. Compare the operation of a busline system with a hard-wired one.
7. List the various functions that are usually processed by a PLC operating in a plant that comprises CNC machines, robots, and automatic guided vehicles.
8. In a combined CNC/PLC control system, how are the various control functions normally apportioned?
9. What is the single most important factor that should be remembered when drawing up any PLC specification?

CHAPTER 17

DIRECT NUMERICAL CONTROL (DNC)

After studying this chapter you should understand:

1. The differences between CNC and DNC.
2. The range of facilities offered by modern DNC installations.
3. Situations where DNC would be ideally suited.
4. The important criteria to be considered when contemplating the installation of a DNC system.

The automatic bidirectional data interchange between CNC machine tools and their dedicated host computer brings so many substantive advantages that every potential CNC user should consider fully all the potential opportunities in this area at an early stage. Most current numerical controllers have a DNC interface, or are provided with facilities for subsequent DNC interfacing.

17.1 INTRODUCTION

Virtually all NC machine tools now have powerful computing facilities incorporated within their controllers (CNC). They are therefore capable of stand-alone operation, and have full NC programming ability together with limited program storage capacity.

Direct numerical control (DNC) is a totally different approach to computer management of NC machine tools in that all CNCs are directly linked and controlled from a common host computer having a prodigious memory capacity.

A DNC system consists of a computer, bulk memory capable of storing NC part programs for transmission to different NC machines on demand, communication stations providing an interface between the machine operator and the host computer, telecommunication lines to transmit program data to remote sites, and the NC machines themselves.

Various approaches to the marriage between DNC and NC/CNC are possible. This may range from the simple downloading of data to an NC/CNC unit from an intelligent terminal to situations where more complex multifunction host computers conduct rich dialogues with NC/CNC units, other automated systems, and computer information networks.

The principal DNC functions are the tapeless downloading of past programs to CNC machine tools from a source remote from the machines, data storage and processing, two-way communication, information collection, and reporting. In contrast, the principal CNC functions are machine control, diagnostics, dynamic program correction, and operating assistance.

Adopting tapeless NC has the following advantages:

- Elimination of preventive maintenance and the cost of repairing tape readers
- Reduction of data-input errors
- Reduction of erroneous data entered because of incorrect tapes
- Simpler program management
- Reduction/elimination of extensive tape libraries

Also, a distinction is made between basic functions and expanded functions of DNC systems.

The basic functions are (*Fig. 17–1*):

- NC program management
- NC data distribution

The expanded functions are:

- NC data correction
- Simulation of NC functions
- Operating data gathering and processing
- Control functions for the flow of material

In order to work without tapes it is necessary to create an additional input channel for the NC data to be fed into the machine control unit. Operational systems frequently do not have such channels and therefore use the already available interface for a punch-tape reader. The NC control information is thus fed into the control directly from the central computer, bypassing the tape reader. The computer in this case simulates the behavior of the tape reader so that the control is unaware of the source of its information. This is referred to as a behind the tape reader (BTR) data input. The advantage of this type of setup is that in case of computer failure it is possible to revert to the tape reader. Obviously, each machine can then only be operated as a stand-alone system. Another advantage is the replacement of as many repetitive hardware components as possible with software, thereby reducing costs, that is, a single computer program replaces duplicated hardware components for each control.

The prime task therefore assigned to the central host computer is to

FIGURE 17–1   DNC basic functions dependent on interconnected NC systems.

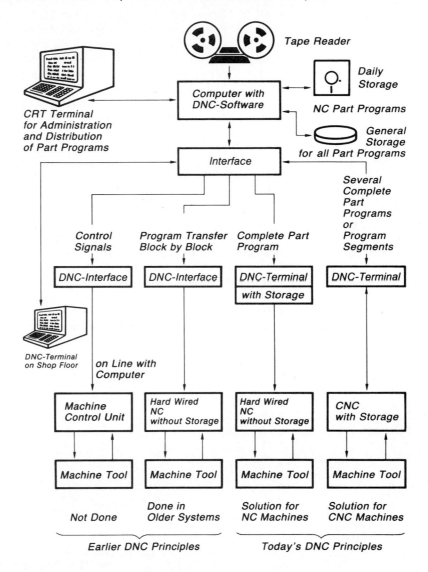

provide all the linked machines with both control information and part programs as and when required.

● ●

17.2 CURRENT DNC CONCEPTS

Based on past experience, and taking into consideration the large program memory capacities now available, the following requirements may be expected from current DNC systems:

- NC program data management must be capable of safely managing and classifying thousands of part programs via program number, program name, machine tools that can be assigned to run any specific program, and preparation date.
- There must be a provision for header information, which includes the part number, drawing number, NC machine tool selection, and required tools, fixtures, and clamping devices.
- Depending on the application, it may be advantageous to transfer NC parts programs from the mass memory disk (10–80 Mbytes) to smaller daily or weekly program memory disks (approximately 160–512 Kbytes) and to hold them ready for instant call-up.
- NC part programs must have built-in security flags, such as specialized release or blocking flags, in order to prevent unauthorized use.
- The initiation or call-up of NC part programs must be simple and easily handled by operating personnel. Also, the initiation of programs must be multiple, that is, they must be able to be run sequentially on several NC machines so that the machining of a given workpiece can progress through a number of machines.
- In the case of complex and decentralized DNC production installations, the data transmission system between the individual controls and the production computer is important. This can be handled by either a loop or a radial data transmission network depending on the DNC manufacturer. A four-wire cable should suffice as the data line (*Figs. 17–2 and 17–3*). This is dealt with in more detail in Chapter 19.

FIGURE 17–2 DNC system with a loop data transmission network.

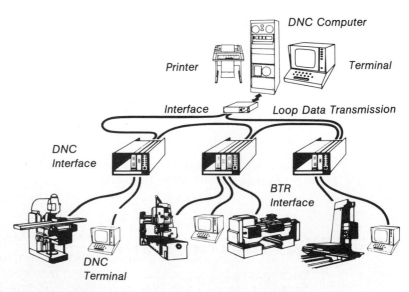

FIGURE 17–3   DNC system with radial data transmission network.

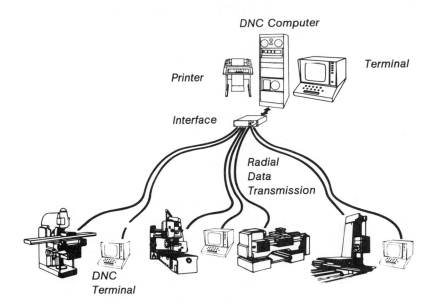

- It must be possible to interconnect numerically controlled machines manufactured by different vendors. For example, if the memory capacity of a connected CNC is smaller than the total program length, the DNC computer must be able to supply the NC part program in several smaller, storable subsets.
- Cabling should be carried out in such a way as to supply several machines with information simultaneously and to retain flexibility to support future expansion without difficulty.
- CNC machines generally offer the possibility of editing a program while it is in the memory of the machine control unit. Therefore the capability must exist to transfer the edited (optimized) program from the machine back to the host computer for storage.
- In addition to the part programs, other information is required at the machine, namely, tool adjustment and/or clamping strategies. In DNC operation, this information is also stored in the computer and called up on request.
- The ability should exist to use the DNC computer for gathering management information such as operating schedules, work loadings, and so on.
- DNC systems should have the capability to directly interconnect the DNC computer to an already existing programming system.
- Under appropriate security conditions, the DNC computer must be capable of fully or partially deleting any NC part program.
- The DNC computer must be able to produce management data listings with the following information, as needed:

All current program numbers
All released programs with related machine identification

All programs scheduled for the next shift/week
The last call-up date of each program and the machine operator
Annual frequency of call-ups
Programs not called up or used in the last *n* months
Program running time
Tools list for any part program
Operator instructions for any part program

- The system must be designed in such a way that, in the event of a DNC computer breakdown, the programs stored locally in the CNCs will ensure continued operation.
  Under emergency conditions, reloading of programs should occur via backup storage media (a daily storage disk and a portable disk reader, for example).
- Machine performance data gathering should also take place in the DNC system (*Fig. 17–4*). Data concerning operating conditions of the machine control unit, machine tool, and terminal should be gathered, stored, and edited according to predetermined criteria, regarding: downtime and causes; service life; number of finished items; current machine utilization, that is, which program is currently being run on which machine; and load factor.
- It is advantageous if the DNC supplier has a computer-aided programming system available which can be implemented on the DNC computer. This additional capability makes even major program alterations easy. It also has the advantage that, in the event of machine breakdown, an alternative program can be quickly generated for each suitable substitute machine by means of a run on the appropriate post-processor.
- The DNC system supplier should be familiar with the hardware and software involved in the installation of the total DNC system and be able to carry out any user-specific modifications required.
- The CNC manufacturer must also take into consideration software and hardware matters involved in the control of the overall DNC system. For a DNC operation to run effectively, it is not only necessary to transmit NC control data bidirectionally, it is also necessary to continuously monitor all other operating parameters.

17.3 COMPARISON OF OLD AND NEW DNC OPERATIONS

From a technical point of view, modern DNC operations offer the advantage of coupling machine tools and computers in a more flexible configuration. Also, for an uninterrupted production run it is not necessary to maintain a connection between computer and machine tool during the entire machining process as was the case in the past. It is now sufficient to establish the connection for only the relatively short period of time during which data is transmitted to the machine controller

FIGURE 17–4   Extended DNC system with integrated computer-assisted programming and management-information data collection.

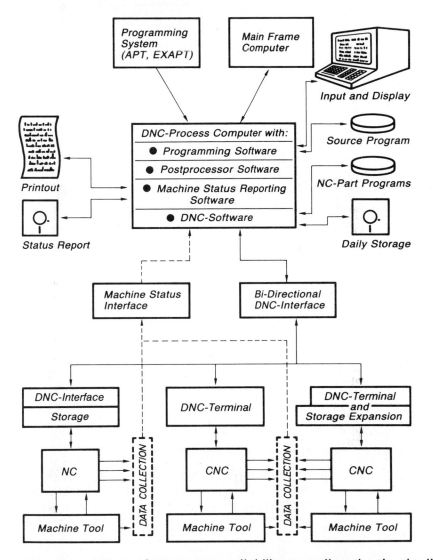

memory. The problem of computer availability as well as the timely distribution of control data thereby becomes less important.

From a profitability point of view, current DNC systems are essentially more efficient and flexible than they were five to ten years ago and can be offered at more economical prices.

As modern DNC systems control data distribution and data management, by using the existing communications systems, additional process tasks, such as operational data collection, optimization of machining, and material flow control will all be integrated in the future. The system components required for such tasks are shown in Figure 17–5, *p. 284.*

FIGURE 17–5   DNC system components.

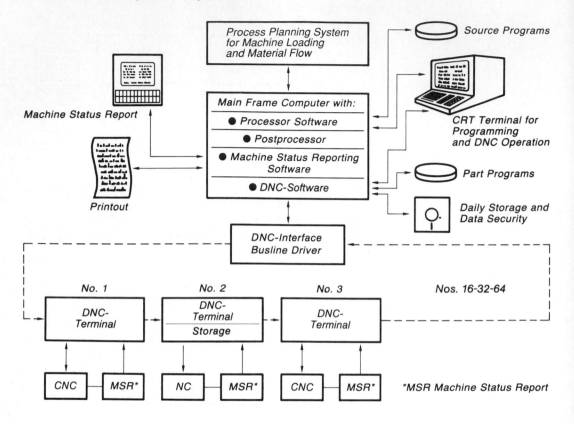

By linking the NC/CNC machines to an automatic material-handling system, and by linking the production and operational computers, a computer-aided manufacturing system (CAM) can be designed that is also capable of computer-assisted production control and job scheduling.

17.4 AREAS OF APPLICATION

DNC systems have found technically satisfactory and economically justified application under the following conditions:

- When the volume of information to be handled by controls is very large and each NC program can be processed quickly
- When the NC/CNC machining equipment is linked to automated materials handling devices, forming a flexible manufacturing system

A DNC system correctly planned and designed offers the following advantages:

- Simple program data management
- Rapid availability of NC data
- Greater security in data transmission
- Fully automatic, flexible operation of the linked NC machines
- Continuous status monitoring and machine utilization and a breakdown of statistics, when expanded to include operational data collection

17.5 APPLICATION CRITERIA FOR DNC SYSTEMS

A DNC installation offers several advantages, as previously mentioned, yet preparation for the application of DNC must be carefully planned. For this reason the following guidelines are proposed:

- Number of machine tools. The minimum number of interconnected machine tools/controllers is important both for productivity and for reasons of economics. Usually four to six NC machines are considered the minimum, although in a few instances two to three machines have proven economical.
- NC programs. The greater the NC part-program-management problem (due to wide ranging and/or long programs), the more one should consider DNC. However, if current CNC local computer memories are substantially full, the possibility of first expanding these memories should be examined, before making a final decision to implement a DNC system.
- Frequent program changes in production. The smaller the lot size and the shorter the program tapes, the greater the difficulty of having the correct tape available on the correct machine at the correct time. With DNC this problem is eliminated, and any program can be immediately downloaded to any machine as often as is required.
- Flexible production systems. With flexible production systems, the complete machining of a component is usually divided up between several machines. Pallets must therefore arrive at the individual machine tools in the correct sequence, and within precise timing if queuing problems are to be avoided.

Basically one may conclude that DNC application becomes increasingly attractive as the use of discrete tapes leads to bottlenecks on the shop floor. Usually such congestion can be eliminated via host computer part-program management, resulting in increased machine running times and improved profitability, particularly when a full management data feed-back system is incorporated.

17.6 COSTS AND PROFITABILITY

A DNC system capable of generating, storing, and distributing part programs costs between $40,000 and $90,000, with connection to each machine tool costing between $2000 and $9000.

Since operational efficiency of CNC machine tools is increased by 10 percent or more when operated within a DNC network, if operation of a CNC machine tool costs $85 per hour, an increase in productivity of only 2 percent would be sufficient to recover the installation costs of a DNC network within approximately one year of two-shift operation.

17.7 THE FUTURE

Since about 1968 DNC systems have been the subject of development by many suppliers, with the result that the number of features and the power and hardware sophistication of these systems has increased dramatically since the early days.

Workshops equipped with a large number of stand-alone CNC machines are already on the correct path towards DNC networking and could readily enjoy the benefits that DNC operation offers; this is even more true where flexible manufacturing cells have been installed. However it is impossible to achieve the maximum flexibility if all the necessary part programs and other supplementary information (such as tool management data) are not readily available. Indeed the efficient use of a computerized tool management system is the first step towards DNC, and usually consists of a dedicated tooling computer linked directly to the CNC machine.

Today almost all DNC systems permit centralized collection and automatic data evaluation related to both the manufacturing processes and the individual machine tools. The DNC computer employs special software for this purpose and usually displays the results via multicolor diagrams and tables.

The combination of today's DNC systems with the latest available computers offers solutions to virtually any application problem with price being determined by the desired technical requirements.

QUESTIONS FOR CHAPTER 17

1. What are the main advantages offered by tapeless NC operation?
2. What are the principal functions of a DNC host computer?
3. Are powerful CNCs made obsolete by the introduction of DNC linking?
4. How is DNC linking of NC machines normally achieved?
5. Do you think there is a conflict between DNC and manual data input (MDI) operation of NC machines?
6. Is there a limit to the number of NC devices that may be connected to a DNC computer network? If so what is it?
7. Briefly describe the difference between loop and radial data transmission networks.
8. In what ways do modern DNC systems differ from earlier versions?

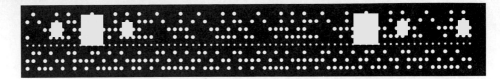

CHAPTER 18

CNC's ROLE IN FLEXIBLE MANUFACTURING SYSTEMS

After studying this chapter you should understand:

1. What is meant by a flexible manufacturing system.
2. The difference between flexible manufacturing cells and islands.
3. The two principal ways that flexible manufacturing systems may be configured.
4. How component transportation and call-up is achieved in cells, islands and systems.
5. The principal functions of the host computer in flexible manufacturing systems.
6. Why system simulation is important.
7. Some of the most significant design problems that arise when planning flexible manufacturing systems.

The availability of reliable CNC machine tools at competitive prices resulted in their rapid spread throughout the machine shops of the world. The logical next step was to link them together by a central control system and common NC devices for component and tool handling to form what is now called a flexible manufacturing system (FMS). Possible combinations of CNC machine tools, piecepart transfer mechanisms, control systems, and computer control formats are nearly limitless and are constrained only by human ingenuity.

18.1 WHAT IS AN FMS?

A basic flexible manufacturing system (FMS) may be defined as a group of numerically controlled machine tools linked by a common materials-handling transport system and controlled via a central computer. This computer is used to exercise overall system control, as well as to provide a centralized part program storage facility similar to that provided for DNC operation (Chapter 17).

Highly integrated systems may also include automated materials storage, on-line inspection by coordinate measuring machines preceded on occasion by an automatic wash/dry unit, and adaptive tool control during machining. Such a system closely corresponds to the concept of a "flexible transfer line" suitable for machining small- to medium-batch sizes.

The use of numerically controlled machine tools allows adaptation to different configurations of workpieces without the time-consuming setups inherent in transfer lines. Flexible manufacturing systems like these can process single parts in random order cost effectively, without being restricted to certain minimum batch sizes (*Fig. 18–1*).

FIGURE 18–1 Application criteria for flexible production systems.

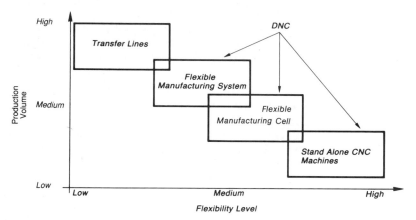

Systems of this type are in use in Japan, the United States, and Western Europe. FMSs can be used for machining either symmetrical or asymmetrical parts by including appropriate materials-handling systems and machine tools. Symmetrical parts may be transported between machine tools by conveyor belts or containers, but asymmetrical parts must be clamped onto pallets in order to ensure proper orientation. At each machining station, symmetrical parts are loaded into, and unloaded from, the machine holding device (such as the chuck on a lathe) by automatic handling equipment. Asymmetrical parts are introduced to, and removed from, each machine tool via pallet changers—see Section 18.5.

FMSs can be particularly attractive when a specific set of machining operations needs to be completed on a family of components in random order and lot sizes.

From an economical point of view, such systems must meet the following special manufacturing requirements:

- Automated, yet flexible, production for a family of parts (that is, a number of parts with similar shape and and/or machining steps)
- Adaptability in the geometry and the number of units to be produced in order to respond rapidly to changes in market demand
- Fully automated operation with minimal human intervention (thereby making the remaining jobs more humane by removing people from the repetitive tasks in a normal manufacturing process)
- Ability to expand without causing a complete shutdown or alteration of the present system
- Adequate flexibility of machine tools to allow continued operation of the system by the remaining machines in the event of unit breakdown
- Easily serviceable installation in order to simplify preventive maintenance and troubleshooting

In the light of the above requirements, an analysis of the workpieces to be manufactured must be completed (see Chapter 23, "Group Technology"), before any FMS can be designed. These data are usually collected with respect to part family attributes, such as the number of components, geometry, size and weight ranges, tolerances, sequence of operations, and the number of tools required. Once this information has been compiled, the type, number, size, and configuration of the machine tools required can then be ascertained. The initial analysis of this type of system should be made without considering the implementation and integration of existing equipment. This approach will deliver a less distorted picture of the potential cost effectiveness of the proposed system. It may be possible, however, to integrate existing CNC machines into the new system. On the other hand, integration of manually operated or mechanically programmed machines is impractical because they lack pallet-changing equipment and are rigidly programmed. However under certain circumstances, special CNC machines (machines with multispindle drilling-heads and drilling-head changing equipment) can be a cost-effective part of a flexible manufacturing system.

FMSs can therefore be considered to be an orchestration of the following components:

- NC machine tools
- materials-handling systems
- workpiece loading and unloading equipment
- a central control system integrated with the above components in such a way that economical automatic production of small and medium-size lots is possible.

18.1.1   APPLICATION CRITERIA

Individual, or "stand-alone" NC machine tools are normally used for the production of similar parts in medium to relatively large lot sizes. Once the holding fixtures and tools are prepared and the program tape is read

into the NC unit, high machine utilization is possible. If processing of the part requires the use of several machines, the in-process parts must be temporarily stored between operations (*Fig. 18–2a*).

Machining and turning centers (*Fig. 18–2b*) are typically used in the production of medium lot sizes of dissimilar parts with close tolerances that preclude reclamping of the workpiece. Short machining times create a need for additional pallet-changing equipment which can be used to allow waiting parts to be loaded and unloaded during machining.

The production of dissimilar items in small lot sizes with varying specifications requires a manufacturing system with great flexibility, and FMSs are ideally suited for this type of production. The major challenge in these systems is to achieve the best combination of component, machine tool, and NC program in order to ensure optimum utilization of this expensive equipment.

18.2 MACHINE TOOL SELECTION AND LAYOUT

The design of an FMS, and especially the selection of the machines to be used, is directly dependent on component geometries and the consequent machining operations to be performed.

Machines may be either a suitable selection of standard CNC machine tools, or a mixture of standard and "special," or customized, CNC machines. Ideally they should all be from the same manufacturer to minimize intercommunication problems, but this is seldom possible in practice. It is thus advisable for the design and construction of an FMS to be commissioned to a general contractor who can pass orders to subcontractors. In this way, the main responsibility for the functioning of the entire system lies with one party. This approach is also advisable for secondary operation equipment such as wash tanks, inspection devices, and load/unload stations. This way, the effectiveness of the general contractor can be easily judged after the entire system has been installed and commissioned. It is generally advisable to use no more than two or three basic types of standard machines, and the use of specials is best avoided if possible. In the event of a machine breakdown, a system equipped in this way can then remain operational by rerouting machining operations to the remaining machine tools. It can also be more easily expanded as a result of increased market demand or changed as necessitated by major component design changes.

After the number and types of machines to be employed have been decided, consideration should be given to the layout of the system and the materials-handling system(s) which will be used. One may choose from three different possibilities:

1. Serial layout (*Fig. 18–2c, p. 291*)
2. Parallel layout (*Fig. 18–2d and Fig. 18–3 p. 292*)
3. Combination layout (serial/parallel)

FIGURE 18–2a   Production with mix of NC and conventional machine tools.

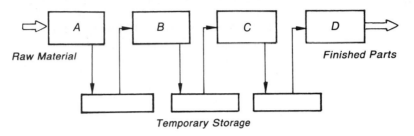

Note: A, B, C, and D refer to the various manufacturing processes performed on the pieceparts produced.

FIGURE 18–2b   Production with CNC machining centers but without automatic piecepart transportation system.

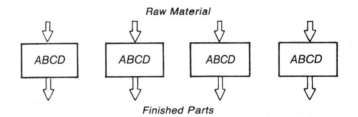

FIGURE 18–2c   Production via two forms of serial FMS layout with integral piecepart transportation system.

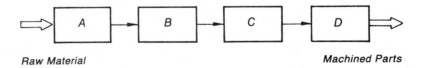

FIGURE 18–2d   Production via parallel FMS layout with integral piecepart transportation system.

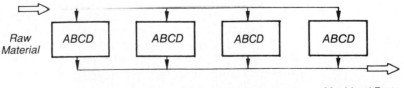

In a serial layout, which utilizes sequentially arranged machines, each component is cycled from machine to machine for processing as it would be in a transfer line *(Fig. 18–2c)*.

FIGURE 18–3   Production via a parallel FMS layout consisting of six CNC machine tools (MT-1 to MT-6 inclusive).

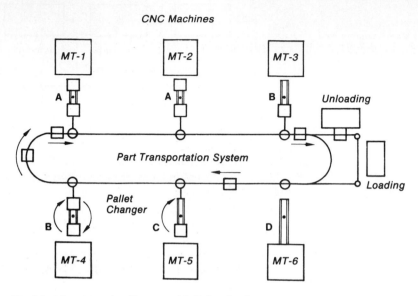

Flexible Manufacturing System with Pallet Coding

The selection of machines which may be used is dictated by the layout. At each station, supplementary machining, which may be dependent on the previous machines and operations, occurs.

In a serial layout, complementary machines are predominantly used. However this complementary interdependence has serious disadvantages, such as:

- The slowest machine or longest operation determines the cycle time, and this results in the faster machines having periodic idle times.
- If a station breaks down, the entire production line stops.
- Substitute programs must be kept on hand. This facilitates the transfer of an operation to another station in the event of a machine breakdown. In order to have this kind of substitute program backup, considerable programming effort must be provided, as must substantial memory capacity.

Because of these disadvantages, modern flexible manufacturing systems usually feature a parallel layout of machines *(Fig. 18–3)* with components being directed, as needed, to any one or more of several machines until machining is complete. Depending on the complexity of the process plan and the workpiece, a parallel machine-tool layout allows for complete machining of a component with one setup on one machine tool or through a sequence of operations on various machine tools. The latter method may be advantageous if high-precision machine tools are a part of the system, as the piecepart may be rough-machined on less accurate machines and finish-machined on the precision machine tools.

•••
18.3   FLEXIBLE MANUFACTURING CELLS

A simpler and less expensive, but much more limited, concept than either the series or parallel FMS arrangement of machine tools, is the flexible manufacturing cell (FMC). There is no precise definition for this term, but it is generally associated with one, or maybe two, CNC stand-alone machines, complemented by ancillaries for unmanned operation for a limited period, and capable of completely machining a very restricted family of components.

FMCs require most of the following features:

- An adequate supply of parts mounted on pallets or single part storage devices for one complete operating shift
- Automatic loading and unloading of each workpiece into the machine tool(s)
- An automatic cutting-tool control system to monitor tool wear and/or fracture, with the ability to call up replacement sister tooling as required
- The ability to monitor and control the dimensions of the machined piecepart in the machine tool via inspection probing, or externally by means of separate measuring equipment, possibly with automatic feedback of correction values to the machine, or ultimately with a stop command in case of unacceptable deviations
- Automatic transportation of finished parts to and from the machine tool
- Automatic stop of the machining operation when the entire supply of parts has been machined (Loading and unloading of pallets is usually carried out manually by the operator.)

The capacity of workpiece storage required in a given cell is mainly dependent on the average machining time per part. About 30 minutes per pallet has proved to be the optimum for palletized operation, and under these circumstances 16 pallets are normally sufficient for an eight-hour machining shift. In the case where workpieces are loaded individually, the minimum machining time per part should be three minutes, that is, approximately 160 parts must be loaded or unloaded per eight-hour shift.

Shorter machining times require bigger pallet and workpiece stores for an operating shift of eight hours, and it is questionable whether such application is then economical.

In order to limit the number of different workholding devices required they should be designed to be multipurpose, that is to be used to machine several different parts. This creates the need for significant program storage capacity in the CNC, or for a DNC system with automatic downloading of programs to the CNC machines.

It is convenient if pallet codes can be changed after machining so that the danger of accidentally reentering a pallet into a machine tool is avoided, and that protection is provided against any false machining operations being carried out in the event that accidental reentry actually occurs.

Turning centers as well as machining centers can be incorporated into flexible machining cells. Machines for cylindrical machining of bulk material as well as those with special chucks, those for shaft turning, and those having power tooling plus ancillary workchanging equipment, cater for a wide range of extended application.

However, in contrast to machining centers, turning centers are not suitable for machining a large variety of parts in random sequence, because the workpieces cannot be so readily coded, and the range of available tooling is more limited (Figs. 18–4a and 18–4b, p. 295).

18.4 FLEXIBLE MANUFACTURING ISLANDS

Until recently a flexible manufacturing island (FMI) was considered to be the next step after an FMC on the road to a full FMS installation. This has now changed and today an FMI is taken to refer to a segregated area of the workshop wherein several CNC machine tools and associated equipment are dedicated to the complete machining of a range of specially selected parts. The main characteristic of the FMI is its isolation from the rest of the general machine shop area, and it is designed and organized specifically for the complete manufacture of a specific family of parts.

The staff assigned to the island organize their own work and its control, and work demarcation is virtually nonexistent. FMIs therefore have a distinct attraction when manufacturing requirements demand the facilities offered by a highly motivated, multiskilled, and flexible staff unit.

18.5 COMPONENT HANDLING

Automatic component materials-handling capability from loading station to the machining stations and back to an unloading station is a necessity in any flexible manufacturing system. Usually, coded pallets are employed to transport each item through the system. Asymmetrical parts are manually bolted onto these pallets to ensure proper location and torquing, while symmetrical parts are stacked in suitable containers that allow automatic materials-handling devices to load and unload the machines as required.

An encoding device on the pallet identifies the component that is clamped to it. By scanning this coding, the control system identifies the component located on the pallet and transmits its location to the overall system controller.

The materials-handling system represents an essential part of the total system from both a technical and an economic point of view. Therefore, appropriate attention must be given to the materials-handling question before a final system selection is made.

FIGURE 18-4a   Flexible manufacturing cell for prismatic parts.

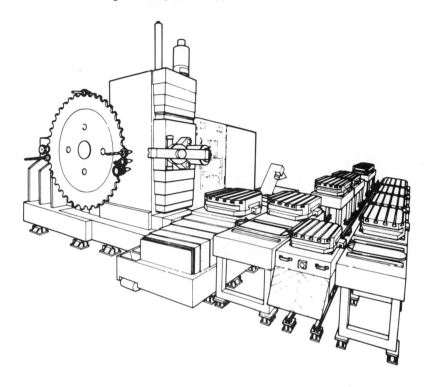

FIGURE 18-4b   Flexible manufacturing cell for turning work.

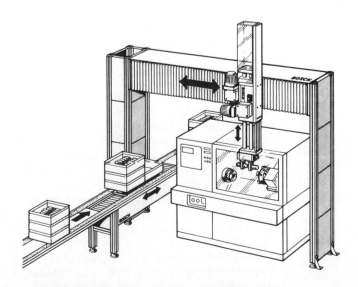

A materials-handling system for asymmetric parts should meet the following functional requirements:

- Efficient, reliable, and flexible handling of components from station to station
- Consideration of safety requirements
- An economical solution to materials-handling needs while satisfying system requirements for simplicity of maintenance, flexibility of control, and adaptability to the various conditions of the machining stations
- Guaranteed machining accuracy for the workpiece mounted on pallets, that is, the pallet guidance or indexing system must not be subject to wear due to continuous transport system
- Capability of providing for buffer stations or loops between and/or in front of the individual machine tools or operations in order to avoid or minimize waiting or nonproductive idle times at the machines
- Simple handling for loading, unloading, cleaning, and inspection at the appropriate stations
- Modular expansion capability
- High serviceability without undue interruption of the workflow

Based on the layout of the machine tools and the design of the control system, organization of the materials-handling system may take one of three forms:

1. A once-through pass (cycle) for machines placed in sequential order
2. A search pass, where the pallet searches for one or several sequentially free machining stations in the prescribed order that corresponds to its encoded requirements—see Section 18.6.1.
3. A target pass, where the control system assigns the pallet to a specific machine tool or work stations in a given sequential order—see Section 18.6.2.

Automatic pallet cycling occurs as follows in parallel layouts:

Parts are manually clamped onto pallets and, with the aid of an encoding device, each pallet is addressed to match the machine tools which are to be approached during that specific run.

The reader heads on the individual machine tools identify the code number and trigger appropriate positioning commands to the materials-handling system. Hence each pallet locates the designated machine.

When leaving the machine tool, the corresponding address is erased from the encoding device on the pallet. This prevents repeated approaches to the same machining station. During transport the encoding device is read by a mechanical, photoelectric, or magnetic reader device. Addressing for the next cycle takes place automatically on leaving the previous work station. Through the utilization of such a materials-handling system, the sequence of operations to be performed can easily be changed to suit the needs of each workpiece.

Various pallet transport methods are available depending on component size and weight. Direct pallet transport is a useful method for smaller units. With this method, the pallet is moved along on a conveyor system made up of individually driven rollers. The individual conveyor sections have their own drives and the movement of pallets is caused, for example, by friction between the conveyor rollers and the pallet. To avoid bottlenecks or collision of pallets it is usual to divide the transport system into single "blocks" similar to the strategy used in railroad networks.

Rotary pallet-changer stations *(see Fig. 12–19)*, located in front of machine tools, at junction points, and at the limits of the transport path make directional changes possible.

One example of a transport system for larger pallets is a four-wheel cart *(Fig. 18–5)*. It is moved along a wire-guided transport-control system built into the floor, different set frequencies of the power supply enable more than one vehicle or track section to be used simultaneously.

Closed loop rail-guided systems are also popular as these may be sited at ground level or above the machine tools if necessary *(Fig. 18–9)*.

FIGURE 18–5   Automatic guided vehicle (AGV) for pallet transportation.

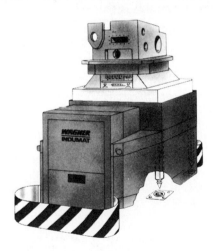

18.6 SYSTEM CONTROL OPTIONS

The performance of individual machine-tool controls is largely dependent on the machine tools to which they are connected and the machining tasks to be performed. All machine tools included in an FMS should have fully expanded numerical controls with as many options as possible, including punch-tape readers. This is not a necessity for automatic operation, but it does make it possible for the system to be manually operated in the event of a malfunction of the central control system, thereby avoiding costly downtime while the control is being repaired. Experience has shown that trunk controls which include the machine control logic as a part of the central host computer are not very effective because they cause the control system to be complicated, difficult to service, and overly dependent on the central computer.

In principle, most types of controls are suited to numerical control. This is true from the simplest point-to-point control with straight cut ability up to complex CNC with continuous path control. CNC controls also offer the ability to safeguard against component damage by means of specialized software modules.

The capability to edit programs at the machine-tool level is not necessary in these systems, especially if the workpieces are processed sequentially on several machines. Program changes should only be made in a central location in order to take into account the effects on all machining stations. This approach also avoids the need to upload corrected programs to the central process computer. However, edited programs should be thoroughly verified before being released into the system.

Two different methods for delivering programs to machining stations are discussed in Sections 18.6.1 and 18.6.2.

18.6.1   PROGRAM CALL-UP THROUGH THE PIECEPART

With this method of program delivery (*Fig. 18–6*), a recycling pallet searches for an empty machine and determines its suitability to perform the needed operation by comparing the barcoding on the pallet with the machine number. In order to avoid waiting time, the program

---

FIGURE 18–6   Program call-up through the piecepart (pallet encoding). Sequence: (1) identification of the pallet number, (2) report to the DNC computer, (3) search for program, (4) identification of program, (5) program to CNC, (6a) pallet to machine, (6b) machine occupied or incorrect, pallet again in search cycle.

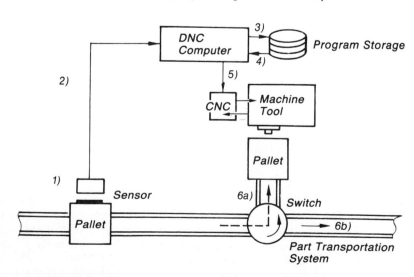

must be delivered to the appropriate machining station during the time it takes for the pallet to enter the machine's working envelope and be secured (a few seconds). The control system for such an FMS needs to be a DNC system in which the process computer takes over the identification-search-preparation-transfer functions. The disadvantage with this method is that no defined workpiece order is possible. Specially required compensations such as feed rate, rpm, or other functions cannot take place at the machine-tool level. Instead, they must be stored centrally and then downloaded to the appropriate machine via the control program.

The process computer controlling this must also assign the machining program to whichever machine tool becomes available, since the selection of machines on this principle is left to chance.

18.6.2   PIECEPART CALL-UP THROUGH THE PROGRAM

This method (*Fig. 18–7*) is a simpler solution to the control problem from a technical point of view. The machining program for a component is downloaded into the memory of the CNC unit at the machine tool. The control reads the code numbers of all pallets as they pass, compares them with the stored program number, and when a match is found guides the pallet to the machine by operating the appropriate switching mechanism. Before the finished part leaves the machine, the pallet address is automatically erased in order to prevent a repeat approach of the same pallet to that machining station. This control method does not incur the disadvantages of program call-up through the part, and so operates with much less data traffic between the cen-

FIGURE 18–7 Component call-up through the program stored in the CNC. Sequence: (1) program to CNC; (2) inquiry of pallet number; (3a) pallet code corresponds to program number, pallet goes to machine; (3b) pallet code does not correspond to program number, so pallet is again in search cycle.

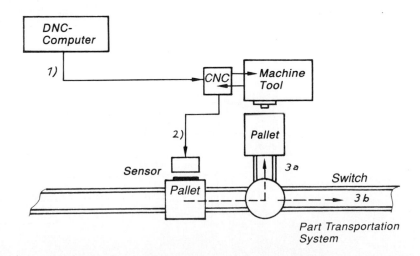

tral computer and control unit. Compensation values pertaining to the machine, tool, or component is directly entered into the CNC unit at the machine tool level, which does unfortunately introduce a degree of inflexibility.

18.7 THE SYSTEM HOST COMPUTER

The use of a computer in an FMS in no way replaces or alters the independent numerical controls of the machine tools. Through the use of BTR (behind the tape-reader) input, machining data may originate not only from punch tapes but can also be directly assigned by the host computer via external data carrier inputs (*Fig. 18–8*). The individual controls, independent and self-sufficient, still permit tape operation under certain circumstances, and this option can prevent a complete shutdown of the installation in the event of a malfunction of the central processing host computer.

FIGURE 18–8 Computer control of a flexible manufacturing system. **DNC computer:** Parts program storage, data transfer to the CNC, operating data collection, pallet-transport monitoring, tool-life monitoring.
FMS computer: Material flow control, pallet conveyor system, workpiece assignment, production priorities, production monitoring, information reporting.

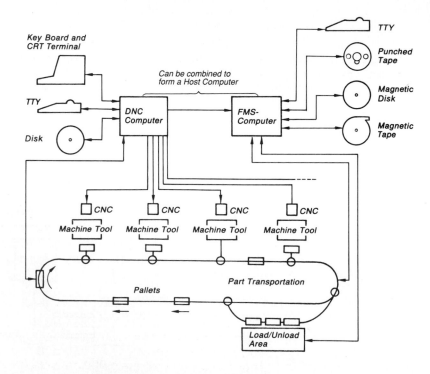

The first responsibility of the host computer in DNC is to provide smooth data transmission, without interruptions, to the individual machine tools. In addition, the computer also offers the capability of monitoring pallet transport through the system, the machining status of each item in the system, the number of pieces completed or in process, and machine utilization. Furthermore, utilization and downtime statistics are automatically compiled, and causes of malfunction are traced. All these statistics can be displayed at any time via interfaced page printers or display screens. Minor program corrections or compensations can be made in the central program memory with the aid of a data terminal and the central process computer, but if extensive changes are necessary, it may be prudent to consider a completely new program.

If individual tool cutting times are being monitored, required tool replacement information can also be made available. This information can be queued to a printer to produce a report including information such as the machine number, tool number, anticipated life span of the tool, its hours in service, and a suggested time for tool change. Because of the large number of tools used in an FMS, automatic tool service life monitoring is almost a necessity.

The amount of memory capacity required for the central process computer is affected by the size of the operational software and the total quantity of control data which must be managed by the computer.

Larger production systems often use a second process computer to control and monitor the entire system. If a machine tool temporarily breaks down, the computer will direct the workpiece to another machine tool and download the necessary replacement program, thereby averting a potential bottleneck.

Constant monitoring and central display of the operating condition indicators is important to the smooth operation of any FMS, and this is an additional task for the central host computer. Typical data of importance to monitoring personnel are:

- Station ready for use or not ready for use
- Pallet released or returning
- Program number or pallet number at each machining station
- Number of parts in circulation

Although the use of a central master computer has obvious advantages, the installation of such a computer is not a necessity in every FMS, and properly designed systems without such host computers do function without significant loss in flexibility or productivity. However, further development of such systems leads to computer-aided manufacturing (CAM) and this requires a central computer to execute the following functional assignments:

Operational Control

- Machine ready for use or machine down
- Proper functioning of coolant and chip removal system—usually via an automatic conveyor belt system
- Proper functioning of the pallet conveyor
- Proper functioning of pallet changer, switching stations, and so on

Production Control

- Number of pallets in circulation
- Required rate of production, parts per day
- Number of unmachined parts on hand
- Number of in-process parts on hand
- Number of parts machined at any given time
- Program numbers of the parts being machined

Management Data

- Tool service life
- Finished/in-process parts log
- Breakdown of downtime and causes
- Malfunction time/downtime/production time per machine
- Required maintenance operations

18.8 SYSTEM-DESIGN PROBLEM AREAS

The range of possible problems associated with the successful implementation of an FMS is far too great to be dealt with adequately in a book of this general nature.

Cutting tool supply is one of the most difficult areas. First and foremost, the design of components should be oriented towards the use of standard tooling to avoid excessively large tool stores being required; a central tool store may help if the number of tools required per system/cell becomes large. With machining operations involving relatively short tool service lives it is essential that a continuous automatic supply of sister tooling be provided, and this task is best controlled by the host manufacturing computer. This is why emergency operation of an FMS via punch-tape readers proves to be rather difficult in such circumstances.

Once a system is designed for operation via host computer control, the job of coordinating the entire system manually is prohibitively complex, even when operating each system component with separate programs. Hence operations cannot normally be transferred from units which have failed to those which are still operational without very great difficulty, even via standby programs. This is not only due to limited program storage capacity but also to the assignment of tooling to different machining processes.

It is usually advisable to build up a full FMS using the approach of progressive cellular extension, especially for small-and medium-sized factories. Thus each installment of capital outlay should already be providing a financial return before the next step is embarked on. However it is a fundamental prerequisite that a basic plan be made at the beginning of the project and adhered to throughout the whole progressive buildup of the complete installation.

18.9 SYSTEM SIMULATION

In the context of FMS systems, simulation is not a physical mockup of the system under consideration, but rather a description of system logic in the form of a mathematical model held in a computer.

It is not, to date, possible to use this mathematical model for system design optimization (there are too many complex variables involved and financial data is not included in the modeling), but it is a means of answering "What if?" type questions, such as "What happens if a machine tool or AGV breaks down?" or, "What happens if we wish to add another machine tool later?". In other words, simulation quantifies alternative operating strategies and conditions and measures the dynamic behavior of the whole system, but it does not identify the best solution.

The choice of the best solution is a management decision based on an evaluation of all available information, much of which can be provided quickly via simulation.

Because of the huge financial investments involved in new FMS installations, it is now regarded as a vital stage in the system design process to employ, and demonstrate at the bidding stage, a graphic simulation of the complete system proposal. Thus from the beginning a customer can experiment and see, with some confidence, how the many variables, complex relationships, random events, and numerous other options affect component cycle times, percentage utilization of the various items comprising the system, and so on.

However it should be remembered that the answers obtainable from a simulation can only be as reliable as the mathematical system modeling employed is realistic.

18.10 SUMMARY

The trend towards a buyer's market results in a demand for products of increasing variety, and it is thus becoming uneconomical to manufacture large batch sizes and to store them for long periods before they are sold. This is one of the main driving forces towards automating the manufacture of smaller batch quantities.

FMSs are capable of fulfilling most of the requirements generally demanded of them, yet there is no optimum design for "the" FMS. For economic reasons, only systems tailored to individual company requirements are likely to be profitably operated. It should be remembered that systems are only as flexible as their constituent parts and associated software allow.

Indeed there is a current trend away from the multimillion-dollar full FMS installation in favor of the much less expensive flexible manufacturing island. For example one can now purchase an FMI comprising two CNC machine tools, a rail-guided vehicle material transport system and a comprehensive host computer system complete with operating software and full tooling, for less than a million dollars.

These islands can then be expanded/combined in various ways at a later date, but only if operating experience suggests that this is economically justified. Thus the overall final investment required can be distributed over several years. Furthermore, gradually increasing operating experience builds up confidence and makes it easier to assess profitability in relation to the rapidly changing markets of today.

The application of FMSs requires a thorough analysis of the total manufacturing requirement, taking fully into account likely company growth profile and future market trends. To assist in these analyses universities and certain software houses have developed simulation packages which help to check and study the impacts of the various pertinent parameters—see Section 18.9.

As long as the selection and arrangement of the machine tools required is clear-cut, it is only the software of the control system that is most likely to cause problems in the detailed operations planning and subsequent commissioning. Operating control systems that are too novel tend to require too much computer assistance, and often prove to be unsuitable for a production environment, due to a great extent to the lack of existing software and the great expense of generating it—costs as high as $200 per hr. are not unknown! It is therefore advisable to check whether any existing software packages are suitable or readily adaptable, and to compare their costs with special software, prior to concluding contracts for a final system design. Only on the basis of such comparisons can decisions with regard to maximum flexibility and minimum costs be confidently taken.

18.11 TYPICAL EXAMPLES OF FMI AND FMS INSTALLATIONS

FIGURE 18–9 Flexible manufacturing island (FMI) comprising three turning centers and a rail-guided pallet-conveyor system.

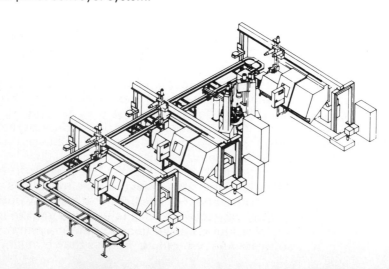

FIGURE 18-10   Flexible manufacturing system (FMS) comprising four machining centers, an AGV transport system, and a manual load/unload station.

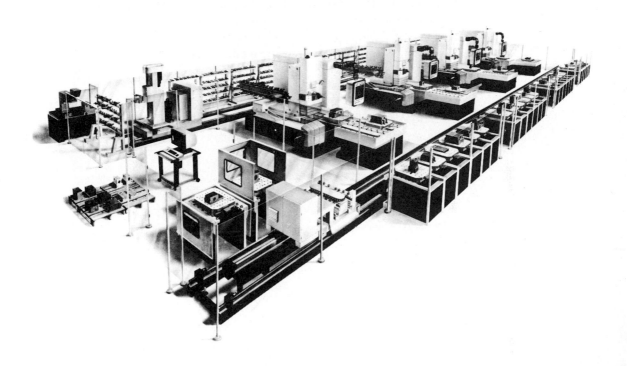

QUESTIONS FOR CHAPTER 18

1. Define the term flexible manufacturing system. What special characteristics make it different from a flexible manufacturing cell or island?
2. List at least six attributes necessary for an FMS to be operated economically.
3. Explain the difference between serial and parallel FMS operations. Use simple sketches to illustrate your answer.
4. What are the principal differences in the criteria for judging the successful operation of stand-alone and grouped CNC machine tools?
5. Describe ways in which the movement of component material may be achieved within a typical FMS installation. How is it likely to differ in FMCs and FMIs?

6. Why are rail-guided vehicle transport systems now finding more favor than AGVs?

7. What is a pallet and why are pallets so necessary in FMSs?

8. Describe in detail the two system call-up options used in FMSs. What are the main advantages and disadvantages of each?

9. What is a system host computer and what are its prime functions?

10. Why is it not always wise to follow the host computer method of system control? What are the alternatives?

11. What are the most common system-design problems encountered when making FMS proposals?

12. Why is system simulation so important? What can it not tell you, and why? What is its most severe limitation?

13. Is a typical FMS really flexible and, if so, from where does its flexibility basically emanate?

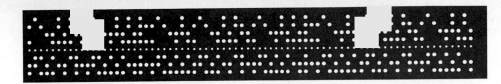

CHAPTER 19

COMPUTER-INTEGRATED MANUFACTURING (CIM)

After studying this chapter you should understand:

1. Why CIM is only a philosophy in the foreseeable future.
2. That there are various stages of CIM.
3. The current situation regarding communication protocols.
4. How to approach the introduction of CIM in the workplace.

The logical progression, after linking a plant's CNC machines together to form a flexible manufacturing setup, is to then link it up with as many of the other company functions as possible. Computer-aided design (CAD) is usually the first candidate, followed by other activities involved in order execution, from receipt through dispatch. Development in this direction is currently hampered due to the lack of internationally agreed-on computer formats and protocols, thus making intercommunication between different computer systems within a given installation difficult or even impossible.

19.1 WHAT IS CIM?

The linking of all of a company's operating and control data into a totally interactive system is clearly the ultimate goal in computer-integrated manufacturing (CIM).

Every engineer in the NC field has his or her own ideas and definition of CIM, but it should be stressed that integration is not limited to the successful interconnection of various computer-assisted/controlled functions—it also entails achieving information flow within a system in a rapid, universally comprehensible, and multidirectional manner.

The integration of the design, production engineering, production control, and manufacturing functions is a good basis on which to build a complete CIM system. Ultimately, however, such areas of company organization as sales and marketing, financial control, administration, and maintenance must all be incorporated within the overall computer-assisted control facility in order to manage the company's business most effectively.

19.2 CIM—ILLUSION OR REALITY?

All the technology necessary to install complete CIM systems is both understood and broadly available. However, we are still in the early developmental stages of large-scale integrated communications network systems, and the manufacturing industry is only now beginning to have fully operational FMSs in any significant numbers—and in many cases these have been created from combining two or more success-proven flexible manufacturing cells.

CAD and CAM, while both proven and being adopted in ever increasing numbers—this is especially true of CAM—have still not become totally integrated via full, unaided, computer-based component operations planning that goes directly from the digitally stored CAD drawings through to NC machine-tool control-tape generation. There are a few exceptions to this but they are confined to very special systems installed to provide a limited range of products. Certainly CIM is no illusionary pipe dream, but as yet it is only a philosophy and it will not be fully attained until the following conditions are met:

- The manufacturing industry must pass through the CAD/CAM learning curve, thus gaining confidence and beginning to reap the commercial benefits.
- Current electronic interfacing problems associated with differing computer formats and protocols must be resolved with the development of internationally agreed-on standards—see Section 19.5.2.
- Proven software packages that cover some of the function areas which, so far, have attracted little attention from software houses, must become readily available.
- In-house programming confidence and capacity must increase.
- Greater computing and data storage capacity per unit cost must become a reality.

But the potential benefits of CIM as outlined below are so attractive that its attainment at a commercially viable cost is eventually inevitable.

19.3 POTENTIAL BENEFITS OF CIM

The potential benefits to a manufacturing plant of installing FMS have already been discussed in Chapter 18. Clearly, by introducing more and more of the company's other operating functions into the host computer's overall control program, the more realistic and comprehensive will the outputs from that computer become. Indeed, if all activities are accurately programmed to simulate the true situation in each area, then computer outputs should similarly approximate very closely to actuality. With such closeness to the real life situation the company directorate is provided with a most powerful managerial tool, outputting rapidly the effects of any chosen course of action upon all other aspects of the business. Changing customer needs may even be predictable at an early stage and hence an opportunity is provided to possibly gain a useful advantage over one's competitors.

With host computer software being as complete and realistic a mirror image representation of the total business organization's operating structure as possible, it becomes feasible to precisely optimize the overall functioning of the entire business enterprise. With rapid interactive data available to all levels of management, one can immediately respond to any new operating situation, anticipated or otherwise, in the most efficient manner and in the confident knowledge that all factors influenced by any given decision have been considered.

It needs little imagination, when comparing such a powerful, computer-based management modus operandi with the more usual "paper and people" based system of operation (still very much the norm in most of the manufacturing industry), to realize just what a quantum leap CIM in its fullest sense will be. However one should always be aware that every function area influences directly or indirectly a company's overall operating efficiency, and accordingly the maximum benefits of CIM can only be achieved if the maximum number of function areas are taken account of within the computer-assisted management system package. Unfortunately this may prove prohibitively expensive for many companies to achieve in the foreseeable future.

19.4 DATA COMMUNICATION AND COMPREHENSION

The difference between communication ability and comprehension should be clearly appreciated, for example, communication across international boundaries is rarely a difficulty but comprehension cannot be automatically assumed!

Communication, in the context of NC machine tools, would be typified by the transmission of NC data to the machine tool from the controlling computer and/or feedback of status data from the machine tool back to the computer. However without "sympathetic comprehension" between the two units, clearly the feedback status from the machine tool would be negative to say the least, and the computer would not even know! While this is perhaps an oversimplified example, it should be understood that communication with full comprehension and total data conversational interchange ability is a prerequisite for all forms of computer-interfaced equipment.

Unfortunately to date no universal standardization of computer formats and protocols exists, and those companies that have traveled the greatest distance down the CIM road have done so by either developing their own interfacing to permit comprehension between existing equipment, or they have done so with the help of equipment suppliers and associated software houses that were anxious to in be the vanguard of CIM development.

19.5 CIM DATA COMMUNICATION

19.5.1 CURRENT SITUATION

Provided a company acquires items of NC equipment and associated controllers from the same manufacturer, it is unlikely to experience too many problems in data interchange and comprehension between the individual units and the control computer. However, any departure from that supplier in favor of alternative vendors for additional equipment will invariably cause data protocol problems between the different suppliers' products. But as long as individual islands of automation suffice, there are few data interchange difficulties within any given island.

If CIM is to achieve its fullest potential, clearly these islands, at the very least, must be able to communicate comprehensibly with one another. Preferably, however, any piece of NC equipment and the associated computers involved should also be able to communicate intelligibly and with complete freedom, with full open intercommunication to the host computer taking place only when necessary.

However it has previously been stated in Section 19.4 that, due to the present lack of compliance to protocol communication standards even at the national level, cross-communication between different suppliers' equipment is rarely easy to accomplish, and it frequently proves to be prohibitively expensive. Even upgrading using the same vendor can prove troublesome.

19.5.2 ESTABLISHMENT OF INTERNATIONAL PROTOCOL STANDARDS

In the United States, General Motors first tackled the problem of equipment communication compatibility by setting up a working group in 1980 to develop and define specification details for a universal protocol to which all future NC equipment to be supplied to them should conform. This project, known as MAP (Manufacturing Automation Protocol), was so successful that GM's proposed standards have now been adopted by the ANBS (American National Bureau of Standards), and in 1985 an operating system, based on MAP, was exhibited.

Like the United States, European engineers have also initiated a program to establish common data communication protocols. This project is committed to ensuring that European proposals are fully compatible with the MAP/ANBS specifications, and its work is intended to complement, not duplicate, the MAP program.

New ISO standards are emerging, but it will be some time before true universal flexibility in selecting automation equipment, without the risk of intercommunicative comprehension problems, becomes a reality—and with it the benefits of CIM are made readily available.

19.5.3 LAN TECHNOLOGY

Even with equipment that conforms to a common communications protocol standard and is hence capable of being fully interlinked, how this interconnection is to be carried out, even at the DNC/shop-floor level, should be the subject of much deliberation. One option could be, for example, via serial lines (*Fig. 19–1, p. 312*), with each item of NC equipment being individually linked to the DNC control room computing and coordinating processor facilities.

An alternative, however, could be linkage to the DNC control via a local area network (LAN) (*Fig. 19–2. p. 313*)—a principle not unlike that used for domestic electrical supply distribution. The advantages of a LAN in terms of flexibility, simplified connecting hardware, and peer communication facility other than via the DNC every time, are obvious when comparing these two linking systems.

Unfortunately LAN technology is considerably more complex than would appear from Fig. 19–2, *p. 313*. For example, one may select from either bus or ring formats, employ fiber optics or coaxial cabling, operate on a collision detect or token passing access system, and so on. All such decisions have the potential of making an installation easy to install, maintain, and modify, or conversely they may be a root cause of endless difficulties.

19.6 HOW TO APPROACH CIM

To answer the question of whether a particular plant should consider CIM clearly requires detailed knowledge of the company concerned, and particularly its experience and involvement in NC to date. If such experience is nonexistent, for reasons of protocol standardization alone one can only recommend a company-phased development plan which provides initially for a somewhat less sophisticated entry into the world of numerical control technology. By the time that confidence has been built up, the present rapidly developing CIM scene will, hopefully, be both standardized worldwide, and systems will be on offer that are sufficiently flexible to be readily adaptable to most companies' special requirements, even if they never prove to be quite as all embracing as one would wish.

FIGURE 19–1 Serial line networking.

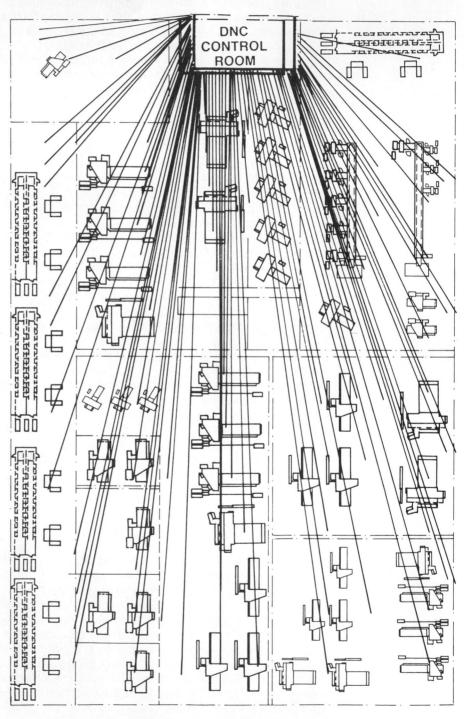

FIGURE 19–2   LAN linking.

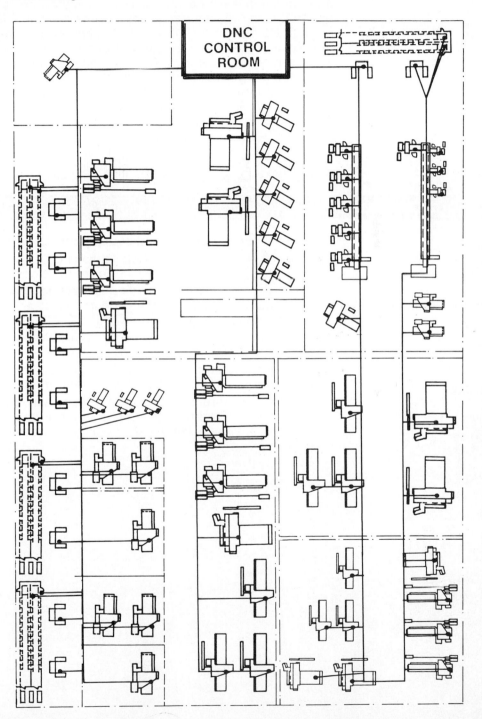

For those companies already well versed in NC equipment, the recommendation must be cautious but steady progress towards a full CIM operation but only insofar as it is commercially justifiable.

Any attempt to rush into full CIM, however experienced a company may be in NC technology, instead of proceeding via a more moderate approach, will surely result in computer induced misery rather than computer integrated manufacturing!

It is a popular view that the optimum batch size for FMS is one, and although this is not necessarily always true, the smaller the average batch size becomes, the greater are the attractions of CIM control of the complete business enterprise.

QUESTIONS FOR CHAPTER 19

1. Define what you understand by the term "CIM."
2. Why is it that CIM in its fullest sense is unlikely to be only commercially attractive to a very few large corporations?
3. What is the difference between connecting CNC machines via LAN and serial line methods of linking and what are the advantages and disadvantages of each method?
4. Discuss the potential benefits of a total CIM system from the standpoint of overall company management.
5. What is the greatest problem area facing potential CIM installers? What is being done to help alleviate this situation?
6. The board of directors of your company asked you to carry out an appraisal of whether CIM should be introduced, write a brief summary of the main factors that would constitute the basis of your study.

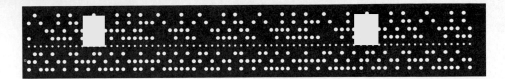

CHAPTER 20

PERSONNEL AND TRAINING REQUIREMENTS

After studying this chapter you should understand:

1. The importance of keeping staff informed at all levels.
2. That adequate planning and preparatory training are vital.
3. The need to train maintenance personnel in the new technology at an early stage, and to update their training regularly.
4. The significance of total teamwork.

To ignore the needs and expectations of one's employees when introducing new technology is extremely foolish. Keeping staff fully informed and gaining their enthusiastic support and cooperation are equally as important as adequate preparatory practical training, if a new CNC installation is to be commercially successful.

20.1 KEEPING STAFF INFORMED

A smooth transition from conventional machine-tool manufacturing to NC production requires extensive staff preparation and training. One should bear in mind that management will have been discussing and concerning themselves with the possible problems of transition to numerically controlled machine tools for some time. Thus the remaining staff due to be affected by extensive operational changes must therefore be systematically familiarized with the new conditions that are scheduled to be introduced. It is vital to make it clear that the effect of the introduction of numerically controlled machines will not be to leave qualified personnel unemployed. On the contrary, the more complex the facility, the more familiar the staff must become with its capabilities and technology in order to make the most efficient use of the advantages presented. Only then can the higher productivity and profitability associated with NC machines be achieved, and this cannot occur without full utilization of the wealth of experience which each member of the staff has acquired through many years of working with conventional machine tools.

It is unwise to shroud the considerations involved in deciding on whether or not to purchase NC machine tools in a cloak of secrecy. Indeed the greatest difficulties and obstacles will always arise if the willingness to cooperate is undermined by false rumors and half-truths about automation and resulting wholesale job losses. Enthusiasm for the new technology should be fostered via provision of detailed technical information in the form of pamphlets, films, illustrative material, and lectures. It should be made clear that in most instances nobody is likely to lose their present job. However, if this should prove inevitable in individual cases, equivalent employment possibilities will be offered. Staff should also realize that their status will be enhanced by the new operations because they will acquire new skills, and their abilities will thus be expanded and developed. Furthermore, the competitive edge of the firm's operations will be improved and this should mean greater job security, not less.

Even if the lead-times quoted by machine-tool suppliers seem infinitely long, experience indicates that it will always be too short for adequate preparation. Therefore one must start as early as possible to orient staff to the changing conditions. Even if employees are generally well organized, it is not sufficient for a few people to have heard and read "one or two things" about NC machines, there being no substitute for detailed and soundly based knowledge to ensure a smooth transition. Organizational plans and schedules have to be prepared, fields of activity and responsibility must be determined, and reclassification of staff must also be carried out.

Getting organized early means having sufficient time for providing information and training. It should be remembered that the learning process takes longer if the people affected have performed mainly manual and repetitive activities for many years. Even the ability to learn must be relearned!

At a very early stage the following positions and departments should be filled by suitable people, with the first appointment being that of the overall project coordinator.

20.2 OVERALL PROJECT COORDINATOR

The person occupying this vital position must be versatile, judicious, well acquainted with the capabilities of the organization, and, preferably, should have risen through the ranks. This person should be appointed as soon as possible and be involved in all aspects from the start. He or she must not only have the required skills, but should also supply the necessary authority at all times. Only in this way will the person be able to effectively coordinate all the participating areas of the company, and be able to make independent decisions and act responsibly in all situations.

The specialized technical knowledge required can be obtained in various ways if it does not already exist. For example, machine-tool manufacturers, control equipment companies, and various formal educational institutions offer informative material and programs, technical seminars, and courses.

Software requirements should be discussed jointly with the computer, machine-tool, and NC suppliers, and areas of specific contractual responsibility must be clearly defined and agreed to by all parties at an early stage.

20.3 PRODUCTION PLANNING

The number of employees placed in this area depends entirely on the scope and size of the installation and the complexity of the planned NC production. These employees must, of course, be provided with thorough and detailed training. A major difference when comparing NC with conventional machining is that of the much higher machining speeds involved, which results in greatly increased output and correspondingly increased material requirements. The hourly machine rate of an NC machine is understandably higher than that of conventional installations, so machine-tool idle times resulting from planning errors have a proportionally more significant effect on costs.

One advantage offered by the NC machine tool is that any fixtures required for parts machining can be manufactured on the NC machine tool itself.

Simple, fast program and tape production leads to short preparation times, and as soon as planning has determined the possible production capacity of the NC installation, workloads can be quickly balanced and optimized.

20.4 PROGRAMMING

This is probably the only completely new function to arise from the acquisition of NC machine tools and related technology. Existing members of the staff should also be used in this area if at all possible. Basic qualifications required are:

- A sound knowledge of machine tools and the various machining operations
- A knowledge of mathematics specifically in the areas of geometry and trigonometry
- A basic understanding of computer systems and their functions, and detailed knowledge of any in-house computer(s)

- A comprehensive knowledge of tape preparation and editing procedures
- A detailed knowledge of computer programs and, in particular, the proposed programming language. (Courses should be made available for this.)

In order to have tapes available to begin production immediately after installation and startup of the NC facility, early appointment and training of programmers is essential, and any delays will adversely affect the profitability of the new installation.

FIGURE 20–1 Fortunately, the player piano has never replaced the concert pianist and CAM technology will never replace the creative professional.

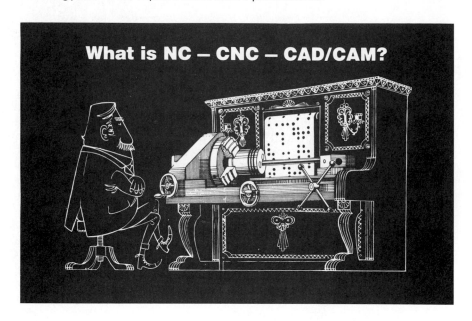

20.5 MAINTENANCE

In the event of problems, service is, in most instances, available free from the NC equipment supplier for the first year. Nevertheless, the electronic complexity of the equipment involved requires the employment of highly skilled technicians for even routine maintenance, and, if at all possible, they should already have some experience in industrial electronics. Every opportunity should be taken to increase and safeguard the level of knowledge of these and all other maintenance technicians, as this is the most inexpensive way to secure troublefree NC operation. Also imperative is a well-stocked replacement parts supply. Plug-in electronic subassemblies have been developed for quick replacement, repairs taking place later when the machine is back in operation. If one has a comprehensive supply of replacement parts, the

FIGURE 20–2   This universal drilling, boring, grinding, milling, tapping "supermachine" is still under development.

education of electronic, hydraulic, and mechanical maintenance staff can be devoted exclusively to intensive diagnostic training aimed at rapid fault recognition, isolation, and rectification. This important topic is dealt with in more detail in Section 21.6.

20.6 MACHINE OPERATORS

A skilled operator is the best backup insurance, even if the NC system itself recognizes malfunctions and avoids the creation of rejects by suitable responses. The people entrusted with the new equipment must keep a watchful eye on tool/workpiece interface, have a good memory for the program sequence, possess a sixth sense for possible error conditions, and, last but not least, have a desire for responsibility and a constant willingness to learn as much as possible about the new technology. The operator's continued education will normally take place via the machine-tool manufacturer.

The preceding important divisions of activity, recommended when installing new NC machine tools and associated equipment, have been adopted successfully by many users. However, if the size of the firm does not justify this type of investment in personnel, one might consider employing the services of, say, a subcontract programming office to assist for an initial period. Certain disadvantages in this approach do exist, such as geographical inconvenience and resultant time delays, but they can be more than offset by benefiting from the extensive experience of such specialists. Also modern controls offer the possibility of correcting faulty programs, produced from whatever source, at the machine tool and producing new, corrected tapes immediately.

Service contracts are usually available from most NC manufacturers. This may save on staffing, but in the event of malfunction, nonproductive periods can increase due to the immediate nonavailability of a service technician. If the technical level of one's own electronics technicians is not sufficiently high to isolate and resolve problems as they arise, they should be encouraged to work closely with the supplier's service technicians, especially during the first year's warranty period. This is, by far, the best and least expensive form of training.

20.7 TOTAL TEAMWORK

Without a doubt, the introduction and application of NC technology requires teamwork and demands the full cooperation of everyone from the most senior manager to the machine-tool operator if the installation is to operate in the most efficient manner possible.

QUESTIONS FOR CHAPTER 20

1. Prepare an agenda for a first meeting with union leaders at which you are to announce the company's decision to introduce CNC technology. What typical questions do you expect to be asked?
2. What attributes would you look for in selecting a new NC project coordinator?
3. Discuss ways of overcoming programming bottlenecks during the early stages of operating a new NC shop.
4. What should be the main thrust of training programs for maintenance personnel responsible for keeping an NC installation operating 24 hours a day?
5. Is it better to retrain conventional machine-tool operators to work CNC machines, or to train new staff from scratch?

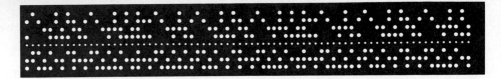

CHAPTER 21

PREVENTIVE MAINTENANCE AND SERVICING OF NC MACHINE TOOLS

After studying this chapter you should understand:

1. The special importance of efficient preventive maintenance when using NC equipment.
2. The most effective ways of minimizing machine downtime.
3. The fundamentals of selecting and training NC maintenance technicians.
4. The importance of negotiating the right maintenance and service contracts.

NC machine tools are technically complex systems and therefore can be sensitive and unreliable if inadequate care and attention is paid to preventive maintenance. It is essential that those working with such machine tools give attention to this aspect if expensive breakdowns are to be avoided.

21.1 THE NEED FOR MAINTENANCE

Developments in electronics and machine-tool design have made it possible to build economical and reliable NC machine tools. With the increasing cost of skilled labor and keener international competition, the NC machine, with its high degree of efficiency and accuracy and high tool utilization, now makes a valuable contribution towards more economical production. This is true in spite of its higher investment cost and technical complexity. However, the trend towards greater NC production can only be encouraged and justified if the NC equipment can be serviced in such a way that downtime is minimized.

The increasing application of NC is focusing the attention of management to in-house maintenance and repair. Unfortunately in some production shops, certain machines represent a production bottleneck, due to persistent downtime. This has a direct negative influence on productivity and, as a result, the bottom line profitability of the firm, but the problem could be avoided through adequate preventive maintenance, quick diagnosis, and elimination of malfunctions by a properly trained maintenance department. Many firms, however, still operate without scheduled preventive maintenance and seem to prefer to concentrate on eliminating malfunctions as they occur. They recognize either too late or not at all that this approach encourages a continuous source of nonproductive downtime.

21.2 PREVENTIVE MEASURES

Earlier NC systems suffered from development and reliability problems. This frequently caused users, especially those with limited self-help capabilities, to lose confidence in this type of equipment, but the reliability of modern controls has increased greatly since the initial development of NC systems. However, NC has also become more complex, which has made it imperative for every shop to have well-trained maintenance technicians to keep downtime to a minimum. Furthermore system builders have countered this increasing complexity by offering diagnostic aids and simplified serviceability to an extent that was previously unknown.

It is unrealistic to expect the often cited "reliability of space-age electronics" at a price which the manufacturing industry is normally willing to pay. However, some internationally competitive machine builders have started a trend towards providing this reliability at reasonable prices.

Irrespective of the level of reliability available, the users of these systems must nevertheless take the initiative to include preventive maintenance and servicing of their NC machines in their operational planning.

The first rule for preventive maintenance of numerical controls is to follow the recommendations of the manufacturer as precisely as possible. Most controls are sensitive to poor environmental conditions such as heat, dampness, vibration, and voltage fluctuations. Some of the limits on environmental conditions that are normally recommended by NC machine tool manufacturers are:

- Ambient temperatures between 50–122° Fahrenheit (10–50° Celsius)
- Relative humidity under 95 percent
- Vibrations under 0.5 g
- Voltage fluctuations no greater than ± 10 percent

Adherence to these limits greatly reduces environmentally caused downtime, but in cases where difficult ambient conditions exist and cannot easily be changed, preventive measures must be found and carried out in agreement with the manufacturer.

Adverse conditions exist in environments such as tropical climates, and in buildings with high air pollution levels from cutting oil, water, organic liquids, dust, and so on. Special seals to prevent penetration by these damaging materials, air conditioners, installation of NC units in protected areas, and other countermeasures all help to reduce downtime in these types of hostile environments.

Brief power failure or momentary power surges often lead to inexplicably faulty operation of numerical controls, but a standby power supply can help to alleviate this problem. Large NC users also use isolated power sources to which their electronic systems and devices can be connected. In this way, electrical interference from induction instruments, thyristor amplifiers, or welding equipment is reduced or eliminated. Such basic considerations should be included during the planning phase.

Large NC users with capable in-house maintenance personnel often specify extensive alterations to machines to satisfy their own specific needs. In this case consideration must be given to machine warranty, maintenance service, and replacement parts, as it can become very expensive for the purchaser to rely exclusively on service from the manufacturer. The manufacturer certainly has the service personnel with the required understanding of the equipment, but this service is not always available when needed. As a result, several hours or days of production might be lost due to minor errors which could have been discovered and eliminated by in-house repair personnel. Maintenance contracts do not protect against this type of avoidable downtime, even though they are being signed in increasing numbers. As is often the case, teamwork between user and manufacturer is often more satisfactory than any contract.

Some of the guidelines recommended by knowledgeable and experienced NC practitioners are:

- Use similar systems as much as possible. This facilitates familiarization on the part of personnel and recognition of possible weak areas.
- The selection of criteria for an NC should be more in the direction of "tried and true" rather than "modern and futuristic." Although these criteria may seem conservative, better productivity will result in the long run.
- Pay special attention to service and diagnostic aids offered by the manufacturer and include them in future planning.
- Organize courses to train programming, operating, and maintenance personnel at an early stage in the implementation process.
- Obtain a full range of documentation from the manufacturer and have it thoroughly examined by your own personnel.
- Have an organized method of storing and updating documentation for making it readily available to repair personnel.

21.3 REPLACEMENT PARTS INVENTORY

Most NC manufacturers have lists recommending the most frequently needed replacement parts. Parts less frequently needed are normally available from the manufacturer within 24 to 48 hours.

In Japan, potential NC users are already purchasing complete reserve controls from which parts can simply be taken as needed. This process simplifies and accelerates repair from many points of view:

- Any required part is always available.
- The hardware costs for a complete control are less than for replacement parts.
- Downtime is kept to a minimum.
- In the event of significant malfunctions, damage, or total breakdown of the control, the complete controller can be exchanged.
- The standby control is available for testing purposes and for comparative research.
- The control can be used to train operating and maintenance personnel.

Considering the potentially enormous cost of NC machine breakdown, the Japanese idea appears to be a good one. The following prerequisites do apply, however:

- The price for the spare controller(s) is justifiable.
- The user has several similar NCs in use.
- The NC manufacturer will sell the reserve NC at a lower price since no software costs are involved.
- Qualified personnel are available.

The Japanese example seems to have set a trend because several large NC users in Germany, the UK, and the United States have now adopted this approach.

21.4 THE LEVEL OF MAINTENANCE OPERATIONS

Figure 21–1 shows an analysis of the requirements for maintenance, broken down into two main areas:

- Planned and preventive maintenance
- Repair of breakdowns

The size of the firm usually has a great impact on its ability to maintain and repair modern NC equipment. Larger firms are more likely to have an adequate number of skilled, trained, and experienced repair personnel than smaller firms. As smaller companies have to accept a lower level of repair capability, preventive maintenance is even more important to them. Obviously, the degree of repair capability by in-house personnel is also dependent on the number, complexity, and

FIGURE 21–1   Basic concept of maintenance.

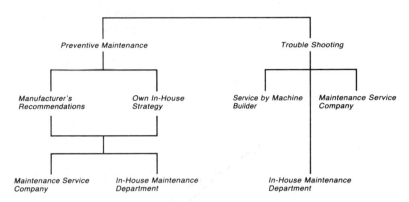

variety of machines installed. The experience of large NC users in the United States has shown that one technician is able to master approximately four different hard-wired NC systems but only two different CNC systems. Although theoretically all NCs are very similar, there are enormous differences in technical documentation, drawings, troubleshooting manuals, diagnostic aids, measuring points, and so on.

Furthermore, familiarity with a specific controller plays an important role in the speed of error diagnosis and elimination.

The first level of preventive maintenance, and a vital one, is routine maintenance of the machine. This includes checking oil levels and hydraulic and pneumatic pressures, and inspecting and changing air filters.

There are many ways of drawing up a simple but effective controller preventive maintenance program, and such routine inspections should lie within the capabilities of most users. The required instructions and guidelines for such programs are obtainable from the equipment manufacturer or may be worked out by the user with the help of the manufacturer's personnel during the installation period. A checklist with the daily, weekly, monthly, and yearly operations to be carried out should also be prepared along the lines of that proposed in Section 21.9.

Typical guidelines are:

- If the power supply for the electronics does not always deliver a perfectly stable voltage, voltage fluctuations, electrical noise, or brief power failure can occur. Excessive voltages can cause damage, especially to ICs and other electronic components. Low voltage and interference voltages are often the cause of malfunctions which appear intermittently and are hard to locate. Therefore, the power supply should be checked every three to six months and compared with the manufacturer's specifications. Ripple voltage or bad connections can then often be identified before they cause major breakdowns.
- The so-called "clock oscillator" and other frequency generators which control feed rate and system frequencies can drift with

time. This can result in irregular machine movements or measurement deviations caused by sinusoidal changes in the resolver or inductosyn measuring voltages. Therefore, frequency regulation testing should also take place every six to twelve months.

- Faulty feedback signals are often a cause of positioning errors. First, the tachometer voltage should be checked for uniformity and absolute value. If the brushes are uneven or if the slip ring is dirty, strong voltage interference can result, and this "noise" is amplified even more by the control loop which, in turn, can cause rough machine feeding, hard stops, or triggering of safety devices.

  It is therefore recommended that brushless tachometers be used on the original installation or as replacement parts. Defective optical encoders can also produce similar malfunctions and their power supplies should be checked every three to six months for proper voltage levels.

- The servoamplifier is balanced for drift, amplification, and machine dynamics at the time of installation. This balancing procedure should be repeated every three months in order to determine whether its ratio has changed in any of the axes. Drift can change data position and path precision, leading to overshoot and damage to drive components.

- A quarterly function check of the overtravel limit switches and emergency stop switch is vital. These switches and cams should be checked for correct actuation and proper, secure mounting. Malfunctioning of such a limit switch can lead to expensive machine damage but can be avoided by performing a simple preventive maintenance check.

- One of the most frequent causes of failure can be avoided by routinely checking the data input devices on the NC. This should include cleaning, lubricating, and adjusting any tape readers and spoolers. Indicator lamps should also be checked to ensure that they light promptly to indicate danger and/or functional status to the operator.

- Documentation is another important area. All malfunctions and maintenance operations should be accurately recorded in a maintenance log located at every NC. Recurring serious areas of malfunction can then be quickly noted. Such a log also provides a valuable maintenance history.

If all of the above maintenance measures are carried out regularly, the mean-time-between-failure (MTBF) will be significantly lengthened.

21.5 FUNDAMENTALS OF NC MAINTENANCE

Technical maintenance familiarity with numerical controls requires a basic knowledge of analog and digital technology. The digital knowledge would cover the tape reader, switches, and all logic circuits in which the data are processed. This takes place via five basic types of logic element: AND, OR, NOR, NAND, and EXCLUSIVE OR.

Their output signal assumes the value 1 if all input signals are in the proper position. Additionally, there are the memories, also referred to as "flip-flops," which can store a 1 or 0 signal until it is erased or changed to the alternative value.

Through the combination of these memory and logic elements, the more complex circuits such as counters, storage registers, adders, and comparators are formed. There are also complex computer functions such as those used for path compensations. Digital encoders provide the axial position feedback signals for closed loop servocontrol.

The portion of numerical controls using analog technology consists of the error signal which the digital portion of the NC produces by comparing target and real position values. The error value then controls the axial drive amplifier which may have been designed as a hydraulic servovalve, a thyristor amplifier, or a transistor SCR amplifier. A tachometer provides actual voltage feedback for the analog speed control loop, and resolvers or inductosyn scales provide actual axial position feedback values for the analog closed loop position control. Analog feedback devices are often preferred by the machine tool users for reliability and parts compatibility.

The NC maintenance specialist must also be familiar with transistors and ICs.

With CNCs, a fundamental understanding of computer technology, including software and data storage, is necessary. Mini- and microcomputer CNCs offer good diagnostic routines which are either built in (resident) or implemented on a temporary basis as needed. These routines vary from simple error alarms to logic analysis, program testing, and external testing of modules.

Continuous or blinking signal lamps indicate the most important emergency conditions such as servo failures, voltage fluctuations, parity check errors, low battery alarms, and excessive temperatures. More extensive, specialized diagnostic software is available when standard diagnosis is not sufficient to identify the cause of a malfunction. It is also essential that the in-house service technician be familiar with this software.

Clearly the NC maintenance technician must possess knowledge and experience in a number of areas. The following qualifications are essential:

- A knowledge of electronics—both theory and practice
- Two or more years of practical experience with NC
- A knowledge of digital technology
- Experience in working with electronic measuring and test equipment
- A desire to enhance current knowledge through continuous training
- A knowledge of basic minicomputer/microcomputer fundamentals

Since without these advantages, maintenance technicians may quickly become discouraged, they should be supported in their efforts to gain increased knowledge. NC manufacturers offer training courses which explain the functional components of NC systems as well as some simple measures which may be used for fault diagnosis. But before taking these courses basic knowledge and experience should be acquired through practical experience with the equipment.

21.6 SELECTION OF MAINTENANCE PERSONNEL

This is perhaps the most difficult task and should be approached by first making decisions regarding the following issues:

- What level of repair should be carried out by in-house personnel?
- What is the total scope of maintenance operations which should be carried out?
- Who is responsible for repairs?

Additionally, the following questions must be answered:

- What training and qualifications should the repair technician have?
- What additional training is necessary?

Experience suggests that a theoretical or academic education in itself is not a basic prerequisite; it is rather an indication of a possible aptitude. A good candidate for the complex function of NC maintenance would be a skilled worker or technician with a strong desire to expand his experience and knowledge, combined with the ability to approach and solve problems in an orderly and logical fashion.

The main steps in solving NC problems are a systematic search for malfunctions, followed by their logical identification and evaluation. The technician must also have the ability to make diagnoses based on symptoms described to him by operating personnel.

If there are only a small number of NC machines in a shop or the selection of potential maintenance technicians is limited, the simplest answer may be to select a suitable electrician for further training in maintenance functions. The electrician, due to his familiarity in dealing with abstract quantities, is more likely to establish a source of error by logical thought rather than to seek it visually.

21.7 TRAINING

If a company has decided to handle its own maintenance and servicing of NC machines, and has appointed personnel responsible for these functions, it must provide these people with the necessary training. The technical knowledge which most of today's technicians have acquired in their original training is too general. Hybrid training is necessary, the type and depth of which will depend on the degree of responsibility to be borne by the maintenance technician. The basic training necessary is shown in Fig. 21–2, *p. 329.*

FIGURE 21-2   Educational plan for the interdisciplinary training of NC technicians.

Mechanical: Machine Tool Elements
The Operation of the Machine Tool
Machine Tool Geometry
Setup and Maintenance of Machine Tools
Elements of Hydraulics and Pneumatics

Electrical: Electrical and Electronic Modules
Logic Functions
Probes and Sensors
Drives
Open and Closed Loop Systems

Circuit Logic: Electric and Electronic Modules
Logic Functions
Magnetics
Displays
Measurement

Control Technology: Fundamentals
Measuring Devices and Transducers
Fundamental Principles of Machine Tool Controllers
NC Technology

Programming: Fundamentals of NC Programming
Part Programming Diagnostics
Manual Data Input
Familiarity with Tooling
Program Edit

Diagnostics: Theory of Problem Identification
Formal Logic Systems
Hands-on-Training

**Maintenance
Planning:** Documentation of Preventive and Non-Preventive
Maintenance, Update of Documentation

NC-Terminology: Definition of Terms, Fundamental Understanding
of Related Technical Terms

After basic training, technicians are equipped to undertake the manufacturer's course in order to become familiar with the details of the installation of which they will later be responsible.

During the assembly of the new machines they should be given the opportunity to take part in, and become familiar with, all the activities carried out by the manufacturer's personnel. Personal contact with these people as well as an understanding of how things fit together will lead to a better grasp of the entire installation. Even though this cannot be referred to as formal training, the time spent will provide a wealth of experience which will be of great value later, and the costs for this training will be recovered by a reduction in downtime during the first one or two years of operation. Even though the manufacturer's installation personnel may resent a constant observer, this training opportunity should not be missed!

21.8 MAINTENANCE AND REPAIR

The NC machine is an electromechanical installation which encompasses a wide range of technologies, including mechanical machine components, hydraulics, pneumatics, electrotechnology, and electronics. As a result, the repair of NC machines demands a high standard of knowledge and experience on the part of maintenance technicians.

Training programs for NC maintenance technicians often go into too much detail. A classic example would be the study of interpolator logic for linear/circular-interpolating continuous path control. The explanation of this principle, which often takes one or two days, serves only to satisfy the technical curiosity of trainees and does nothing to assist in elimination of NC malfunctions.

Caution should be exercised with respect to randomly exchanging "plug-in" modules; this can be a costly practice. Components may be damaged during the exchange process, an inventory of parts will grow containing damaged components, and more damage may be done to the machine.

The systematic approach of error location is much better. In this context, NC machines can be divided into three main groups:

Group 1: Machine tool: axis and spindle drives, machine components, hydraulics, and pneumatics.

Group 2: Measuring systems and control loops including transfer systems.

Group 3: Electronic control: technology for digital and data processing, logic links, input and output units.

Through intensive cross-linking of these three groups—through control loops, measuring circuits, feedback circuits, and interlocks, for example—an error can become visible in one part of the system which is not directly linked to the defective part. This necessitates a complete understanding of the total system before a satisfactory error search can be performed.

Fig. 21–3 shows the categories of common causes of failures in NC machines. It is clear that peripheral devices and modules predominate.

FIGURE 21–3   Typical causes of failure on NC machines.

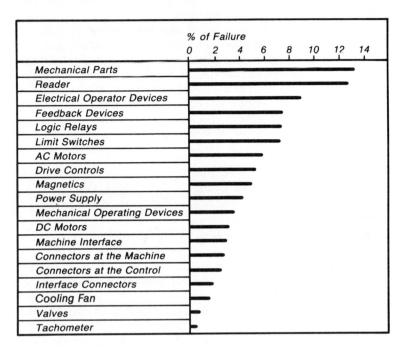

21.9 PREVENTIVE MAINTENANCE PROGRAMS

From evaluation of previous experience in preventive NC maintenance, the following guidelines are suggested:

- Leave well-functioning components alone! Do not alter any settings, and do not dismantle or rebuild any devices without good reason.
- Each time the system is serviced, pay special attention to signs of possible future malfunctions: corrosion, loose connections, discolored contacts, and any material which may be present whose origin is unknown.
- The three most important preventive maintenance functions to be carried out on a timely basis are cleaning, lubricating, and inspecting as prescribed by the manufacturer.
- Use only as much lubricant as needed. Excess oil, grease, or graphite should be carefully wiped off. Too much lubrication is sometimes as damaging as too little!
- Diagnosis and electrical testing should only take place in accordance with appropriate written instructions. Deviations noted should be corrected immediately, if possible.
- Preventive maintenance should reduce downtime to a minimum. Therefore use available replacement parts as much as possible and repair defective parts in your shop or send them back to the manufacturer once the machine is back in operation.

A typical preventive maintenance program looks like the following:

Weekly

- Run a short test program and alter the feed rate override control between minimum and maximum.
- Test deficiencies and complaints noted by the operator; search for causes and correct them, if possible.
- Check all fans for operation and pay attention to good air circulation.
- Check the appearance and functioning of any tape reader paying special attention to wear of drives and reeler, cleanliness of read head, and alignment of channel and transport tracks.

Monthly

- Test a part program without using a workpiece and observe the axes for stability, uniform movement, positioning behavior, and so on.
- Oil all fans, if applicable.
- Make sure that all plug-in circuits are correctly positioned in the contact strips and that retainers are in place.
- Check moving cables and plugs for worn or damaged wires and connections.
- Remove the cover of each measuring system and check for dirt, cable condition, and condition of connections.
- Reorder replacement parts for those which have been used.
- Check maintenance logs for problems noted by operating personnel—especially repetitive problems.

Semiannually

- Measure the mutual dependency of speed/tachometer voltage and following error as a function of the command voltage. Compare the measured values with values measured at the time of installation.

Annually

Environmental conditions of the NC system may even dictate more frequent checks!

- Test each circuit board for perfect seating in its contact strip.
- Inspect all contact strips for damage or breakage.
- Check doors, seals, and screw fittings for loose connections.
- Clean console with vacuum cleaner and soft brush, as necessary.
- Test tape reader mechanics for good working condition.
- Test functioning and precision of the NC.
- Test power supply for correct voltage output.
- Complete functional test of the NC by processing a test part program with and without a workpiece.

The question of availability of maintenance personnel arises when considering preventive maintenance and repair. NC machines are generally operated in more than one shift per day and therefore may require repair outside of the normal day shift working hours. The demand for multishift scheduling of NC maintenance personnel is understandable from a production standpoint. However, for the practical reasons listed below, the trend frequently has not been in this direction except in the case of large-volume manufacturers for whom continuous use of capital assets is an economic necessity.

- Service assistance is not normally available at night, from manufacturers, co-workers, mechanics, or programmers.
- The repair of many problems is usually left to the day shift.
- It is often more difficult to find qualified service technicians who are willing to work shifts.
- One NC service technician is often not enough at night, since various NC systems are usually present.

It may be preferable to set up a group of on-call staff which can be reached by telephone when needed.

21.10 TELEPHONE DIAGNOSIS

Several NC manufacturers have set up telephone diagnostic centers. User evaluation has been quite varied and suggests that up to 50 percent of the problems reported by telephone diagnosis can be detected and solved. Furthermore, the effectiveness of the NC manufacturer aiding client maintenance personnel on the telephone is very dependent on the ability of the operator to properly evaluate and explain the problem. A study performed in the United States a few years ago revealed interesting information regarding service calls which can be handled over the telephone (*Fig. 21–4 p. 334*). According to this study, the success rate was highest for trained maintenance technicians who had replacement parts at their disposal. In such cases, after an average telephone conversation of 10 minutes, 80 percent of the reported errors were eliminated. However, the effectiveness dropped to about 25 percent when calls were from nontrained maintenance technicians without replacement parts. This held true even after an hour-long telephone conversation.

21.11 MAINTENANCE CONTRACTS

It is advisable to clarify the question of minimum possible downtime at the time of purchase negotiations with the supplier. The following points should be considered:

- Exchange service for defective components
- Repair and return of defective components with the shortest possible delay
- A checklist for locating errors
- A list of measured values and test points for later comparative testing

FIGURE 21–4   Effectiveness of telephone maintenance assistance.

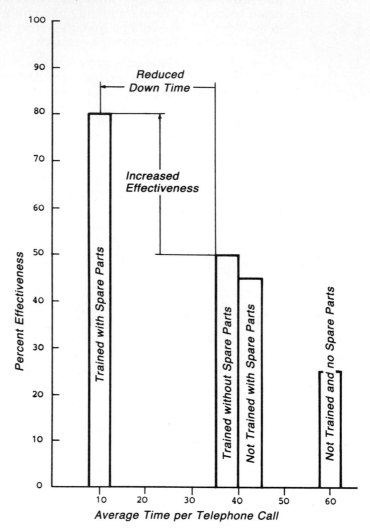

- A part program test tape containing values measured at the time of machine acquisition for future comparison
- The fastest form of delivery for replacement parts
- Availability of replacement parts for at least five years
- Reasonable notification of model or series discontinuation for replacement parts ordering
- Complete plans, circuit diagrams, maintenance and inspection instructions, recommended spare parts lists, programming and operating instructions at least four weeks before delivery of the machine
- Warranty agreement covering reimbursement for a technical breakdown rate in excess of an agreed maximum

- Guaranteed service after the warranty period expires
- Maintenance contract for annual inspection and, if required, maintenance of the entire machine or system

21.12 RETROFITTING

When an older CNC machine tool is still in good mechanical condition, it is sometimes commercially attractive to replace its original controller with a new, up-to-date one. This generally increases the machine's computing power, programming capabilities, and its ability to handle a wider range of ancillary control functions such as tool management activities.

Increased reliability of modern controllers, coupled with their improved user-friendliness and enhanced facilities, all contribute to making the retrofitted machine tool much more adaptable and cost effective to operate. Furthermore, the self-diagnostic capabilities of modern controllers make troubleshooting much simpler and quicker (see Section 21.13).

Unfortunately the upgrading of the controller is usually not sufficient to upgrade the whole machine to modern CNC machine-tool specification. It is also important to consider the following additional points:

- The machine's measuring system must also be up-to-date. New, encapsulated rotary encoders with spindle error compensation might be worth considering, as older measuring systems were rarely protected against the ingress of dirt.
- Current CNC machine interfaces may be similar to the older unit being replaced; however if this is not the case the original relay logic should be changed to a modern programmable control logic system, the costs of the new software required being quickly recovered by greatly increased efficiency of operation.
- If the machine tool incorporates hydraulic drives these should be replaced by modern, brushless servodrives, which offer completely maintenance-free operation, are much quieter, and dissipate far less heat.

21.13 CNC SELF DIAGNOSTICS

In addition to providing color screen displays of controller faults and menu style diagnostic assistance to speed up rectification, the latest CNCs also offer sophisticated system self-diagnostic capabilities, ranging from the dynamic display of input and output signals from the programmable control, to optimization of control circuits during commissioning, and observation of the dynamic behavior of axes via screen enlargement of the areas of interest.

Indeed, much of the reduced downtime in today's CNC workshops can be attributed to the self-diagnostic capabilities provided by modern

CNCs. They offer maintenance and service personnel efficient and rapid assistance in both diagnosing and establishing the most appropriate course of corrective action that should be taken in any given situation.

QUESTIONS FOR CHAPTER 21

1. Why is preventive maintenance so vital when working with NC machines?
2. In the event of an NC machine making an unexpected stop during a cutting operation, what should the operator do and not do? What should the maintenance technician do and not do?
3. Briefly describe how the latest CNC controllers greatly simplify fault diagnosis.
4. Is telephone diagnosis a good facility?
5. What environmental conditions are particularly injurious to NC machines? How would you overcome such conditions?
6. Discuss at least six fundamental recommendations that you would make to potential maintenance technicians.
7. In what ways do the skills of an NC technician differ significantly from those of a maintenance technician in a shop operating only non-NC machine tools?

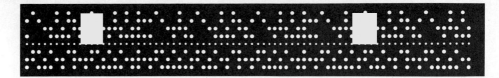

CHAPTER 22

INDUSTRIAL ROBOTICS— CURRENT AND FUTURE APPLICATIONS

After studying this chapter you should understand:

1. What an industrial robot (IR) really is, and its prime functions.
2. The function of each of an IR's principal elements.
3. The most important characteristics of the three main IR types.
4. How IRs are controlled.
5. What sensors are used in IRs, and their main functions.
6. An appreciation of typical industrial applications for IRs.

Industrial robots and CNC machine tools have similar characteristics and they operate via similar numerical control technology. Indeed their application and operating modes are frequently planned by the same personnel. However a robot can never replace a CNC machine tool. It can, however, act in a supportive role in order to increase the degree of automation possible.

22.1 INTRODUCTION

When discussing robots the first picture that usually comes to mind is a humanoid with two legs, two arms with hands, a body, and—most important of all—a head, with eyes and ears replaced by photocells and antennae. This image was formed long before the industrial application of these "machine men" and it has been sustained by science fiction ever since. Initial impressions of death and destruction and of a creature superior to its rivals and subservient only to its inventor still persist, and this view of industrial robots may be responsible for the defensive reactions shown by many workers and unions.

In contrast to these impressions, the industrial robot of today has an entirely new role and different characteristics:

- Helper (not rival)
- Machine (not person)
- Programmed (not intelligent)
- Flexible (not innovative)

The notion that some day all of the operating personnel of an industrial production facility will be replaced by robots is obviously false.

The ability of human beings to make use of all of their sensory functions cannot be duplicated by robots that have neither consciousness nor the creativity that would enable them to deal with unstructured problems.

In November 1979 the Robot Institute of America defined a robot as "a programmable, multifunctional manipulator designed to move material, parts, tools, or specialized devices through variable programmed motions to accomplish a variety of tasks."

Nevertheless, robots are being increasingly considered for use in production, and it is estimated that more than 100,000 robots will be used in the near future.

The majority of these robots will be simple operating devices, so-called pick-and-place units, for loading and unloading machines, and completely programmable, universally applicable devices will represent only 20 percent of this robot population. Further development of sensor technology is continuing to enable robots to "see" and "feel" so they can perform increasingly complex activities.

22.2 INDUSTRIAL ROBOT DESIGN

An industrial robot (IR) consists of six principal elements (*Fig. 22–1, p. 339*).

22.2.1 MECHANICS/KINEMATICS

Mechanics/kinematics refers to the physical hardware for the required movements within a given work area (*see Fig. 22–2, p. 340*). The three main or basic axes are designed to be either linear or rotational depending on the IR design. As shown in Fig. 22–2, *p. 340,* the robot construction with three rotational axes has the largest work envelope relative to its physical size.

22.2.2 GRIPPER OR HAND

The gripper is used to grip, hold, and transport the workpiece or tool and to position it in the desired location. Normally, three axes are needed to execute unrestricted tipping (pitch), turning (roll), and pivoting (yaw) "hand" movements.

FIGURE 22–1   Principal elements of industrial robots.

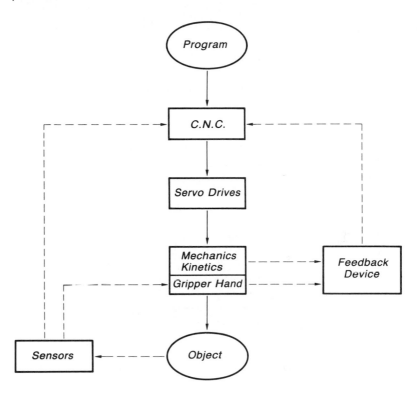

22.2.3   CNC

The control system is used for input and storage of the various programming cycles, taking into account the required links, priorities, and sequence of the program cycle. Entry of the control programs via the manual "teach-in" process, as well as the capability to call up the stored programs in any order, are fundamental requirements.

22.2.4   DRIVES

Drives are used to control the operation of each axis and to maintain a specified approach position. The dynamic performance of the drive is very critical because highly variable dynamic behavior is required of the robot while it is coping with differing component weights.

22.2.5   MEASURING FEEDBACK SYSTEM

The measuring feedback system measures the position, displacement speed, and acceleration of each axis. Incremental or cyclical absolute feedback measuring systems are mainly used in the primary axes, while only absolute feedback measuring systems are used in the hand axes. The reason for this is that the primary axes can be traversed relatively easily towards a reference position and set to some arbitrary

FIGURE 22–2 Kinematic concepts of a three-axis industrial robot and the resulting working envelopes.

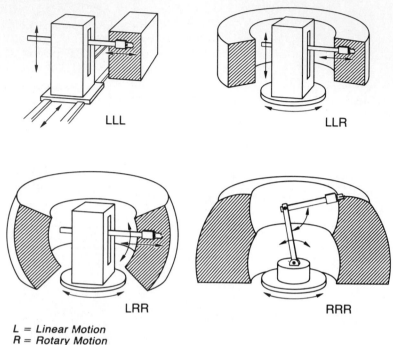

LLL

LLR

LRR

RRR

L = Linear Motion
R = Rotary Motion

zero, but the location of the hand in the work space must be known as soon as power is supplied to the robot.

22.2.6 SENSORS

Sensors are used to identify and evaluate any interactions such as position changes, pattern deviations, or externally occurring malfunctions.

22.3 BASIC CHARACTERISTICS OF INDUSTRIAL ROBOTS

According to the definition given above, industrial robots are freely programmable handling devices with several axes of freedom which can be equipped with grippers or tools. Depending on the control used, they are able to carry out highly complex movements and tasks.

The performance of IRs with respect to range, slide path, speed, and precision depends mainly on the design details and differs widely from application to application.

IRs are classified by application function as either pick-and-place units, point-to-point control units or continuous path units.

The general requirements for integrating IRs into systems with machine tools is very diverse. Basically, the robot's arm must be able to reach all machining stations and also be able to accurately grip all parts of a predetermined size and weight. There is a wide variety of grippers available but, depending on the application, it may be possible for the same gripper to be used to hold and place various types of components.

FIGURE 22–3   Industrial robot—six-axis type (courtesy of Cincinnati Milacron Inc.).

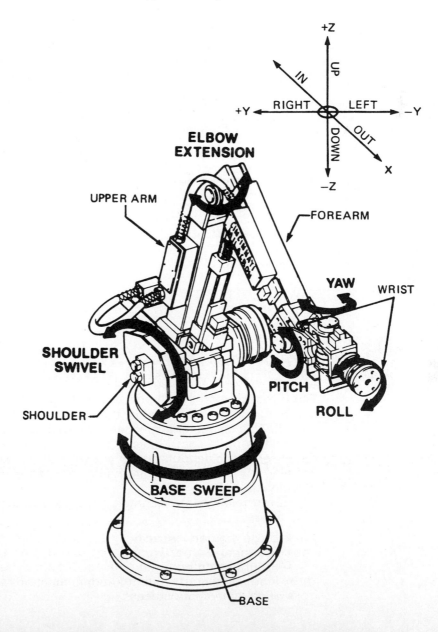

TABLE 22-1 Important robot features.

THE MOST IMPORTANT CHARACTERISTICS OF A ROBOT WITH CONTINUOUS PATH CONTROL ARE *(see figure 22-3, p. 341):*	THE MOST IMPORTANT CHARACTERISTICS OF A ROBOT WITH POINT-TO-POINT CONTROL ARE:
■ Up to 6 or 7 independently controllable movements between the main structure and the gripper of the robot (3 basic axes, 3 hand axes, 1 slide travel axis) ■ Fast programming using a manual teach-in method ■ Repeatability of between 0.06 in. and 0.004 in. in the work area of the gripper ■ Work speed equal to or greater than that of the operator, especially in continuous operation ■ Arbitrary program selection by external signals ■ Subprograms for acquiring and depositing various tools ■ Internal and external program memory storage ■ High reliability—at least 400 hr. mean time between failures (MTBF) ■ Linearization of joint axis movement *(Fig. 22-4, p. 343)* ■ Sensor inputs to provide automatic adaptation to changing conditions ■ Computer interface for connection to DNC systems	■ System operation of up to 4 axes ■ Manual teach or external programming ■ Gripper position repeatability of between 0.02 and 0.004 in. ■ High displacement speed ■ Fast conversion or switching of programs ■ Palletizing program for pickup and depositing of parts ■ Internal program storage capability ■ High reliability (a minimum of 1000 hours MTBF) ■ Dual gripper for 2 parts (machined/not machined) ■ Automatic identification of part location and stacked parts when removing or depositing them

22.4 CONTROL OF INDUSTRIAL ROBOTS

The most important attribute contributing to the cost-effective application of IRs is flexibility (that is, the ability to adapt to changing requirements). This characteristic is determined in the IR by the programming capabilities of its control system. The NCs that are normally supplied for use on machine tools are only marginally suitable for controlling IRs as they have control requirements that differ widely from those of machine tools.

Nevertheless some common requirements for both IR and other NC devices are:

- Large memory capacity
- Subroutine programming
- Program editing facility
- Inputs and outputs for additional functions
- High-speed data processing

Optional features which are not absolutely necessary are:

- Display screen on the control
- S- and T-functions (speed and tool change)
- Built-in control panel with keyboard
- Tape reader
- Linear and circular interpolation (This cannot be used if the kinematics of the IR are designed for discrete joint motions.)

Additional necessary requirements on IRs are:

- Program input using a "teach-in" method
- Linearization of circular and joint axes (that is, the robot hand travels along a straight line while the basic axis motion is rotary). (*See Fig. 22–4.*)
- Automatic compensation for axis acceleration forces (independent of part weight, construction, or distance moved)

FIGURE 22–4   Linearized motion.

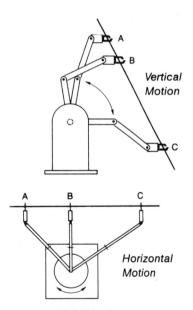

Vertical Motion

Horizontal Motion

22.4.1   SIMPLE PLACEMENT

Devices which traverse preset motion sequences in two, three, or sometimes four axes according to a fixed program are called pick-and-place units. Path limitations in the individual axes can be regulated by adjustable, fixed limits, but control of intermediate positions is not possible. These devices have very simple controls with no instrumentation or servocontrol of the individual axes. Axis movement is usually achieved via pneumatic or hydraulic cylinders.

The axes can be moved in either direction between fixed limits, the move cycle being programmed with a plugboard control or pneumatic components (fluidics). These robots are simple, inexpensive devices offering high-speed motion and accurate positioning in a maximum of up to four axes. They are thus ideally suited to the loading and unloading of machine tools, and to simple repetitive assembly work in mass production environments.

22.4.2   POINT-TO-POINT

Robots which traverse a path by moving between discrete, programmed points are called point-to-point units. Each axis has a feedback system and a servodrive, but the motion occurs from one discrete point to the next independent of other points along the traverse path. Program steps are generated using either a teach-in method or manual data input of the coordinates for the individual positions required. The control system for this application is relatively simple, and such robots are therefore ideally suited to workpiece handling on NC machine tools.

22.4.3   CONTINUOUS PATH

Robots which traverse a path in a controlled manner with programmable motion in all axes (usually up to seven) have continuous path control. Each axis has a position measuring system and a servodrive and can be programmed to any value between its end limits. These devices differ from pick-and-place and point-to-point units by their ability to perform functions, such as fusion welding or spray painting due to their continuous path control capability.

Programs are developed through the teach-in method which is performed as described in Section 22.5.4.

Automatic execution of this type of program occurs with the block-by-block loading of the data into the working memory and most basic IRs produced today operate in this manner. The use of additional memory in the control provides for input and storage of several programs, and this is particularly useful in such applications as the automatic welding of different chassis parts in the area of automobile assembly.

By using edit functions on modern controllers, programs can be easily modified, requiring only keyboard input plus a CRT terminal temporarily connected to the control. These input devices are not needed in the subsequent operation of the IR and may thus be used for programming other IRs.

Robots which have cylindrical, spherical, or joint coordinates also may require linearization of movement (*Fig. 22–4, p. 343*). This is best achieved by causing the displacement to occur along a straight line by programming end positions A and C and keeping the slide speed of the part constant. In this way the robot hand should lead the tool (a welding torch or spray nozzle, for example) from the beginning point to the end point at a constant angle to the part. However, this function requires a fast computer to provide input to the control.

Another IR control function is synchronization to allow operations on a moving object (that is, an object being processed by the robot while moving past it along a conveyor belt). In this case the position of the part must be constantly monitored and related to robot axis movement.

FIGURE 22–5   Four of the most common forms of industrial robots.

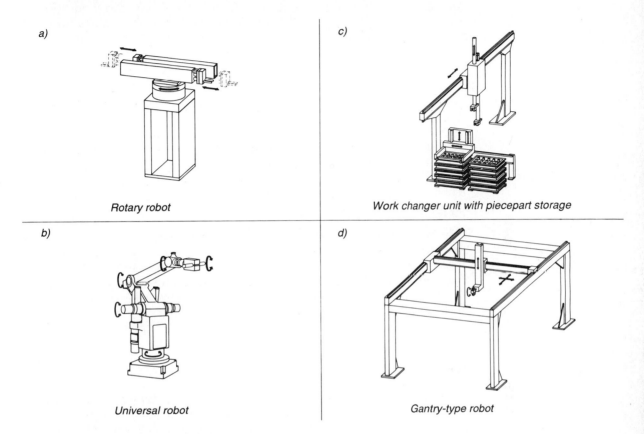

a)

Rotary robot

b)

Universal robot

c)

Work changer unit with piecepart storage

d)

Gantry-type robot

22.5 IMPORTANT CHARACTERISTICS OF NUMERICAL CONTROLS FOR IRs

The five most important NC specification areas relative to robot application are memory, path functions, sequence control, teach-in software, and sensor interface.

22.5.1 PROGRAM MEMORY

This part of the control contains the entire program sequence with all path functions and additional data. In most cases the memory capacity is designed to store several programs which can be called up as needed by the process.

Modifying stored programs and duplicating them on punched or magnetic tape is just as important as erasing old programs and loading new ones. And a readout that is capable of displaying stored program numbers is needed so that the operator is always aware of programs that are available for use.

22.5.2 PATH FUNCTIONS (G-FUNCTIONS)

The same considerations as for machine tools apply here, and they are specified in the Electronic Industries Association (EIA) standard. Additional path functions which result from IR functional requirements include:

- Linearizing rotating axis motion
- Following moving parts
- Stacking and palletizing parts
- Waiting for and acknowledging function instructions for individual cycles
- Changing inertia due to arm extensions and part weights
- Compensating for tolerance with predetermined compensation values
- Processing sensor inputs

22.5.3 SEQUENCE CONTROL

The most important control is the emergency stop to prevent the robot arm from entering a danger zone where it could cause damage to itself or to its environment. Further, the pauses necessary for processing and program changes are scheduled as required. The reaction of the robot to internal and external signals is not generally part of the operating program; it is separately programmed by the user.

22.5.4 TEACH-IN PROGRAMMING

It is practically impossible to manually program a six-axis robot for, say, spot welding an automobile chassis or for fusion welding. Instead, the teach-in method is regarded as the most suitable type of programming. An example of this technique in welding would be a situation wherein the electrode holder of the IR is manually directed along each line of weld, and the corresponding axis movement coordinates are then digitized and stored automatically. This programming method is not applicable to machine tools and must be added to existing NC systems for IR applications.

22.5.5 SENSOR INPUT

Provision for external sensor inputs is required to effect automatic correction of programmed moves due to changing process requirements.

22.6 SENSORS

The increase in robot use in the future will depend significantly on the development of specialized sensors. Sensors are transducers which emulate human senses and perceptions in machine applications. All human senses operate over a limited range, and if the stimulus is below a certain threshold, the person perceives nothing; if it is above the threshold, a warning occurs: pain, for example.

Sensory organs are localized functional devices in animals and humans, situated at certain body locations, particularly in the head. They serve to pick up specific stimuli and thus make it possible for human beings to be in contact with their environments. All perceptions provided by the sensory organs converge in the brain and effect an appropriate bodily response process. Neither humans nor animals are capable of existence without sensory organs.

If one considers what a robot needs in order to completely replace human effort, one realizes that it is sensory organs or equivalent capabilities as well as the automatic learning ability to store and process experience. It would be extremely helpful if an IR could see, and the emulation of the sense of touch and weight perception would also be advantageous, but without sensory feedback the applicability of the IR is extremely limited.

For an IR to operate within constantly changing environmental conditions, the sensory functions of humans must be emulated by technological sensors (Table 22-2). The control must react to these sensory signals as quickly as possible to correct the program cycle automatically. Thus, with an optical sensor, the IR can determine positional changes of the part to be gripped and extend its hand precisely to pick it up. It might even be able to identify different parts and to differentiate and grip only the desired one from a random assortment possibly via image digitization (see *Fig. 22–6, p. 348*).

22.7 TYPICAL INDUSTRIAL ROBOT APPLICATIONS

The concept of the industrial robot was introduced in 1954 with a patent application by George C. Devol. It described the design of a digitally controlled mechanical arm and its use in place of human labor in a

TABLE 22–2 Examples of sensory perception.

ACTION	SENSE	ORGAN	TECHNICAL SENSOR	SENSATION
Hear	Hearing	Ear	Microphone	Sound
See	Sight	Eye	Photocell	Light
Feel	Temperature Load/Force Touching	Skin Muscle Nerves	Thermometer Scales Probe/Feeler Switch	Heat Weight/Pressure Contour/Form/ Position
Smell	Smelling	Nose	Special Smoke or Smell Detector	Smell
Taste	Tasting	Taste buds	————	Taste

FIGURE 22–6   Digitized image before and after computer processing.

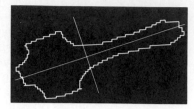

few elementary industrial applications classified as "materials handling." This included the loading and unloading of components, that is, the supply and removal of parts in the following sequence:

- Remove part from pallet.
- Wait until completion of part just machined.
- Grip and remove finished part.
- Load next part to be machined.
- Place finished part on another pallet or transfer it to the next machining station.

This is how the classical arrangement of a robot in the center of a circular configuration of machines and pallets evolved. Figure 22–7 illustrates the layout.

Parts are first placed into a machine to process their ends; they are then fed one after another into the chucks of two lathes. Next, they are transported to a drilling machine, inspected, and finally stacked on a finished parts pallet.

The number of machines that can be tended by one robot is determined by the cycle time of each machine, but the multiple activities of the robot should not be a limiting factor and so adversely affect the productivity of the manufacturing island (*Fig. 22–7, p. 349*).

If the cycle time per part is very long and the circular arrangement of the machines in the work envelope of the robot is not large enough to accommodate additional machines, a linear rail-guided arrangement is often used instead (see *Fig. 22–8, p. 349*). In this way the slide path for the longitudinal movement of the robot can be placed either on the floor or above the machines.

If the cycle time for each part is too short for one IR, several robots of the point-to-point type can be used to load and unload the machines. Each IR has not one, but two grippers which can independently grip raw and finished parts. This makes possible the fast handling of both nonmachined and finished parts at each machine. Such a typical industrial installation involving milling machines is shown in Fig. 22–9, *p. 350*. Another increasingly popular IR application area is for the deburring of components after machining.

The general distribution of IRs in industry today is shown in Table 22–3, *p. 351*.

FIGURE 22–7   Circular flexible manufacturing island serviced by an industrial robot.

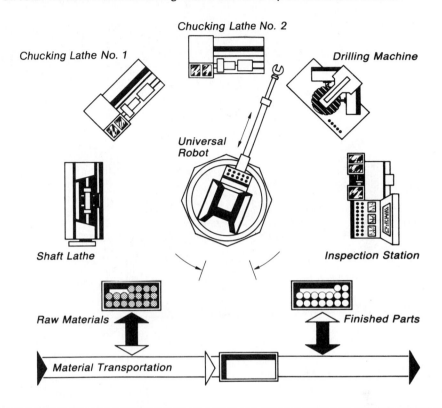

FIGURE 22–8   Rail-guided machine arrangement serviced by an industrial robot.

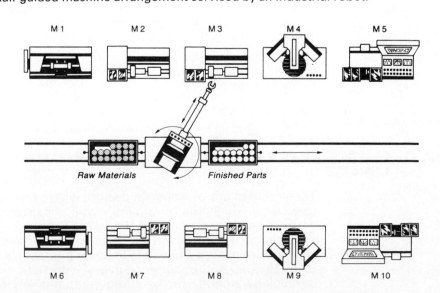

FIGURE 22–9   Universal load/unload robot for milling machines.

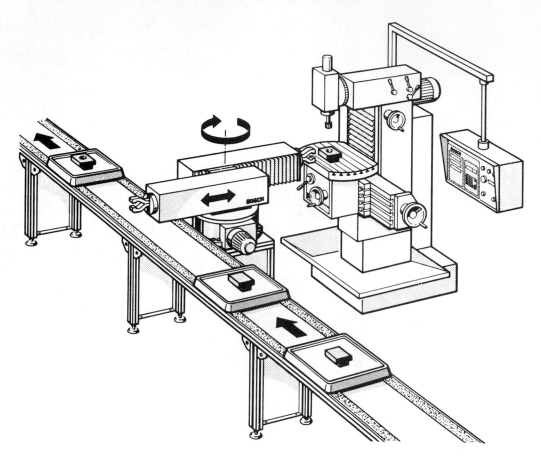

The simple IR used for pick-and-place duties is not included in Table 22–3. However, it is applied in very large numbers due to its comparatively low cost.

22.8 GANTRY-TYPE ROBOTS AND WORKCHANGER UNITS

These robots are of a special design, where the robotic unit is attached to a beam which sits on a gantry-type construction with a height normally of between 8 and 13 ft (*Fig. 22–10*).

The robot approaches all objects from above and this specific design feature makes it possible to cover a relatively large working area of up to 15 x 100 ft, thus serving several workstations. These units are also particularly suitable for handling comparatively heavy parts weighing up to 150 lbs.

TABLE 22–3   Typical current robotic applications.

APPLICATION	PERCENTAGE	TYPE OF CONTROL
Welding	28%	Point-to-Point and Continuous Path
Application of surface coatings paints, plasma arc spraying, etc.	21%	Playback
Loading/unloading of Injection Molding Machines	12%	Simple Sequence
Loading/unloading of punches	19%	Simple Sequence
Tool handling at machine tools	8%	Simple Sequence
Miscellaneous	12%	Miscellaneous

The robots have three linear main axes (X, Y, and Z), and one or two swivel axes (A and B), for orientation of the gripper. The required grippers or multiple-grippers are tailored to specific handling tasks and they can be changed automatically if necessary while also incorporating automatic zero point adjustment.

Their control differs from that of machine tools and has to meet special requirements. Typically, operational sequences must be performed accurately in both forward and backward directions. In case of

FIGURE 22–10   Gantry-type robots do not need a large floor area. They approach machines from the top (not from the side), and are capable of handling parts weighing up to 150 lbs.

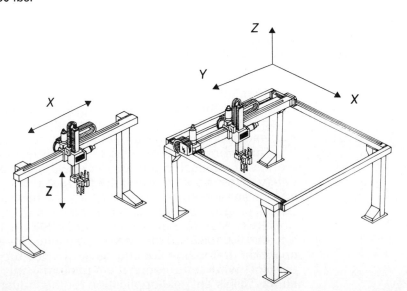

an interruption, or during the setup procedure, the robot must move backward along exactly the same path as it has moved forward in order to reduce the danger of collisions during manual operation.

The handling of fragile parts is feasible as it is possible to program not only maximum speed but also maximum acceleration, thus avoiding damage due to dynamic loads arising during transportation by the robot.

Programming is usually a mixture of remote office programming and shop-floor teach-in. The general structure of the program is conceived in the planning office, with dummy parameters replacing real positional values. The exact positional values (with reference to the gripper, for example) are then precisely specified in the workshop by "over teaching" the previous dummy parameters.

Gantry-type handling robots require programs for a structure comprising a main program which frequently calls up automatic subroutines apart from the transport and positioning tasks, as well as powerful subroutines for pallet management. These subroutines must be able to locate pallets or shelves after a power outage in order to restart the program at the correct point, and if the parts are stacked, the robot must be capable of recognizing the stack height.

Some applications require sensors whose operation is controlled by the program. The sensors are used for determining the position or orientation of pieceparts, feedback of load, pressure, or optical data signals.

In a few cases absolute path measuring systems are advantageous, but due to their much lower cost, relative path measuring systems are normally used—(see Chapter 4). These are equipped with battery-powered buffer memories which enable them to retain information for up to an hour after a power outage, including noting any positional changes that might have occurred during the power loss, and thus permitting immediate restart without having to reset axis zero points.

22.9 INDUSTRIAL ROBOT APPLICATION CRITERIA

It is desirable for both humane and economic reasons to relieve a person from the monotony of operating a machine with a fixed time cycle. Also, when the cycle time of the machine exceeds human ability, or when the environmental conditions of the workplace are unreasonably hot, damp, or dangerous, an IR application is called for.

Thus workers are relieved of unhealthy, monotonous, or dangerous work, and expensive production equipment can be better utilized. The safety of the workplace and the firm's status in the employment market is also enhanced. Such considerations have resulted in the so-called Delphi prognosis which was carried out and published by the American Society of Manufacturing Engineers (SME) in 1977. This report projected that by 1987, 20 percent of machine investment costs would be spent on materials-handling devices since they would operate around the clock whereas personnel are generally only available during the day shifts. This is an ideal application for the industrial robot.

The task of the robot—to the extent that it can still be defined as an individual device in an automated environment—can be quite diverse, and can range from being part of the production process (for welding, assembly, or painting), to handling the transportation of parts in various areas of the plant.

22.10 SUMMARY

In reviewing robots offered by vendors today, one finds over 100 types of robots produced by around 50 manufacturers. The various designs differ mainly with respect to:

- Size and load-bearing capacity
- Kinematics and number of axes
- Control specifications

It is noteworthy that robot manufacturers offer their equipment with only one control and thus spare the purchaser the problem of having to make a choice. This is also not surprising when one considers the enormously high software development costs for an optimal adaptation of a CNC to a specific robot.

In principle, numerically-controlled industrial robots use the same basic control concept as NC machines, in that positional data are numerically entered, classified in the memory according to program numbers, and executed in steps when called up. Each degree of freedom of the robot corresponds to a numerically controlled axis of the machine tool with its own servodrive and feedback measuring system.

In FMSs, robots work together with NC machine tools or are used directly in the processing of workpieces.

Apart from their mechanical construction, IRs vary considerably as to their control (simple program cycle, point-to-point, or continuous path control), the type of control being dependent on the function of the IR. As with an NC machine tool, the IR assumes that the environmental conditions remain the same over time.

QUESTIONS FOR CHAPTER 22

1. Briefly describe what you understand by the term "industrial robot."
2. What are the three main forms of IR? Briefly describe the differences between them, and tell where each has its own most appropriate area of application.
3. Where are IRs most commonly used in combination with CNC machine tools?
4. Describe the principal elements of IRs and, using a line diagram, explain how each element interacts with the others.

5. What are the five most important NC specification areas with respect to robotic operation?
6. What is meant by the term "teach-in" programming when used in the context of IRs?
7. Why is linearized motion of joint axis movement of importance?
8. What is meant by "working envelope?" Which type of IR has the most versatile envelope?
9. How many basic sensory activities can you think of that are monitored by robots? Compare manufactured and human organs used for environmental sensory detection.
10. What particular attractions does the gantry-type robot have over other formats?

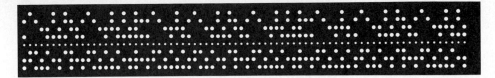

CHAPTER 23

GROUP TECHNOLOGY

After studying this chapter you should understand:

1. The fundamental philosophy of group technology and its paramount importance in planning for CNC manufacture.
2. The difference between functional and cellular plant layout.
3. The importance of grouping components into families.
4. The principles associated with the three main methods of family grouping.
5. The potential benefits of a comprehensive parts coding/classification system.

The manufacturing industry has long wished that the production efficiency and consequent financial benefits that are normally associated with mass production might be achieved in batch and jobbing shop situations as well. Group technology (GT) has played a significant role in the effort to bring this about, and it has become increasingly important with the introduction of high-cost CNC machines.

23.1 TRADITIONAL METHODS OF PLANT LAYOUT

Apart from the continuous process manufacture associated with the production of, for example, petrochemicals, the manufacturing industry has evolved to utilize two distinct methods of plant layout: line flow and functional.

Line flow is traditionally associated with the mass production of large volumes of virtually identical goods. Typical examples of products made by this type of manufacture include automobiles and domestic appliances. This production method is the most cost effective yet devised, but it accounts for approximately only 25 percent of all manufacturing output and has some major limitations, such as:

- It is, by design, almost totally inflexible.
- The rate of production is determined by the speed of the slowest operation on the line.
- Large amounts of capital are tied up in the product's highly specific hardware.
- Even small problems or delays on the line can bring it to a halt; buffer stocks between the different processes can help to alleviate this but will increase work-in-progress.
- Servicing and maintenance is complex as multiskilled staff are required to be on hand 24 hours a day.
- To justify capital outlay the lines must generally operate 24 hours a day.

Functional layout, where the plant is laid out by grouping machines of a similar type together, has traditionally been considered as the most suitable for batch and jobbing production. Certainly most of the limitations associated with line manufacture are not applicable, but here too there are limitations:

- While highly flexible, a large volume of work-in-progress is involved.
- Piecepart movement is often extensive. It is not uncommon to find a component spending up to 95 percent of its total time in the workshop being moved from machine to machine, waiting to be worked on, being inspected, and so on.
- Floor-space requirements are high compared to that needed for comparable line-flow layouts.
- Throughput time is high, largely due to the inordinate waiting times between operations.
- Cost of material handling can be high when pieceparts are physically large and heavy.
- Production control is complex.
- Batch sizes are normally controlled by economic batch quantity theory which is heavily influenced by setup times.

23.2 THE PHILOSOPHY OF GROUP TECHNOLOGY

Ideally one would like to achieve the production efficiency of line-flow manufacture but with the flexibility offered by machines laid out functionally. This is precisely what GT strives to achieve. To examine how such a situation can be achieved one must consider what makes the line flow system so economically efficient. The answer lies, of course, in the obvious benefits to be gained from a stable demand for very large quantities of an identical product. Going from a minimum jobbing batch size of one to a line flow batch size of infinity, using infinity in its broadest sense, results in unit costs dropping dramatically.

Clearly one can only achieve the benefits of mass production (high machine utilization, minimal setup times and work-in-progress), if the marketplace demands production volumes that justify such manufacturing methods. Thus the further one can move away from "one-offs" in the direction of mass production, the lower will become the unit cost of manufacture.

Increasing batch sizes without a market need to support such output will result in any benefits in production costs to be more than offset by costs of maintaining much higher stock levels. However if it were readily possible to identify all those small batch items that needed similar process requirements, they could be grouped together to make up much larger batch sizes than would otherwise be possible. This would then justify the installation of self-contained machine cells comprising all the machine tools necessary to completely make each family of components. This is the basic principle of GT.

Many definitions of GT have been proposed but one of the most succinct is perhaps:

> Group technology is the technique of identifying and processing the largest possible batch sizes of components requiring similar manufacturing processes, in order to bring the benefits of large-scale production to batch-type manufacture.

The advent of CNC machines has made the GT approach even more attractive as quite significant variations between items in a given grouped batch are more readily catered to by a CNC machine than by an equivalent manually-operated machine tool. Thus batch sizes can be even bigger.

23.3 THE PRACTICALITIES OF IMPLEMENTING GROUP TECHNOLOGY

The introduction of GT into a manufacturing plant involves two fundamental steps:

- Identifying components with similar manufacturing requirements and then grouping them into families.
- Designing and installing new workshop layouts to cater to the identified component families.

23.3.1 ESTABLISHING FAMILY GROUPS

Faced with an extensive range of components produced by any manufacturing workshop of significant size, the task of identifying related components can be daunting if not approached in a reasoned and systematic manner. Numerous approaches have been proposed, depending on the level of commitment to the GT philosophy required, but there are three generally accepted approaches.

In increasingly sophisticated order and rising cost of implementation these are:

1. Subjective assessment based on extensive experience of the component range produced
2. Production flow analysis (PFA)
3. Introduction of a comprehensive coding and classification system to cover the whole range of parts produced

No attempt will be made here to provide an exhaustive exposé of these methods, and only a sufficiently brief description of each is given to enable the reader to appreciate the principles and significance of each approach.

1. Subjective Assessment

While it is the least expensive to implement, subjective assessment is highly personal and might even border on being intuitive, depending on the level of in-depth knowledge, with respect to the company's overall component range, possessed by the planning staff involved. Furthermore, it is more natural to select components that are physically similar, as it is much more difficult to identify items which require a similar sequence of manufacturing operations when their visual features are very diverse.

The integration of new components into established groupings is also difficult to implement as the design engineer will not necessarily have knowledge of existing part family characteristics.

2. Production Flow Analysis

Originally proposed by Burbidge in 1963, PFA has stood the test of time, in part due to the cost attractiveness of its half-way-house approach. Implementation costs are moderate while its logical, diagrammatically analytical approach leads the planning engineer to very definite component family groupings. The procedure involved is best illustrated via a simple example.

Example:

Assume that a sample of 10 items are to be machined using the following conventional machine tools: lathes, millers, drilling and boring machines, and grinding and honing machines. Also considered are materials preparation, dispatch, and the inspection departments. Examination of the planning sheets for all 10 components provided operational sequence data for each item, and these are tabulated in Fig. 23–1.

The first step is to construct a simple PFA matrix table; this provides the first indication of component operational similarities. The matrix table for this example is shown in Fig. 23–2, *p. 359*.

As all raw material, castings, or forgings emanate from the goods inwards area (Gi) and finish up in the dispatch department (Gd), for the purposes of this simplified example these two end locations may be disregarded. By examining the remaining five rows in Fig. 23–1, *p. 359*, representing machine tool and inspection centers, one can draw up a common location chart. Such a chart, covering each of the components featured in this example, is shown in Fig. 23–3, *p. 360*.

The common location chart (*Fig. 23–3, p. 360*) clearly indicates the existence of two family groupings—family X and family Y.

FIGURE 23–1 Operational sequence table.

ITEM NO.	ROUTING SCHEDULE
1	Gi/T/I/DB/M/I/GH/I/Gd
2	Gi/T/I/M/I/Gd
3	Gi/T/I/GH/I/Gd
4	Gi/T/I/M/I/Gd
5	Gi/DB/I/GH/I/Gd
6	Gi/T/I/Gd
7	Gi/M/T/I/Gd
8	Gi/T/I/T/M/I/Gd
9	Gi/DB/I/GH/I/Gd
10	Gi/DB/I/Gd

Where
Gi = Goods inwards/materials prep. and release area.
Gd = Dispatch department.
T = Turning section
DB = Drilling and boring section.
M = Milling section.
GH = Grinding and honing section.
I = Inspection department.

FIGURE 23–2 PFA matrix table.

LOCATION	ITEM NUMBER									
	1	2	3	4	5	6	7	8	9	10
Gi	●	●	●	●	●	●	●	●	●	●
T	●	●	●	●		●	●	●●		
M	●	●		●			●	●		
DB	●				●				●	●
GH	●		●		●				●	
I	●●●	●●	●●	●●	●●	●	●	●●	●●	●
Gd	●	●	●	●	●	●	●	●	●	●

Components in family X all require lathe and milling operations in addition to inspection, while components in family Y all require drilling/boring and grinding/honing work plus inspection facilities.

Unfortunately, items 1 and 3 do not fully fit into either family, but the degree of flexibility associated with the PFA approach may well permit item 1 to be turned and milled in the family X cell before being moved to the family Y cell. Similarly item 3 could possibly also be accommodated. If, however, the volume required of either items 1 or 3 can justify it, then a specific cell for that component may be the best solution. Alternatively, the routing of items 1 and 3 could be examined to establish whether replanning would enable them to be more readily incorporated into one of the two cells already established for the X and Y families. The term "cell" has already been introduced, implying the

FIGURE 23–3   Common location chart.

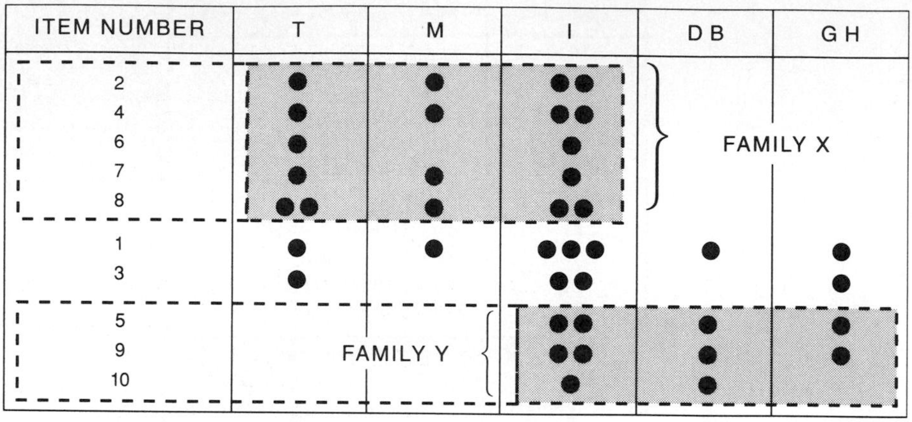

ITEM NUMBER	T	M	I	D B	G H
2	●	●	● ●		
4	●	●	● ●		
6	●		● ●		FAMILY X
7	●	●	● ●		
8	● ●	●	● ●		
1	●	●	● ● ●	●	●
3	●		● ●		●
5			● ●	●	● ●
9	FAMILY Y		● ●	●	● ●
10			●	●	●

grouping together of specific machine tools into one area for the purpose of producing a particular family of parts. This approach is commonly referred to as cellular manufacture.

The shop-floor layout implications of the cellular technique are illustrated for this example in Figs. 23–4, *p. 361* and 23–5, *p. 361*. Comparison with functional layouts is discussed in Section 23.5 of this chapter.

Two important factors must not be overlooked when examining the results of a PFA exercise as presented by a common location chart. No account has been taken of any differences in component size. Obviously, every machine has its capacity limitations (its working envelope, for example), and even though two items may require an identical machining sequence, if they are vastly different in scale then a given group of machine tools is unlikely to be capable of catering to both. Secondly, one should be cognizant of the fact that the PFA approach relies on existing production planning data. Are present methods always the best?

3. Coding and Classification Systems

One component differs from another because of one or more differences in physical shape, material used, surface finish required, specified tolerance levels required, and so on. If one could devise a numerical or alphanumeric coding system to precisely describe each and every feature of any piecepart, examination of this code number would instantly provide a comprehensive description of the component concerned. The degree of detail retrievable from such a numerical specification is clearly a function of the complexity of the coding system employed; one could even extend the code to include other factors such as data concerning manufacturing methods used, for example.

Obviously, to examine and code every component made in a particular plant would be a tedious and time-consuming exercise, but in order to reap the maximum benefits from GT there is little alternative. However one should not begin without first giving much thought to the

FIGURE 23–4   Functionally laid-out shop.

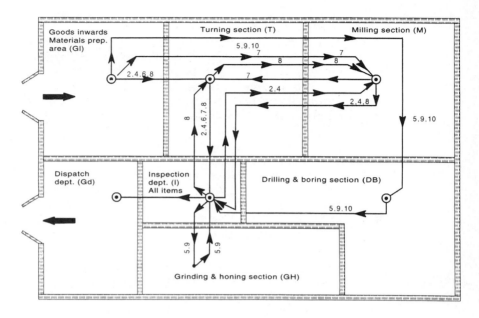

FIGURE 23–5   Cellular shop layout.

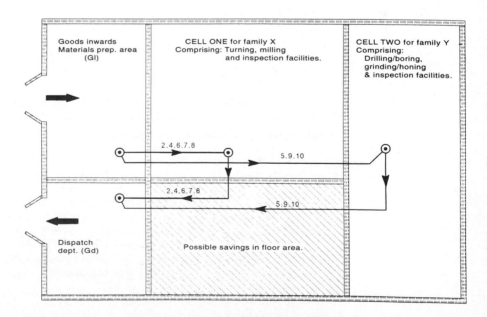

coding system to be used. The more complex the code employed, the more specific can be the subsequent grouping exercise using the designated item codings, but the more time consuming and costly will be the coding activity.

Many workers worldwide have proposed coding systems, most notably, Germany's Opitz (1946), Brisch (1957), Mitrofanov (1966), and Bobrowicz (1975) in association with Manufacturing Data Systems Inc.

No universal or standardized system has evolved, in part due to the great diversity of products made from company to company, but examination of systems proposed by these researchers and others does suggest that they fall into just two categories, normally referred to as hierarchic and chain-type codes.

Brisch's proposals are certainly hierarchical in form in that each code digit is dependent on the one preceding it. The chain format, where each digit is independent and represents some designated component characteristic, was favored by Opitz and Bobrowicz among others, although their systems did incorporate certain hierarchical features.

The data-sorting power of modern computers is prestigious, but the larger and more complex the code number the greater the risk of typographical and other human errors. Thus while one must ensure that the coding system selected is sufficiently comprehensive to cover all the required aspects of both current and future components, it should not be more complex than absolutely necessary for the needs of the particular plant concerned. Whether one enlists the assistance of specialist consultants or develops one's own code is a matter for individual assessment.

23.4 ADDITIONAL BENEFITS OF COMPREHENSIVE CODING SYSTEMS

The benefits of an all embracing coding system, while expensive to introduce, do extend far beyond the facility to group components for the purposes of improving manufacturing efficiency via GT.

Depending on the complexity of the coding system employed, because of its totally numeric or alphanumeric format, the use of a computer enables both design and production planning departments to easily:

- Identify existing component similarities within proposed new designs
- Simplify and speed up costings of new items by extracting relevant data applicable to similar items already in existence
- Avoid duplication at both the production planning stage of new parts and when designing the associated tooling/fixturing

As in other spheres of life, one only gets what one pays for, and these additional valuable peripheral benefits are only available if the coding system used is sufficiently comprehensive. One has therefore to make a balanced appraisal at the outset between code system complexity and the cost of its implementation. Such an assessment should, of course, consider whether a coding system is appropriate at all or whether PFA, or even subjective analysis, would be more appropriate to the shop in question.

23.5 COMPARISON BETWEEN FUNCTIONAL AND CELLULAR LAYOUTS

When compared with the traditional functionally based workshop layout, considerable space savings are possible by employing the "family of grouped parts" or "cellular manufacture" method of production.

Referring to the earlier example used to demonstrate the principle of PFA, and assuming that the size of all 10 items falls within the working envelopes of the machine tools used, if generous space is provided for each of the two cells X and Y, significant savings in floor area is made. Figures 23–4, *p. 361* and 23–5, *p. 361* clearly illustrate this, as well as showing the drastic reduction in component mobility when converting to a cellular workshop layout. For diagrammatic clarity, and to avoid speculation regarding the possible movements of items 1 and 3, only the movements of 8 of the 10 components are shown.

23.6 GROUP TECHNOLOGY AND CNC MANUFACTURE

One form of highly flexible manufacturing cell is typified by the modern CNC machine. The degree of flexibility within the machine's working envelope, whether machining or turning center, is a matter of conjecture, but current developments in CNC machine tool design, where such traditional subdivisions are eliminated, will certainly provide even greater flexibility in the future.

Many of the more productive cells in use today consist of one or two CNC machines fed by dedicated robotic loading/unloading devices. It is therefore clear that the process of component family grouping is the essential first step towards the introduction of cellular manufacture employing either conventional, CNC, or a mixture of both forms of machine tool.

However, as the investment involved in the purchase of CNC machines is so high, it is often this factor alone which acts as the necessary catalyst to trigger an organization into formally analyzing its products with a view to family rationalization. Certainly no CNC machine should ever be purchased without first having clearly identified the family of parts for which it is to be used.

23.7 PRINCIPAL BENEFITS OF THE GROUP TECHNOLOGY APPROACH TO MANUFACTURE

GT, like many innovations introduced to improve organizational efficiency and/or productivity, is usually best implemented in stages. Apart from the opportunity to make any modifications found necessary as implementation proceeds, as in the case of the progressive introduction of CNC technology, the instigator is able to enjoy the benefits to be gained from each stage of implementation.

Indeed it would be extremely difficult to convert a complete manufacturing facility from functional to cellular production in one step. For example, what happens to manufacturing output during the change-over period involving wholesale relocation of machine tools and associated backup services? Subcontracting is not always possible or desirable.

With this general proviso, the principal benefits associated with GT may be summarized as offering:

- Greatly reduced work-in-progress
- Much lower component stock levels
- Greater efficiency in the use of available floor space
- Reduction in the number of setups required
- Shorter throughput times, thereby improving speed of response to customers' needs
- Greatly reduced piecepart handling
- More flexible workforce with a greater sense of purpose due to the increased variety of tasks available and a feeling of team spirit within the cell group
- Lower tooling and fixturing costs
- Less paperwork due to reduced component mobility and the larger batch sizes possible with GT
- More positively directed equipment maintenance which can be readily directed towards the most important items of equipment within a given cell
- Greater willingness from design through manufacture to maximize component standardization

With such an impressive array of potential benefits, it is not surprising that GT has remained a popular and essential manufacturing strategy, especially when using CNC machines, despite the not inconsiderable implementation costs associated with the more sophisticated coding and classification systems.

QUESTIONS FOR CHAPTER 23

1. What is meant by GT?
2. What is the essential first step to be taken when contemplating the purchase of CNC machines?

3. What effect is the next generation of CNC machines likely to have on cellular manufacture?

4. Under what circumstances would cellular manufacture be inappropriate?

5. What are the principal benefits of a cellular workshop layout compared with either line flow or functional formats?

6. What are the major benefits of adopting the GT philosophy?

7. When assessing whether a manufacturing plant would benefit from cellular manufacture, what features would you look for during your examination of their product range? If CNC machines were being considered, how would this affect your appraisal?

8. Why is "working envelope" of importance when designing manufacturing cells?

9. Briefly describe the three principal methods of coding and classifying a company's range of components.

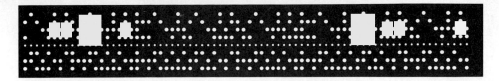

CHAPTER 24

COMPUTER-AIDED DESIGN AND MANUFACTURE— CAD/CAM

After studying this chapter you should understand:

1. The difference between CAD and CAM.
2. What is meant by computer-aided engineering (CAE).
3. The operating principle of CAD and how CAD workstation designs are digitally transferable to CNC machines.
4. The types of input and output devices commonly used on CAD systems.
5. The principal factors to be considered when contemplating the installation of CAD/CAM and CNC facilities.

If the drawing of a component can be stored in digital format, that is, if all geometric data can be digitally described, then it should be possible to use this data directly from the production planning stage through to final NC machine-tool program generation or even assembly. The elimination of the common practice of duplicating drawings in various formats in successive departments results in enormous savings of both time and money along with savings made possible by the elimination of manual process planning.

24.1 INTRODUCTION

Most chapters in this book have been concerned, in one way or another, with computer-aided manufacture (CAM).

However premanufacturing stages have also benefited from advances in computer technology, with one result being that the face of traditional design and drawing offices are being changed forever. Rows upon rows of drawing boards is rapidly disappearing and being replaced by CAD workstations. Disappearing too are such unproductive chores as the endless redrawing of layouts and component details in order to accommodate design changes.

We are still not quite at the point where digitally stored workpiece design data can be freely converted, without human intervention, to part program production, incorporating all the required technological cutting data automatically from the appropriate data file banks. This would result in production planning becoming totally computer based. But this step is only a matter of time away, and we therefore turn our attention in this final chapter to CAD and its integration with CAM.

24.2 DEFINITIONS

The concept of CAD and CAM has been evolving over the past 30 or more years and will continue to develop and expand. Initially, the acronyms CAM and CAD were used independently to describe computer-aided part programming and computer-aided drawing or graphics. However, the two terms have become linked over the years to form CAD/CAM, representing an integrated approach to the use of computers in the total production process, encompassing both the design and the manufacturing phases. Today, CAD embraces all the activities involved in the computer-aided production of engineering data such as drawings, geometric models, finite element analysis, parts lists, work schedules, and NC control information. CAM encompasses all the applications of computers to a wide variety of manufacturing functions, such as process planning, production scheduling, NC, CNC, quality control, and assembly.

The goal of the integration of CAD and CAM is the systemization of the flow of information from the preliminary design phase of a product through to the completion of its production. The series of steps beginning with the entry of component descriptive data, continuing with their storage and further processing, and ending with the conversion of these data into control information for production machinery, materials handling, and automatic testing equipment is known as computer-aided engineering (CAE) and may be considered to be the result of linking CAD with CAM.

The purpose of CAE and CAD/CAM technology is not to replace human effort with computerized equipment, but to enhance the human propensity to invent and create new ideas and products. Furthermore, time-consuming, labor intensive tasks, such as the storage and retrieval of engineering drawings and other pertinent design or manufacturing data, can now be carried out quickly and accurately by electronic devices.

• •

24.3 CAD COMPONENTS

A modern CAD workstation, often part of a turnkey system, contains several components interconnected by computer software and it is capable of accepting input, processing data, and displaying output. The traditional drawing board has been replaced by a data tablet (*Fig. 24-1*) which is usually divided into sections representing different shape functions such as the circle, line, point, or spline. To produce a drawing,

---

FIGURE 24–1   Electronic board plotter and board with menu fields.

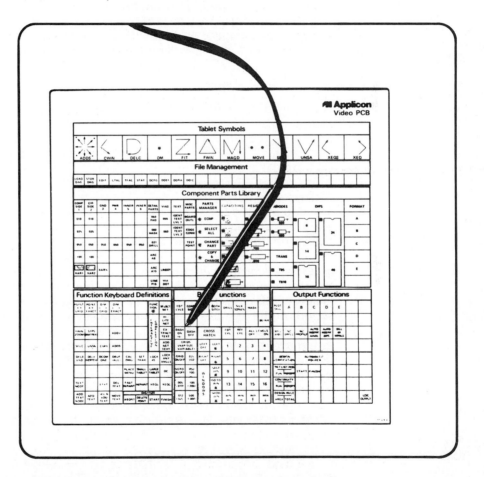

the designer activates these functions by touching the desired menu item on the tablet and then enters information specific to that geometric profile, such as its size and relative position, through an input keyboard. By the combined use of the tablet and keyboard the designer can tailor the standard menu items to fit specific applications. A separate alphanumeric color graphics screen is usually provided for display of the dialogue entered via the keyboard and the data tablet.

•••

24.4 VISUAL DISPLAY UNITS

Visual display units (VDUs), or graphics screens, operate in a number of different ways. The cathode ray tube (CRT) display technology has been dominant in this field, and it has benefited from ergonomic concerns in the design of workstations, and advances in associated technologies (mainly television).

A CRT uses a heated cathode which emits a continuous stream of electrons. These electrons are formed into a beam, accelerated, and focused at a point on the display screen surface. This beam is rapidly scanned across the phosphor-coated face of the tube and its current is increased or decreased to create brighter or darker points.

The three main types of CRTs are raster-scan tubes, direct-view storage tubes (DVST), and directed-beam refresh tubes (DBRT).

24.4.1 RASTER-SCAN TUBES

A raster-scan display screen has a set number of dots or locations arranged in a fixed array of rows and columns known as the "raster." As the raster is scanned (usually from top to bottom and left to right), each dot, or pixel, is either illuminated or not, depending on current flow. Scanning is a continuous process which refreshes the display at a minimum rate of 60 Hz—sufficiently fast for the human eye not to perceive flickers. The versatility of this pixel-by-pixel addressing, combined with full color capability (developed for television receivers) has gained it wide acceptance. However, raster-scanning is a memory intensive activity and this causes it to be expensive. All available addressing information must be transferred from memory to monitor each time the screen is refreshed. Increasing the resolution of raster-scans by increasing the number of pixels on the screen is also costly, as doubling resolution quadruples the number of pixel values which must be calculated, stored in memory, and transferred to the monitor screen. One method used to improve vision quality without increasing resolution is called antialiasing. This method makes the edges of diagonal lines, which normally appear jagged on low resolution screens, look less rough by illuminating the jagged parts at lower intensities. This slightly blurs the image but tends to make lines appear straighter. Due to these limitations, raster-scan CRTs are used more for applications that require good color, interactivity, and imaging capabilities rather than high resolution.

24.4.2 DIRECT-VIEW STORAGE TUBES

A direct-view storage tube (DVST) is a CRT which preserves an image for extended periods of time. The surface of a DVST screen is kept at a neutral (zero volt) potential by a number of flood guns which continuously bombard the phosphor surface with electrons. A negative potential "writing" gun illuminates images on the screen by charging the phosphor where it strikes. The phosphor, due to its bistable property, is sustained by the energy from the flood guns and thus remains visible until erased. Portions of the picture can be refreshed without erasing the stored image if only a part of the image is to be changed or deleted. These refreshed portions are stored in memory and rewritten many times a second. Powerful user interaction is made possible by the size of this refresh memory, and the user can highlight or isolate desired portions of the image using a second color. DVST units produce a very high resolution picture, which makes them particularly useful in CAD/CAM applications. Eye strain is also reduced because the image on the screen is stable and unchanging, an improvement over raster-scan display units from which users sometimes experience flickers as the image is being refreshed.

24.4.3   DIRECTED-BEAM REFRESH TUBES

A directed-beam refresh tube (DBRT) combines some of the features of both raster-scan and DVST CRTs. A DBRT is similar to a DVST, except that it cannot store images. Therefore it must continuously retrace the display at a rate above the flicker threshold of the human eye. Animation is facilitated with this type of display unit because a new image is traced with each retrace cycle. The complex circuitry required to maintain the retrace cycle is expensive, but the high resolution and wide spectrum of colors available with DBRTs make them well suited to CAD/CAM and finite element analysis applications.

24.5 INPUT DEVICES

CAD systems utilize a large variety of devices to assist the user in telling the computer what type, size, position, and orientation of geometric construction it should display on the graphic screen. The keyboard was the most common of these devices, and the user would convey the above information to the computer in a dialogue form by choosing options from a displayed menu. Since these dialogues can be time-consuming, many CAD stations now use other input devices to facilitate the communication of this information. The most popular of these is the data tablet mentioned earlier in Section 24.3.

A digitizer is an input device which can be used to input large quantities of graphical data from existing paper documents into a CAD system. It consists of a surface on which the document is placed and a cursor which is placed on the document and used to trace out and digitize particular features.

A light pen is a stylus-type input device which operates as an electronic pencil and can be used to digitize lines, circles, arcs, and other geometric features. Data entered through the use of a light pen are simultaneously reproduced on the graphics display screen and digitally stored in the computer.

A trackball is an input device which consists of a small sphere which is housed beneath a flat surface. The user transmits vector information to the computer by rolling the trackball with the palm of his hand.

A mouse, so named because of its vague resemblance to a real mouse, is a hand-held device with numerous buttons on top and a trackball underneath. This device has gained widespread acceptance due to its versatility and ease of use.

24.6 OUTPUT DEVICES

There are also a large variety of output devices available for producing printed output, or hard copies, from CAD systems. A CAD workstation, including some of the typical peripheral equipment, is shown in Fig. 24-2.

The five major types of hardcopy devices available are pen plotters, printer/plotters, CRT copiers, impact graphics printers, and camera systems. Pen plotters are available in two different configurations, flatbed or drum, and can be used to reproduce vectors and characters directly from computer output or a magnetic storage device. A flatbed plotter moves the pen along two perpendicular axes over a stationary flat sheet of paper. The drum plotter rotates the paper which is wrapped around a cylinder, while moving it under a pen which in turn moves along an axis parallel to the rotational axis of the oscillating cylinder. These pen plotters are available in a wide range of sizes to suit most design needs of the user. Flatbed plotters may be fitted with multiple pens for specific applications. An example of the output generated by a pen plotter is shown in Fig. 24-3, *p. 373*.

Printer/plotters produce images electrostatically on paper which is coated with a dielectric. They are relatively large and expensive, but they produce high-quality black and white copies.

CRT copiers reproduce images directly from the graphics screen or memory using either thermal, electrophotographic, or electrostatic technology.

Impact graphics printers use the dot-matrix impact approach to reproduction.

FIGURE 24–2 CAD workstation.

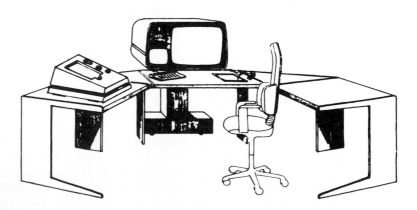

FIGURE 24–3   Production drawing prepared with CAD (Computervision) system and printed using a pen plotter.

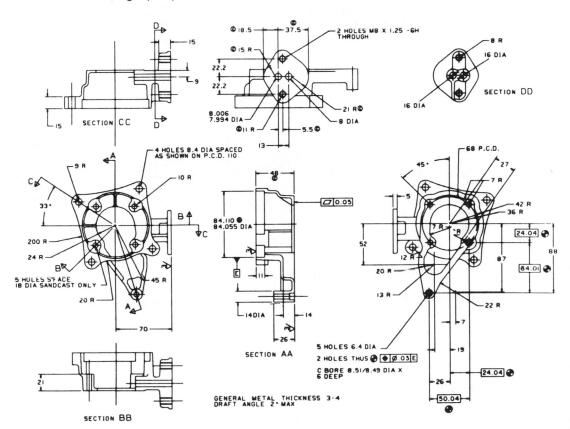

24.7 CAD OPERATING PRINCIPLE

The component geometry entered by the operator at the CAD workstation is converted by the computer into a digital representation. This data volume is referred to as the internal computer model.

It is necessary to differentiate between two-dimensional (2-D), two-and-one-half dimensional (2½-D), and three-dimensional (3-D) models in computer representations (*Fig. 24-4, p. 374*). These designations specify whether only profile representations of objects (2-D) or volume representations (3-D) are stored. In the case of 3-D models, a further distinc- tion is made between line (wire frame) representation and surfaceoriented and volume-oriented model representations. The models differ in terms of the amount of data which must be entered and stored in the internal computer.

Line or wire frame models are less informative than volume models, wire models becoming very ambiguous in certain cases and therefore having limited application in design and production.

FIGURE 24–4 Geometry model classes for CAD.

		Description of Elements	Internal Computer Representation
2D lateral model	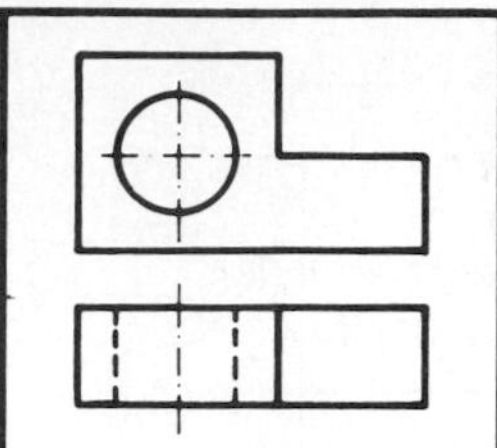	as 2D profile with 14 profile elements	14 profile elements 13 point elements
2 1/2 D profile body	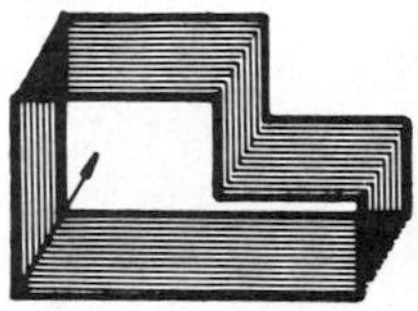	as profile body with 6 profile elements and recessing info	1 volume element 8 surface elements 18 profile elements 12 point elements
2 1/2 D rotating body	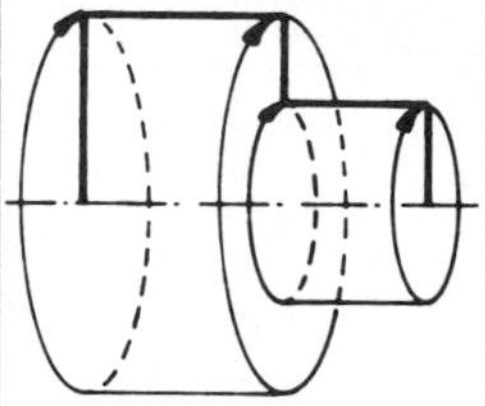	as rotating body from 6 profile elements and angular rotation	1 volume element 5 surface elements 5 profile elements 6 point elements
3D lateral model	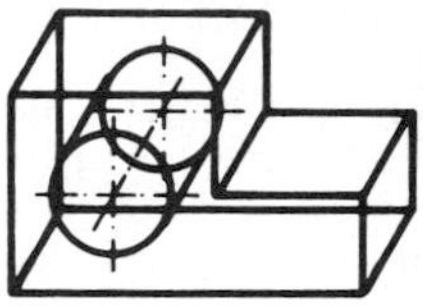	as 3D profile with 22 profile elements	22 profile elements 18 point elements
3D surface model	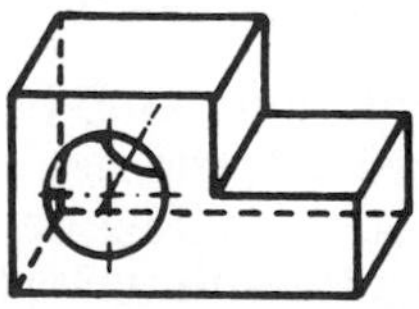	closed surface with 8 planes and 1 cylindrical surface area	9 surface elements 19 profile elements 14 point elements
3D solid model	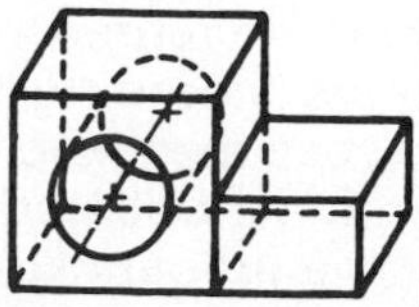	volume body with 2 right parallel-epipids & 1 cylinder (substracted)	3 volume elements 9 surface elements 19 profile elements 14 point elements

In generating a component representation as a 2½-D model, for example, one can use a 2-D profile representation (contour drawing) and by moving that 2-D surface representation along the Z axis generate a 2½-D volume. On symmetrical parts the 2-D profile can be rotated 360° about its own axis to represent a 2½-D volume. Most CAD systems for mechanical design today are 2½-D systems with wire frame philosophy which can be expanded, in part, with surface elements.

Development is clearly in the direction of 3-D solid modeling (3-D geometric models) which provide a total 3-D volumetric and geometric definition. Having a 3-D mathematical internal definition of the volumetric geometry provides entirely new engineering opportunities from two points of view: upward compatibility with analytical packages, and downward compatibility to the production of manufacturing programs.

The generation of component geometry can be achieved with 2-D or 3-D basic elements (*Fig. 24-5, p. 376*). The description of a workpiece is possible using these primary elements (straight line, circle, plane, cylinder, and so on), but they use a large amount of data memory. Although this represents the transfer of previously manual work to the computer, it basically maintains the same design thought processes. In order to reduce input time, user-selected elements can be stored in the CAD data base as geometric macros to cover those standard parts or representations that are frequently used.

These macros can be compared to the templates used in the old work method.

For parts families, similar shapes are grouped and are easily called up to make minor dimension or form parameter changes.

Functions for manipulating geometric elements should be included in the geometric capabilities of the system. They are particularly important in order to modify and adapt the entered model data until an optimally designed product has been achieved. These system functions include rotation, translation, mirroring, intersection, duplication, scaling, and other miscellaneous functions. The usefulness of any CAD system is assessed, in part, by the number of these functions it offers.

While the generation of a single element is not necessarily faster compared with manual drafting, the advantages become rather impressive in terms of speed and accuracy when elements are reproduced and in descriptions of the whole component utilizing component symmetries in combination with scaling and duplicating functions.

The workpiece geometric description data developed during the design process also embodies specifications for production of the part. In manual design, this is documented in the form of technical drawings, and all subsequent process steps (parts list preparation, process plan preparation, NC part programming, coordinate measuring machine programming, and so on) are all based on, and refer back to, these drawings. Therefore, in manual procedures, the technical drawing is the primary data source, but in CAD/CAM applications, the conventional technical drawing loses its significance as the main data carrier. The data describing the geometric and technological information (including surface finish and tolerance) are now available within the internal computer model. The total description of the geometric model is therefore stored in the system data base and is readily accessible for the production of NC part programs, scheduling, and materials ordering. The geometric model thus forms the basis for a completely integrated CAD/CAM system that provides for the control and processing of all design and manufacturing data (*Fig. 24-6*).

FIGURE 24–5 Systemization of description elements for CAD.

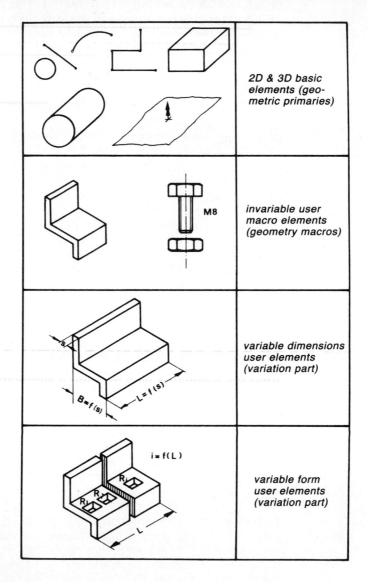

2D & 3D basic elements (geometric primaries)

invariable user macro elements (geometry macros)

variable dimensions user elements (variation part)

variable form user elements (variation part)

FIGURE 24–6   Representation of geometric data flow.

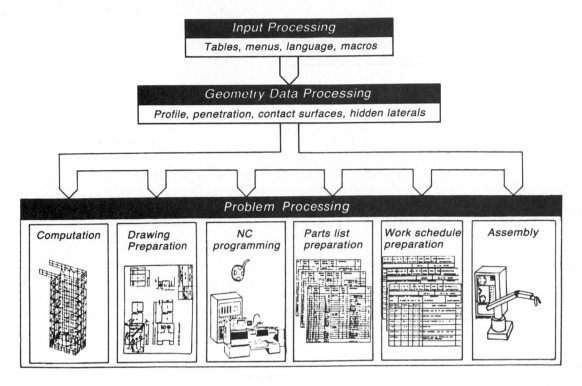

24.8 NC PART PROGRAMMING WITH CAD

After the geometric data defining a component have been stored internally in the computer, this stored data can then be used for computer-aided process planning and NC part programming. Chapter 11 dealt with computer-assisted NC part programming but focused mainly on the conversion of information from the technical drawing into an NC program. This required either the utilization of an NC programming language, such as APT, ADAPT, or COMPACT II, or manual data input directly into the CNC. However, with an integrated NC part programming capability within a CAD system, the tool-path program may be generated directly from the geometrically-verified, internally-stored computer model by means of a conversion program. The NC programmer calls up from a previously established tool data file, details of all the tools necessary to machine the item. Then the internally-stored computer model of the part is extracted from the CAD system data base and displayed on the VDU screen. Depending on the machining process, various tool-path-control sequences can be generated from the stored tool geometry files, especially prepared for:

- Point-to-point controls
- 2½-D axis controls for profile machining processes

- 3-axis controls for surface machining
- 5-axis controls for 3-D surface and pocket machining

The tool-path description is determined by the user via a graphic-interactive dialogue at the CAD workstation. The whole tool-path sequence can either be completely determined by the NC part programmer, including the optimization of the NC part program, or the programmer can have the tool-path sequence and number of cuts generated automatically by the CAD system (that is, with surface or pocket milling). The tool-path data are computed from the part geometry as a function of the tools to be used, and are dependent on the surface or contour geometry, tool diameter and corner radii, machining allowances, and tolerances.

The graphics capabilities of a CAD system make it simple to carry out visual verification of the tool-path description and to check for collision of tools with clamping devices and other obstructions. The NC programmer can also easily change or edit the tool path at a later time or can adapt it to different geometry. To speed up programming work, it is possible to use the group technology principles described in Chapter 23 in preparing NC user macros or NC variant programs for part families.

After tool-path geometry has been generated and stored it must be supplemented by production technology values (practical cutting parameters, for example). Elements of the part geometry are automatically provided with symbolic labels by most CAD systems (*Fig. 24-7*), and these labels serve to identify the tool paths associated with the geometric elements within the NC source program.

Tool paths can also be addressed on an interactive-graphic basis by touching the displayed tool path line with an appropriate input device.

With the editing function of the CAD system, the NC programmer can finally insert the remaining technological specifications such as rapid traverse rpm, feed rates, and coolant ON/OFF. Thus the programmer completes the generation of the NC program for the component.

The output format of the NC program is, in the case of most modern CAD systems, an APT source code or a CLDATA file, and, depending on further processing intent, it can be listed, produced as punch tape, or copied onto magnetic tape or hard disk. In any event, the data must be further processed through a postprocessor for each specific NC/CNC system, although postprocessors can be integrated into the CAD system so that machine-specific NC programs are produced directly.

Two possibilities exist for the transmission to the production machinery of NC programs generated in a CAD system (*Fig. 24-8, p. 380*). The first method consists of transmission by intermediate data carriers, such as punch tapes, magnetic tapes, and floppy disks. This is referred to as off-line operation. The second possibility for data transmission is by direct on-line operation, and this is achieved by coupling the CAD system directly to the production units via data cables.

By coupling the production machinery to the CAD system, part geometries can be called up and part programs generated, or completed programs can be immediately downloaded to the NC/CNC machines. Such a tight coupling of CAD system and production unit appears visionary at first, but it really serves to illustrate the logical continuation

FIGURE 24–7   An example of APT labeled geometry generated by the Applicon CAD system.

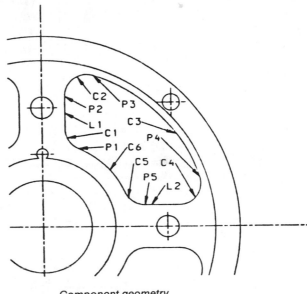

Component geometry

```
INOUT V1H

PARTNO 123456789
P1=POINT/-7.3972,1.3723,0.9740
C1=CIRCLE/-7.2450,1.7150,0.9740,0.3750
L1=LINE/-7.6200,2.2863,0.9740,-7.6200,1.7150,0.9740
P2=POINT/-7.6200,2.2863,0.9740
C2=CIRCLE/-7.2450,2.2863,0.9740,0.3750
P3=POINT/-7.1293,2.6430,0.9740
C3=CIRCLE/-7.9799,0.0201,0.9740,2.7574
P4=POINT/-5.3570,0.8707,0.9740
C4=CIRCLE/-5.7137,0.7550,0.9740,0.3750
L2=LINE/-6.2850,0.3800,0.9740,-5.7137,0.3800,0.9740
P5=POINT/-6.2850,0.3800,0.9740
C5=CIRCLE/-6.2850,0.7550,0.9740,0.3750
C6=CIRCLE/-8.0120,-0.0120,0.9740,1.5148
FINI
```

of the CAD + CAM = CAE concept. It represents the integrated data flow between the application areas of CAD and CAM, where the NC/CNC machine configuration can be considered to act only as a terminal to the CAD system, allowing for two-way communication between the CAD/CAM and NC/CNC systems.

Such configurations have only been achieved in a very few special-ized plants to date, worldwide. Furthermore, the profile format generat-ed in the design computer by the CAD process is completely different from the profile format required by the CAM process for its production computer. Interfacing computer networks are therefore the most likely

FIGURE 24–8 Computer integration for CAD/CAM application.

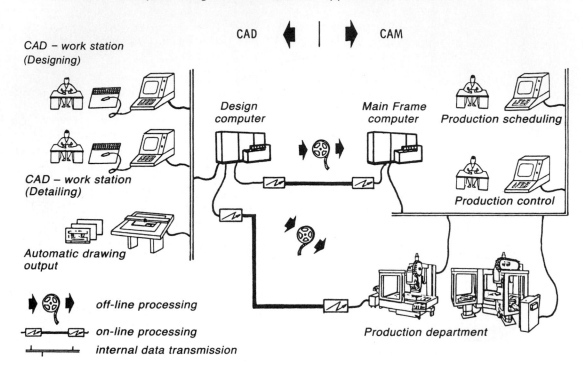

development, making possible the linking together of function computers for CAD and in-process computers for CAM. Design data already prepared are then easily transferable via data links or via a standardized geometry interface to the master production computer.

This production computer manages all NC program data and assigns them to the appropriate CNC production machines, as well as handling tasks such as machine tool operational data collection and sequential control functions.

24.9 THE FUTURE

The realization of an integrated data flow system between heterogeneous components of hardware and software is not available at the moment. However, actual examples of current CAD/CAM usage have highlighted two factors. First, it is increasingly necessary to shorten the job throughput time as much as possible, and this is greatly helped with the turnkey CAD systems which are available today. Second, data transmission must be more effectively formatted on an internal computer basis in order to achieve easier data transfer between CAD and CAM.

The use of CAD systems guarantees greater efficiency not only for drawing preparation, but also through tighter coupling to the CAM area. It also causes the two technical areas to exert a stronger positive influence on one another. Designers and drafters on the one hand and production planners and NC programmers on the other then enjoy a facility that virtually guarantees the following:

- Faster development, planning, and production times
- Better quality products by assessing alternate solutions and reducing transmission errors
- Greater flexibility due to the possibility of considering modifications right up to the point of manufacture, thanks to the speed with which computerized preparation of engineering specifications can be processed through to NC part programs

24.10 GUIDELINES FOR IMPLEMENTATION OF CAD/CAM

While few companies will have the luxury of reorganizing and retooling to accommodate new technologies, it is nevertheless worthwhile to explore the optimum environment for implementation of CAD/CAM, NC, CNC, DNC, and robotics. It is no exaggeration to suggest that management structures and existing policies, procedures, practices, and systems may be the largest stumbling block to widespread application of emerging technologies.

We have all been trained to analyze investment opportunities to determine their effects on profitability. While this concept will be the mainstay of industry for the foreseeable future, it presents a dichotomy to decision makers who are considering implementation of CAD/CAM and other new factory automation technologies. Although some short-term savings can be accurately predicted with these systems, there is general agreement among managers that the greatest benefits are related to improved product quality and cost, as well as to greatly reduced lead times.

Few companies faced with the pressures of inflation, high interest rates, and declining profits are prepared to risk the very large expenditures often necessary to apply these technologies when the return on investment cannot be realized for 5 to 10 years. On the other hand, most managers recognize that without the efficiency made possible by CAD/CAM, NC, and so on, they cannot expect to compete in the international marketplace of the '90s. It is this dilemma that has made many companies, large and small, decide to take only small exploratory steps into the CAD/CAM area.

Furthermore, many companies have very structured policies and procedures regarding the acquisition of computer systems and their operation. These procedures, developed over the past 20 years with business data processing systems, are often too restrictive to allow for experimentation and hands-on use of CAD/CAM computers by engineers.

Beyond the questions concerning economics and policy remain the considerable challenges of planning for CAD/CAM, NC, robotics, and related technologies. The starting point for this planning effort should be the formation of a multidisciplinary task force which includes representatives from both corporate and operating units. This task force should be charged with the responsibility for developing objectives for factory automation and for drawing up a general strategy for accomplishing these objectives. Involvement of qualified outside consultants may be advisable during this phase to ensure that the plan takes full advantage of state-of-the-art technology and avoids mistakes made by other companies.

Following acceptance of the strategic plan by management, organizational responsibility for CAD/CAM technology should be decided. Only at this point can specific work plans be laid out to evaluate, acquire, and install the systems. These work plans should provide for heavy involvement of system end users in the selection and application of systems, as well as for major programming efforts. The implementation plan should include provisions for training and preventive maintenance, as well as a method of measuring the effectiveness of new system installations.

A critical factor in successful implementation of CAD/CAM, NC, CNC, DNC, and robotics is the general level of understanding of the technology across the entire company. From the executive office to the shop floor, people need to know enough about the various systems and machinery to avoid the apprehension that is certain to result from lack of understanding. The early installation of pilot systems for the sole purpose of allowing people to become acquainted with terminology and functions is worthwhile. No amount of literature search or visits to suppliers or other plants can serve this familiarization objective as well as actually watching a system run your own parts in your own shop. This hands-on perspective is critical to proper decision making and planning for broad-based installations.

The actual selection of various components of hardware and software should be assigned to committees of technically qualified people who will be responsible for the eventual implementation. People directly involved in the decision to purchase or develop a system are much more likely to make it work than if they inherit someone else's choice! Any company considering purchase of equipment will find a mature sales force in place at most suppliers. These sales engineers can be most helpful in providing product specifications and arranging tests. The prospective buyer must be on guard constantly, however, to determine whether features and capabilities actually exist in a system at present or are only at the planning stage. Buying a system based on promised future capabilities is extremely risky in today's explosion of computer technology. Heavy emphasis should be placed on the stability of the supplier's business and the depth of commitment to product support.

A final word of caution to prospective systems buyers. A system demonstration is not always what it appears to be! It may be difficult to determine if the clever program you observe at a demonstration is really the result of a completed piece of software or the result of a canned demonstration tape. A seemingly stand-alone computer may in fact be networked to a development center at a remote location. The actual hardware itself may look like a production unit from the outside, but may be a first "breadboard" prototype inside. A few pointed questions about where other units are installed, and when you can actually buy and install your own, will normally clarify such issues.

Most suppliers are reputable and will not purposely misrepresent their products or capabilities, but many cannot resist the temptation to sell tomorrow's technology today. This is true of CIM at the present time because of the problems of equipment intercommunication which have yet to be fully resolved—see Chapter 19.

Finally, it should be clearly appreciated that manufacturing systems are, and can only be, as flexible as the individual items of NC equipment contained within the complete system.

QUESTIONS FOR CHAPTER 24

1. Is a CAD system little more than an expensive but versatile NC programming facility?
2. What are the principal components of a CAD system and what are their functions?
3. Why are CAD systems frequently used in close conjunction with CAM systems?
4. Describe briefly the basic steps that occur between a CAD-generated component drawing and the production of the required CNC program.
5. What type of CAD graphics display is preferred? Why?
6. What do you understand about a $2\frac{1}{2}$-D model?
7. Using a suitable shape, illustrate how a CAD system would display it in 2-, $2\frac{1}{2}$- and 3-D modes.
8. Describe how CAD systems use, to great advantage, the systemization of basic engineering elements.
9. What are the two greatest impediments to a much more general adoption of fully integrated CAD/CAM systems worldwide?

APPENDIX 1

Glossary of NC, CNC, and CAM Terminology

Absolute Coordinate System
All coordinates are measured from a fixed data or zero point for each axis.

Absolute Data Input
All programmed geometric data are related to a fixed zero point for each axis.

Absolute Measuring System
A measuring system in which all positions of an axis are measured from a fixed zero point. For absolute measuring the following measuring devices can be used: inductosyn, resolvers, absolute coded rotary encoders, potentiometers, and absolute coded linear scales.

Access Time
The time interval between the time at which data are called for from a storage device and the time delivery is completed.

Accuracy
(1) The degree of freedom from error: that is, the degree of conformity to truth or to a rule. (2) The difference between the target and the average from that target plus or minus three standard deviations for a confidence limit of 99.9 percent. The averages and deviations are found by making many identical programmed moves and then correlating them. See also, repeatability.

Active Memory
The part of the control logic in which data are stored as they are being executed.

Actual Position
The actual positional value of an axis fed back by the measuring system to the controller.

Adaptive Control (A/C)
(1) A control method using sensors for real time measurement of process variables with calculation and adjustment of control parameters as a means of achieving near optimum process performance. (2) Machine control units for which fixed speeds and feeds are not programmed. The control unit, working from feedback sensors, is able to optimize situations by automatically controlling these operating parameters.

Address
A coded identification, as represented by a name, label, or number for a register, location in storage, or any other data source to indicate the destination of data, such as the location of a station in a communication network.

Address Format
The assignment of data contained on a tape to the different commands and functions of the machine. The five types of address formats are word address, TAB sequential, fixed sequential, TAB ignore, and variable block format.

Algorithm
A prescribed set of well-defined rules or procedures for the solution of a problem in a finite number of steps.

Alphanumeric
Referring to the totality of characters that are either alphabetic or numeric.

Amplifier
A device for amplifying the output of an electrical signal. In a numerical control this is normally a servosystem which amplifies the error signal of a measuring system.

Analog
(1) Pertaining to representation by means of continuously variable physical quantities. (2) Using physical variables such as distance or rotation to represent and correspond to numerical variables that occur in

a computation. (3) A system which utilizes electrical voltages or ratios to represent physical axis positions.

Analog-to-Digital (A/D) Converter
A device which converts an analog input signal to a digital output signal.

ASCII
American Standard Code for Information Interchange. A data transmission code which was standardized by the American Standards Association. Seven bits are used to represent a character, with the eighth bit providing for an even number of punched holes per character parity check.

Assembler
(1) A translation program which converts program code written in assembler to machine code. (2) A machine-specific, low-level programming language. The commands for the machine are written in a mnemonic code which the computer can identify by a specific bit-pattern.

Asynchronous Axes
The control of these axes is independent of that of the main axes. For example, they might be auxiliary axes of a handling robot fitted to an NC machine.

Automatic Guided Vehicle (AGV)
Computer-controlled vehicle which needs no rails, and which is used for the transportation of pieceparts (and cutting tools in some installations) in flexible manufacturing systems. It is usually guided by a signal from an inductive wire buried in the shop floor.

Automation
The use of machines for the performance of repetitive tasks. The jobs can be physical or mental work, and often have to be carried out in sympathy with other equipment. Automated operations are often controlled by a program which automatically checks the sequence validity and corrects deviations.

Auxiliary Functions (M)
All functions which are programmed under the M-address (miscellaneous functions).

Axis
(1) One of the reference lines of a coordinate system. (2) One of the lines of motion on a machine. (3) A coordinate reference on a graphical device. (4) A general direction along which the relative movements of the tool and workpiece occur.

Axis Calibration
Some CNC systems offer an axis calibration feature which permits the compensation of systematic measuring errors of axes, and thereby increases axis accuracy. For each axis, error values are stored, which are then added to, or subtracted from, the measured value, depending on the position and orientation of the axis.

Axis Control
A numerically controlled machine axis which is permanently connected to the control unit is designated an NC axis. If the control unit is only temporarily or intermittently switched to an axis, this is referred to as a "half numerically controlled axis" or $\frac{1}{2}$ axis. A numerical control which controls two axes in an alternating fashion is designated $2 \times \frac{1}{2}$ axis. The simultaneous control of two axes with an additional axis switched on temporarily is referred to as a $2\frac{1}{2}$ axes system.

Axis Lag
The dynamic difference between the calculated position target value and the actual position value of a machine axis during feed or rapid traverse. At high speeds, axis lag can cause geometric errors in the contour of the component.

Backlash
Movement between interacting mechanical parts resulting from looseness and deflections.

Backlash Compensation
Electronic compensation of backlash in the mechanical drive train of an axis feed.

Ball-Screw/Nut Axis Drive
A leadscrew with ultra-low friction between the spindle and the drive nut. An additional advantage is the high accuracy of the pitch and minimal play between spindle and nut. It is mainly employed for the precision movement of NC machine slideways, and has a high mechanical efficiency of about 98 percent.

BASIC

Short for Beginner's All Purpose Symbolic Instruction Code, this is a high-level programming language which is easy to learn and particularly suited to solving mathematical problems.

Batch Processing

(1) The technique of executing a set of programs so that each is completed before the next program is started. (2) A method of processing jobs on a computer where they are organized and handled sequentially. This is the opposite of timesharing where there is ready access to a computer.

Baud

Transmission speed of data, measured in bits per second.

BCD

Binary coded decimal. Each digit of a decimal number is represented by a binary number of at least 4 bits: 379 in BCD notation is 0011 0111 1001, for example.

Bidirectional Flow

In flowcharting, flow that can be extended over the same flowline in either direction.

Binary

(1) Pertaining to a characteristic or property involving a selection, choice, or a condition in which there are two possibilities. (2) Pertaining to the numbering system with a radix of two.

Binary Numbers

A numerical system in base 2 (as opposed to the conventional decimal system in base 10). The place value of each individual digit is given by a positive or negative power of the number 2. For example, in the usual decimal notation $51 = (5 \times 10^1) + (1 \times 10^0)$, while the binary number is:

$$110011 = (1 \times 2^5) + (1 \times 2^4) + (0 \times 2^3) + (0 \times 2^2) + (1 \times 2^1) + (1 \times 2^0) = 32 + 16 + 0 + 0 + 2 + 1 = 51$$

Since only two characters are used (0 and 1), binary numbers can be easily represented—for example, by the position of an ON/OFF switch or by hole/no hole in a punch tape or punched card. By the arrangement 1 = hole, 0 = no hole, individual characters can be represented in encoded form via various hole patterns.

Bit

A contraction of binary digit, this is the smallest unit of information, usually expressed as 1 or 0.

Block

(1) A group of words, characters, or digits handled as a unit. (2) A collection of contiguous data recorded as a unit. Blocks are separated by block gaps and each block may contain one or more units of data. (3) A group of bits or binary digits transmitted as a unit. An encoding procedure is generally applied to the group of bits or binary digits for error control purposes. (4) Sometimes means 128 bytes of storage area.

Boolean Algebra

A process of reasoning, or a system of theorems, using a symbolic logic and dealing with classes, proposition, or ON/OFF circuit elements. It employs symbols to represent operators such as AND, OR, NOR, or NAND to permit mathematical calculation.

BTR Input

Abbreviation for behind the tape-reader input. Connection for the direct input of control data via data lines "behind" the punch-tape reader. It is used, for example, in DNC systems.

Bus (Business Line)

A bidirectional data transmission link between several modules or components of a processor-controlled electronic system. Mostly a busline is divided into address bus, data bus, control bus, and so on.

Byte

Group of 8 bits. A sequence of adjacent binary digits operated on as a unit. A series of computer binary bits organized together to hold a symbol letter or number in a computer. Sometimes called a "word." A word may be comprised of 9, 12, or 15 bits, for example. In describing the memory or logic capacity of a computer, terminology such as "8K, 9-bit words" could be used.

CAD

Abbreviation for computer-aided design.

CAM

Abbreviation for computer-aided manufacturing, denoting the use of computers in different areas of manufacturing, such as for the control of material flow or machine control.

CAM-I

Abbreviation for Computer Aided Manufacturing International, Inc., the continuation in development of, and the replacement for, the APT long range program.

Canned Cycle (Fixed Cycle)

Several fixed, frequently used machine or program functions, such as tool changing, pallet changing, or drilling operations, which are permanently stored in the control and which can be initiated by a single command in the part program (G-function).

Cartesian Coordinates

The definition of a point in space by means of a system of three orthogonal axes, designated X, Y, and Z.

Cell

The smallest flexible manufacturing unit, consisting of one or two CNC stand-alone machines, complemented by ancillary equipment (such as auto-tool change), and providing unmanned operation for a very limited period.

Channel Structure

The structure of a CNC which permits the distinction between synchronous main axes, which require coordinated interpolation, and the asynchronous auxiliary axes.

Character

A letter, digit, or other symbol that is used as part of the organization, control, or representation of data. A character is often in the form of a spatial arrangement of dots or connected strokes.

Chip

(1) In machining, a particle of material removed from a workpiece as a result of a processing operation to alter the shape of the raw material. (2) In electronics, an integrated circuit mounted on a base to enable connection into a larger circuit.

CIM (Computer-Integrated Manufacture)

No universally accepted definition exists, but CIM is generally taken to imply computer-assisted monitoring and control of all aspects of a manufacturing business, thereby providing a source of rapid information flow from which optimal operating decisions can be made.

Circular Interpolation

The calculation of the points on a circular contour, which is specified only by the start and end points and center point or radius. Usually, circular interpolation is performed in a two axis plane (XY, XZ, YZ) and not in free space.

Closed-Loop On/Off

A control circuit, where a feedback signal is used to switch something on or off when a certain target value is reached.

C MOS

Abbreviation of "complementary MOS," a semiconductor drawing negligible current.

CNC

Numerical control with one or more integrated microcomputers, used to perform all control functions. Also called "softwired NC" because of the capability to change software in the computer memory.

Code

A set of unambiguous rules specifying the way in which data may be represented.

Code Converter

Converts digital input signals of one code into digital output signals of another code.

Code Format

The arrangement of hole combinations in a column of a punch tape to represent a specific character.

Code Inspection

NC control function of a programming device in order to eliminate incorrect characters from the punch tape. Every step of the punch tape input is checked for: a) an odd number of holes for a character in the EIA code (parity check) and, b) the meaning of each character, that is, testing for a hole combination permitted by the programming protocol.

A deviation triggers the tape error or programming error indicator and stops the programming equipment or control. Path or switching data with incorrect values are not identified by code inspection.

Command

(1) An item of information which determines which branch of an algorithm or application program will be used. Vaguely distinguishable from an instruction by being in data stream rather than in the text or by being specified on-line rather than off-line. Distinguishable from data which usually does not affect the branching in an algorithm. (2) A control signal. (3) An instruction in machine language. (4) A mathematical or logic operator.

Comparator

A computer program used to compare two versions of the same computer program under test.

Compatibility

The degree to which output languages/programs from punch tapes or magnetic tapes, and components from different systems can freely interact. Two devices are compatible if they can communicate without any additional interfacing equipment being necessary.

Compiler

A computer translator program that transforms a higher-order language source program into an assembly language format for subsequent transformation to machine language by an assembler.

Computer

Basically, a computer is a data processing device with the capability of carrying out calculations and logic operations. After specific input data is provided, the computer will process the data to provide the desired output.

Computer-Aided. . . (CA. . .)

Abbreviation for all computer-aided technologies, for example:
CAD = Computer-aided design
CAE = Computer-aided engineering
CAM = Computer-aided manufacture
CAPP = Computer-aided process planning
CAQ = Computer-aided quality assurance

Computer-Aided Programming

Preparation of a part program with the aid of a computer. Again with computer aid, a processor and postprocessor program is then produced in a special programming format suitable for input into the NC machine tool.

Console

(1) The main operator control center of the computer. Usually, the results of all operations, indicators, and general conditions are available at the console. (2) That part of a computer used for communication between the operator and the computer. (3) Usually the unit containing the external side of a device where controls and indicators are available for manual operation of that device.

Continuous Path Control

A form of numerical control where the relative movement of tool and component along the required path is continuously controlled. Continuous path control is achieved by the coordinated simultaneous operation of two or more machine axes. Path controllers employ interpolators for this purpose. They calculate the exact path contour according to the start and end points of the path elements. (For circular paths either the center point or the radius is also required.)

Controller

An apparatus of unitized or sectional design, through which commands are introduced and manipulated.

Control Loop Circuit

A system in which an output signal is fed back to the input point and then compared with the input signal.

Converter

A device capable of converting impulses from one mode to another, such as analog to digital, parallel to serial, or one code to another.

Coordinate

An ordered set of data values, either absolute or relative, which specifies a particular location.

Coordinate Measuring Machine (CMM)

A computer controlled measuring machine which can be used to inspect a workpiece, whereby the individual coordinate values are measured numerically and indicated digitally.

Core Memory

A read-write memory which consists of ferromagnetic rings arranged in a wire matrix. Each ring stores one bit of data.

Counter

A device such as a register or storage location used to represent the number of occurrences of an event.

CPC/CPL

Abbreviation for customer programmable cycles or customer programmable language. This is a feature offered by most modern CNCs, enabling customers to write their own machining cycles or macros in a high-level programming language (BASIC, PASCAL, or a hybrid language).

CPU

Abbreviation for central processing unit. The CPU is the heart of any computer, and consists of the processor, controller, and register. A CPU can be made up of either discrete components, an IC, or a microprocessor with memory modules.

CRT (Cathode Ray Tube)

A vacuum tube, much like a television screen, within which a beam of electrons is focused to a small spot on a luminescent screen and deflected by high voltage to trace output graphics. Some CRTs, called storage tubes, can hold images on the screen continuously without electron-beam retracing.

Cursor

A movable electronic pointer on a VDU screen, generally displayed as a blinking point or dash. It helps the operator with orientation on the screen, especially during editing of input data.

Cutter Compensation

A means of adjusting the cutter on a numerical control system to compensate for the variance in actual cutter radius from the normal programmed cutter radius.

Cutter Location File (CL File/CL Tape/CL Data)

A data set which defines the cutter centerline path. This data must be postprocessed in order to convert the CL data into a part program for a specific machine tool.

Cutter Path

The path followed by the center line of a cutting tool as the part is being cut to the desired dimensions.

Cycle

Any set of operations that is repeated regularly in the same sequence. The operations may be subject to minor variations on each repetition.

Cycle Time

(1) An interval of time in which one set of events or phenomena is completed. (2) The minimum time necessary for a CNC to prepare program blocks for their processing. When processing time is shorter than cycle time the machine is stationary until the next block can be processed, and the resulting operating data downloaded. However, such standstill situations can be avoided by reducing machine feed rate.

Data

A representation of fact, concepts, or instructions in a formalized manner suitable for communication, interpretation, or processing by human or automatic means.

Data Carrier

A physical medium on which data can be stored for later retrieval; punch tape, magnetic tape, or diskette, for example.

Data Processing

Carrying out a systematic series of calculations or other logical operations according to specific data to derive further data, to place them in a certain format, or to control other devices—numerically controlled machine tools, for example.

Data Resolution

The minimum resolution of a control or measuring system, for example, 0.0001 in.

Data Storage
The electronic storage of data on a data carrier or other storage device, from which they can be retrieved at will.

Datum Offset (Zero Offset)
The capability of shifting a datum point.

Datum Point
A particular point from which individual coordinate dimensions are referenced. See also, zero reference point.

Dead Zone
A well-defined zone in which a change of input signal does not cause a change in output signal.

Debugging
The process of identifying errors in programs by means of either special debugging programs, or by laborious manual means. See also, editing.

Decade
The distance between two variables in a relationship of 10:1.

Decade Switch
Has ten switching positions, with values from 0 through 9. They are often employed in decade switch groups, thus permitting the manual setting of a parameter to any required numeric value, provided the number of switches equals the number of digits of the decimal number. They are mostly used for the presetting of target values for certain machine positions or tool compensations.

Decimal Point Programming
Path measurement input using decimal points instead of leading or trailing zeros.

Examples:

417 instead of	417 000
.75 instead of	750
.1 instead of	100
.001 instead of	1

The advantage of decimal point programming is not that tapes are shorter, but that manual data input is more convenient and less prone to error.

Dedicated Computer
A computer which is dedicated to a specific task. For example, in a DNC installation a computer is dedicated to a group of machines, whereas in a CNC it is dedicated to a single machine.

Deviation
Deviation of an actual value from its target value. An example is the difference between the actual path and the programmed path of a cutting tool (defined as dynamic path deviation), which impairs piecepart contour accuracy.

Diagnosis
A special feature of computers or CNCs which permits the localization of program errors with the aid of the screen display. Software features such as logic analyzers, PLC monitor, multiple channel oscilloscope, comparison of target and actual values, and graphic display of measured values all belong in this category.

Dialogue
In relation to NC, the designation of a data input method in which the operator is "led" by the control, that is, the data required for positions, parameters, and additional information are requested from the operator by the NC unit via a display screen menu.

Differential Resolver
A position encoder consisting of a transformer with two secondary windings in which reciprocal voltages are produced and are dependent on the position of the primary winding or the magnetic core.

Digit
(1) A symbol that represents one of the nonnegative integers which is smaller than the base. For example, in decimal notation, a digit is one of the characters from 0 through 9. Synonymous with numeric characters. (2) See binary numbers.

Digital
Relating to digits, operating by the use of discrete signals to represent data in the form of numbers or other characters. The display of information as numbers in a specific code.

Digital Data
Information represented in a discrete (discontinuous) form and transmitted by such

means as the presence or absence of a voltage, the presence or absence of a hole on a punched tape or card, or a contact in the open or closed position.

Digital Input
Input data in the form of digits which are entered manually or automatically via punch tapes or from a magnetic storage medium.

Digital Readout, Numerical Display
The desired target location or the actual location of one or more axes is visually displayed as a decimal number.

Digital-to-Analog (D/A) Converter
A device which transforms digital data into analog data.

Digital Measuring System
A measuring system which measures discrete values in either incremental or absolute format.

Digitizer
(1) A device for converting positional information into digital signals. Typically, a drawing or other graphic is placed on the measuring surface of the digitizer and traced by the operator using some form of cursor or stylus. Frequently, an alphanumeric or function keyboard is also provided for inserting supplementary information which aids in defining the elements of the drawing. A digitizer may output to any standard peripheral device such as a card punch or magnetic tape unit. It can be interfaced directly to a computer and used interactively in conjunction with a display. (2) A device that converts graphic representations to digital form, i.e., Data Tablet.

Direct Measurement
A measuring system which does not convert linear slide movement into a rotary movement.

Direct Numerical Control (DNC)
The use of a shared computer for distribution of part program data via data lines to remote machine tools, and other NC equipment in the system.

Diskette
A flexible disk of oxide-coated mylar stored in paper or plastic envelopes. The entire envelope is inserted in the disk unit. When the diskette is being read or written to, the plastic disk is rotated within a disk drive unit. Diskettes provide low cost storage for microcomputers and minicomputers.

DOS
Abbreviation for disk operating system; a disk-orientated operating system for computers which predominantly uses disks for storage of programs and data.

Dwell
A timed delay of programmed duration, not cyclic or sequential, that is, not an interlock or hold. Dwells of specific durations may be specified by preparatory G-function G04.

Editing
The process of correcting or optimizing a part program by adding, removing, or modifying individual characters, words, or blocks of information in the program. See also, debugging.

EIA Standard Code
A standard code for point-to-point, linear path, and continuous path controls proposed by the U.S. Electronic Industries Association in their standard RS 244. It uses a punched tape input medium which is one in. wide and has eight tracks.

Electronic Handwheel
A small integrated handwheel found on the operating panel of modern CNC controllers. It can be used in the setup operating mode to finely adjust individual axes, and is the electronic equivalent of the mechanical handwheels found on conventional machine tools.

Encoder
A type of transducer commonly used to convert angular or linear position into digital data. See also, resolver.

Encoding
Translation of data from a program tape onto a punch or magnetic tape.

End of Block (EOB or $) Character
A character entered on a program tape to denote the end of a block of data.

End-of-File Mark (EOF)
A code which signals that the last record of a file has been read.

EPROM, EEPROM
Electronic memory module which permits the deletion of data stored on it, either electronically (EEPROM) or by means of ultraviolet light (EPROM).

Error-Detecting Code
A code in which each expression conforms to specific rules of construction. Therefore, if errors occur in an expression, their presence is detected.

Error Signal
Differential voltage which is produced by the positional deviation between a preset target value and the actual value measured.

Executive Program
The software for the microprocessors of a CNC, which achieves its desired functionality. It contains all the operational features of the controller and is developed by the CNC manufacturer.

External Interpolation
(1) A computer which is separate from the CNC performs all interpolations for linear, circular, or parabolic cutter paths. The resulting path data are then entered into the CNC where they can be more quickly processed. A storage medium commonly used for this purpose is magnetic tape. (2) An external calculation which deduces larger linear and circular paths for a sequence of points, and thus reduces the amount of input data to a path-control system with internal interpolation.

External Storage
Data storage which is not integrated into the central processing unit of a computer, often designed as mass storage (disk, tape, or RAM).

Family of Parts
A group of parts of similar geometry, which can be machined by similar machines and tooling without major changes to the setup of the machine tools. See also, group technology.

Feedback
(1) Change in input information of a system as a function of the output information of that system. (2) The concept of obtaining information from real experience and feeding it back into the planning and appropriate initial stages to improve system efficiency.

Feedback Loop
The part of a closed-loop system which feeds back a measured actual value for comparison to the target value.

Feed-Rate Control
A capability for controlling the feed rate manually or via tape.

Feed-Rate Override
A function which allows the operator to manually alter the feed rate by a desired percentage (usually 10–120 percent) of its programmed value.

File
Precisely defined region in the memory of a computer where data which are to be reused are stored. Typical NC examples are tool data files, material specification data files, and cutting tool data files.

Firmware
The control functions which are stored in the read-only memory (ROM), or in the microprogram of the CPU, are referred to as firmware and include functions like multiplication and division. In contrast to the operating system of a computer, firmware is not considered to be part of the operating software.

Fixed Sequential Format
An NC tape format whereby each word in the format is identified by its position. Every word must be stated even though it is repeated from the previous block.

Fixture
A mechanical device for holding a piecepart in a precisely defined position during the machining process.

Flexible Manufacturing System (FMS)
Machine tools which are closely linked to each other, for example by means of robots or automatic guided vehicles for component handling, and controlled by comput-

ers which coordinate the operation of all the items in the system. FMSs are employed in the automated manufacture of part families of any lot size.

Floating Zero
A characteristic of a numerical control system which allows the zero reference point to be established at any position over the full travel of the machine tool. See also, zero offset.

Floppy Disk
Another name for a diskette.

Flow Chart
A diagram which shows the structure and organization of a computer program and which specifies the sequence in which individual steps and subroutines are performed.

Format
A specific arrangement of data; the physical arrangement of data on a program tape and the overall pattern in which it is organized and presented.

Geometric Data
All information in a part program which describes tool traverse motions.

G Function
A preparatory code in a program tape to indicate a special function. The code consists of the letter G and two digits, which are preassigned to various functions, such as motion, delay, dimensional data coordinates, and feed rates.

Graphics
The use of a VDU screen as part of a CNC or an independent programming facility to provide graphics display of data. Typical examples are: input graphics for programming tasks including display of input corrections; simulation graphics for program testing, sometimes with dynamic display of cutting tools used; auxiliary graphics for rapid ancillary information retrieval to help the operator/programmer; and diagnostic graphics as a debugging aid.

Group Technology
The technique of grouping parts together that require similar manufacturing operations and not necessarily based on component shape. See also, family of parts.

Handling Unit
A robot or other mechanized device used for loading and unloading a machine, or for parts assembly.

Hard Disk
Encapsulated magnetic system for large-scale storage of data (sometimes called a Winchester disk). It has a much higher memory capacity than a diskette, and is permanently installed in the computer.

Hardware
(1) Physical equipment and peripherals of a computer system, including mechanical, magnetic, electrical, or electronic devices. Contrast with software. (2) The tangible instruments of a data processing system.

Hard-Wired
A CNC system which processes control data via hard-wired circuits and logic modules. Modification of the system is only possible by physically changing the wiring or exchanging modules.

Hexadecimal
A number system having the base of 16, predominantly used in computing. One hexadecimal digit is equivalent to a group of four bits. For the first ten digits the numbers 0 through 9 are used, the further six digits being represented by the first six letters of the alphabet (written in upper case letters A to F).

Decimal	Four Bit Group	Hexadecimal
0	0000	0
1	0001	1
3	0011	3
7	0111	7
9	1001	9
10	1010	A
11	1011	B
12	1100	C
13	1101	D
14	1110	E
15	1111	F

Home Position
The fixed "datum position" of each machine axis. It is generally the position in which the axis is completely retracted so

that maximum physical access to the machine is possible. The home position is often coincident with the zero point of the axis.

Host Computer
The computer which is highest in the hierarchy of an FMS. It coordinates all program data flow, piecepart transportation, tool management, materials handling, and inspection, as well as creating management reports as required.

Impulse
Short electrical signal (μs, ms) for the control of certain functions, numbering processes, and so on. Examples: Read impulse from a reader into the data memory; path measurement impulses from an incremental measuring system to the counter in the control. For interference-free processing of impulses it is necessary to have the highest possible signal-to-noise ratio of utilization signal to interference signal.

Increment
The quantity by which the value of a variable increases or decreases from one position or step to the next.

Incremental Coordinates
In computer graphics, the coordinate measured from the preceding coordinate in a sequence of values.

Incremental Dimension
A dimension measured from the preceding point in a series of points as opposed to an absolute dimension in which each point in a series would be dimensioned from a single reference point.

Incremental Jog
The capability of displacing distance in small increments.

Incremental System
(1) A control system in which each coordinate or positional dimension, both input and feedback, is taken from the last position rather than from a fixed datum point. (2) Programming whereby each coordinate location is given in terms of distance and direction along rectangular axes from the previous position and not from a fixed zero location.

Indirect Measurement
Measuring principle in which a rotating measuring system is driven via screw/nut or rack and pinion devices. Inaccuracies of the mechanical transmission elements impair measurement accuracy.

Inductosyn
Trademark for Farrand Controls analog position transducer. Available in linear and rotary versions for high precision positional measurement. The electrical output signal is produced by inductive coupling between scale and slider.

In-Process Gaging
Measurement control of a workpiece during computer-aided machining. Adaptation to numerically controlled machine tools enables the controls to compensate for external influences like tool wear, thermal expansion, and other factors which are not controlled on conventional machines.

Input
(1) Set of possibilities. (2) Pertaining to a device, process, or channel involved in the insertion or transfer of data or information into a computer or machine control unit.

Input Data
Coded instructions for the input into an NC controller via punch tape, magnetic tape, diskette, downloading from a DNC link, or direct manual input at the machine tool's controller.

Integrated Circuit (IC)
A circuit made up of semiconductors integrated into a single chip of standardized size.

Interface
The I/O module between different parts of a system, particularly between a machine tool and its control. Its functions are to decode, interpret, combine, and match electronic signals. Modern controls use programmable interfaces, where these functions are achieved via software.

Internal Interpolation
The calculation of the points on a linear,

circular, or parabolic contour carried out within the numerical controller itself. The start and end point of the contour, plus any necessary auxiliary points, are the only input data required by the CNC.

Interpolation

The passing of a curve or surface precisely through a set of data points, and/or by the insertion of intermediate information based on an assumed order or computation (for example, cutter paths are controlled by interpolation between fixed points by assuming intermediate points are on a line, a circle, or a parabola). In NC, curved sections are approximated by a series of straight lines or parabolic segments.

Interrupt

The interruption of a program at a specified position for a finite period of time for the call-up of a subroutine, for example. After the interruption, the program is continued from the interrupt point.

Island

A segregated area of the shop wherein several CNC machines and associated equipment are dedicated specially to machining a specific family of parts.

ISO Code

Standardized 8-track punch tape code with 7 data bits and one test bit in track 8.

KByte

Abbreviation of kilobyte; unit of the storage capacity of a computer. One kilobyte contains 1024 bytes (2 to the power of 10).

Language

A set of symbols, conventions, and rules used to convey information.

Light Emitting Diode (LED)

A semiconductor which emits a colored light beam, and can be used instead of colored light bulbs.

Linear Interpolation

The calculation of the points on a straight line, defined only by the start and end points. A distinction is made between linear interpolation by switching from one plane to the other ($2\frac{1}{2}$ -D), and linear interpolation in space (3-D).

Linear Path System

A point-to-point control with the capability of controlling the feed rates for movements in directions parallel to the axes of a machine, for straight-line milling, for example. The principle of linear path control is the control of parallel axis movement.

Logic

A system of computational components based on the basic switches either/or, on/off, and so on. Since only two conditions are possible, bistable devices can be used (relays, diodes, and so on).

Looped Tape

A system in which punch paper tape drops into a chute after its pass through the reader without being respooled. The beginning and end are joined together so that a continuously repeating pass-through is possible.

LSI

Abbreviation for large scale integration which denotes the integration of several chips into one single complex chip.

Machine Reference

A machine position which can always be located by the measuring system, even after power failure or program cancellation.

Machining Center

A multifunctional NC machine tool with automatic tool changing, automatic workpiece changing, and the capability of a wide variety of operations on up to five sides of a prismatic workpiece in a single setup.

Macro

A sequence of instructions (control data) which are stored and called up as one integral unit, canned cycles, for example.

Magnetic Tape

A data carrier or data storage medium which consists of a plastic tape with a ferromagnetic surface coating. It is generally used in the form of standard or minicassettes or cartridges for data input and output to and from NCs.

Management Information

General term to encompass information covering all aspects of, in this context, manufacturing management, such as materials handling operations, transportation times, setup and machining times, downtimes and their causes, lot sizes processed, manufacturing quality statistics, and assembly times.

Manual Data Input (MDI)
Manual insertion of part program data into the controller at the machine tool. Modern MDI controls have integrated programming aids and a graphics screen to simplify parts programming at the machine tool.

Manual Programming
The preparation of a part program in program format for a certain machine/NC combination without use of computer aids.

Manuscript
A form used by a part programmer to organize workpiece machining instructions. From this a program tape is punched or a computer program is prepared.

MAP
Abbreviation for manufacturing automation protocol. MAP is the name of a project initiated by General Motors to link independent manufacturing islands, thereby permitting continuous data flow throughout the company. It has now been internationally adopted. MAP also aims to ensure that all data and information from the order receiving department through job planning, materials handling, manufacturing, quality assurance, and accounts shall all use universally exchangeable data bases, via the use of standardized manufacturer-independent interfacing.

Measuring System
A transducer or a system of transducers necessary for measuring a machine's movements.

Menu
A selection of instructions or possibilities offered to the user by the computer and displayed on a VDU screen in the most user-friendly form.

M Function
Under the miscellaneous M address, programmable on-off functions such as spindle stop, coolant on/off, and tool changing are controlled. Also called auxiliary functions.

Microcomputer
A microprocessor with program memory, working memory, and an input/output unit is termed a microcomputer, and is the minimum configuration of a working system. Additionally, every microcomputer also needs the appropriate software to control it in the performance of its required tasks. Memory capacity ranges from 640 to 4000K bytes.

Microprocessor
A large scale integrated circuit performing the basic functions of the central processing unit of a computer. It basically consists of an arithmetic unit, various working registers, and a sequence control. To work correctly, a microprocessor needs additional memory modules for program and data storage.

Milling Cutter Radius Compensation
A manual adjustment or regulating capability for varying milling cutter radii which arise, for example, from regrinding or use. With this capability, the path of the milling cutter center point can be altered to allow for unavoidable deviations from the nominal size used in the program.

Minicomputer
The size of a computer is not determined by its physical dimensions but by its memory storage capacity. Minicomputers have a memory capacity of approximately between 8000 and 256,000K bytes, while mainframe systems have a minimum capacity of about 512,000K bytes. Such large computers permit the rapid processing of extensive and complex calculations.

Mirror Image Operation
By reversing the direction of only one axis of a machine tool, two mirror image workpieces can be produced from the same input data. Mirror images can be produced in all quadrants.

Modal
The structure of NC data blocks permits the use of two types of words. Commands in the form of modal words remain effective

until they are deleted or replaced by other commands. Nonmodal words are effective only once in an instruction, and have to be repeated if required again.

Modem
Abbreviation for modulator/demodulator; a device used for data transmission. It converts data from one format to another, for example, it converts characters in an 8-track code into bit-serial impulses for data transmission down telephone lines.

Moire Fringe
An effect caused by the opposing movement of two similar optical grids perpendicular to the grid lines. This interference effect consists of alternating light and dark patterns or bands which produce a cyclical bright/dark image as movement proceeds. Since these lines are basically enlarged pictures of the pitch (grid constants), they can be read by a photoelectric system and differentiated based on movement direction. This results in a highly accurate measuring method for small movements.

Monitor
VDU screen for the display of operations, results data, and so on in the form of text or graphics.

MOS
Abbreviation for metal oxide semiconductor; a semiconductor with a very high electrical input resistance.

Numerical Control (NC)
An electronic system to control movements of a machine tool through the insertion of numerical data. The system interprets these data and converts them into the appropriate electrical signals in order to cause the desired movements or actions at the machine tool.

Numerically Controlled Tool Change
A system which allows different cutting tools to be located and placed in the machine spindle on demand.

Object Program
A program in the binary code which can be loaded directly into a computer and is thus immediately executable. The output of an assembler processor is always an object program.

Off-Line Operation
An operation carried out independently of the main computer. (1) Pertaining to equipment or devices not under direct control of the central processing unit. (2) The CPU or MCU operates independently of the time base of the actual inputs; that is, considerable time may elapse between an input to the computer and the resulting output. It can also mean operation of peripheral equipment independent of the central processor of a computer system.

On-Line Operation
An operation carried out within the main computer system. (1) Pertaining to equipment or devices under direct control of the central processing unit. (2) Operation where input data is fed directly from measuring devices into the CPU or MCU. Results are obtained in real time; that is, computations and operations are based on current data to permit effective control action. It can also mean the operation of peripheral equipment in conjunction with the central processor of a computer system.

Open Loop System
A system which generates output signals but relies on the integrity of the system to execute them. There is no feedback for monitoring purposes.

Operating System
One or more programs which control the operation of a computer. It is the operating system that makes the processing of specific programs possible and manages the operations of the computer.

Output Signal
Current or voltage output, or mechanical force, provided by a control in order to meet a specific function.

Overshoot
The condition that occurs when a variable exceeds its target value.

Pallet
A portable piecepart holder. Jobs are usu-

ally loaded and unloaded remotely from CNC machines, and they remain on their respective pallet throughout the machining procedure. The use of programmable automatic pallet changers now makes it possible to cut to a minimum unproductive machine downtime normally required to align, clamp, load, and unload each job .

Parallel Axis

The simultaneous control of two or more mechanically independent axes which are parallel to each other. For example, if parallel motion to Z is desired, such as in the control of two spindles on one machine tool, then a secondary axis must be designated as being parallel to Z, which in this case would be W.

Parallel Data Input

The simultaneous transmission and input of information in the 8-track or 16-bit format via 8 or 16 parallel channels — the alternative to serial data input.

Parallel Input Mode

In this programming mode new part programs are written via a CNCs manual data input control, at the same time as the NC machine continues to produce a different part, controlled via the same NC controller.

Parametric Programming

NC programming by means of parameter input only—for example, the relevant parameters for holes on a certain pitch circle diameter are the pitch diameter, the number of holes, start and increment angles, and the appropriate drilling cycle. The system then automatically determines all necessary data from just these few input parameters.

Parity Check

A method for checking binary data for syntax errors, that is, to identify incorrect characters in a punch tape or in data transmission. An additional bit, the so-called "parity bit," is added to certain characters in order to keep the number of bits per character even (ISO Code) or odd (EIA Code).

Part Program

Specific and complete set of data and instructions for the purpose of manufacturing a part on an NC machine tool.

Path Data

All data which are necessary to achieve a certain relative position or movement between tool and workpiece. The programmability of dimensional numbers (geometrical data) is a basic characteristic of numerical control. The path data are taken by the programmer from the design drawings of the component to be machined, and then they are entered in such a way that the paths or positions of the tools with respect to the piecepart are clearly described.

Path Measuring

Path measuring with electrically usable signals or voltages is the basis of numerical control. The relative movements between tool and workpiece are measured in Cartesian or polar coordinates and compared with the preset target position in the control. If the target value and actual value are the same, the machine movement stops.

Path Measuring System

There are two different types of system:
1. The position measuring system issues the coordinate value of a machine axis position in absolute form, e.g., via encoded measuring systems or a resolver.
2. The path measuring system measures the increase in travelled distance of each axis movement, e.g., through an incremental impulse encoder in combination with an electronic forward/reverse counter.
A stationary, path measuring system is needed for each numerically controlled axis.

Peck Feed

An automatically programmable feed system for deep hole drilling, where the normal feed rate movement is interrupted by rapid reverse in the direction of feed at preset intervals in order to allow the generated chips to be removed from the hole. The drill then returns to its last cutting position where it begins to operate at the normal cutting feed rate for another period of time.

Peripheral Equipment

Any unit of equipment, distinct from the central processing unit, which may provide the system with outside communication.

Photoelectric Line Tracer
A device used for copying profiles directly from the drawing or controlling the path of a burning head of a NC flame cutting machine.

Pitch Correction Unit
A unit in a control which enables the correction of a pitch error in a lead screw or a rack and pinion gear.

Playback
The generation of control data for repeated automatic machining by manually machining the first workpiece.

Plotter, XY
A device used in conjunction with a computer to plot coordinate points graphically.

Pocketing
A capability for removing (usually by end-milling) metal from an enclosed surface up to a certain depth using a single instruction instead of programming each single step.

Point-To-Point Control System
An NC system which controls motion only to reach a given end point but exercises no path control during the transition from one end point to the next.

Point-To-Point Control With Straight Cut
A point-to-point control with the additional capability to control feed rate along the coordinate axes. Such a system can be used for straight milling operations parallel to the direction of the coordinate axes.

Polar Axis
Axial designation for circular tables, rotational axes, and joint axes.

Polar Coordinates
A mathematical system of coordinates for locating a point in a plane by the length of its radius vector and the angle this vector makes with a fixed line.

Position Readout
The visual display of the relative position of a machine axis (the distance from its zero point), which is measured by a resolver or encoder.

Positive Positioning
A movement in the positive direction with reference to an absolute zero point.

Postprocessor
One of the most misunderstood terms used in NC. It is not a piece of hardware, but a computer program that takes a generalized part program output and adapts it to a particular machine control unit/machine tool combination.

Processor
In hardware, a data processor. In software, a computer program that includes the compiling, assembling, translating, and related functions for a specific programming language; normally precedes postprocessing.

Program
A collection of one or more computer-executable (directly or indirectly) procedures. In general, the execution of a program results in the execution of one main procedure and a number of subprocedures.

Program End
A function which causes the shutdown of the machine after the last block of a program has been processed. The shutdown includes machine functions like coolant off, spindle off, tool retraction, and retraction of the machine axes to their initial positions.

Programmable Logic Controller (PLC)
A sequence control which works like a relay control, but with a computerlike structure. For programming the control functions a special programming device is needed. The program logic is stored in RAM, PROM, or EPROM, and defines the sequence and the manner in which inputs and outputs are to be connected.

Programming
The preparation of a listing of a sequence of events necessary to carry out a given task. The listing is written in a form that can be readily interpreted and processed by a computer or NC unit.

Programming Aids
Computer-assisted systems or devices, which facilitate the programming of an NC

machine. They perform geometric calculations and check programs for bugs and syntax errors related to a specific NC controller/machine tool combination.

Programming Language
An artificial language for writing computer programs.

Programming Method
The way a program is structured. Manual programming leaves much methodology freedom to the programmer, that is, the programmer can decide the order of the programming steps. Interactive programming systems with computer assistance determine the programming step order automatically.

Programming System
Comprises all the components that a part programmer needs to fulfill his task. For example, an EXAPT programming system consists of a computer, processor, postprocessor, and all data files and associated software packages, as well as a puncher, plotter and printer. However, a TELEAPT system only comprises the input device, telephone modem, a puncher, and a printer.

Programming Technique
The structured technique which is used for producing part programs, and which depends on the programming system used. With manual programming systems the program sequence is written in the form of blocks in a format suitable for direct input into the NC at the machine tool, but with computer-aided programming systems the manufacturing process is described in a high-level programming language. With interactive programming systems the description of the part contour is by means of either geometric elements or the geometric data of the contour itself.

Programming Unit
The combination of an electric typewriter, a puncher, and a reader for the production of punch tapes (can punch, check, copy, and print out the information data in a readable format).

Program Stop
An instruction in an NC program that will automatically stop the machine (M00, for example).

PROM
Abbreviation for programmable read-only memory; an electronic memory module which retains the once-and-for-all programmed data, and permits its reading but not its editing or deletion.

Protocol
An agreed-on set of rules by which data interchange between computers and related numerically controlled devices is formatted to enable them to freely communicate with total comprehension.

Punch Card
An input medium in the form of a card in which holes can be entered in certain patterns for storage and transmission of data; now a largely obsolete data-carrier system.

Punching
Putting encoded data on a card or a punch tape in the form of punched holes.

Punch Tape
An input medium consisting of a paper or plastic strip in which encoded instructions are entered in the form of punched holes. The tape contains eight possible data tracks as well as a transport track.

Quadrant
One of the quarters of the rectangular or Cartesian coordinate dimensioning system.

RAM
Abbreviation for random access memory; an electronic volatile semiconductor memory module which permits random access. This is in contrast to a magnetic tape which permits only sequential access. Thus each sector or segment can be addressed, for both reading and writing, individually.

Rationalization
The elimination of unnecessary equipment, personnel, or processes from a factory, in order to make it more efficient. Rationalization makes it possible to save on raw material, capital, labor, and time. Automation is a final step in rationalization.

Reference Point
A point defined within the limits of travel to

locate an axis or the spindle in relation to the part.

Repeatability
(1) A measure of hardware repeatable accuracy. (2) Closeness of agreement of repeated positional movements to the given indicated location. See also, accuracy.

Reproducibility
The closeness of agreement between repeated output measurements for a given input value made under the same operating conditions over a period of time, approaching from either the positive or negative direction.

Resolution
(1) The fineness of detail in a reproduced spatial pattern. (2) The degree to which a system or a device distinguishes fineness of detail in a scanned or generated spatial pattern. (3) The smallest increment of distance that can be read and acted on by a numerical control system.

Resolver
A rotary feedback device which converts mechanical motion into analog electronic signals that represent motion or position. See also, encoder.

Retrofitting
The act of modifying or improving the design or construction of a piece of equipment in order to take advantage of improvements in technology. For example, the replacement of an outdated NC unit with a more modern CNC.

Robot
An automatic device that performs functions ordinarily ascribed to human workers.

ROM
Abbreviation for read only memory; an electronic memory module which is programmed with a special programming device, making it impossible to modify the information stored on it.

Scaling
The capability for altering axes' dimensions by means of a given multiplication factor.

Scanner
Equipment to digitize coordinate values and store them in a data carrier. It is a device which traverses a measuring sensor in order to collect and store those data which, after further processing, can result in tape geometric data needed to control an NC machine.

Sensing Probe
High precision probe finger equipped with a contact switch system offering high reproducibility. Some types of probes can be inserted into the spindle of a machine tool to perform measuring tasks both before and after machining operations. They are also used for the identification of part position/orientation, and for quality control purposes.

Sensitivity
The ratio of a change in steady-state output to a corresponding change of input.

Sensor
A measuring probe or feeler which monitors technical procedures and determines values of pressure, temperature, position, angle, and so on.

Serial Data Input
The transfer of information, in digital format, serially bit by bit. Transfer speed (bits per second) is referred to as baud rate; an alternative to parallel data input.

Serial-to-Analog Converter
Stores digital format signals transmitted in serial mode, and then converts them into analog signals.

Sequential Control
A positioning system in which movements occur sequentially along the various axes.

Sequence Number
A number identifying the relative position of a block of data.

Sequence Search
A program tape is advanced by means of a manual or programmed specific search command. While the search is being performed, the requested block number is displayed, and execution of intervening machine commands is blocked.

Servomechanism
(1) A feedback control system in which at

least one of the system signals represents mechanical motion. (2) An automatic control system incorporating feedback that governs the physical position of an element by adjusting either the values of the coordinates or the values of their time derivatives. (3) A powerful amplifying device which takes an input signal from some low-energy source and directs it to an output delivering much larger power. Power steering in automobiles is an example.

Shaft Encoder (Rotary Encoder, Optical Encoder)
A device for converting analog data which are received in the form of angular position of a shaft into encoded digital data.

Silicon Controlled Rectifier (SCR) or Thyristor
An electronic device which is generally used in control systems for high power loads such as electric heating elements or direct current motors. Its operation is similar to a transistor.

Simulation
A mathematical logic model held in a computer which provides a means of studying the interactive effects of variables in a complex system. It is not a system design optimization tool, but rather it provides answers to the "what if" question.

Simultaneous Control
The simultaneous control of multiple axes.

Single Block Operation
Operational mode in which only one block of a part program is executed. The execution of each subsequent block must be individually started by the operator.

Skip
To ignore one or more instructions in an operational sequence.

Slash Code
A switch or signal input which can be used by the programmer to cause the NC unit to suppress all blocks which begin with a slash character before the N address.

Softkeys
Mechanical or electronic keys installed adjacent to the screen display of a CNC. There are usually between five and eight, and their functions may be preset by the operator. Softkeys can replace over a hundred hardware keys associated with fixed, discrete functions.

Software
Programs necessary for executing tasks with the hardware of a computer. In connection with CNC, for example, the software is the operating program for the built-in microprocessor or minicomputer. It basically determines the specifications and capabilities of the control. Included are testing software, DNC software, postprocessor software, and so on.

Soft-Wired NC
An NC whose features are specified by the software (that is, by the programs of a CNC computer) and not by the hard-wired circuits of the constituent CNC components.

Spindle Orientation
The positioning of the main spindle of the machine tool in a certain established angular position. This procedure may be necessary prior to the retraction of single-edge cutting tools from a bore or for automatic tool changing.

Spline Interpolation
Concatenation of third order polynomials which have tangential intersections. Spline interpolation is a mathematical function within the CNC and is for conveniently defining complex curves in space.

Stepping Motor
An electric motor in which the rotary movement takes place in small, predetermined angular steps. The steps are controlled by a series of electrical impulses which are transmitted to the stator windings via a control device. The angle of rotation corresponds to the applied, number of impulses, while the rotational speed corresponds to the impulse frequency.

Storage
(1) In data processing, a device into which data can be entered and stored, and from which the data can be retrieved when required. (2) In production, an area or device in which parts or materials may be stored

for later use.

Subroutine
A routine that is part of another routine.

Symmetrical Switching
A method used to produce components which are symmetrical in nature. This method corresponds in principle to mirror-imaging.

Syntax
The basic rules for the structure of commands in a programming language.

Tachometer
A device for measuring speed; in NC, mainly a DC voltage generator for feedback of actual feed rate or spindle speed.

Tape-Control System
A control system in which punch tapes or magnetic tapes are used as the data input medium.

Tape Duplication
Production of a duplicate tape from an original or master tape.

Tapeless Numerical Control
A programmable control system capable of controlling a machine tool which has no tape-input medium. This type of control uses digital input switches, a keyboard, or a DNC interface.

Tape Perforator, Tape Punch
A device used to punch holes that represent coded instructions into tapes. Punching devices can be manually or electronically operated. A manual device uses a typewriter keyboard to activate the punch, while an electronic device uses signals emitted directly from a computer.

Tape Reader
Equipment for the collection and transmission of stored instructions on a tape. With magnetic tape, the device automatically scans and reads the magnetized tape; the punch holes in a punch tape can be read mechanically, pneumatically, electrically, or optically via photocells. The encoded signals are then used as input to the computer or to a numerical control unit.

Teach-in Programming
Programming technique for NC machines and NC robots. Axes motions are manually carried out, then the movements are automatically digitized, and finally they are stored in the memory of the CNC for subsequent repeated replay.

Teletype
An automatic typewriter containing an 8-track punch tape reader and puncher. It produces readable hard copy of the program at the same time as it produces the associated punch tape. It can also read a punch tape and produce readable hard copy, or it can print out a program from a CNC memory and produce an equivalent punch tape.

Timesharing
The use of a computer memory for two or more purposes during the same time period.

Tool Call-up
A T-word (based on the EIA word address code) for searching and preparing the next tool to be used in the tool magazine. Placing the tool in the spindle occurs via the tool changer with a programmed "M06 command."

Tool Changer
A mechanical device for automatic tool change on NC machines, and tool retrieval from the tool magazine, in accordance with the part program instructions.

Tool Compensation
A manual data input into the CNC to compensate the machine movement because of the difference between programmed and actual tool dimensions.

Tool-Length Compensation
Manually controlled deviation from the programmed cutting depth intended to compensate for the difference between the actual length of a cutting tool and its programmed length.

Tool Management
A feature of a CNC which permits the monitoring of all tooling with respect to life, wear, and breakage, and can call up sister tooling when required. In a FMS a central tool computer performs all administration tasks which are not carried out internally within the CNC, such as exchange of tools

that are no longer needed for the machining of subsequent parts.

Tool Monitoring

A CNC function for monitoring of the acceptable life of each individual tool in the magazine of an NC machine. The NC keeps a running total of the cutting times of each individual tool, and continuously compares this total with the tool's programmed acceptable life. The operator receives warning messages when tool life has expired.

Tool Nose Compensation

Equidistant path compensation for turning machines to compensate for the tool nose radii of curring tools.

Track

Any one of eight paths parallel to the edges of a punch tape. Coded instructions and information are stored in these tracks (also referred to as channels) through the presence or absence of punched holes.

Transducer

(1) A device for converting energy from one form to another. (2) In NC, a device that measures an output and converts it into a signal that is normally linked to an error-detection device.

Turning Center

A numerically controlled turning machine with automatic tool-changing capability. Common machining capabilities include external and internal turning, thread cutting and drilling. With the addition of auxiliary power tooling equipment, these centers may also be used for surface milling, offcenter drilling, and automatic workpiece clamping.

Turnkey System

Delivery of a computer, DNC, or FMS system with one supplier having total responsibility for production, installation, testing, and functioning of the entire system.

Variable Block Format

A tape format that allows the number and order of words in a block of tape to vary from one block to the next.

Verifier

A device or equipment for testing reproduced tape for accuracy—for example, a character-by-character comparison of a punch tape copy and the original tape.

Volatile Memory

A memory which loses its data when the power supply is switched off, RAM, for example.

Word

A character or bit string representing the basic unit in which a machining instruction may be stored, transmitted, or acted upon.

Word Address Format

A tape format where each word in a block of tape is identified by a preceding character.

X, Y, Z Axes

The three letters used for the notation of the three principal linear axes on NC machine tools.

Zero Offset

A feature of an NC unit which permits the zero point on an axis to be located anywhere within a specified range while still retaining information of the "permanent zero." See also, floating zero.

Zero Reference Point

The point in a measuring system to which all coordinate values are referenced.

In order to assist industry to readily locate guidelines in the fields of CAD/CAM and associated topics, standards have been drawn up. The following standards are organized under various topic headings, beginning with a short explanation of the principal abbreviations used.

ABBREVIATIONS

AGMA   American Gear Manufacturers Association

AIA   Aerospace Industries Association

ANSI   American National Standards Institute

ASME   American Society of Mechanical Engineers

BSI   British Standards Institution

CAMI   Computer Aided Manufacturing International

EIA   Electronic Industries Institute

GKS   Graphical Kernel System

IPC   Institute for Interconnecting and Packaging Electronic Circuits

MIL   Military Standard

NAPLPS   North American Presentation—Level Protocol Syntax

CAD STANDARDS

ASME Y14.26 m   Digital representation for communication of product definition data, engineering drawing, and related documentation practices

IPC 10   CAD printed wiring design guide

IPC 10.1.1   Applications of CAD

IPC 10.1.3   Variations of CAD

IPC 10.1.6   Establishing CAD capability

MIL-STD-960   Standards and specifications

CAM STANDARDS

CAMI R-76-SC02   Computer-assisted speed and feed selection for automated process planning

CAMI R-78-SC01   Glossary of CAM terms

CAMI ST-79-SC01   Documentation standards

CNC STANDARDS

MIL-L-80053   Lathes, turret, horizontal

MIL-L-80053a   Lathes, turret, horizontal

MIL-L-80053c   Lathes, turret, horizontal

MIL-L-80257   Lathes, turret, horizontal, bar and chucking, $1\frac{3}{4}$ in. capacity

MIL-M-80255   Machining centers, vertical single speed

AGMA p 129.26   Gear cutting, generating machine

AIA NAS 875   Drilling, reaming, and countersinking

AIA NAS 995   CNC specifications

DNC STANDARDS

AIA NAS 993   DNC systems

EIA RS-484   Electrical and mechanical interface characteristics and line control protocol using communications control characters for serial data link between a DNC system and NC equipment employing asynchronous full duplex transmission

GRAPHICS STANDARDS

NAPLPS North American Presentation-Level Protocol Syntax

GKS Graphical Kernel System

VDI Virtual Device Interface

VDM Virtual Device Metafile

PHIGS Programmer's Minimal Interface for Graphics

ANSI X3H3

GSX Graphic System Extension

NUMERICAL CONTROL STANDARDS

EIA Standards

RS 273-A Interchangeable perforated tape variable format for positioning and straight cut numerically controlled machines

RS 274-B Interchangeable perforated tape variable block format for contouring and contouring/positioning numerically controlled machines

RS 281 Construction standards numerical machine tool control

RS 326 Interchangeable perforated tape fixed block format for positioning and straight cut numerically controlled machines

AIA Standards

NAS 911 Milling machine airframe skin, nonferrous

NAS 913 Milling machine automatically controlled profiling and contouring

NAS 938 Machine axis and motion nomenclature

NAS 943 Interchangeable perforated tape standards variable block format for positioning and straight cut numerically controlled equipment

NAS 948 Printed circuit board drilling machine—numerically controlled

NAS 953 Numerical control system

NAS 954 Automatic horizontal boring, drilling and milling machine

NAS 956 Tube bender—precision aircraft type for thin wall, ferrous and nonferrous alloys

NAS 957 Numerically controlled drafting line plotter

NAS 960 Drilling machines-numerically controlled

NAS 963 Numerically controlled horizontal and vertical jig-boring machines

NAS 966 Lathe, precision—numerically controlled

NAS 971 Measuring inspection, machine precision

NAS 972 Glossary of manufacturing equipment terms

POSTPROCESSOR STANDARDS

BSI BS 5510: part 2 Programming languages for the numerical control of machines

ISO ISO 4343 Numerical control of machines—NC processor output

LANGUAGE STANDARDS

BSI BS 5110 Programming language constraints

BSI BS 5110A Updated constraints and recommendations

ROBOTIC STANDARDS

AIA NAS 875 Manipulator regulations and standards

EI 8310-088144 Explanations of standards